Adventure, Mystery, and Romance

Adventure, Mystery, and Romance

Formula Stories as Art and Popular Culture

John G. Cawelti

The University of Chicago Press
Chicago and London

For Betty, Donald, and Florence Cawelti

Who cannot be held responsible for my taste in literature,
but who have had a great deal to do with everything else

The University of Chicago Press, Chicago 60637
The University of Chicago Press, Ltd., London

80 79 78 77 76   987654321

The following publishers have generously given permission to use
extended quotations from copyrighted works: From *Farewell, My
Lovely,* by Raymond Chandler. Copyright 1940 by Raymond Chandler
and renewed 1968 by the Executrix of the Author, Mrs. Helen Greene.
Reprinted by permission of Alfred A. Knopf, Inc. From *Red Harvest,*
by Dashiell Hammett. Copyright 1929 by Alfred A. Knopf, Inc. and
renewed 1957 by Dashiell Hammett. Reprinted by permission of the
publisher. From *I, The Jury* by Mickey Spillane. Copyright 1947 by
E. P. Dutton & Co.; renewal © 1975 by Frank Morrison Spillane.
Reprinted by permission of the publishers, E. P. Dutton & Co., Inc.

**Library of Congress Cataloging in Publication Data will be found at the
end of this book.**

Contents

Acknowledgments   vii

Introduction: The Design of This Book   1

1 The Study of Literary Formulas   5
    Formulas, Genres, and Archetypes 5
    The Artistic Characteristics of
        Formula Literature 8
    Formulas and Culture 20

2 Notes toward a Typology of Literary Formulas   37
    Adventure 39
    Romance 41
    Mystery 42
    Melodrama 44
    Alien Beings or States 47

3 The Mythology of Crime and Its Formulaic
  Embodiments   51
    The Godfather and the Literature of Crime 51
    Elements of the New Formula 65
    The Cultural Function of Popular Crime Formulas 76

4 The Formula of the Classical Detective Story   80
    Patterns of the Formula 80
    Cultural Background of the Formula 98

5 The Art of the Classical Detective Story   106
    Central Artistic Problems of the Genre 106
    Artistic Failures and Successes: Christie and
        Sayers 111
    The Art of Simenon 125
    Detective Stories and Detection as an Element
      in Other Literary Genres 222

The Future of the Classical Detective Story   136

6   The Hard-Boiled Detective Story   139
           Hard-boiled and Classical Detective Stories   139
           Patterns of the Formula   142
           Cultural Background of the Formula   156

7   Hammett, Chandler, and Spillane   162

8   The Western: A Look at the Evolution of a Formula   192
           Cooper and the Beginnings of the Western
              Formula   194
           Nick of the Woods and the Dime Novel   209
           Wister's *Virginian* and the Modern Western   215
           Zane Grey and W. S. Hart: The Romantic Western
              of the 1920s   230
           The Classic Western: John Ford and Others   242
           The Jewish Cowboy, the Black Avenger, and the
              Return of the Vanishing American: Current Trends
              in the Formula   252

9   The Best-Selling Social Melodrama   260
           The Social Melodrama   260
           The Aesthetics of Social Melodrama   263
           The Evolution of Social Melodrama   268
           Irving Wallace   284

         Conclusion   296

         Notes   303

         Bibliographical Notes   319

         Index   330

Acknowledgments

First, I would like to express my gratitude to my colleagues at the University of Chicago who have given me so many ideas about popular literature over the years. In particular I offer thanks for ideas or bits of information to say nothing of general support and encouragement to Walter Blair, Norman Maclean, Wayne Booth, Edward W. Rosenheim, Jr., Robert Streeter, Charles Wegener, Keith Cushman, Arthur Heiserman, David Bevington, John Wallace, William Ringler, Janel Mueller, Sheldon Sacks, Jay Schleusener, Jerome McGann, Stuart Tave, Mark Ashin, Peter Homans, Gwin J. Kolb, Elder Olson, Joseph Williams, Merlin Bowen, William Swenson, Kenneth Northcott, Peter Dembowski, and Robert Rosenthal.

William Veeder not only offered a flow of helpful ideas about popular forms but also read and criticized much of the manuscript. I'm also grateful to Peter Rabinowitz for his careful reading of the chapters on detective fiction.

Like most scholars, my students have taught me most of what I know. Since I cannot list twenty years of class rosters, I would like to implicate with special thanks as symbols for all the rest, Barbara Bernstein, Charles Flynn, Randolph Ivy, Horace Newcomb, Steven Weiland, Virginia Wright Wexman, Johnnine Hazard, Malachy Walsh, Nancy Huse, Kay Mussell, Gordon Kelly, Suzanne Asher, William Duffy, and Gary Wolfe.

Harold and Marylynn Boris have talked through so many parts of this book with me that they might rightly be listed as coauthors.

Friends from other institutions have offered me guidance above and beyond what I have learned from their published works and for this I would particularly like to thank Russel B. Nye, Ray Browne, Marvin Felheim, Marshall Fishwick, Carl Bode, Joshua C. Taylor, George Grella, Alan M. Fern, John Raeburn, Larry Mintz, Morton Ross, Reuel Denney, Stephen B. Wood, Robert Corrigan, J. Fred MacDonald, and Patrick Morrow.

My ideas about the western have profited greatly from conversations with Richard Etulain, Delbert Wylder, Frederick Manfred, Allen Slickpoo, and William Stafford.

Without many conversations with Stuart Kaminsky, Gerald Temaner, Steve Fagin, Gerald Peary, Ralph Amelio, Dudley Andrew, and Russell Merritt my ignorance about popular film genres would be much greater than it is.

Two former teachers, Alexander C. Kern and Napier Wilt, were particularly influential in arousing my curiosity about the problems dealt with in this book. I would also like to express my great debt to the late Ronald S. Crane, who gave me encouragement and advice at a crucial time.

Earlier versions of some parts of the present book have appeared in various publications and I would like to thank the editors of *The Journal of Popular Culture, The University of Chicago Magazine, The Velvet Light Trap, Boundary 21,* and the *Indiana Social Studies Quarterly* for giving some of my ideas an initial hearing.

Various parts of the manuscript were typed by Jennifer Bell, Marcia Baker, Diane Durante, Karen Weil, Deborah Kurland, Christine Michael, and Carol Sykes, to whom I am everlastingly grateful for their patience in deciphering the illegible.

Finally, I would like to express my special admiration and thanks to Henry Nash Smith, not only because his own great work *Virgin Land* set me off after popular formulas, but because he read and gave wonderfully helpful criticisms to all but one chapter of my manuscript. To him and all the others who have been so generous with help and encouragement: Friends, I absolve you from the errors and limitations of this book, but I hope you can take some pleasure in your contribution to its merits.

Introduction

The Design of This Book

Our earliest experiences of literature involve us in the different pleasures and uses of novelty and familiarity. As children we learn new things about the world and ourselves from stories. By hearing about creatures and events that transcend the limits of space and time allotted to us we widen the range of our imagination and are prepared to deal with new situations and experiences. But children also clutch at the security of the familiar. How often a child rejects a new story, preferring to hear one he has already been told a hundred times. And as he hears again the often-heard, his eyes glaze over with pleasure, his body relaxes, and, the story ends in peaceful slumber. The recurrent outlines of a familiar experience have returned. In that well-known and controlled landscape of the imagination the tensions, ambiguities, and frustrations of ordinary experience are painted over by magic pigments of adventure, romance and mystery. The world for a time takes on the shape of our heart's desire.

Older children and adults continue to find a special delight in familiar stories, though in place of the child's pleasure in the identical tale, they substitute an interest in certain types of stories which have highly predictable structures that guarantee the fulfillment of conventional expectations: the detective story, the western, the romance, the spy story, and many other such types. For many persons such formulaic types make up by far the greater portion of the experience of literature. Even scholars and critics professionally dedicated to the serious study of artistic masterpieces often spend their off-hours following a detective's ritual pursuit of a murderer or watching one of television's spy teams carry through its dangerous mission. An enormous percentage of books, magazines, films, and television dramas depend on such formulaic structures. Thus these formulaic stories are artistic and cultural phenomena of tremendous importance.

Because of their association with the times of relaxation, entertainment, and escape, this type of story has been largely ignored by literary scholars and historians or left to the mercy of sociologists, psychologists, and analysts of mass culture. These disciplines have produced many interesting analyses of various literary formulas, but have largely treated them as ideological rationalization, psychological stratagems, or opiates for the masses. Such

1

approaches oversimplify the problem by translating or reducing an artistic phenomenon into other terms. To fully understand and interpret the phenomenon of formulaic stories we must treat them as what they are: artistic constructions created for the purpose of enjoyment and pleasure. To come to some insight into their cultural significance we must arrive at some understanding of them as a form of artistic behavior. Because formula stories involve widely shared conventions, what one could call a form of collective artistic behavior, we must also deal with the phenomenon in relation to the cultural patterns it reveals and is shaped by, and with the impact formula stories have on culture.

This book, then, is a study of popular story formulas, those narrative and dramatic structures that form such a large part of the cultural diet of the majority of readers, television viewers, and film audiences. As my readers will soon discover, I consider these popular formulas to be of more complex artistic and cultural interest than most previous commentators have indicated. To substantiate this general thesis, I have chosen to deal rather intensively with a few major formulas—various forms of detective and crime stories, the western, and the best-selling social melodrama. I have not attempted to present an overall account of popular formulas or genres—the reader will quickly note such obvious omissions as all types of comedy and romance, the horror story, science-fiction, and many other important areas of popular narrative and drama. Even in the case of those formulas I do analyze, I have not attempted anything like a complete historical survey. Instead, the organizing principle of this book is theoretical: I have tried to define the major analytical problems that confront us when we seek to inquire more fully into the nature and significance of formulaic literature, and to use a variety of different formulas to illustrate with some specificity how these problems might be explored. Thus, I hope the book will combine some of the advantages of generality and particularity. It develops a general methodology that can, I believe, be profitably applied to popular formulas other than those treated in this book. It also presents a number of detailed and specific analyses of certain major formulas and individual writers that I hope will be of interest to those who are as fascinated as I am by such artistic types as the detective story and the western, by such important creators as Agatha Christie, Dashiell Hammett, Owen Wister, and John Ford, and by the relation between these types and the cultures that create and enjoy them.

As a hasty road map, let me offer the following guide. The first chapter is definitional and contextual. It sets out to define the notion of literary formulas from various perspectives and to relate formulaic analysis to such other modes of literary and cultural exploration as genre study, myth and symbol analysis, communications research, and social-psychological criticism. I offer various notes on method as well as a number of speculations about the phenomenon of artistic popularity, the relationship between artistic expression and other forms of behavior, and such other large and difficult questions as the study of formulas inevitably must encounter. In particular, this chapter introduces the notion of the formula as a synthesis of cultural mythology with archetypal story pattern that will be more fully developed in chapters 2 and 3.

Chapter 2 is a tentative attempt to define the major archetypal patterns that underlie the particular story formulas of many different cultures; in other words, to abstract those patterns that are common to such evidently similar types of story as the American western, the H. Rider Haggard type of adventure in Darkest Africa, the historical swashbuckler, the knightly romance, and the folkish hero-tale, and to enumerate the other archetypal story patterns that recur in many different cultures.

Chapter 3 begins as an examination of the contemporary popularity of *The Godfather*, primarily as a springboard for a discussion of the ways in which the same basic cultural mythology—in this case the great modern cluster of myths that focus on crime, criminals, detectives, and the police—can become synthesized with different archetypal patterns. An attempt is made to illustrate how the changing story patterns through which this mythology is dramatized relate to cultural changes. This chapter also attempts to set the two major detective story formulas that will be the subject of the next four chapters into a broader cultural and historical perspective and to consider the puzzling question of our extraordinary affection for literature about crime.

Chapter 4 is my first full-scale attempt to define a particular formula in depth. For this purpose I have chosen what is perhaps the most highly formalized and ritualistic of all popular formulas, the pattern that underlies the classical detective story genre. The major elements of this pattern and their relationship to each other are examined at length and an attempt is made to account in psychological and cultural terms for the great appeal of this genre during the period in which it flourished most extensively.

The fifth chapter looks at the classical detective story from another perspective, raising the problem of its distinctive artistic problems and potentialities. While a story formula reflects the psychological needs and cultural attitudes of its period, it also has certain artistic limitations and potentialities that may be handled skillfully or clumsily in particular cases. In this chapter I attempt to define some of these characteristics by comparing successful and unsuccessful Poirot mysteries by Agatha Christie and by considering the different ways in which Christie, Dorothy Sayers, and Georges Simenon deal with the possibilities of their genre.

Chapter 6 is intended to parallel chapter 4 by developing a comparative discussion of two closely related popular formulas: the classical and hard-boiled detective stories. As in the case of the classical genre, I also attempt to explore the psychological and cultural significance of the hard-boiled story.

In chapter 7 I am concerned as I was in chapter 5 with the artistic potentialities of popular formulas. In this case, I deal with a different aspect of this problem: the way in which formulas may be used on different artistic levels and for very different and expressive purposes. The basis of this discussion is a treatment of three major hard-boiled writers, two of whom, Dashiell Hammett and Raymond Chandler, are considered significant artists by many persons and the third, Mickey Spillane, is usually viewed as the apotheosis of non-art. I offer the view that there is a kind of artfulness involved in Spillane's work, though it is certainly a different kind than that for which we value the stories of Hammett and Chandler.

When literary formulas last for a considerable period of time, they usually undergo considerable change as they adapt to the different needs and interests of changing generations. Chapter 8 is an analysis of this evolutionary process using the western as a case study. In this discussion which moves from James Fenimore Cooper's Leatherstocking saga to the western films of the early 1970s, I attempt to show how the western formula has responded to changing American attitudes by a continual reinterpretation of its basic elements.

Since most of my examination of the various dimensions of formulaic literature has concerned itself with formulas embodying the archetypes of adventure and mystery, I have had little opportunity to consider with any intensity the great range of formulas that depend primarily on the archetypal patterns of romance, melodrama, and alien beings and states. While a full treatment of these areas would expand this study beyond reasonable limits, I feel that we must examine at least one aspect of this area of popular literature. Therefore I have chosen, in chapter 9, to explore one melodramatic formula, the best-selling "blockbuster" or social novel. In this chapter I have tried to indicate, in briefer form, how the various perspectives and methods of analysis developed in the preceding nine chapters might be applied to this complex formula. I consider the definition of the blockbuster formula, its character as art, its relation to its cultural background and audience, and some suggestions as to how we might begin to trace its evolution.

Chapter 9 can serve as a summary of the various problems explored in this book. The conclusion is reserved for my attempt to define the major inadequacies and limitations of this work, not so much to forestall my readers, who will certainly have their own sense of this book's shortcomings, but because, having lived with this inquiry for some years, I do have a peculiarly poignant vision of its strengths and weaknesses. I try to articulate this sense as clearly as I can in the conclusion, along with some suggestions for further inquiry.

One

The Study of Literary Formulas

Formulas, Genres, and Archetypes

In general, a literary formula is a structure of narrative or dramatic conventions employed in a great number of individual works. There are two common usages of the term formula closely related to the conception I wish to set forth. In fact, if we put these two conceptions together, I think we will have an adequate definition of literary formulas. The first usage simply denotes a conventional way of treating some specific thing or person. Homer's epithets—swift-footed Achilles, cloud-gathering Zeus—are commonly referred to as formulas as are a number of his standard similes and metaphors—"his head fell speaking into the dust"—which are assumed to be conventional bardic formulas for filling a dactylic hexameter line. By extension, any form of cultural stereotype commonly found in literature— red-headed, hot-tempered Irishmen, brilliantly analytical and eccentric detectives, virginal blondes, and sexy brunettes—is frequently referred to as formulaic. The important thing to note about this usage is that it refers to patterns of convention which are usually quite specific to a particular culture and period and do not mean the same outside this specific context. Thus the nineteenth-century formulaic relation between blondness and sexual purity gave way in the twentieth century to a very different formula for blondes. The formula of the Irishman's hot temper was particularly characteristic of English and American culture at periods where the Irish were perceived as lower-class social intruders.

The second common literary usage of the term formula refers to larger plot types. This is the conception of formula commonly found in those manuals for aspiring writers that give the recipes for twenty-one sure-fire plots—boy meets girl, boy and girl have a misunderstanding, boy gets girl. These general plot patterns are not necessarily limited to a specific culture or period. Instead, they seem to represent story types that, if not universal in their appeal, have certainly been popular in many different cultures at many different times. In fact, they are examples of what some scholars have called archetypes or patterns that appeal in many different cultures.

Actually, if we look at a popular story type such as the western, the detective story, or the spy adventure, we find that it combines these two sorts of literary phenomenon. These popular story patterns are embodiments of archetypal story forms in terms of specific cultural materials. To create a western involves not only some understanding of how to construct an exciting adventure story, but also how to use certain nineteenth- and twentieth-century images and symbols such as cowboys, pioneers, outlaws, frontier towns, and saloons along with appropriate cultural themes or myths—such as nature vs. civilization, the code of the West, or law and order vs. outlawry—to support and give significance to the action. Thus formulas are ways in which specific cultural themes and stereotypes become embodied in more universal story archetypes.

The reason why formulas are constructed in this way is, I think, fairly straightforward. Certain story archetypes particularly fulfill man's needs for enjoyment and escape. (I offer some speculations about the psychology of this in chapter 2.) But in order for these patterns to work, they must be embodied in figures, settings, and situations that have appropriate meanings for the culture which produces them. One cannot write a successful adventure story about a social character type that the culture cannot conceive in heroic terms; this is why we have so few adventure stories about plumbers, janitors, or streetsweepers. It is, however, certainly not inconceivable that a culture might emerge which placed a different sort of valuation or interpretation on these tasks, in which case we might expect to see the evolution of adventure story formulas about them. Certainly one can see signs of such developments in the popular literature of Soviet Russia and Maoist China.

A formula is a combination or synthesis of a number of specific cultural conventions with a more universal story form or archetype. It is also similar in many ways to the traditional literary conception of a genre. There is bound to be a good deal of confusion about the terms "formula" and "genre" since they are occasionally used to designate the same thing. For example, many film scholars and critics use the term "popular genre" to denote literary types like the western or the detective story that are clearly the same as what I call formulas. On the other hand, the term is often used to describe the broadest sort of literary type such as drama, prose fiction, lyric poetry. This is clearly a very different sort of classification than that of western, detective story, spy story. Still another usage of genre involves concepts like tragedy, comedy, romance, and satire. Insofar as such concepts of genre imply particular sorts of story patterns and effects, they do bear some resemblance to the kind of classification involved in the definition of popular genres. Since such conceptions clearly imply universal or transcultural conceptions of literary structure, they are examples of what I have called archetypes. I don't think it makes a great deal of difference whether we refer to something as a formula or as a popular genre, if we are clear just what we are talking about and why. In the interests of such clarification let me offer one distinction I have found useful.

In defining literary classes, it seems to me that we commonly have two related but distinguishable purposes. First of all, we may be primarily interested in constructing effective generalizations about large groups of literary works for the purpose of tracing historical trends or relating literary production to other cultural patterns. In such cases we are not primarily interested in the artistic qualities of individual works but in the degree to which particular works share common characteristics that may be indicative of important cultural tendencies. On the other hand, we use literary classes as a means of defining and evaluating the unique qualities of individual works. In such instances we tend to think of genres not simply as generalized descriptions of a number of individual works but as a set of artistic limitations and potentials. With such a conception in mind, we can evaluate individual works in at least two different ways: (a) by the way in which they fulfill or fail to fulfill the ideal potentials inherent in the genre and thereby achieve or fail to achieve the full artistic effect of that particular type of construction. These are the terms in which Aristotle treats tragedy; (b) by the way in which the individual work deviates from the flat standard of the genre to accomplish some unique individual expression or effect. Popular genres are often treated in this fashion, as when a critic shows that a particular western transcends the limitations of the genre or how a film director achieves a distinctive individual statement. This is the approach implicit in much *"auteur"* criticism of the movies, where the personal qualities of individual directors are measured against some conception of the standard characteristics of popular genres.

The concept of a formula as I have defined it is a means of generalizing the characteristics of large groups of individual works from certain combinations of cultural materials and archetypal story patterns. It is useful primarily as a means of making historical and cultural inferences about the collective fantasies shared by large groups of people and of identifying differences in these fantasies from one culture or period to another. When we turn from the cultural or historical use of the concept of formula to a consideration of the artistic limitations and possibilities of particular formulaic patterns, we are treating these formulas as a basis for aesthetic judgments of various sorts. In these cases, we might say that our generalized definition of a formula has become a conception of a genre. Formula and genre might be best understood not as denoting two different things, but as reflecting two phases or aspects of a complex process of literary analysis. This way of looking at the relation between formula and genre reflects the way in which popular genres develop.

In most cases, a formulaic pattern will be in existence for a considerable period of time before it is conceived of by its creators and audience as a genre. For example, the western formula was already clearly defined in the nineteenth century, yet it was not until the twentieth century that the western was consciously conceived of as a distinctive literary and cinematic genre. Similarly, though Poe created the formula for the detective story in the 1840s and many stories and novels made some use of this pattern throughout the later nineteenth century, it was probably not until after Conan Doyle that the detective story became widely understood as a specific genre with its own special limitations and potentialities. If we conceive of a genre as a literary class that views certain typical patterns in relation to their artistic limitations and potentials, it will help us in making a further useful clarification. Because the conception of genre involves an aesthetic approach to literary structures, it can be conceived either in terms of the specific formulas of a particular culture or in relation to larger, more universal literary archetypes: there are times when we might wish to evaluate a particular western in relation to other westerns. In this case we would be using a conception of a formula-genre, or what is sometimes more vaguely called a popular genre. We might also wish to relate this same western to some more universal generic conception such as tragedy or romance. Here we would be employing an archetype-genre.

These, then, are the major terms that I propose to employ in the study of formulaic literature. As I have indicated, I hold no special brief for this particular terminology, but I do believe that the implied distinctions between the descriptive and the aesthetic modes of generalization and between the cultural and universal conceptions of types of stories are crucial and must be understood in the way we use whatever terms we choose for this sort of analysis. In the remainder of this chapter I will deal with what can be said in a general way about the analysis of formulaic structures.

The Artistic Characteristics of Formula Literature

Formula literature is, first of all, a kind of literary art. Therefore, it can be analyzed and evaluated like any other kind of literature. Two central aspects of formulaic structures have been generally condemned in the serious artistic thought of the last hundred years: their essential standardization and their primary relation to the needs of escape and relaxation. In order to consider formula literature in its own terms and not simply to condemn it out of hand, we must explore some of the aesthetic implications of these two basic characteristics.

While standardization is not highly valued in modern artistic ideologies, it is, in important ways, the essence of all literature. Standard conventions establish a common ground between writers and audiences. Without at least some form of standardization, artistic communication would not be possible. But well-established conventional structures are particularly essential to the creation of formula literature and reflect the interests of audiences, creators, and distributors.

Audiences find satisfaction and a basic emotional security in a familiar form; in addition, the audience's past experience with a formula gives it a sense of what to expect in new individual examples, thereby increasing its capacity for understanding and enjoying the details of a work. For creators, the formula provides a means for the rapid and efficient production of new works. Once familiar with the outlines of the formula, the writer who devotes himself to this sort of creation does not have to make as many difficult artistic decisions as a novelist working without a formula. Thus, formulaic creators tend to be extremely prolific. Georges Simenon has turned out an extraordinary number of first-rate detective novels, in addition to his less formulaic fiction. Others have an even more spectacular record of quantity production: Frederick Faust and John Creasey each turned out over five hundred novels under a variety of pseudonyms. For publishers or film studios, the production of formulaic works is a highly rationalized operation with a guaranteed minimal return as well as the possibility of large profits for particularly popular individual versions. I have been told, for instance, that any paperback western novel is almost certain to sell enough copies to cover expenses and make a small profit. Many serious novels, on the other hand, fail to make expenses and some represent substantial losses. There is an inevitable tendency toward standardization implicit in the economy of modern publishing and film-making, if only because one successful work will inspire a number of imitations by producers hoping to share in the profits.

If the production of formulas were only a matter of economics, we might well turn the whole topic over to market researchers. Even if economic considerations were the sole motive behind the production of formulas—and I have already suggested that there are other important motives as well—we would still need to explore the kind and level of artistic creation possible within the boundaries of a formula.

Robert Warshow in his essay on the gangster film effectively defined the special aesthetic imperatives of this sort of literary creation:

> For such a type to be successful means that its conventions have imposed themselves upon the general consciousness and become the accepted vehicle of a particular set of attitudes and a particular aesthetic effect. One goes to any individual example of the type with very definite expectations, and *originality is to be welcomed only in the degree that it intensifies the expected experience without fundamentally altering it.* Moreover, the relationship between the conventions which go to make up such a type and the real experience of its audience or the real facts of whatever situation it pretends to describe is only of secondary importance and does not determine its aesthetic force. It is only in an ultimate sense that the type appeals

to its audience's experience of reality; more immediately it appeals to
previous experience of the type itself: it creates its own field of reference
[italics mine].[1]

Since the pleasure and effectiveness of an individual formulaic work depends
on its intensification of a familiar experience, the formula creates its own
world with which we become familiar by repetition. We learn in this way
how to experience this imaginary world without continually comparing it
with our own experience. Thus, as we shall see in a few moments, formulaic
literature is a most appropriate vehicle for the experiences of escape and
relaxation. Let me first examine some of the artistic problems generated by
the fundamental formulaic imperative of intensifying an expected experience.
In this type of literature, the relationship between individual work and
formula is somewhat analogous to that of a variation to a theme, or of a
performance to a text. To be a work of any quality or interest, the individual
version of a formula must have some unique or special characteristics of its
own, yet these characteristics must ultimately work toward the fulfillment of
the conventional form. In somewhat the same way, when we see a new
performance of a famous role like Hamlet, we are most impressed by it if it is
a new but acceptable interpretation of the part. An actor who overturns all
our previous conceptions of his role is usually less enjoyable than one who
builds on the interpretations we have become accustomed to. But if he adds
no special touches of his own to the part we will experience his performance
as flat and uninteresting. The same thing is true of variations on a theme as in,
for example, a jazz performance. The soloist who makes us completely lose
our sense of the tune may create a new work of considerable interest, but it
will lose the special pleasure that comes with our recognition of new
emphasis and intensity given to a melody we already know. On the other
hand, an improvisation that simply repeats the tune or "noodles" around it
arouses very little excitement. This artistic principle of variations on a theme
is clearly one of the fundamental modes of expression in popular culture, as
can be seen from the tremendous importance of performance in almost all of
the popular media. From this point of view a new detective story by, say,
Agatha Christie, is comparable in many ways to a successful production of a
familiar play by a gifted cast and a talented director.

It is not easy to put into words the rather subtle and even fleeting qualities
that make one performance stand out over another. In a later chapter, I will
discuss this problem in connection with the formula of the classical detective
story. There the quality of the individual work depends on the author's
ability to invent some ingenious new type of mystification while still working
within the conventional structure of rational detection. Each formula has its
own set of limits that determine what kind of new and unique elements are
possible without straining the formula to the breaking point. We can point to
at least two special artistic skills that all good formulaic writers seem to
possess to some degree: the ability to give new vitality to stereotypes and the

capacity to invent new touches of plot or setting that are still within formulaic limits.

The power to employ stereotypical characters and situations in such a way as to breathe new life and interest into them is particularly crucial to formulaic art of high quality since the creator of a western or detective story cannot risk departing very far from the typical characters and situations his audience has come to expect. In a western, for example, if the creator employs such stereotypical situations as the chase on horseback, the barroom brawl, and the shootout, and such conventional characters as the school-marm from the East, the dance-hall girl, the slick gambler, the crooked banker, the seedy doctor or lawyer, and the cowboy hero, he will have the advantage of heightening his audience's immediate response through the recognition that comes from many previous encounters with these characters and situations. But the good writer must renew these stereotypes by adding new elements, by showing us some new and unexpected facet, or by relating them to other stereotypes in a particularly expressive fashion. The ultimate test of a truly vitalized stereotype is the degree to which it becomes an archetype, thereby transcending its particular cultural moment and maintaining an interest for later generations and other cultures. As structural stereotypes that have pleased audiences over a number of years, formulas themselves have much of this power. The western has been a successful formula for over a hundred years and is now a genre of worldwide popularity. Individual instances of a formula generally tend to be limited in their appeal either to a particular period or a particular culture. And yet, many individual formulaic works contain vitalized stereotypes that survive beyond their historical moment.

Two sorts of stereotype vitalization seem particularly effective. The first is the stereotypical character who also embodies qualities that seem contrary to the stereotypical traits. For example, Sherlock Holmes is the stereotype of the rational, scientific investigator, the supreme man of reason. Yet, at the same time, his character paradoxically incorporates basic qualities from a contrary stereotype, that of the dreamy romantic poet, for Holmes is also a man of intuition, a dreamer, and a drugtaker, who spends hours fiddling aimlessly on his violin. This combination of opposing stereotypical traits is one of the things that made Holmes such a striking literary character. A similarly paradoxical mixture marks the portrayals of some of the great western stars. Gary Cooper, for example, is typically a man of violence, enormously skilled with guns and fists and faster on the draw than anyone else; yet he also plays a character of great shyness and gentleness. Because Cooper so effectively embodied these stereotypical opposites in his manner and physical presence, he became perhaps the greatest of the western stars, for this same mixture marks the hero of some of the most effective western stories—Max Brand's *Destry Rides Again*, Jack Schaefer's *Shane*, Owen Wister's *The Virginian*.

A second mode of stereotype vitalization is the addition of significant touches of human complexity or frailty to a stereotypical figure. This is a very delicate matter, for if a character becomes too complexly human he may cast a shattering and disruptive light on the other elements of the formula. Many works fail rather badly because they develop characters and situations that are too complex for the formulaic structure they are part of, without becoming sufficiently individualized to support a nonformulaic structure of their own. The film director John Ford has always been a master of this sort of stereotype treatment. Working with a group of stereotypical characters, he is able to suggest scenes and gestures to his performers that add rich touches of human complexity to his characters. One exemplary scene is the great church dedication sequence in *My Darling Clementine* where the stereo-typical western hero, Wyatt Earp, suddenly finds himself accompanying a lady to a church meeting and a dance. The wonderfully awkward and clumsy gestures that Ford worked out with Henry Fonda, who played the part, add a delightfully warm sense of human comedy to Earp's heroic stature, without in the least undercutting the quality of nobility called for in the formula. Another example of this kind of portrayal, very much in the Ford tradition, is Sam Peckinpah's treatment of two aging western heroes in *Ride the High Country*. The sore feet, aching backsides, and arthritic twinges with which Joel McCrea and Randolph Scott comically contend in the course of their heroic mission make them much more interesting and memorable characters without ultimately detracting from their stereotypical heroism. In fact, these moments really intensify, in Warshow's sense, our pleasure in the work's fulfillment of the heroic pattern of the western formula.

The sort of uniqueness of plot and setting appropriate to formulaic structures is analogous to the artistic value of stereotype vitalization. Elder Olson once remarked to me that he thought the real difference between mystery or adventure stories and "serious" literature was that the latter worked toward the representation of universal characters and situations while the former reached its highest success by creating something unique. At first glance, this observation seems contrary to the formulaic emphasis on conventional structures. Nevertheless, we do value a certain kind of unique-ness in formulaic literature precisely because the type is so highly standard-ized. This is not the creativity of a work that breaks through the conventions of a particular cultural milieu. A successful formulaic work is unique when, in addition to the pleasure inherent in the conventional structure, it brings a new element into the formula, or embodies the personal vision of the creator. If such new elements also became widely popular, they may in turn become widely imitated stereotypes and the basis of a new version of the formula or even of a new formula altogether. Dashiell Hammett's stories and novels transformed the detective story by creating a new kind of detective in a new kind of setting. Because these new elements were widely imitated, Hammett's work actually led to the development of a new detective story formula that is, as we shall see, quite different from the classical detective story. At many points in the history of the western, a new work has given rise to a new version of the formula. Just recently, for example, Thomas Berger's *Little Big Man* and the highly successful movie based on that novel have already been widely imitated in their handling of western conventions. Another current example of a work whose success probably marks the emergence of a new version of a traditional formula is *The Godfather*.

Another major characteristic of formula literature is the dominant influence of the goals of escape and entertainment. Because such formulaic types as mystery and adventure stories are used as a means of temporary escape from the frustrations of life, stories in these modes are commonly defined as subliterature (as opposed to literature), entertainment (as opposed to serious literature), popular art (as opposed to fine art), lowbrow culture (as opposed to highbrow), or in terms of some other pejorative opposition. The trouble with this sort of approach is that it tends to make us perceive and evaluate formula literature simply as an inferior or perverted form of something better, instead of seeing its "escapist" characteristics as aspects of an artistic type with its own purposes and justification. After all, while most of us would condemn escapism as a total way of life, our capacity to use our imaginations to construct alternative worlds into which we can temporarily retreat is certainly a central human characteristic and seems, on the whole, a valuable one.

In order to short-circuit such implicitly evaluative oppositions as low and high or popular and serious literature, I propose to proceed on the basis of a loose categorization of mimetic and formulaic literature, using the distinction suggested by Warshow when he says,

> the relationship between the conventions which go to make up such a type and the real experience of its audience of the real facts of whatever situations it pretends to describe is only of secondary importance and does not determine its aesthetic force. It is only in an ultimate sense that the type appeals to its audience's experience of reality; much more immediately, it appeals to previous experience of the type itself; it creates its own field of reference.

The mimetic element in literature confronts us with the world as we know it, while the formulaic element reflects the construction of an ideal world without the disorder, the ambiguity, the uncertainty, and the limitations of the world of our experience. Of course, the mimetic and the formulaic represent two poles that most literary works lie somewhere between. Few novels, however dedicated to the representation of reality, do not have some element of the ideal. And most formulaic works have at least the surface texture of the real world, as Mickey Spillane's heroic detective stories are full of the grittiness and sordidness of the corrupt city. It is possible that in earlier periods the dominant literary forms so balanced mimetic and formulaic elements that a specialized literature of escape was unnecessary. But the formulaic constructions of the last century or so, with which we are primarily concerned in this study, do tend to have overall structures of a conventional character that differentiate them from contemporaneous mimetic works.

What, then, are the aspects of formulaic literature that constitute what we might call the artistry of escape? First of all, I think we can say that formulaic works necessarily stress intense and immediate kinds of excitement and gratification as opposed to the more complex and ambiguous analyses of character and motivation that characterize mimetic literature. It is almost a cliché that formulaic works stress action and plot, particularly of a violent and exciting sort, i.e., actions involving danger or sex or both. In order for us to temporarily forget about our own existence and enter fully into an imaginary world, we require the strongest kinds of interest and stimulus. In relation to this particular aspect of the escapist experience, the structure of pornographic literature might serve as an ideal type. Pornography is perhaps the most completely formulaic of literary structures in that all its various elements are oriented toward one purpose, the narration or presentation of scenes of sexual activity in such a way as to create in the audience a pleasurable state of sexual excitation so direct and immediate that it is physical as well as mental, i.e., a state of tumescence. The experience of pornography can be an extremely effective form of escape from the limitations of reality into a fantasy world of totally submissive females readily willing or forced to submit to sexual activity with lustful enthusiasm. While pornography is doubtless an effective escape formula for many people, however, it has too many limitations to be a fully effective formulaic art. Aside from the fact that many people find the pornographic world immoral or distasteful and thus reject it from the outset, the escape experience offered by pornography is really too immediately physical to be sustained for any substantial period of time. In effect, the only possible consequences of a pornographic episode are orgasm or detumescence, both of which lead inevitably back to the world of reality. The creators of pornography have attempted to overcome this difficulty by developing a narrative and dramatic structure that seeks to sustain and intensify sexual excitation through a series of increasingly complex and perverse episodes of sexual activity. Many pornographic books or films begin with masturbation and proceed through normal heterosexual intercourse, followed by cunnilingus and anal intercourse to a grand climactic orgy involving several persons. Yet I would hazard the guess that the actual experience of pornography for most people consists of moments of pleasurable excitation interspersed with long stretches of boredom and frustration, rather than a sustained and completed experience that leaves one temporarily satisfied.

Thus while the experience of escape requires the sort of intense interest and excitement that can be briefly generated in a receptive audience by pornography, the weakness of pornography is that it arouses an excitation so intense and uncontrolled that it tends to force immediate gratification outside itself.

Then frustration and boredom set in until nature takes its course and the physiological cycle begins anew. Clearly a more artful and ultimately satisfying form of escape is one that can sustain itself over a longer period of time and arrive at some sense of completion and fulfillment within itself. We might take as our model of this sort of experience a good thriller or detective story, where the interest and excitement, though perhaps not as physically intense as in the case of pornography, are sustained over a much longer cycle and resolved without the requirement of physical action outside the imaginary world. Despite the ready availability of pornography in recent years, the great majority of people clearly continue to prefer other kinds of formulaic structures such as thrillers and detective stories for most of their moments of relaxation and entertainment. If my speculations about the artistry of escape are correct, this will probably continue to be the case, even if pornography becomes still more widely acceptable on moral grounds.

Some people have argued that there is a pornography of violence as well as of sexuality and that many current films with their graphic portrayal of death should be considered as analogous to the pornographic representation of sexual activity. No doubt violence, like sex, plays an important role in formulaic structures because of its capacity to generate the kind of intense feelings that take us out of ourselves. But the effects of the representation of violence seem considerably more obscure and complicated that those of sex.

Seeing pictures or reading accounts of sexual activity will tend to arouse sexual excitation that in turn causes a desire for release through orgasm. At least this holds true for the majority of men, who are still the prime consumers of pornography. It is by no means certain that the representation of violence has any comparable effect. While some recent studies suggest that certain children seek physical release by aggressive behavior after seeing a representation of violence, there is certainly no clear-cut physiological cycle involved in such responses as there is in the case of sexuality. For some people violence is sexually exciting; others react to it with a feeling of intense disgust or horror. Perhaps the most we can say on this subject in our present state of understanding is that if there is a pornography of violence the same observations can be made about it that I have suggested in connection with sexual pornography. Because it arouses extreme feelings, the representation of violence is an effective means of generating the experience of escape. And yet a mere sequence of violent episodes is not likely to be fully effective in sustaining and completing the experience.[2]

I think that our fuller understanding of the art of literary escapism involves recognizing two rather different psychological needs, both of which play an important part in shaping the kind of imaginative experiences we pursue for relaxation and regeneration. First of all, we seek moments of intense excitement and interest to get away from the boredom and ennui that are particularly prevalent in the relatively secure, routine, and organized lives of the great majority of the contemporary American and western European public. At the same time, we seek escape from our consciousness of the ultimate insecurities and ambiguities that afflict even the most secure sort of life: death, the failure of love, our inability to accomplish all we had hoped for, the threat of atomic holocaust. Harry Berger nicely described these two conflicting impulses in a recent essay:

> Man has two primal needs. First is a need for order, peace, and security, for protection against the terror or confusion of life, for a familiar and predictable world, and for a life which is happily more of the same.... But the second primal impulse is contrary to the first: man positively needs anxiety and uncertainty, thrives on confusion and risk, wants trouble, tension, jeopardy, novelty, mystery, would be lost without enemies, is sometimes happiest when most miserable. Human spontaneity is eaten away by sameness: man is the animal most expert at being bored.[3]

In the ordinary course of experience, these two impulses or needs are inevitably in conflict. If we seek order and security, the result is likely to be boredom and sameness. But rejecting order for the sake of change and novelty brings danger and uncertainty. As Berger suggests in his essay, many central aspects of the history of culture can be interpreted as a dynamic tension between these two basic impulses, a tension that Berger believes has increased in modern cultures with their greater novelty and change. In such cultures, men are continually and uncomfortably torn between the quest for order and the flight from ennui. The essence of the experience of escape and the source of its ability to relax and please us is, I believe, that it temporarily synthesizes these two needs and resolves this tension. This may account for the curious paradox that characterizes most literary formulas, the fact that they are at once highly ordered and conventional and yet are permeated with the symbols of danger, uncertainty, violence, and sex. In reading or viewing a formulaic work, we confront the ultimate excitements of love and death, but in such a way that our basic sense of security and order is intensified rather than disrupted, because, first of all, we know that this is an imaginary rather that a real experience, and, second, because the excitement and uncertainty are ultimately controlled and limited by the familiar world of the formulaic structure.

As we have seen, the world of a formula can be described as an archetypal story pattern embodied in the images, symbols, themes, and myths of a particular culture. As shaped by the imperatives of the experience of escape, these formulaic worlds are constructions that can be described as moral fantasies constituting an imaginary world in which the audience can encounter a maximum of excitement without being confronted with an overpowering sense of the insecurity and danger that accompany such forms of excitement in reality. Much of the artistry of formulaic literature involves the creator's ability to plunge us into a believable kind of excitement while, at the same time, confirming our confidence that in the formulaic world things always work out as we want them to. Three of the literary devices most often used by formulaic writers of all kinds can serve as an illustration of this sort of artistic skill: suspense, identification, and the creating of a slightly removed, imaginary world. Suspense is essentially the writer's ability to evoke in us a temporary sense of fear and uncertainty about the fate of a character we care about. It is a special kind of uncertainty that is always pointed toward a possible resolution. The simplest model of suspense is the cliff-hanger in which the protagonist's life is immediately threatened while the machinery of salvation is temporarily withheld from us. We know, however, that the hero or heroine will be saved in some way, because he always is. In its crudest form the cliff-hanger presents the combination of extreme excitement within a framework of certainty and security that characterizes formulaic literature. Of course, the cruder forms of suspense—however effective with the young and the unsophisticated—soon lose much of their power to excite more sophisticated audiences. Though there are degrees of skill in producing even the simpler forms of suspense, the better formulaic artists devise means of protracting and complicating suspense into larger, more believable structures. Good detective story writers are able to maintain a complex intellectual suspense centering on the possibility that a dangerous criminal might remain at large or that innocent people might be convicted of the crime. They sustain uncertainty until the final revelation, yet at the same time assure us that the detective has the qualities which will eventually enable him to reach the solution. Alfred Hitchcock is, at his best, the master of a still more complex form of suspense that works at the very edge of escapist fantasy. In a Hitchcock film like *Frenzy*, reassurance is kept to a minimum and our anxiety is increased to the point that we seriously begin to wonder whether we have been betrayed, whether evil will triumph and the innocent will suffer. After we have been toyed with in this way, it is a powerful experience when the hero is finally plucked from the abyss.

Complex as it is, the suspense in a work like Hitchcock's *Frenzy* is different from the kind of uncertainty characteristic of mimetic literature. The uncertainty in a mimetic work derives from the way in which it continually challenges our easy assumptions and presuppositions about life. This tends to reduce the intensity of suspense effects since, if we perceive the world of the story as an imitation of the ambiguous, uncertain, and limited world of reality we are emotionally prepared for difficulties to remain unresolved or for resolutions to be themselves the source of further uncertainties. But if we are encouraged to perceive the story world in terms of a well-known formula, the suspense effect will be more emotionally powerful because we are so sure that it must work out. One of the major sources of Hitchcock's effects is the way in which he not only creates suspense around particular episodes, but suggests from time to time that he may depart from the basic conventions of the formulaic narrative world. Of course, we don't really think he's going to, but the tension between our hope that things will be properly resolved and our suspicion that Hitchcock might suddenly dump us out of the moral fantasy in which mysteries are always solved and the guilty finally identified and captured can be a terrifying and complex experience of considerable artistic power. At the climactic moment of *Frenzy* the protagonist escapes from the prison to which he has been wrongfully condemned and sets out to murder the man who is truly guilty, but finds himself beating an already murdered victim in such a way that circumstantial evidence will certainly condemn him as the murderer. This is an extraordinary suspense effect because, in the few moments before the final appropriate resolution, we are suspended over the abyss of reality. Such a moment would be less powerful if we were not ultimately expecting and anticipating the formulaic resolution.

The pattern of expectations with which we approach an individual version of a formula results both from our previous experience of the type and from certain internal qualities that formulaic structures tend to have. One of the most important such characteristics is the kind of identification we are encouraged to have with the protagonists. All stories involve some kind of identification, for, unless we are able to relate our feelings and experiences to those of the characters in fiction, much of the emotional effect will be lost. In mimetic literature, identification is a complex phenomenon. Because mimetic fictions aim at the representation of actions that will confront us with reality, it is necessary for writers to make us recognize our involvement in characters whose fates reveal the uncertainties, limitations, and unresolvable mysteries of the real world. We must learn to recognize and accept our relationship to characters, motives, and situations we would not ordinarily choose to imagine ourselves as involved in or threatened by. "There but for the grace of God go I." Ordinarily I would prefer not to think of myself as a murderer, as a suicide, or as a middle-aged failure cuckolded by his wife. Yet in Dostoevsky's *Crime and Punishment*, Faulkner's *The Sound and the Fury*, and Joyce's *Ulysses* I am forced to recognize and come to terms with my participation in the fate of Raskolnikov, of Quentin Compson, and of Leopold Bloom. The process of identification in a mimetic fiction involves both my recognition of the differences between myself and the characters and my often reluctant but rather total involvement in their actions. I have at once a detached view and a disturbingly full sympathy and understanding.

Because of its escapist thrust, formulaic literature creates a very different sort of identification between audience and protagonists. Its purpose is not to make me confront motives and experiences in myself that I might prefer to ignore but to take me out of myself by confirming an idealized self-image. Thus, the protagonists of formulaic literature are typically better or more fortunate in some ways than ourselves. They are heroes who have the strength and courage to overcome great dangers, lovers who find perfectly suited partners, inquirers of exceptional brilliance who discover hidden truths, or good, sympathetic people whose difficulties are resolved by some superior figure. The art of formulaic character creation requires the establishment of some direct bond between us and a superior figure while undercutting or eliminating any aspects of the story that threaten our ability to share enjoyably in the triumphs or narrow escapes of the protagonist. Several means have developed for accomplishing this purpose. By giving narrative emphasis to a constant flow of action, the writer avoids the necessity of exploring character with any degree of complexity. Second, the use of stereotyped characters reflecting the audience's conventional views of life and society also aids the purpose of escapism. Formulaic literature is generally characterized by a simple and emotionally charged style that encourages immediate involvement in a character's actions without much sense of complex irony or psychological subtlety. As a model of the simplest and crudest form of immediate identification between protagonist and reader, I might cite the narrative methods of Mickey Spillane, which will be discussed in a later chapter.

While Mickey Spillane does represent a kind of narrative art that has been enormously successful with a certain kind of audience, I would guess that the formulaic writers of most lasting interest and consequently of greatest artistic importance are those who achieve the escapist form of identification in more complex and subtle ways that can withstand a certain degree of scrutiny. This can be accomplished through the creation of an imaginary world that is just sufficiently far from our ordinary reality to make us less inclined to apply our ordinary standards of plausibility and probability to it. If we become immersed in such a world, it is easier for us to escape from ourselves into identification with a story's protagonists. Many of the most successful and long-lasting formulas such as that of the western, or various other forms of historical adventure, involve the creation of just such an integral fantasy world, just as many of the best writers are very skillful in fleshing out the atmosphere of their imaginary universe. For example, many readers of Conan Doyle's Sherlock Holmes stories find renewed pleasure in rereading them because of Doyle's remarkable ability to evoke an imaginary vision of a whole bygone world. Something of the same sort can be said about the continued popularity of such works as Margaret Mitchell's *Gone with the Wind*, or Owen Wister's *The Virginian*. Despite the fact that these works are permeated with stereotypical characters, unlikely situations, and obsolete themes and values, they retain a hold on later generations because their fantasy world seems so complete and interesting in itself that it is still possible to enter into an effective escapist identification with the protagonists.

In general, the escapist aspect of formulaic art makes it analogous to certain kinds of games or play. In fact, if we look at television schedules, we find that they contain a predominance of spectator sports and formula stories. Like such games as football or baseball, formula stories are individual versions of a general pattern defined by a set of rules. While the rules remain the same, the highly varied ways in which they can be embodied in particular characters and actions produce a patterned experience of excitement, suspense, and release that, as in the case of the great games, can be perennially engrossing no matter how often the game is repeated. In the formula world, as in play, the ego is enhanced because conflicts are resolved and inescapable tensions and frustrations temporarily transcended. Piaget's general description of play applies completely to the escapist dimension of formulaic art:

> Conflicts are foreign to play, or, if they do occur it is so that the ego may be freed from them by compensation or liquidation whereas serious activity has to grapple with conflicts which are inescapable. The conflict between obedience and individual liberty is, for example the affliction of childhood and in real life the only solutions to this conflict are submission, revolt, or cooperation which involves some measure of compromise. In play, however, the conflicts are transposed in such a way that the ego is revenged, either by suppression of the problem or by giving it an effective solution. . . . it is because the ego dominates the whole universe in play that it is freed from conflict.[4]

Thus there are a number of distinctive problems and techniques characteristic of formulaic art. In general, the most significant formulaic artists are those who effectively solve these problems in a way that balances the claims of escapism and the fulfillment of a conventional experience with the artistic interests of revitalized stereotypes, some degree of originality, and as much plausibility as the boundaries of the formula will permit.

Formulas and Culture

Formulas are cultural products and in turn presumably have some sort of influence on culture because they become conventional ways of representing and relating certain images, symbols, themes, and myths. The process through which formulas develop, change, and give way to other formulas is a kind of cultural evolution with survival through audience selection.

Many different sorts of stories are written about a great diversity of subjects, but only a few become clearly established as formulas. For instance, out of the vast number of potential story possibilities associated with the rise of urban industrialism in the nineteenth century, relatively few major formulaic structures have developed, such as the detective story, the gangster saga, the doctor drama, and various science-fiction formulas. Other story types have been repeated often enough to become partly formulaic, such as the story of the newspaper reporter and the scoop, or the story of the failure of success as represented in the figure of the great tycoon. But these two types have never had the sustained and widespread appeal of the western, the detective story, or the gangster saga. Still other potential story topics have never become popular at all. There is no formula for the story of the union leader—despite the best efforts of "proletarian" critics and novelists in the 1930s. There are no formulas with politicians or businessmen as protagonists, though they are social figures of major importance. Farmers, engineers, architects, teachers, have all been treated in a number of individual novels but have never become formulaic heroes.

What is the basis on which this process of cultural selection of formulas takes place? Why do some sorts of stories become widely popular formulas while others do not? How do we account for the pattern of change within formulas, or for the way one formula supersedes another in popularity? What does popularity itself mean? Can we infer from the popularity of a work that it reflects public attitudes and motives, or is it impossible to go beyond the circular observation that a story is successful with the public because the public finds it a good story?

First of all, we can distinguish, I think, between the problem of the popularity of an individual work and the popularity of a formula. Determining why a particular novel or film becomes a best-seller is problematic because it is difficult to be sure what elements or combination of elements the public is responding to. For example, in the case of the enormously successful novel *The Godfather*, is it the topic of crime and the portrayal of violence that made the book popular? Probably not, since there are many other novels dealing with crime in a violent way that have not been equally successful. Thus it must be something about the way in which crime and violence are treated. Only if we can find other books or films that treat the topic of crime in a similar way and also gain a considerable measure of popularity can we feel some confidence that we have come closer to isolating the aspects of *The Godfather* that are responsible for its public success. (I attempt to do this for *The Godfather* in chapter 3.) Clearly, we can only explain the success of individual works by means of analogy and comparison with other successful works, through the process of defining those elements or patterns that are common to a number of best-sellers.

A formula is one such pattern. When we have successfully defined a formula we have isolated at least one basis for the popularity of a large number of works. Of course, some formulaic writers are more successful than others, and their unique popularity remains a problem that must be explored in its own right. During his heyday, Mickey Spillane's hard-boiled detective stories sold far better than those of any other writer in the formula, and Spillane's success was certainly one main reason why other writers continued to create this type of story. Yet quite apart from Spillane's own personal popularity, the hard-boiled detective formula, in the hands of writers as diverse as Dashiell Hammett, Raymond Chandler, Carter Brown, Shell Scott, Brett Halliday, and many others, in hard-boiled detective films by directors like Howard Hawks, John Huston, Roman Polanski, and in TV series like "Cannon," "Mannix," and "Barnaby Jones," has been continually successful with the public since the late 1920s. When it becomes such a widely successful formula, a story pattern clearly has some special appeal and significance to many people in the culture. It becomes a matter of cultural behavior that calls for explanation along with other cultural patterns.

Unfortunately, to construct such an explanation requires us to have some notion of the relation between literature and other aspects of culture, an area which remains rather impenetrable. Are literary works to be treated primarily as causes or symptoms of other modes of behavior? Or is literature an integral and autonomous area of human experience without significant effects on political, economic, or other forms of social behavior? Do some works of literature become popular primarily because they contain a good story artistically told or because they embody values and attitudes that their audience wishes to see affirmed? Or does popularity imply some kind of psychological wish-fulfillment, the most popular works being those which most effectively help people to identify imaginatively with actions they would like to perform but cannot in the ordinary course of events? We certainly do not know at present which, if any, of these assumptions is correct. Persuasive arguments can be made for each one. Before attempting to develop a tentative method for exploring the cultural meaning of literary formulas, let us look briefly at what can be said for and against the principal methods that have been used to explore the relation between literature and other aspects of human behavior.

Three main approaches have been widely applied to explain the cultural functions or significance of literature. These may be loosely characterized as (1) impact or effect theories; (2) deterministic theories; and (3) symbolic or reflective theories.

1. Impact theories are the oldest, simplest, and most widespread way in which men have defined the cultural significance of literature. Such theories assume basically that literary forms and/or contents have some direct influence on human behavior. Naturally, the tendency of this approach is to treat literature as a moral or political problem and to seek to determine which literary patterns have desirable effects on human conduct and which have bad effects, in order to support the former and suppress or censor the latter. Socrates suggested in *The Republic* that it might be necessary to escort the poet to the gates of the city since his works stimulate weakening and corrupting emotions in his audience. Over the centuries, men of varying religious and political commitments have followed this advice by seeking to censor literary expression on the ground that it would corrupt the people's morals or subvert the state. Today, many psychologists study what effects the representation of violence has on the behavior of children. Presumably if they are able to demonstrate some connection between represented violence and aggressive behavior, the widespread clamor against film and television violence will increase and laws will be passed regulating the content of these media.

The impact approach also dominated mass communications research in its earlier years, when sociologists were primarily interested in propaganda and its effects. Propaganda research sought to show just how and in what ways a literary message could have an effect on attitudes and behavior. This research discovered, for the most part, that insofar as any effect could be isolated, propaganda simply caused people to believe and act in ways they were already predisposed toward. It became evident to most researchers in this area that their original quest for a direct link between communication and behavior oversimplified a more complex social process. Much of the more interesting recent research has tended to focus on the process of communication rather than its impact, showing the ways in which mass communications are mediated by the social groups to which the recipient belongs, or by the different uses to which communications are put. But the more complex our view of the process of communication becomes, the less meaningful it is to speak of it in terms of cause and effect.

Another basic weakness of impact theories is that they tend to treat literary or artistic experience like any other kind of experience. Since most of our experience does have an immediate and direct effect on our behavior, however trivial, the impact theorists assume that the same must be true of literature. The difficulty with this view is that our experience of literature is not like any other form of behavior since it concerns events and characters that are imagined. Reading about something is obviously not the same thing as doing it. Nor are the very strong emotions generated in us by stories identical with those emotions in real life. A story about a monster can arouse fear and horror in me, but this is certainly a different emotion than the one I feel when confronted by some actual danger or threat, because I know that the monster exists only in the world of the story and cannot actually harm me. This does not mean that my emotion will necessarily be less strong than it would be in reality. Paradoxically, feelings experienced through literature may sometimes be stronger and deeper than those aroused by analogous life situations. For instance, I am inclined to believe that the fear and pity evoked by literature is more intense for many people than that generated in real-life experiences. That literature can give us such intensified emotions may be one of the reasons we need stories. Yet, no matter how strong the feeling aroused by a work of literature, we do not generally confuse it with reality and therefore it does not affect us as such. There are probably some important exceptions to this generalization. Unsophisticated or disturbed people do apparently sometimes confuse art and reality. The same is apparently true of many younger children. There are many instances where people treat characters in a soap opera as if they were real people, sending them gifts on their birthdays, grieving when they are in difficulties, asking their advice and help. Some of this behavior is probably an unsophisticated way of expressing one's great pleasure and interest in a story, but some of it may well indicate that a person does not make our ordinary differentiation between imagination and reality. For such people literature may well have a direct and immediate behavioral impact. I suspect that this is particularly the case among relatively disturbed children. Not surprisingly, it is here that recent studies may indicate a causal connection between represented violence and violent behavior. Nonetheless, for most people in most situations, the impact approach assumes much too simple a relationship between literature and other behavior to provide a satisfactory basis for interpreting the cultural significance of any literary phenomenon.

If such reflections lead us to question the idea that literature has a direct causal effect on behavior, this does not mean that we must take the position that literature causes nothing and is only a reflection of reality without further consequence than the evocation of some temporary state of feeling. Such a view seems just as implausible as the notion that art directly and immediately changes attitudes and behavior. One of my colleagues has often remarked that all of us carry a collection of story plots around in our heads and that we tend to see and shape life according to these plots. Something like this seems to me to be the basic kernel of truth in the impact theory. Our artistic experiences over a period of time work on the structure of our imaginations and feelings and thereby have long-term effects on the way in which we understand and respond to reality. Unfortunately, no one has ever managed to demonstrate the existence of such long-term effects in a convincing way, in part because we have never been able to define with any precision just what are the most common and widespread patterns of literary experience. The analysis of formulas may be a promising method of beginning to study long-term effects, for formulas do shape the greater part of the literary experiences of a culture. If we can clearly define all the major formulas of a particular culture, we will at least know what patterns are being widely experienced. It may then be possible to construct empirical studies of the relation between these formulas and the attitudes and values that individuals and groups show in other forms of behavior. David McClelland and his associates managed to isolate a particular pattern of action in stories that they correlated with a basic cultural motive for achievement. In cross-cultural studies reported in *The Achieving Society*, McClelland suggests that the presence of this pattern of action in the stories of a particular culture or period is correlated with a definite emphasis on achievement in that culture or in a succeeding period. Some of the cases McClelland cites could be instances where the stories heard most often by children did have a long-term impact on their behavior as adults; it is, of course, difficult to determine the extent to which these story patterns were causes or symptoms, but this, I feel, is a problem that can never be solved. If we can establish correlations between literary patterns and other forms of behavior, we will have done all we can expect to do by way of establishing the long-term impact of literature. The reason for this can be best understood by turning to the second major approach that has been employed to explain the cultural significance of literature: the various theories of social or psychological determinism.

2. These deterministic theories—the most striking being various applications of Marxian or Freudian ideas to the explanation of literature—assume that art is essentially a contingent and dependent form of behavior that is generated and shaped by some underlying social or psychological dynamic. In effect, literature becomes a kind of stratagem to cope with the needs of a social group or of the psyche. These needs become the determinants of literary expression and the process of explanation consists in showing how literary forms and contents are derived from these other processes.

The deterministic approach has been widely applied to the intepretation of all sorts of literature with interesting if controversial results ranging from the Oedipal interpretation of *Hamlet* to interpretations of the novel as a literary reflection of the bourgeois world view. When used in conjunction with individual masterpieces, the deterministic approach has been widely rejected and criticized by literary scholars and historians for its tendencies toward oversimplification and reductionism. And yet the method has gained much wider acceptance as a means of dealing with formulaic structures like the western, the detective story, and the formula romance. Some scholars see the whole range of formulaic literature as an opiate for the masses, a ruling-class stratagem for keeping the majority of the people content with a daily ration of pleasant distractions. Others have interpreted particular formulas in deterministic terms: the detective story as a dramatization of the ideology of bourgeois rationalism or as an expression of the psychological need to resolve in fantasy the repressed childhood memories of the primal scene.

All such explanations have two fundamental weaknesses. (*a*) They depend on the a priori assumption that a particular social or psychological dynamic is the basic cause of human behavior. If it is the case that, for example, unresolved childhood sexual conflicts generate most adult behavior, then it does not really explain anything to show that the reading of detective stories is an instance of such behavior. The interpretation does not go beyond the original assumption, except to show how the form of the detective story can be interpreted in this way. But the only means of proving that the detective story *should* be interpreted in this way is through the original assumption. Because of this circular relationship between assumption and interpretation, neither can provide proof for the other, unless the assumption can be demonstrated by other means. Even then there remains the problem of showing that the experience of literature is the same as other kinds of human activity. (*b*) The second weakness of most deterministic approaches is their tendency to reduce literary experience to other forms of behavior. For example, most Freudian interpretations treat literary experience as if it could be analogized with free association or dream. Even if we grant that psychoanalysis has proved to be a successful approach to the explanation of dream symbolism, it does not follow that literature is the same or even analogous. Indeed, there seems to me to be as much reason to believe that the making and enjoying of art works is an autonomous mode of experience as to assume it is dependent, contingent, or a mere reflection of other more basic social or psychological processes. Certainly many people act as if watching television, going to the movies, or reading a book were one of the prime ends of life rather than a means to something else. There are even statistics that might suggest that people spend far more time telling and enjoying stories than they do in sexual activity.[5] Of course, the psychological determinist would claim that listening to a story is in fact a form of sexual behavior, though stated in this way, the claim seems extreme.

Though there are many problems connected with the psychoanalytic

interpretation of literature, it is difficult to dismiss the compelling idea that in literature as in dreams unconscious or latent impulses find some disguised form of expression. Formula stories may well be one important way in which the individuals in a culture act out unconscious or repressed needs, or express latent motives that they must give expression to but cannot face openly. Possibly one important difference between the mimetic and escapist impulses in literature is that mimetic literature tends toward the bringing of latent or hidden motives into the light of consciousness while escapist literature tends to construct new disguises or to confirm existing defenses against the confrontation of latent desires. Such a view might be substantiated by the contrast between Sophocles' play *Oedipus the King* and a detective story. In the play detection leads to a revelation of hidden guilts in the life of the protagonist, while in the detective story the inquirer-protagonist and the hidden guilt are conveniently split into two separate characters—the detective and the criminal—thereby enabling us to imagine terrible crimes without also having to recognize our own impulses toward them. It is easy to generate a great deal of pseudopsychoanalytic theorizing of this sort without being able to substantiate it convincingly. Nevertheless, I think we cannot ignore the possibility that this is one important factor that underlies the appeal of literary formulas.

Thus, though we may feel that most contemporary deterministic approaches oversimplify the significance of literary works by explaining them in terms of other modes of experience, I think we cannot deny that stories, like other forms of behavior, are determined in some fashion. Though artistic experience may have an autonomy that present theories of social and psychological determinism are not sufficiently complex to allow for, I presume that, as human behavior in general is more fully understood, we will also be better able to generalize about how social and psychological factors play a role in the process by which stories and other imaginative forms are created and enjoyed. In the present state of our knowledge, it seems more reasonable to treat social and psychological factors not as single determinant causes of literary expression but as elements in a complex process that limits in various ways the complete autonomy of art. In making cultural interpretations of literary patterns, we should consider them not as simple reflections of social ideologies or psychological needs but as instances of a relatively autonomous mode of behavior that is involved in a complex dialectic with other aspects of human life. It is reasonable to see collective attitudes entering into the artistic works created and enjoyed by a particular group as a limit on what is likely to be represented in a story and how it is likely to be treated. What we must avoid is an automatic reading into a story of what we take to be the prevailing cultural attitudes or psychological needs. This has been too often the path taken by the deterministic approach and in its circularity it tells us nothing about either the literary work or the culture.

3. A third approach to the cultural explanation of literary experience—symbolic or reflective theories—rejects the more extreme forms of reductive

determinism by granting a special kind of autonomy to artistic expression. According to this approach, the work of art consists of a complex of symbols or myths that are imaginative orderings of experience. These symbols or myths are defined as images or patterns of images charged with a complex of feeling and meaning and they become, therefore, modes of perception as well as simple reflections of reality. According to this approach, symbols and myths are means by which a culture expresses the complex of feelings, values, and ideas it attaches to a thing or idea. Because of their power of ordering feelings and attitudes, symbols and myths shape the perceptions and motivations of those who share them. The flag is a relatively simple example of a symbol. Though nothing but a piece of cloth made in a certain pattern of colors and shapes, the flag has come to imply an attitude of love and dedication to the service of one's country that has even, in many instances, motivated individuals to die in an attempt to protect that piece of cloth from desecration. In recent years this symbol has in turn become a counter-symbol for some groups of an unreasoning and destructive patriotism, and this implication has motivated other individuals to risk danger and even imprisonment to desecrate the same piece of cloth. The first usage of the flag illustrates a class of symbolism that poses relatively few problems of analysis and interpretation since the meaning of the symbol is more or less established by some specific enactment, in this case laws designating a specific design as the national emblem. In this sense the flag has an official status with a designated set of meanings, as indicated by the fact that it is against the law to treat the flag in certain ways. But the second usage of the flag as counter-symbol of regressive or false patriotism is of a different sort altogether. This symbolism was not created by specific enactment and has no official status. It emerged as one means of focusing and representing the rejection by certain groups of actions and attitudes taken in the name of the country and defended by traditional claims of patriotism. I don't know whether it is possible to determine who first conceived of using the flag as a symbol of this sort, but it is clear that throughout the 1960s, particularly in connection with the agitation against the Vietnam war, this new symbolism of the flag became a powerful force, generating strong feelings and even violent actions both in support of and in opposition to this new form of symbolism.

These two types of symbolism indicate the great significance that symbols have for culture and psychology. In fact, the concept of symbolism seems to resolve some of the problems we have noted in connection with the impact and deterministic approaches to explaining the cultural significance of literary experience. The symbolism of the flag suggests how it is possible for an image both to reflect culture and to have some role in shaping it. Not surprisingly, some of the most influential studies of American culture in the past two decades have been analyses of symbols and myths primarily as these are expressed in various forms of literature. And yet there remain a number of problems about this approach, many of which have been effectively articulated in a critique of the myth-symbol approach by Bruce Kuklick in a recent issue of *American Quarterly*. Kuklick defines two kinds of objection: the first concerns certain confusions in the theoretical formulations of the leading myth-symbol interpreters, while the second involves a number of problems of definition and method. Since the formula approach that I am using in this study is essentially a variation of the myth-symbol method of interpretation, I feel we must examine the most important of Kuklick's objections to it.

Essentially, Kuklick argues that certain theoretical confusions in the myth-symbol approach prevent it from being a meaningful way of connecting literary expression with other forms of behavior. He points out that the myth-symbol critics assume the existence of a collective mind (in which the images, myths, and symbols exist) that is separated from an external reality (of which the images and symbols are some form of mental transmutation). This separation is necessary, he suggests, in order for the interpreter to determine which images are real and which are fantastic or distortions or value-laden. Unfortunately, this separation of internal mind from external reality leads the method right into the philosophical trap of the mind-body problem, as exemplified in what Kuklick calls crude Cartesianism. The result is as follows:

> A crude Cartesian has two options. First, he can maintain his dualism but then must give up any talk about the external world. How can he know that any image refers to the external world? Once he stipulates that they are on different planes, it is impossible to bring them into any meaningful relation; in fact, it is not even clear what a relationship could conceivably be like. Descartes resorted to the pineal gland as the source and agent of mind-body interaction, but this does not appear to be an out for the [myth-symbol interpreters]. Second, the Cartesian can assimilate what we normally take to be facts about the external world—for example, my seeing the man on the corner—to entities like images, symbols and myths. . . . Facts and images both become states of consciousness. If the Cartesian does this, he is committed to a form of idealism. Of course, this maneuver will never be open to . . . Marxists, but it also provides problems for the [myth-symbol interpreters]: they have no immediate way of determining which states of consciousness are "imaginative" or "fantastic" or "distorted" or even "value-laden" for there is no standard to which the varying states of consciousness may be referred. On either of these two options some resort to platonism is not strange. A world of suprapersonal ideas which we all share and which we may use to order our experiences is a reasonable supposition under the circumstances. But this position, although by no means absurd, is not one to which we wish to be driven if we are setting out a straightforward theory to explain past American behavior.[6]

According to Kuklick, the only solution to this dilemma is to give up using symbols and myths to explain all kinds of behavior. Instead, he says, we should postulate mental constructs like images and symbols only as a means of describing a disposition to write in a certain way. In other words, a symbol or a myth is simply a generalizing concept for summarizing certain recurrent patterns in writing and other forms of expression. Insofar as it explains anything, the myth-symbol approach simply indicates that a group of persons has a tendency to express itself in certain patterns:

> Suppose we define an idea not as some entity existing "in the mind" but as a disposition to behave in a certain way under appropriate circumstances. Similarly, to say that an author has a particular image of the man on the corner (or uses the man on the corner as a symbol) is to say that in appropriate parts of his work, he writes of a man on the corner in a certain way. When he simply writes of the man to refer to him, let's say, as the chap wearing the blue coat, we can speak of the image of the man, although the use of "image" seems to obfuscate matters. If the man is glorified in poem and song as Lincolnesque, we might speak of the author as using the man as a symbol, and here the word "symbol" seems entirely appropriate. For images and symbols to become collective is simply for certain kinds of writing (or painting) to occur with relative frequency in the work of many authors.[7]

I think we must accept Kuklick's contention that insofar as the myth-symbol approach assumes a direct connection between literary symbols and other forms of behavior such as specific political or social actions, it is highly questionable. To explain the American course of action in Vietnam as the effect of the American western myth is to indulge in speculations about causal connections that can never be demonstrated or substantiated and that probably assume an oversimplified view of the relations between art and other kinds of experience. Yet, to take the further step of insisting that the myths and symbols found in written (and other forms of expressive) behavior can only be understood as a generalization about that specific kind of behavior seems contradictory to experience, for we can all think of many ways in which our lives have been shaped by the symbolic or mythical patterns we have encountered in various forms of literature. The problem is to arrive at some better and more complex understanding of the way in which literature interacts with other aspects of life, for I think we can grant that imaginative symbols do not have a direct and immediate causal effect on other forms of behavior. Otherwise the impact approach to interpreting the cultural significance of literature would long since have proved more fruitful.

The resolution of the problems posed by these criticisms of the myth-symbol approach lies, I think, in replacing the inevitably vague and ambiguous notion of myth with a conception of literary structures that can be more precisely defined and are consequently less dependent on such implicit metaphysical assumptions as that of a realm of superpersonal ideas, which Kuklick rightly objects to. One such conception is that of the conventional story pattern or formula. This notion has, in my view, two great advantages over the notion of myth. First of all, the concept of formula requires us to attend to the whole of a story rather than to any given element that is arbitrarily selected. A myth can be almost anything—a particular type of character, one among many ideas, a certain kind of action—but a formula is essentially a set of generalizations about the way in which all the elements of a story have been put together. Thus it calls our attention to the whole experience of the story rather than to whatever parts may be germane to the myths we are pursuing. This feature of the concept leads to its second advantage: to connect a mythical pattern with the rest of human behavior requires tenuous and debatable assumptions, while the relation between formulas and other aspects of life can be explored more directly and empirically as a question of why certain groups of people enjoy certain stories. While the psychology of literary response is certainly not without its mysteries, it seems safe to assume that people choose to read certain stories because they enjoy them. This at least gives us a straightforward if not simple psychological connection between literature and the rest of life.

Beginning with the phenomenon of enjoyment, we can sketch out a tentative theory for the explanation of the emergence and evolution of literary formulas. The basic assumption of this theory is that conventional story patterns work because they bring into an effective conventional order a large variety of existing cultural and artistic interests and concerns. This approach is different from traditional forms of social or psychological determinism in that it rejects the concept of a single fundamental social or psychological dynamic in favor of viewing the appeal of a conventional literary pattern as the result of a variety of cultural, artistic, and psychological interests. Successful story patterns like the western persist, according to this view, not because they embody some particular ideology or psychological dynamic, but because they maximize a great many such dynamics. Thus, in analyzing the cultural significance of such a pattern, we cannot expect to arrive at a single key interpretation. Instead, we must show how a large number of interests and concerns are brought into an effective order or unity. One important way of looking at this process is through the dialectic of cultural and artistic interests. In order to create an effective story, certain archetypal patterns are essential, the nature of which can be determined by looking at many different sorts of stories. These story patterns must be embodied in specific images, themes, and symbols that are current in particular cultures and periods. To explain the way in which cultural imagery and conventional story patterns are fitted together constitutes a partial interpretation of the cultural significance of these formulaic combinations. This process of interpretation reveals both certain basic concerns that dominate a particular culture and also something about the way in which that culture is predisposed to order or deal with those concerns. We must remember, however, that since artistic experience has a certain degree of autonomy from other forms of behavior, we must always distinguish between the way symbols are ordered in stories and the way they may be ordered in other forms of behavior. To this extent, I think Kuklick is correct in suggesting that the existence of symbols and myths in art cannot be taken as a demonstration that these symbols are somehow directly related to other forms of behavior and belief. Yet there are certainly cultural limits on the way in which symbols can be manipulated for artistic purposes. Thus our examination of the dialectic between artistic forms and cultural materials should reveal something about the way in which people in a given culture are predisposed to think about their lives.

As an example of the complex relationship between literary symbols and attitudes and beliefs that motivate other forms of behavior, we might look at the role of political and social ideologies in the spy story. Because of its setting, the spy story almost inevitably brings political or social attitudes into play since conflicting political forces are an indispensable background for the antagonism between the spy-hero and his enemy. Thus, in the espionage adventures written by John Buchan and other popular writers of the period between World Wars I and II—"Sapper," Dornford Yates, E. Phillips Oppenheim, and Saxe Rohmer, for instance—one dominant theme is that of the threat of racial subversion. The British Empire and its white, Christian civilization are constantly in danger of subversion by villains who represent other races or racial mixtures. Saxe Rohmer's Fu Manchu and his hordes of little yellow and brown conspirators against the safety and purity of English society are only an extreme example of the pervasive racial symbolism of this period. It is tempting to interpret these stories as reflections of a virulent racism on the part of the British and American public. There is no doubt some truth in this hypothesis, especially since we can find all kinds of other evidence revealing the power of racist assumptions in the political attitudes and actions of this public. Yet few readers who enjoyed the works of Buchan and Rohmer were actually motivated to embark on racist crusades, for it was in Germany rather than England and America that racism became a dominant political dogma. Even in Buchan's case, many of the attitudes expressed in his novels are far more extreme than those we find in his nonfiction and autobiographical works, or in his public life and statements. It is a little difficult to know just what to make of this. Was Buchan concealing his more extreme racist views behind the moderate stance of a politician? Or is the racial symbolism in his novels less a reflection of his actual views than a means of intensifying and dramatizing conflicts? Umberto Eco in a brilliant essay on the narrative structure of the James Bond novels suggests that something like this may well be the case with Ian Fleming's "racism."

> Fleming intends, with the cynicism of the disillusioned, to build an effective narrative apparatus. To do so he decides to rely upon the most secure and universal principles, and puts into play archetypal elements which are precisely those that have proved successful in traditional tales. . . . [Therefore] Fleming is a racialist in the sense that any artist is one, if, to represent the devil, he depicts him with oblique eyes; in the sense that a nurse is one who, wishing to frighten children with the bogey-man, suggests that he is black. . . . Fleming seeks elementary opposition: to personify primitive and

universal forces he has recourse to popular opinion.... A man who chooses to write in this way is neither Fascist nor racialist; he is only a cynic, a deviser of tales for general consumption.[8]

As in the case of Fleming, many apparently ideological expressions in Buchan may arise more from dramatic than propagandistic aims. Therefore we must exercise some caution in our inferences about the social and political views that the author and audience of such stories actually believe in. Most audiences would appear to be capable of temporarily tolerating a wide range of political and social ideologies for the sake of enjoying a good yarn. As Raymond Durgnat has suggested, recent spy films with ideological implications ranging from reactionary to liberal have been highly successful. Or to take a different example of the same sort of phenomenon, a number of recent black detective films and westerns, which portray whites as predominantly evil, corrupt, or helpless, have been quite successful with substantial segments of the white as well as the black public.

But even if we grant that the melodramatic imperatives of formula stories tend to call forth more extreme expressions of political and moral values than either author or audience fully accept, there still remains a need for author and audience to share certain basic feelings about the world. If this sharing does not occur at some fundamental level, the audience's enjoyment of the story will be impeded by its inability to accept the structure of probability, to feel the appropriate emotional responses, and to be fascinated by the primary interests on which the author depends. An audience can enjoy two different stories that imply quite different political and social ideologies, so long as certain fundamental attitudes are invoked. Durgnat puts the point rather well in explaining why the same public might enjoy *Our Man Flint*, a spy film with very conservative political overtones, and *The Silencers*, which is far more liberal in its ideology:

> The political overtones of the movies appear only if you extrapolate from the personal sphere to the political, which most audiences don't. The distinct moral patterns would be more likely to become conscious, although neither film pushed itself to a crunch. In other words, the two moral patterns can coexist; both films can be enjoyed by the same spectator, could have been written by the same writer. Both exploit the same network of assumptions.[9]

This "network of assumptions" is probably an expression, first, of the basic values of a culture, and on another level, of the dominant moods and concerns of a particular era, or of a particular subculture. That Buchan is still enjoyed with pleasure by some contemporary readers indicates that there are enough continuities between British culture at the time of World War I and the present day to make it possible for some persons to accept Buchan's system of probabilities and values at least temporarily for the sake of the story. That Buchan is no longer widely popular, however, is presumably an indication that much of the network of assumptions on which his stories rest is no longer shared.

These considerations suggest the importance of differentiating literary imperatives from the expression of cultural attitudes. In order to define the basic network of assumptions that reflect cultural values we cannot simply take individual symbols and myths at their face value but must uncover those basic patterns that recur in many different individual works and even in many different formulas. If we can isolate those patterns of symbol and theme that appear in a number of different formulas popular in a certain period, we will be on firmer ground in making a cultural interpretation, since those patterns characteristic of a number of different formulas presumably reflect basic concerns and valuations that influence the way people of a particular period prefer to fantasize. In addition, the concept of the formula as a synthesis of cultural symbols, themes, and myths with more universal story archetypes should help us to see where a literary pattern has been shaped by the needs of a particular archetypal story form and to differentiate this from those elements that are expressions of the network of assumptions of a particular culture. Thus the spy story as a formula that depends on the archetype of heroic adventure requires a basic antagonism between hero and villain. The specific symbols or ideological themes used to dramatize this antagonism reflect the network of assumptions of a particular culture at a particular time. The creation of a truly intense antagonism may well involve pushing some of these cultural assumptions to extremes that would not be accepted by most people in areas of life other than fantasy.

Most of Kuklick's other criticisms of the myth-symbol approach come down to an attack on the way in which myths and symbols have been defined and interpreted. He argues that most myth-symbol interpreters have defined the central myths of the American past in terms of concerns of the present and argues that they have thereby committed the historical fallacy of presentism. He also points out that they have based their analysis almost entirely on printed literary materials that can be said to relate to only a minority of the population. Indeed, some scholars have based their interpretations on a small number of masterpieces which, despite the argument that great writers have a unique capacity to articulate central cultural myths, cannot really be said to reflect more than the interests and attitudes of the elite audiences who read them. Whether or not these criticisms apply to the myth-symbol interpreters, and I must confess that they do in a number of instances, I think they are largely obviated by the method of formula analysis. First of all, a formula is by definition a pattern characteristic of the widest possible range of literature and other media. Therefore, it does not involve drawing cultural inferences from a few select masterpieces in a medium that does not cover the entire culture. The major formulas we will be studying are basic structural patterns in mass media like the movies and television as well as in printed literature. Therefore, they are understood and enjoyed by the great majority of the population at one time or another. In addition, while the concept of a symbol or myth is vague enough that it can be interpreted in many different ways, the study of formulas has a built-in defense against "presentism" for it forces us not simply to explain the meaning of a single symbol or myth, but to account for the relationship between many different myths and symbols. In doing this, I feel we are inevitably forced to come closer to the original intention. While it may well be possible for us to treat the symbolic figure of Cooper's Leatherstocking in such a way as to lose track of the original meaning he had for Cooper, I think that if we insist upon reading the Leatherstocking tales in the context of all the various characters and situations that Cooper places him in and then upon comparing all this with later embodiments of the western formula, we will certainly find it far more difficult to misread Leatherstocking's original meaning for Cooper. The analysis of a formula always involves us in the exploration of a literary whole, while themes, symbols, or myths are usually only parts of larger patterns. To select a theme or symbol out of a larger whole invariably has an arbitrary aspect that the analysis of formulas avoids.

To understand more fully the relation between artistic and cultural interests involved in the creation of formulas, we need to know more about the range of cultural functions as well as the distinctive artistic qualities of formulaic literature. In an earlier section of this discussion, I suggested that the special artistic quality of formulaic literature was the result of striking a balance, appropriate to the intended audience, between the sense of reality or mimesis essential to art of any kind and the characteristics of escapist imaginative experience: an emphasis on game and play, on wish-fulfilling forms of identification, on the creation of an integral, slightly removed imaginative world, and on intense, but temporary emotional effects like suspense, surprise, and horror, always controlled by a certainty of resolution. Effective formulaic literature depends on a maximizing of this escapist dimension within a framework that the audience can still accept as having some connection with reality.

What, then, can be said of the cultural functions of formulaic literature? I think we can assume that formulas become collective cultural products because they successfully articulate a pattern of fantasy that is at least acceptable to if not preferred by the cultural groups who enjoy them. Formulas enable the members of a group to share the same fantasies. Literary patterns that do not perform this function do not become formulas. When a group's attitudes undergo some change, new formulas arise and existing formulas develop new themes and symbols, because formula stories are created and distributed almost entirely in terms of commercial exploitation. Therefore, allowing for a certain degree of inertia in the process, the production of formulas is largely dependent on audience response. Existing formulas commonly evolve in response to new audience interests. A good example of this process is the recent success with urban audiences of a new kind of black-oriented, action-adventure film. The great majority of these new black films are simply versions of traditional formulas like the western, the hard-boiled detective story, and the gangster saga with an urban black setting and protagonists. These formulas enable the new black self-consciousness to find expression in conventional forms of fantasy not significantly different in their assumptions and value structures from the sort of adventure stories that have been enjoyed by American audiences for several decades. The new black cowboy or gangster or detective hero is the same basic hero type in the same kind of action. Thus, in this case, the evolution of formulas has simply assimilated black needs for some sort of distinctive artistic expression into the shapes of conventional fantasies. It would appear, then, that one basic cultural impetus of formulaic literature is toward the maintenance of conventional patterns of imaginative expression. Indeed, the very fact that a formula is an often repeated narrative or dramatic pattern implies the function of cultural stability. Formulaic evolution and change are one process by which new interests and values can be assimilated into conventional imaginative structures. This process is probably of particular importance in a discontinuous, pluralistic culture like those of modern industrial societies. Therefore, literary formulas tend to flourish in such a society.

I would like to suggest four interrelated hypotheses about the dialectic between formulaic literature and the culture that produces and enjoys it:

1. Formula stories affirm existing interests and attitudes by presenting an imaginary world that is aligned with these interests and attitudes. Thus westerns and hard-boiled detective stories affirm the view that true justice depends on the individual rather than the law by showing the helplessness and inefficiency of the machinery of the law when confronted with evil and lawless men. By confirming existing definitions of the world, literary formulas help to maintain a culture's ongoing consensus about the nature of reality and morality. We assume, therefore, that one aspect of the structure of a formula is this process of confirming some strongly held conventional view.

2. Formulas resolve tensions and ambiguities resulting from the conflicting interests of different groups within the culture or from ambiguous attitudes toward particular values. The action of a formula story will tend to move from an expression of tension of this sort to a harmonization of these conflicts. To use the example of the western again, the action of legitimated violence not only affirms the ideology of individualism but also resolves tensions between the anarchy of individualistic impulses and the communal ideals of law and order by making the individual's violent action an ultimate defense of the community against the threat of anarchy.

3. Formulas enable the audience to explore in fantasy the boundary between the permitted and the forbidden and to experience in a carefully controlled way the possibility of stepping across this boundary. This seems to be preeminently the function of villains in formulaic structures: to express, explore, and finally to reject those actions which are forbidden, but which, because of certain other cultural patterns, are strongly tempting. For example, nineteenth-century American culture generally treated racial mix-

tures as taboo, particularly between whites, Orientals, blacks, and Indians. There were even deep feelings against intermarriage between certain white groups. Yet, at the same time, there were many things that made such mixtures strongly tempting, not least the universal pleasure of forbidden fruit. We find a number of formulaic structures in which the villain embodies explicitly or implicitly the threat of racial mixture. Another favorite kind of villain, the grasping tycoon, suggests the temptation actually acceded to by many Americans to take forbidden and illicit routes to wealth. Certainly the twentieth-century American interest in the gangster suggests a similar temptation. Formula stories permit the individual to indulge his curiosity about these actions without endangering the cultural patterns that reject them.

4. Finally, literary formulas assist in the process of assimilating changes in values to traditional imaginative constructs. I have already given the example of the new black action films as an instance of this process. As I shall show in another chapter, the western has undergone almost a reversal in values over the past fifty years with respect to the representation of Indians and pioneers, but much of the basic structure of the formula and its imaginative vision of the meaning of the West has remained substantially unchanged. By their capacity to assimilate new meanings like this, literary formulas ease the transition between old and new ways of expressing things and thus contribute to cultural continuity.

This analysis of the major ways in which literary formulas relate to the processes of culture is necessarily speculative. And yet it does provide us with some explanatory hypotheses that can be tested both in the analysis of formulaic literature and in investigations of the ways in which creators and audiences relate to these formulas. Since this study is concerned with defining and analyzing some of the major formulas, I must leave the latter kind of inquiry largely in abeyance, though I hope that the preceding outline of a theory of the cultural function of literary formulas will be put to the test by social psychologists or mass communications researchers.

Two

Notes toward a Typology
of Literary Formulas

One of the important problems connected with the study of literary formulas is to arrive at some understanding of the general story types that underlie the diversity of formulaic constructions.[1] I suggested in the first chapter that particular formulas clothe cultural images, myths, and themes in archetypal story forms that appear to be transcultural if not universal. Almost every commentator on the western has noted at one point or another the analogy between the heroic cowboy and the chivalrous knight. Though the specific images and themes of the knightly romance are quite different from those of the western, they are both forms of heroic adventure. Consequently the basic structures of action, the kinds of character relationships and situations they represent, have many things in common. There are several reasons why it is important to gain some clear definition of these archetypal structures. First, because they underlie so many different kinds of stories, these structures probably reflect basic psychological interests and needs and thus can give us insight into the workings of the psyche. Second, to define these underlying forms is a means of clarifying what the artistic boundaries and potentials are for different sorts of formulas. Such definitions can lead us to a better appreciation of the artistic problems involved in the creation of formula literature. Finally, by discovering these more universal story types, we will be better able to differentiate what is particularly characteristic of an individual culture or period from those aspects of formulas that reflect more universal psychological and artistic imperatives.

If we look at the enormous variety of literary formulas, certain general principles seem to emerge. Many types of stories center on heroic action, and these are quite different from stories where the chief interest lies in how a girl meets a boy and love is born. Still another kind of story focuses on the unraveling of some sort of mystery, and while it may well contain elements of both heroism and romance, these are clearly subordinate to the search for truth. Other types of stories derive their fascination from the imaginary encounter with some monster or situation of fantasy. And what do we make of such highly successful dramas as those typically found in soap operas or in many best-selling novels, where different individuals undergo many diverse forms of suffering and unhappiness? Is there any basis on which we can account for the emergence of these formal archetypes?

At first, one is tempted to see these different archetypes as instances of such traditional literary genres as tragedy, comedy, romance, and satire. Thus, a soap opera might be seen as a popular form of tragedy, while the western can certainly be treated as a contemporary form of the romance. Though this approach is doubtless valid in a general way, it does not take into account certain special characteristics of formulaic literature that tend to differentiate it from what we commonly refer to as "serious" or "high" literature. Formulas are more highly conventional and more clearly oriented toward some form of escapism, the creation of an imaginary world in which fictional characters who command the reader's interests and concern transcend the boundaries and frustrations that the reader ordinarily experiences. The hero successfully overcomes his enemies and surmounts great dangers; the lover has his or her desires fully met; the long-suffering saint is finally rewarded. We might loosely distinguish between formula stories and their "serious" counterparts on the ground that the latter tend toward some kind of encounter with our sense of the limitations of reality, while formulas embody moral fantasies of a world more exciting, more fulfilling, or more benevolent than the one we inhabit. In these imaginary worlds we come temporarily nearer to our hearts' desires and escape from the limiting reality around us by imaginatively identifying with characters who have an unusually great ability to deal with the problems they face, or who are so favored by luck or providence that they eventually overcome their difficulties and "live happily ever after." At least until we need another story.

Not that formula literature is totally nonmimetic. A moral fantasy that is incredible to the point that it cannot generate some temporary suspension of disbelief will not serve the function of escape. This is one point where formulas are very closely tied to particular cultures and audiences, for it is the attitudes of particular groups that determine the rudimentary margin of credibility necessary even for the purposes of escape. Formula creators must produce different kinds of heroes for different audiences. Children can accept a Lone Ranger, but, for most adults, such a character is too pure and superheroic to serve the purposes of effective moral fantasy. For many nineteenth-century Americans it was plausible to ascribe certain events to providential action in a way that is totally unacceptable to contemporary audiences.

Moral fantasy can also be distinguished from the more mimetic form of physical or material fantasy in which the writer imagines a world materially different from ordinary reality, but in which the characters and the situations they confront are still governed by the general truths of human experience. *Alice's Adventures in Wonderland*, for example, takes place in a world where objects, time, and space are not governed by the ordinary laws of nature, yet the protagonist's behavior seems remarkably true to our understanding of the psyche of a young lady of her age, while many of the fantastic characters and episodes cast an ironic or satiric light on human nature as we know it. *Alice* is not, in any sense, a moral fantasy. A James Bond adventure, on the other hand, though it exists in a world that materially resembles our own at almost every point, presents a protagonist of extraordinary capacities in a set of circumstances that enable him to face the most insuperable obstacles and surmount them without lasting harm to himself, either morally or physically. This is clearly a special form of moral fantasy.

Mimesis and moral fantasy establish two poles between which there exists a rather complex continuum. Many major mimetic works contain elements of moral fantasy, just as many of the most effective escapist fictions mix a large proportion of human actuality with their fantasies of heroism and a more exciting, glamorous, and secure world. Nonetheless, even the most casual glance at a variety of the major formulaic types suggests that their basic structures involve some kind of moral fantasy. Therefore, it seems possible that an analysis of the moral fantasies underlying some of our major formulaic types might provide us with the basis for a typology of formulaic structures.

In making this analysis I have chosen, for the sake of simplicity, to eliminate from consideration the various forms of comedy. The reason for this selection is twofold. First of all, to add the whole range of comic formulas to what is already an extraordinarily broad and diverse mass of literary materials would make our task of classification and analysis infinitely more complicated than it already is. Second, comedy poses a special problem in connection with the discussion of moral fantasy since even the most mimetic comedies employ conventions that can be seen from certain points of view as examples of moral fantasy: the happy ending, the triumph of the fool, the defeat of the disproportionate. Indeed, if Elder Olson's analysis of the basic structure of comedy is correct and the comic effect is derived from our perception that a circumstance thought to be dangerous and threatening is not so in actuality, then comedy as a whole bears a different relation to escapist fantasies than the variety of noncomic structures.[2] To avoid getting into these complex and difficult questions, I will confine my attention to the typology of such noncomic formulas as the detective story, the spy story, the western, and the gothic romance.

Looking at the whole range of story formulas, we can, it seems to me, discern five primary moral fantasies under which all the formulas I am familiar with can be subsumed. I will first list these fantasies and then try to define them more specifically: Adventure; Romance; Mystery; Melodrama; Alien Beings or States.

Adventure

The central fantasy of the adventure story is that of the hero—individual or group—overcoming obstacles and dangers and accomplishing some important and moral mission. Often, though not always, the hero's trials are the result of the machinations of a villain, and, in addition, the hero frequently receives, as a kind of side benefit, the favors of one or more attractive young ladies. The interplay with the villain and the erotic interests served by attendant damsels are more in the nature of frosting on the cake. The true focus of interest in the adventure story is the character of the hero and the nature of the obstacles he has to overcome. This is the simplest and perhaps the oldest and widest in appeal of all story types. It can clearly be traced back to the myths and epics of earliest times and has been cultivated in some form or other by almost every human society. At least on the surface, the appeal of this form is obvious. It presents a character, with whom the audience identifies, passing through the most frightening perils to achieve some triumph. Perhaps the basic moral fantasy implicit in this type of story is that of victory over death, though there are also all kinds of subsidiary triumphs available depending on the particular cultural materials employed: the triumph over injustice and the threat of lawlessness in the western; the saving of the nation in the spy story; the overcoming of fear and the defeat of the enemy in the combat story. While the specific characterization of the hero depends on the cultural motifs and themes that are embodied in any specific adventure formula, there are in general two primary ways in which the hero can be characterized: as a superhero with exceptional strength or ability or as "one of us," a figure marked, at least at the beginning of the story, by flawed abilities and attitudes presumably shared by the audience. Both of these methods of characterization foster strong, but slightly different, ties of identification between hero and audience. In the case of the superhero, the principle of identification is like that between child and parent and involves the complex feelings of envious submission and ambiguous love characteristic of that relationship. This kind of treatment of the hero is most characteristic of the adventure stories constructed for children and young people. The superhero also frequently embodies the most blatant kind of sexual symbolism. More sophisticated adults generally prefer the "ordinary" hero figure who is dominant in the fictions of those who are usually considered the best writers of "grown-up" adventure stories such as H. Rider Haggard, Robert Louis Stevenson, or, to take a more recent example, Alistair MacLean. Some of the most popular writers of this type have managed to combine the superhero with a certain degree of sophistication as in the James Bond adventures of Ian Fleming.

Beyond the two general adventure patterns of the superhero and the ordinary hero, specific adventure formulas can be categorized in terms of the location and nature of the hero's adventures. This seems to vary considerably from culture to culture, presumably in relation to those activities that different periods and cultures see as embodying a combination of danger, significance, and interest. New periods seem to generate new adventure formulas while to some extent still holding on to earlier modes. Adventure situations that seem too distant either in time or in space tend to drop out of the current catalog of adventure formulas or to pass into another area of the culture. Thus, tales of knightly adventure, still widely popular in the nineteenth century, no longer play much of a role in adult adventure literature. More recent cultural situations—crime and its pursuit, war, the West, international espionage, sports—have largely usurped the battle with dragons and the quest for the grail.

Romance

The adventure story is perhaps the simplest fantasy archetype. Appearing at all levels of culture, it seems to appeal to all classes and types of person, though particularly to men. The feminine equivalent of the adventure story is the romance. This is not to say that women do not read adventure stories or that romances cannot be popular with men; there is probably no exclusive sexual property in these archetypes of fantasy. Nonetheless, the fact that most adventure formulas have male protagonists while most romances have female central characters does suggest a basic affinity between the different sexes and these two story types.

The crucial defining characteristic of romance is not that it stars a female but that its organizing action is the development of a love relationship, usually between a man and a woman. Because this is the central line of development, the romance differs from the adventure story and the mystery. Adventure stories, more often than not, contain a love interest, but one distinctly subsidiary to the hero's triumph over dangers and obstacles. One might put it that in the adventure story the relation between hero and villain is really more important than the hero's involvement with a woman. Romances often contain elements of adventure, but the dangers function as a means of challenging and then cementing the love relationship. For example, in a recent *True Confessions* story— "Raped—Then Thrown in the Drunk Tank to Die"—a young man tells the grim story of how on the eve of their wedding his sweetheart was raped and then underwent a series of further sufferings. But the significance of this episode lies in the way it brings the two lovers to a deeper and more secure love for each other—"For both of us, our wedding night was as perfect as any mortal man and woman could hope for—tender, passionate, wild, beautiful."[3]

The "gothic romance" or "contemporary gothic," one of the most popular present-day formulas, makes extensive use of elements of adventure and mystery. Unlike a straight mystery formula such as the detective story where the solution of the mystery is the dominant line of action, the gothic romance uses mystery as an occasion for bringing two potential lovers together, for placing temporary obstacles in the path of their relationship, and ultimately for making its solution a means of clearing up the separation between the lovers.

The moral fantasy of the romance is that of love triumphant and permanent, overcoming all obstacles and difficulties. Though the usual outcome is a permanently happy marriage, more sophisticated types of love story sometimes end in the death of one or both of the lovers, but always in such a way as to suggest that the love relation has been of lasting and permanent impact. This characteristic differentiates the mimetic form of the romantic tragedy from the formulaic romance. In works like *Romeo and Juliet, Tristan and Isolde*, or *Last Tango in Paris*, the intensity of the lovers' passion is directly related to the extent to which their love is doomed. It simply cannot continue to exist in the fictional situation either for social or psychological reasons and consequently the passion itself brings about the death of one or both of the lovers. In a romance like Erich Segal's *Love Story*, the passion is perfect in itself and redeems the lovers. It is not the inability of love to triumph over obstacles that brings about the death of Jenny, but a biological accident. The result is sentimental rather than tragic; we feel sad that something so perfect cannot continue, but we do not confront the basic irreconcilability of love with other responsibilities and needs, which is the essential tension of romantic tragedy.

Since romance is a fantasy of the all-sufficiency of love, most romantic formulas center on the overcoming of some combination of social or psychological barriers. A favorite formulaic plot is that of the poor girl who falls in love with some rich or aristocratic man, which might be called the Cinderella formula. Or there is the Pamela formula, in which the heroine overcomes the threat of meaningless passion in order to establish a complete love relationship. Another more contemporary formula is that of the career girl who rejects love in favor of wealth or fame, only to discover that love alone is fully satisfying.

There seems little doubt that most modern romance formulas are essentially affirmations of the ideals of monogamous marriage and feminine domesticity. No doubt the coming age of women's liberation will invent significantly new formulas for romance, if it does not lead to a total rejection of the moral fantasy of love triumphant. Just as one can see the increasing significance of antiheroic versions of such traditional adventure formulas as the western and the spy story, so the recent success of antiromantic romances like John Fowles's *The French Lieutenant's Woman* may presage the development of an antiromantic formula.

Mystery

The fundamental principle of the mystery story is the investigation and discovery of hidden secrets, the discovery usually leading to some benefit for the character(s) with whom the reader identifies. The discovery of secrets with bad consequences for the protagonist, as in the case of Oedipus, is indeed the result of a mystery structure, but a use of this structure outside the realm of moral fantasy. In mystery formulas, the problem always has a desirable and rational solution, for this is the underlying moral fantasy expressed in this formulaic archetype.

Unlike adventure and romance, which have spawned a great multiplicity of formulas, mystery has been far more important as a subsidiary principle in adventure stories, romances, and melodramas than as a dominant formulaic principle in its own right, with the single exception of one of the greatest and most fruitful of all formulas, that of the classical detective story. Most other formulas involving a good deal of mystery—such as the hard-boiled detective story, the secret agent story, the gothic romance, or the crime thriller—tend to shade over into adventure or romance, though mystery remains a basic interest and an important secondary principle of the form. The reason for this is probably quite simple. Pursued as an end in itself the search for hidden secrets is primarily an intellectual, reasoning activity. However much it may be the conscious expression of nonintellectual or unconscious interests— some psychoanalytical critics have suggested that our fascination with mysteries can ultimately be traced to our repressed feelings about the primal scene—the actual narrative of a mystery involves the isolation of clues, the making of deductions from these clues, and the attempt to place the various clues in their rational place in a complete scheme of cause and effect. Such an activity, and the underlying moral fantasy that all problems have a clear and rational solution, is necessarily of greatest interest to those individuals whose background and training have predisposed them to give special interest and valuation to the processes of thought. Others, perhaps the majority of people, will rather quickly lose interest in a structure that is predominantly rational and will prefer their mysteries served up as a sauce to heroic or erotic action. Used in this way, mystery can intensify and complicate a story of triumph over obstacles or of the successful development of love by increasing suspense and uncertainty and adding further interest to the final resolution.

Because of the basic intellectual demands it makes on its audience, the pure mystery has become one of the most sophisticated and explicitly artful of formulaic types. Yet its limitations are also great. While the classical detective story was a preeminent type of formulaic literature between the end of the nineteenth century and the time of World War II, and still remains an important formula, it has not shown the same capacity for change and development as the other major formulaic types. It is possible that the heyday of the pure mystery is past. And yet, as an important element in other formulaic types, mystery will undoubtedly continue to be a basic formulaic resource.

The mystery shares many characteristics with the story of imaginary beings or states and thus the term is often applied to ghost stories, to tales of demonic possession or of madness. But there is a fundamental difference that should be borne in mind. The mystery of the imaginary being or state is not resolved. Instead, the human protagonist adapts himself in some fashion to the alien creature, for example, by learning how to control him. Of course, there are ghost stories in which the alien being turns out to be a trick or a deception with the mysterious manifestations being given a rational explanation. This is a mystery formula. In the true story of imaginary beings, the mystery of the alien is never solved, only somehow dealt with. In Bram Stoker's *Dracula*, the alien being is dealt with by a more or less rationalistic-religious technology of vampire control, but the mystery cannot be explained away. The way is prepared for him to rise again and again. This sort of conclusion is the very antithesis of the mystery story where, once discovered and explained, a secret is no longer capable of disturbing or troubling us.

Melodrama

Though the term "melodrama" is sometimes applied to the dramatic productions of a certain period, it also often designates a certain kind of literary structure, and that is what I have in mind here. The structure in question is a somewhat problematic category because it does not appear to reflect a single overriding narrative or dramatic focus such as heroic adventure, the quest for love, the solution of mystery or alien beings and states. But there are formulaic narratives such as various types of best-selling novels, or many nineteenth-century plays commonly designated by the term, which seem to combine more than one of these different fantasies toward some other purpose. For example, if we take a novel like *Peyton Place* we can obviously subsume much of the narrative under the heading of romance, though it is clearly not a romance in the sense that it focuses on the story of a single protagonist or even a couple. The problem is even cloudier if we consider one of the large, messy, but enormously popular canvases of Harold Robbins, such as *The Adventurers*. There we have a great deal of romance, but also a whole structure of adventure, as well as elements that do not readily fit under any of the other categories such as the quasirealistic portrayal of different social structures in Europe and South America. Another kind of formula poses a related difficulty, the classic gangster film with its tale of the rise and fall of a gangster protagonist. In terms of its action content, this type of film might be subsumed under the category of adventure formulas, but there is a very important difference between this formula and the adventure pattern. The classic gangster tale is not a story of heroic triumph but of ultimate defeat. Though it deals with crime and involves police detection and pursuit of the criminals, it is not a mystery either, since no secrets are held from the audience and those who seek a solution of the crime are not protagonists but antagonists.

At first sight works as diverse as *Peyton Place*, *The Adventurers*, and *Little Caesar* do not seem to have much in common. I would like to put forward the argument that they do share one very fundamental pattern: they are all narratives of a complex of actions in a world that is purportedly full of the violence and tragedy we associate with the "real world" but that in this case seems to be governed by some benevolent moral principle. It is not a tragic or a naturalistic world because we can be confident that no matter now violent or meaningless it seems on the surface, the right things will ultimately happen. Melodrama, then, is the fantasy of a world that operates according to our heart's desires in contrast to the other formula types that are fantasies of particular actions or states of being that counter some of our deepest fears or concentrate on particular wishes for victory or love or knowledge. Therefore, melodrama can contain all the other fantasies and often does. In fact, its chief characteristic is the combination of a number of actions and settings in order to build up the sense of a whole world bearing out the audience's traditional patterns of right and wrong, good and evil.

One thing possessed in common by these otherwise very different sorts of stories is the quality that has traditionally been understood as the hallmark of melodrama: the drama of intensified effects (i.e., music, "melos") added to the play to increase its emotional power and intensify its hold on the audience. Therefore, the idea of melodrama has come to be associated with violence and sensationalism—"the plot revolves around malevolent intrigue and violent action, while credibility both of character and plot is sacrificed for violent effect and emotional opportunism."[4] This is undoubtedly one major characteristic of melodrama, but, as I noted in the first chapter, the quest for intensified narrative or dramatic effects is characteristic of the entire range of formulaic types. Particular formulas come into existence and flourish at least in part because they invent heightened narrative or dramatic patterns. In this sense all formulaic stories are melodramatic, and we might look at the various formulaic types—adventure, romance, and mystery—as simply specialized forms of melodrama. Indeed, many of the modern specialized formulas such as the classical detective story, the spy story, the hard-boiled detective story, and the gothic romance did evolve historically from the broader melodramatic forms of the early nineteenth century.

In addition to this basic aspect of melodrama, we can specify a characteristic purpose which differentiates a large class of works that can be called melodramatic from the other major formulaic types. This type has at its center the moral fantasy of showing forth the essential "rightness" of the world order. As the adventure story plays out the fantasy of heroic triumph over insuperable obstacles and the mystery presents the assertion of rational order over secrecy, chaos, and irrationality, the melodrama shows how the complex ambiguities and tragedies of the world ultimately reveal the operation of a benevolent, humanly oriented moral order. Because of this, melodramas are usually rather complicated in plot and character; instead of identifying with a single protagonist through his line of action, the melodrama typically makes us intersect imaginatively with many lives. Sub-plots multiply, and the point of view continually shifts in order to involve us in a complex of destinies. Through this complex of characters and plots we see not so much the working of individual fates but the underlying moral process of the world. In this respect, melodrama sometimes comes close to tragedy. But there is a crucial difference: in tragedy, the protagonist's catastrophe reveals the great gap between human desires and the limitations of the world; in melodrama this gap is bricked over. Melodramatic suffering and violence are means of testing and ultimately demonstrating the "rightness" of the world order. If the melodramatic hero meets a catastrophic end, it is either as a noble sacrifice to some good purpose or because he has become deserving of destruction. Within certain basic limits of plausibility and audience acceptance, the more realistic, tragic, and overpowering the evil plots, the more satisfying the ultimate triumph of the good.

Nothing seems quite so dated as a fifty-year-old melodrama because the moralistic assumptions on which its concept of "rightness" are founded are deeply tied up with culture-bound assumptions and beliefs. Therefore, what may seem the essence of "rightness" to one period becomes morally outrageous or even hilariously funny to another. Throughout most of the nineteenth century, for example, the "rightness" of the world order appears to have hinged on a sort of divine, providential economy that hinted at the direct and continual intervention of God in the affairs of men. Evil actions, defined largely as transgressions against the happiness and respectability of the middle-class family structure, inevitably led to terrible catastrophes for their perpetrators, while the innocent and the good were assured of their reward, if not in this life at least in the hereafter. In *Uncle Tom's Cabin*, the most powerful and most popular of nineteenth-century melodramas, the world we live in is shown to us as full of tragedy and evil; yet it is somehow a benevolent and right world because even the suffering of the good shows the hand of God at work. The death of Little Eva and the martyrdom of Tom are transcended and our tears turn to joy when we are assured that the wracked and beaten body will rise in glory. Certainly much of Mrs. Stowe's skill in organizing and narrating the multiple stories of the novel lies in the way her presentation of a slave society both condemns the transgressors and conveys to us certainty of redemption for the good. The history of *Uncle Tom's Cabin* also reveals to us another aspect of the cultural significance of melodrama. Because it directly implicates a world-view with particular social actions and characters, melodrama has the capacity for enormous social impact. When a new set of social meanings are powerfully involved with traditional structures of value and feeling, as Mrs. Stowe effectively presented black characters in such powerful traditional melodramatic roles as the Christian martyr, the loving mother, and the self-reliant hero, the impact of the work can possibly bring about significant changes in public attitudes. It is hard to be certain that *Uncle Tom's Cabin* had a causal relation to the Civil War, but it is clear that Southern apologists felt that it posed a basic threat to their moral vision of the world.

Of course, few melodramas involve this implication of traditional attitudes with new social meanings. More typical of the formulaic nineteenth-century melodrama is a work like Mrs. E. D. E. N. Southworth's *Ishmael*, where the self-reliant Christian hero suffers a good deal in his early life from the imputation of bastardy before a providential series of circumstances finally reveals that he was born in wedlock and is the legitimate son of a first family of Virginia. Here, as in most melodramas, the universal moral order validates current social attitudes. One can see this principle operating in a contemporary melodramatist like Harold Robbins, even though the conception of providence is no longer part of the vision of the world order. In Robbins's *The Carpetbaggers*, for example, the protagonist tastes extensively of all that enormous riches, power, and erotic delights can offer only to discover in the end that true fulfillment lies in a monogamous love, a simple home, and a family. Popular Freudianism has replaced providence as the primary means of articulating the universal moral order, but the result is essentially the demonstration of a connection between traditional middle-class domestic morality and the operative principles of the cosmos. On the other hand, a work like *The Godfather* may well involve some significant transformations of meaning in the relation between the moral order and received values, but I must deal with this at greater length in another place.

The specific formulas that depend on the basic moral fantasy of melodrama are many and various. Some of the more important contemporary examples are the best-selling panoramic social novel such as those written by Irving Wallace, Harold Robbins, and Jacqueline Susann, the historical spectacle such as *Gone with the Wind*, the soap opera, the gangster saga, the professional drama such as the doctor, lawyer, or teacher story, and many others. Though extremely various in the cultural materials they employ, all these formulas are shaped by the basic qualities of melodrama: the heightening of feeling and moral conflict and multiple lines of action that work together to create a sense of the rightness of the world order.

Alien Beings or States

One of the largest and certainly the strangest of all formulaic types consists of stories dealing with alien beings and states. The horror story, which usually portrays the depredations and ultimate destruction of some monster, is one of the most striking formulas of this type. On the face of it, horror is a most puzzling sort of entertainment, yet, judging from the immense popularity of the formula and the great enjoyment audiences derive from it, people take enormous delight in being scared out of their wits, at least in fantasy. There are a number of ideas that might help to explain this paradoxical feeling. First of all, the very intensity of the emotion of horror may be one reason for its success as escapism, for the more intense our response to a work is, the more it takes us out of ourselves. When audiences shriek and howl with fear as Dracula suddenly appears at the window, fangs dripping with blood, this may be for many people a profound experience of self-transcendence, a complete forgetting of self in the intense and momentary involvement in an external fantasy. The fact that horror seems especially fascinating to the young and relatively unsophisticated parts of the public offers some substantiation for this view. Older, educated people probably learn more sophisticated modes of self-transcendence and become too detached and critical to be terrified by the more primitive modes of monsterdom. For such audiences, and for those to whom the horrific devices of the past have become too familiar, creators must develop new, more refined modes of terror such as madness; Hitchcock's *Psycho* was a brilliant example of the sophisticated refinement of horror that retained much of the primitive intensity of the classic horror story.

But pure intensity of emotion is clearly not the only answer, for the emotion has to occur in some context where it does not become a real threat to the audience. Thus we might make a differentiation between the fear or terror we may experience in connection with tragedies and the sense of horror we feel as we watch or read a monster story. There is something basically comfortable about horror, while terror shakes our whole view of the world. I remember still the terror I experienced as a child when I saw the zombie lurch across the screen in Bob Hope's movie *The Ghost Breakers*. Ironically, this was a totally irrelevant response, since the portrayal was full of comic exaggeration, but I was too unfamiliar with this sort of formula to know that, and I was frightened for months. What really scared me was that I became half-convinced that the monster was real, not in the pleasurable sense of suspended disbelief, but in a terrible confusion of fantasy and reality that left me looking behind doors, fearing shadows, and even being afraid to go to movies. I felt suddenly and very palpably confronted with all the limitations of mortality. I think this was close to a tragic emotion, though it lacked the moral transcendence that derives from the feeling of pity for a defeated protagonist and the sense of acceptance of the limitations of man that tragedy usually creates.

Actually my reaction to that zombie was a direct result of my lack of experience with imaginary creatures of this sort. Therefore, I allowed my fear to turn something I was seeing into something unknown and unknowable, yet nonetheless real. This is what the finest nonformulaic stories of terror such as Henry James's *Turn of the Screw* or Poe's "Fall of the House of Usher" accomplish. They show us the incomprehensibility of the unknown and the limits of the knowable. We know that something terrible is happening around or between the governess and her charges or between Roderick and his sister, but we cannot and never will find out just what, despite the best efforts of generations of critics to find certain evidence as to whether there are or are not supernatural causes at work in those stories. Horror domesticates terror by objectifying it in the form of some clearly defined alien being or state. It is a commonplace that once a terrifying thing is actually seen or experienced, it loses much of its terror, and that is precisely what happens in the various formulas involving horror. For this reason I suggest that the key characteristic of the type is the representation of some alien being or state and the underlying moral fantasy is our dream that the unknowable can be known and related to in some meaningful fashion. The evoking of our fears becomes entertaining when we are assured that we will finally be able to understand and relate to them. Even if the alien creature or state is somehow finally victorious as in Don Siegel's superb film *Invasion of the Body Snatchers*, we still feel the security of understanding what is happening. And the formulaic tendency, of course, is toward the ultimate defeat or at least temporary departure of the alien creature, just as Siegel was pressured to qualify his original bleaker ending to that film.

Viewed in this way, I think we can understand why it is that horror is sometimes so strangely close to comedy, and why the monsters of one generation have a tendency to become beloved quasi-comic heroes for later periods. To objectify a terror by giving it a specific form is closely related to the basic rhythm of comedy in which a situation presented as dangerous or disturbing turns out suddenly to be far less so than we thought. The more we come to know a creature like Dracula, the more domesticated he seems to our imaginations. Inevitably the earlier Dracula films now involve us in a sense of incongruity between how terrifying and unknowable the alien creature seems to the other characters in the film as compared to our comfortable knowledge about the technology of vampire control. This is the feeling that Polanski seized upon so brilliantly in *The Fearless Vampire Killers* by using explicit comedy as a means of re-creating the experience of horror. Other contemporary vampire-film makers have had to resort to a variety of devices to regenerate the sense of horror: updating the vampire figure, creating all manner of gory and bloody effects, inventing quasi-scientific rationales to replace the traditional Christian symbolism of the vampire story.

Horror is not the only mode for stories of alien beings or states. The fantasy of knowing the unknowable through objectification is also the basis of the broad range of stories loosely referred to as science fiction. Though most science fiction does not aim for the effect of horror in the fashion of ghost and monster stories, the close connection between these different modes of using alien experiences is suggested by the role of science in a classic horror story like Mary Shelley's *Frankenstein*, and by the importance of various forms of transcendent, quasi-religious experience in works of science fiction like those of Arthur Clark and C. S. Lewis.

These notes toward a typology of literary formulas are set forth in a tentative and exploratory fashion. There may be other important archetypes of moral fantasy that I have not identified in this system of classification. But it does seem to provide some general classes into which we can loosely differentiate the most common contemporary formulas. Unfortunately, even to treat with some complexity the most important particular formulas that embody the five archetypes would exceed reasonable limits. Therefore, I have chosen to concentrate my attention in the main body of this book on certain key formulas embodying mainly the archetypes of adventure and mystery: the western, the hard-boiled detective story, the classical detective story, and, to some extent, the gangster saga. Only in the ninth chapter will I attempt a discussion of one kind of melodramatic formula, using the various techniques of analysis developed in chapters 3 through 8. The whole complex territory covered by the archetypes of romance and alien beings or states must, alas, be left to later inquiries and to the work of other scholars.

Three

The Mythology of Crime and
Its Formulaic Embodiments

In the first chapter I argued that particular formulas are ways of embodying certain archetypal fantasies in the materials of a specific culture. The second chapter presented a tentative anatomy of these underlying archetypes. In this chapter I will consider more fully the problem of cultural mythology by examining the various formulas that have been generated by the mythology of crime, a great imaginative obsession of the nineteenth- and twentieth-century Englishmen and Americans. To give this rather complex discussion some center, I will let it grow out of a consideration of a current best-seller about crime, Mario Puzo's *The Godfather*. In the course of the analysis I will show how the major nineteenth- and twentieth-century crime formulas compare with *The Godfather* and with each other and will offer some hypotheses about the dialectic between the literature of crime and the contemporary cultures that produce it so prolifically.

The Godfather *and the Literature of Crime*

The best-selling novel and film of the late 1960s and early 1970s was Mario Puzo's *The Godfather*. Its impact has been so great—millions of copies of the book sold in little over three years, and many more millions of movie admissions—that one does not need much prescience to predict that this work will be a major turning point in the evolution of popular literature, perhaps comparable to the significance of Conan Doyle's Sherlock Holmes, certainly as important as Ian Fleming's James Bond. In the wake of *The Godfather*'s enormous success, a film sequel has been produced, while a number of other films about the Mafia such as *The Valachi Papers* have coasted to considerable popularity on its coattails. Publishers have increased their listings of crime fiction, taking advantage of the Godfather craze to reissue in paperback any recent novels that have the slightest connection with the subject of Puzo's book.[1] Everywhere newsstands and marquees are plastered with such come-ons as "more action, sex, and violence than *The Godfather* and *The French Connection* combined" or "The Big New Mafia blockbuster in the searing tradition of *The Godfather*." Though no TV network has yet announced a series called "One Don's Family," I suspect that scores of producers and writers are racking their brains to figure out a formula that will be recognizably like *The Godfather* while avoiding the overt violence and sex that current mores will not sanction on the television screen. With all this activity, is seems clear that *The Godfather* has not only achieved a striking individual success but has established a new fashion in the portrayal of crime.

Of course crime, particularly violent crime, has always been a sure-fire topic for the entertainment of the public. From the beginning of written literature and, one suspects, long before that, human beings have been fascinated by stories of homicide, assault, thievery, and roguery of all sorts. Without exaggeration one can say that crime and literature have been in it together from the beginning. Homer launched the subject with his account of the suitor's conspiracy against Odysseus' homecoming, or perhaps one should give precedence to an even earlier account in *The Iliad* of the rape of Helen. Murder was a favorite subject of the Greek and Roman dramatists and of Shakespeare and other Renaissance tragedians. The development of printed literature led to an even greater and more various flowering of crime stories, from the picaresque tales and outlaw ballads of the sixteenth and seventeenth centuries, down to the innumerable crime and detective stories of our own age. The development of film added to this array the saga of the urban gangster that in various forms has been a staple of the American film since D. W. Griffith's *The Musketeers of Pig Alley* (1912). And, in modern times, while the fictional criminal has been a leading figure in novel, drama, and film, his real-life model has inspired uncountable billions of words in the nonfictional form of accounts of actual crimes and criminals in newspapers, magazines, and books.[2]

Why has the criminal held such an important place in the hearts of the great majority of peaceful and law-abiding citizens throughout the ages? Is it an expression of man's original sin, or some basic instinct toward destruction, or the result of an innate aggressiveness inherited from some primordial animal ancestor? These general answers share a certain unfortunate circularity: man loves crime stories because he has some basic trait that, among other things, manifests itself in a fascination with tales of crime. It may be a matter of great theoretical or metaphysical interest whether this trait is a function of free will, evolution, heredity, or environment, but this question cannot be answered by the analysis of popular literature. Whatever the cause, the end result is the same, a basic human delight in the literature of crime. Granted this basic human interest and leaving its significance for the inquiries of theologians, psychologists, and ethologists, let us turn to a problem that is within our grasp and on which the formulas of popular literature may shed some light: the question of how differing cultures and periods define crime, how they relate it to other elements of their culture, and in what story patterns they embody their fascination with it.

The single aspect of *The Godfather* that seems to have make the deepest impact on the American public is Puzo's use of the central symbol of "the family." This symbol's influence has virtually changed overnight the American public's favorite term for a criminal organization. As Puzo develops it, the symbol of the family is the unifying principle of *The Godfather*. The novel is a tale of family succession, showing the rise of the true son and heir and reaching a climax with his acceptance of the power and responsibilities of Godfather. It tells how Michael Corleone comes to understand his father's character and destiny and then allows himself to be shaped by that same destiny. Most of the novel's major characters are members of the Corleone family, and the main events are key points in that family's history: the marriage of a daughter, the death of a son, the death of the father, the rise of a new generation. Puzo extends the symbolism of the family beyond the actual progeny of Don Vito Corleone to the criminal organization of which he is the leader. In narrating the history of the Corleone family Puzo is also giving an account of the rise, difficulties, and ultimate triumph of a criminal gang. By doing so, he makes the reader view that gang as something more complex than a band of lawbreakers organized for the purpose of committing evil or illegal actions.

Puzo's theme of the family is a significant departure from the representation of crime in earlier periods. Until well into the twentieth century the aspect of crime most fascinating to the public was the exploits of individual criminals and notable crimes, particularly murders.[3] A few major nonformulaic instances immediately spring to mind: Shakespeare's Macbeth, Dostoevsky's Raskolnikov, Stendhal's Julien Sorel, the various murderers in Dickens. These are almost all types of the criminal overreacher with the creator's emphasis on the individual complex of motives that led up to the crime and on the psychological consequences that followed it. Usually, though not invariably, the criminal was finally destroyed by these consequences. The same emphasis on individual criminals and their crimes also dominated the popular formulaic literature of the seventeenth and eighteenth centuries. Popular accounts of crime in the form of broadsheet ballads and later in collections like the Newgate Calendar gave colorful accounts of individual criminals, their deeds, and the ensuing retribution. Archetypally, this broadsheet literature was a very simple form of melodrama, stressing the providential order through which the criminal was inevitably punished. The archetypal form underlying the representation of crime began to change in the later eighteenth century with the emergent gothic novel. Though such gothics as *The Mysteries of Udolpho* and *The Monk* also stressed the evil plots of a master criminal and the inevitable retribution they evoked, this formula gave much greater significance to mystery and even, on occasion, to the archetype of alien beings. By the later nineteenth century in the classical detective story, the archetype of mystery had become the most popular way of fantasizing about crime. It occupied this position until about the third decade of the twentieth century when the emergence of the American hard-boiled detective story and gangster saga gave renewed importance to the patterns of heroic

adventure and melodrama. A closer and more complex look at this development will show how the shift in underlying archetypes was related to changing
attitudes toward crime.

In the seventeenth and eighteenth centuries, crime was still primarily a
religious and moral matter. An offense against the law was also an offense
against God and was given harsh and terrible punishment. This was a period
in which it seemed perfectly natural to most people that capital punishment
should be meted out to a wide variety of crimes including some that would be
classified today as minor felonies or misdemeanors. Because the criminal was
primarily conceived as an individual sinner, the literature about him
consisted largely of accounts of crime and retribution, mirror images, one
might say, of the popular literature of saints and martyrs. Just as the stories
of the sufferings and eventual salvation of the good were set forth as
examples and models for all men, so the evil deeds and terrible punishment of
murderers, thieves, and bandits provided a terrifying paradigm of damnation
or of last-minute grace and repentance. No doubt many readers of broadsheet ballads or of the accounts in the Newgate Calendar found other
interests and satisfactions such as admiration of the criminal as rebel against
social oppression or vicarious pleasure in his acts of violent aggression against
the social order. Yet the vast majority of popular crime stories prior to the
nineteenth century take the form of exemplary warnings. There was little
interest in motivation or in social causation.

Another important aspect of the treatment of crime before the nineteenth
century was its relation to what we would today call class. Noble criminals as
in the plays of Shakespeare and other Renaissance tragedians were frequently
represented with considerable sympathy and a complex attention to motive
and social context, thereby giving their story a tragic dimension. Lower- and
middle-class criminals, however, were almost never represented in this way.
Their deeds were rendered didactically, as horrific examples of sin, or,
satirically, as picaresque tales of roguery, in order to criticize the corruption
and folly of mankind. Occasionally the two modes of moral warning and
satire were combined, a prime example being Fielding's *Jonathan Wild*.
Though there were important differences between tragic representations of
noble criminals and didactic or satiric tales of lower-class crime, there
remained a basic identity in the cultural understanding of crime. Despite his
tragic dignity and the complexity of his motives, Macbeth was a figure of the
evil individual in a morality play, sinning greatly and bringing inevitable
retribution upon himself.

During the nineteenth century, several major changes in the literature of
crime gradually came about. The first was most evident in the emergent
classical detective story, but its signs were apparent in many other aspects of
both popular and intellectual interest in crime. I think we can define this
change most broadly as a shift from an essentially religious or moral feeling
about crime to what might best be called an aesthetic approach to the subject.
The classic detective story is the fullest embodiment of this attitude because it

treats crime as an entertainment, the cycle of crime and punishment becoming an occasion for pleasurable intellectual and emotional stimulation. While residual moral valuations are a significant part of the rhetoric and psychology of the detective story, this is not because writer and reader are primarily concerned with the process of sin and retribution but simply because it increases one's pleasure in a story to be able to sympathize with the innocent and look forward eagerly to the exposure of the guilty. Though the detective story concerns itself with individual crimes, and its underlying psychological power depends on the manipulation of our feelings of guilt, it is nevertheless quite evident that we are more interested in the form of the crime and the process of its solution than in the sinfulness of the criminal and his punishment.

This new attitude toward crime was most definitively and brilliantly set forth long before the full flourishing of the detective story in Thomas de Quincey's essay "Murder Considered as One of the Fine Arts" (1827). The speaker of de Quincey's essay is, of course, perverse, and the thesis he sets forth is doubtless intended to be consumed with a large grain of salt. Yet, at the same time, the argument is a serious one and despite its ironic guise would seem to have the author's fundamental agreement. The essay is thus one of the first major examples of what we would today call a "put-on," a paradoxical and ambiguous way of speaking or behaving that is difficult to know how far to take seriously. Because de Quincey realizes the position espoused in "Murder Considered as One of the Fine Arts" is morally shocking, he sets it forth through a dubious persona; yet, allowing for the speaker's depraved excesses, the essay is a brilliant rationale for a literature like the detective story that transforms the tragic material of crime and sin into an object of mild pleasure and entertainment. De Quincey's essay also suggests how an enjoyment of the aesthetic dimension of crime seems corrupt and depraved from a traditional moral or religious point of view, and thus helps to explain the sense of shame that continues to afflict many of those addicted to the detective story.

De Quincey's speaker begins with the proposition that murder has become so striking an accomplishment in the present day that it ought to receive an adequately serious criticism:

> in this age, when masterpieces of excellence have been executed by professional men, it must be evident that in the style of criticism applied to them the public will look for something of a corresponding improvement, practice and theory must advance *pari passu*. People begin to see that something more goes to the completion of a fine murder than two block-heads to kill and be killed, a knife, a purse, and a dark lane. Design, gentlemen, grouping, light and shade, poetry, sentiment, are now deemed indispensable to attempts of this nature.[4]

To the obvious objection that such an approach to murder is immoral, he insists that "Everything in this world has two handles. Murder, for instance, may be laid hold of by its moral handle ... or it may also be treated *aesthetically*, as the Germans call it—that is, in relation to good taste."[5] Finally, to explain the circumstances in which an aesthetic approach to murder is appropriate, de Quincey's speaker makes a striking series of observations:

> When a murder is in the paulo-post-futurum tense—not done, not even (according to modern purism) *being* done, but only going to be done—and a rumor of it comes to our ears, by all means let us treat it morally. But suppose it is over and done, and that you can say of it ... It is finished ... suppose the poor murdered man to be out of his pain, and the rascal that did it off like a shot nobody knows whither; suppose, lastly, that we have done our best, by putting out our legs, to trip up the fellow in his flight, but all to no purpose.... why, then, I say, what's the use of any more virtue? Enough has been given to morality; now comes the turn of Taste and the Fine Arts. A sad thing it was, no doubt, very sad; but *we* can't mend it. Therefore let us make the best of a bad matter; and as it is impossible to hammer anything out of it for moral purpose, let us treat it aesthetically, and see if it will turn to account in that way. Such is the logic of a sensible man; and what follows? We dry up our tears, and have the satisfaction, perhaps, to discover that a transaction which, morally considered, was shocking, and without a leg to stand upon, when tried by principles of Taste, turns out to be a very meritorious performance. Thus all the world is pleased; the old proverb is justified, that it is an ill wind which blows nobody good.[6]

Whatever degree of irony de Quincey intends with such a statement—and it is difficult to be sure of this—he describes quite brilliantly one major dimension of the popular treatment of crime in the nineteenth and twentieth centuries. With the separation of church and state and the consequent disassociation of religion and law, it became increasingly possible for men to view crime in aesthetic as well as moral terms. This change in attitude is apparent not only in the rise of the detective story but in the treatment of crime in magazines and newspapers. Indeed, it is possible to read de Quincey's essay at least in part as poking fun at the new delight in the picturesque details and striking mysteries of murder that flourished in the nineteenth-century press, a type of literature to which de Quincey himself made important contributions.

The development of an aesthetic delight in unusual crimes was accompanied by two other important nineteenth-century trends in the literary representation of crime. One was the romanticization of crime, the other the development of a scientific approach to crime as a social problem. At first, it is a little difficult to understand how these three rather different trends could have emerged in the same cultural context. The romanticization of crime was primarily a feature of nineteenth-century melodrama, which, following the earlier model of the folk figure of Robin Hood, elaborated a heroic role for the criminal by showing him as victim of and rebel against an unjust or corrupt regime. It is important to note that this figure is almost never shown in the role of urban criminal. Rather, these qualities were ascribed to the noble outlaw or bandit who has withdrawn from urban society to some mountain fastness or forest from which he strikes out against the unjust tyrant and oppressor of the poor. Hobsbawn has shown how the "social bandit" who appears in times of cultural transition throughout history frequently takes on in folklore the qualities of a Robin Hood.[7] But it was in the nineteenth century that this figure became a stock character in melodrama, and in prose fiction. His rationale was almost always the same; a good man, usually of aristocratic origin, whose rightful position had been usurped by evil and treacherous enemies using unjust laws to legitimate their depredations. This heroic outlaw often justified himself in words like those of the title character of G. P. R. James's *The Brigand* (1841):

> "It is because man's law is not God's law that I stand here upon the mountain. Were laws equal and just, there would be found few to resist them. While they are unequal and unjust, the poor-hearted may submit and tremble; the powerless may yield and suffer; the bold, the free, the strong, and the determined fall back upon the law of God and wage war against the injustice of man."[8]

This romantic image of the criminal had great appeal for the public in nineteenth and twentieth-century America and Europe. It was well enough established by the later nineteenth century to serve as a favorite target of burlesque and parody, the supreme instance being Gilbert and Sullivan's *Pirates of Penzance*. Americans, in addition to taking over the already established image of the noble brigand, translated him into the form of the western outlaw. Popular legend and pulp novel transformed criminals like Billy the Kid and Jesse James into figures of romantic rebellion driven to a life of crime by oppressive land barons, grasping railroad tycoons, and crooked, greedy politicians. Later similar legends arose about the bank robbers, kidnappers, and murderers of the twenties and thirties, John Dillinger, Bonnie and Clyde, and Pretty Boy Floyd in particular. Not surprisingly, one can still find many traces of this romantic image of crime in *The Godfather*. When Puzo's protagonist Michael gives his justification for the Godfather's life of crime it is in terms of a view of society quite reminiscent of the nineteenth-century brigand's apologia.

A third major factor in nineteenth-century attitudes toward crime was the rise of a scientific and social approach to the analysis of criminal deeds. The new scientific attitude led to empirical investigations of the causes of crime and to the assumption that crime could be best understood and dealt with not as a moral or religious matter but in terms of its social or physiological background. In this view, criminal acts were not evil deeds but the result of defective social arrangements or heredity. The emerging scientific approach to crime was far-reaching in its impact. It not only stimulated the growth of a scientific criminology and sociology but had a major impact on legal and penological practices. Not surprisingly, the new attitudes had a profound influence on the literary treatment of crime. While one source of the detective story was the aesthetic interest in the picturesque and mysterious forms of criminal acts, another was the model of rational and scientific inquiry that played such an important part in the characterization of the detective of the late nineteenth and early twentieth centuries. In addition, the nineteenth-century novel increasingly concerned itself with the social milieu and institutional factors underlying crime. In novels like *Oliver Twist* Dickens analyzed the terrible social environment that led to urban crime. Later in the century, Zola and his followers wrote novels that specifically tried to demonstrate the environmental and hereditary factors at work in criminal behavior.

Different as they seem, some common elements in the aesthetic, romantic, and scientific images of crime help to account for their more or less simultaneous development. First, all three of these approaches indicate a weakening of traditional religious definitions of crime as sin and the search for alternative modes of explanation and reaction. As the detective story shows, aesthetic and scientific attitudes toward crime are by no means irreconcilable, since both depend on a certain detachment from intense moral feeling. On the popular level, the figure of Sherlock Holmes with his combination of artistic and scientific skills and interests constitutes an imaginative synthesis of aesthetic intuition and empirical rationalism. The romantic image of the outlaw as rebel is, in one sense, an extension of the aesthetic approach, for it differentiates the bandit's admirable nobility of character and intention from the dark reality of his deeds. The romantic image also shares with the scientific approach to crime a concern with criminality as a social phenomenon. For the melodramatist, the brigand symbolized a state of social evil, just as for the scientific criminologist the criminal was evidence of a poor environment or a defective heredity. Though there are perhaps more points of similarity between the various nineteenth-century views of crime than appear on the surface, it is nonetheless quite apparent that, by the beginning of the twentieth century, a number of basic ambiguities had developed in the understanding and representation of crime. Though the concept of crime as a function of social context rather than individual morality was becoming ever more widely accepted, a residual moralism continued to dominate public attitudes. This was especially strong in America where one could find a traditionally religious and moralistic movement like Prohibition existing cheek by jowl with a romanticizing of the bootleggers who evaded that same law. Moreover, in this same period American sociologists made major contributions to the scientific study of crime and punishment. These divergent reactions suggest that the public wanted at once to condemn the criminal, to admire him, and to understand and eliminate the causes of his criminality. On the one hand, many Americans could no longer accept the traditional view of crime as individual evil or sin; yet, at the same time, the general public was not prepared to accept the idea that criminality must be treated as a function of abstract social pressures. There was a further ambiguity in the sociological conception of crime. Paradoxically, as knowledge about the "causes" of crime increased, the rate of crime doubled and tripled. Even specialists in the science and sociology of crime were uncertain whether increasing knowledge could be used to reduce crime. Radzinowicz points out the opposed opinions which the nineteenth-century study of crime had produced:

> Can crime be eliminated? Can it be substantially reduced? On the threshold of the twentieth century there were two opposing opinions to these questions. On the one hand, disappointment that so little had been achieved combined with a fervent belief that crime could be conquered. On the other, a detached examination of crime as an intrinsic part of social life produced the assertion that it must be accepted as a normal, even useful, social fact.[9]

The final result of these complex ambiguities of attitudes and ideology was that the criminal became, for twentieth-century American culture, a new kind of social symbol and scapegoat.

This development is evident in the emergence in the 1920s of two major formulaic figures in the literature of crime: the urban gangster and the hard-boiled detective. Both reflected a new vision of the social significance of the criminal. The hard -boiled detective was a transformation of the English gentleman or scientific amateur detective. The new American-style literary detective took on many characteristics that had heretofore been ascribed to criminals: a penchant toward violence, alienation from society, and rejection of conventional values coupled with adherence to a personal code of ethics. Indeed, one might see the Sam Spades, Philip Marlowes, and Mike Hammers of the hard-boiled tradition as a modern synthesis of Sherlock Holmes with the melodramatic figure of the romantic brigand. The urban gangster was also a striking departure from the nineteenth-century criminal figures of the outlaw and the domestic murderer. His legend was, as Daniel Bell and Robert Warshow have noted, a complex mirror image of the American myth of success and social mobility. Typically, the gangster protagonist of novel and film rose from poverty to great wealth and power and then, overreaching himself, fell to destruction at the hands of the law. The hard-boiled detective, on the other hand, did not become personally involved in the quest for wealth and power. Instead, he served as an appropriate instrument of vengeance against those who used corrupt and perverse means to success. In many cases, his central antagonist was the urban gangster and his organization.

Probably the central model for the gangster legend of the 1920s and 1930s was the actual figure of Al Capone. The Capone legend gained national attention in the twenties through newspaper reports of his deeds and was transmuted into a fictional pattern by writers like Ben Hecht (*Underworld* [1927]) and W. R. Burnett (*Little Caesar* [1929]). Filmmakers quickly discovered an avid public interest in this formula and after a brilliant series of films in the late 1920s and early 1930s—e.g., Josef von Sternberg's *Underworld* (1927), Mervyn Le Roy's *Little Caesar* (1930), William Wellman's *Public Enemy* (1931), and Howard Hawk's *Scarface* (1932)—the gangster film became one of the major genres of the American film industry. The Capone legend was the basis of all the films I have mentioned and continued to be a prime inspiration for the gangster film into the 1960s.[10]

The Capone legend synthesized the various attitudes toward crime that had emerged throughout the nineteenth century. It had a striking aesthetic dimension that would doubtless have appealed to de Quincey, for it was replete with picturesque and dramatic episodes such as the Dion O'Bannion flowershop murder, the assassination of Hymie Weiss on the steps of Holy Name Cathedral, the attack on Capone's stronghold in Cicero, and the climactic Saint Valentine's Day massacre. Capone's story also had the romantic aspect of an outlaw chief at war against a corrupt society, stealing from the rich and powerful so that he might, like Robin Hood, give largess to the poor and downtrodden. Furthermore, the Capone legend provided occasion for the representation of crime as a social phenomenon. The way in which the social experiment of Prohibition gave rise to the Capone organization was invariably a part of the story as was an indictment of the extent to which the criminal gang had become allied with corrupt politicians and policemen. Journalistic and cinematic accounts of the Capone figure often portrayed the slum environment of the American city as the source of the criminal protagonist. But, above all, the Capone legend was the story of a great rise and fall, and in this way it coincided with the traditional moralistic pattern of the destruction of the criminal overreacher and with the archetype of melodrama. The climax of the legend was Capone's imprisonment for income tax evasion, while, in most of the fictional versions of Capone—*Little Caesar* and *Scarface*, for example—the protagonist was killed by the police. Thus the gangster hero became a kind of melodramatic scapegoat for the corruption and violence that surrounded his rise.

Another important aspect of the Capone legend and its offshoots was the lower-class social origin of the protagonist. The nineteenth-century figure of the heroic outlaw was usually an aristocrat forced into exile by evil rivals. Even the benevolent bandit of the American western was typically represented as coming from a respectable social class: his family owned a nice farm until they were dispossessed by a grasping land baron or railroad agent. The Capone hero was blatantly lower-class and despite his rapid rise to wealth and power, he stayed that way. Surely one of his most endearing traits was that he never became assimilated into an upper-class life-style but remained an unregenerate barbarian. Suspicious of culture, art, and manners, he was always ready for a fight, and tough on women, the kind of hero who would smash a grapefruit into the face of a dame who annoyed him. Even dressed in his custom-made suits and silk shirts—he gloried in what Veblen called conspicuous consumption—the Capone hero always betrayed his lower-class origins through speech and actions. Just as the hard-boiled detective tended to take on a purposeful lower-class toughness in order to carry on his quest for justice in a corrupt world, the Capone hero never allowed himself to pretend that he was anything more than a barbarian in the streets of Rome. The imaginative power of the Capone figure as an embodiment of lower-class toughness and unrestrained aggressiveness clothed in an obviously transparent veneer of fancy clothes and expensive accoutrements remains a powerful one. It is interesting to note that Sonny, one of the three Corleone brothers in Puzo's novel, is in this tradition.

Thus, the two major formulaic patterns that emerged in the literature of crime of the 1920s and 1930s—gangster tragedy and hard-boiled detective-hero tale—embodied significant shifts in both archetype and cultural mythology. These new formulas made protagonists or heroes out of lower-class figures characterized by crudeness, aggressive violence, and alienation from the respectable morality of society. Though he was a destroyer of criminals, even the hard-boiled detective-hero had his own code of behavior that did not correspond to that of society in general. The main difference between the hard-boiled detective and the gangster was that the gangster protagonist was supremely egotistical. His actions were solely motivated by the desire to achieve enough wealth and power to impose his own will on the world; because his ambitions were limitless and boundless they could lead only to destruction. He resembled in this way the figure of the overreaching tycoon. At least one major nonformulaic American writer of the 1920s clearly perceived the link between the gangster and the tycoon and used it as a major theme in *The Great Gatsby*. The hard-boiled detective, on the other hand, was motivated not by ambition but by the desire to help or avenge other persons. Aside from this major difference, the moral universe of the two formulas is the same. The social setting of both gangster melodrama and hard-boiled detective story was the corrupt and violent American city ruled by a hidden alliance of rich and respectable businessmen, politicians, and criminals. It is, in effect, the world portrayed in Lincoln Steffens's *Shame of the Cities* and other muckraking works of the early twentieth century. Both gangster protagonist and hard-boiled detective were rebels against this corrupt society, and this was a primary justification for the violence and brutality of their actions. Yet, where the detective sought to avenge particular injustices, the gangster protagonist was driven by a desire to dominate the whole unjust system by himself and this led invariably to his downfall. Even in this corrupt society it did not seem possible to exercise unbounded power.

This latter aspect of the crime formulas of the twenties and thirties is particularly striking when compared with *The Godfather* and other recent crime novels and films. The gangster stories of the twenties and thirties were primarily concerned with the protagonist's rise and fall. Though the gangster protagonist is ostensibly the leader of a criminal organization and rises to power in that organization, we rarely see him in the process of exercising his power. Indeed, once the hero of films like *Little Caesar, Public Enemy*, and *Scarface* has reached a position of real power, the process of his destruction begins. In current crime novels and films, the emphasis is on the organization's power, a power that seems particularly fascinating since, being outside the law, it is represented as being nearly limitless. Thus, in *The Godfather* the story is not structured around Michael Corleone's rise in society but on his apprenticeship to power. Michael learns to accept and to use the extraordinary power bequeathed him by his father. At the story's climax, he directs a bloody series of assassinations that destroy the leaders of rival organizations and make the Corleone family even more powerful than before. This ending is only the culmination of a long series of studies in the family's various forms of power. For example, the novel—and the film—open with a series of exemplary instances of the Godfather's power, largely in response to boons asked by family members and hangers-on during the day of his daughter's wedding. The Godfather arranges for the beating of two young men who have assaulted another man's daughter and then been freed by a sympathetic judge—a case of the power to effect justice when the law has failed. He secures citizenship for a young Italian who wants to marry his boss's daughter—an example of his ability to manipulate the government. Finally, he promises to secure a major part in a new film for his godson, the singer Johnny Fontane—an instance of his control over the worlds of business and the mass media. All these forms of power are unavailable to the ordinary citizen and even, to a considerable extent, to men of authority in government and business. But through his tools of extralegal violence and the hidden character of his organization, the Godfather is easily able to make offers that cannot be refused.

Thus, one central difference between the world of *The Godfather* and that of earlier crime formulas is a complex fascination with power and organization, a fascination that corresponds to new themes in the public definition of crime.

Criminal organizations have existed for centuries but the myth of "organized crime" is a very recent phenomenon. Even the nation's most highly publicized crime fighter, J. Edgar Hoover, rejected the idea of a national crime syndicate until the mid-fifties. Since that time, however, public concern about supposed large-scale crime organization—referred to variously as "Cosa Nostra," "the Mafia," "the Syndicate," or simply "organized crime"—has been increasingly fed by a variety of congressional hearings, grand jury investigations, and sensational publications. It might be argued that this growing public interest is simply a response to the emergence of an important new social phenomenon, yet most serious scholars and historians are dubious that the Mafia is any more powerful now than it was in the 1930s. Curiously enough, the Capone legend, though based on a criminal organization that probably came closer to controlling the life of an entire city than any other such organization before or since, laid far more stress on the rise and fall of Capone than on the power of his organization. Thus there is some doubt that public fascination with the idea of organized crime simply reflects an objective awareness of a dangerous new social phenomenon. Instead, Morris and Hawkins argue rather convincingly that the current flurry of publications and investigations into organized crime have resulted in more fantasy and mysticism on the subject than solid empirical data:

> A perplexing and elusive problem does indeed confront anyone seeking information about organized crime. It concerns the concept "organized crime" itself. A curious feature characterizes almost all the literature on this subject, up to and including the task force report on this topic published by the President's Crime Commission. This is that a large proportion of what has been written seems not to be dealing with an empirical matter at all. It is almost as though what is referred to as organized crime belongs to the realm of metaphysics or theology.[11]

Morris and Hawkins point out that one major characteristic of the Mafia or Syndicate aficionado is his absolute faith in the proposition that the power of the organization is boundless and unlimited, even godlike in its sway. Moreover, the fewer hard facts a devotee can find to support this proposition the more he is convinced of its truth. The lack of evidence becomes a sign for him of the secret organization's power to prevent its deeds from being known. The literature of the Mafia is full of statements like the following, commonly set forth without a single bit of convincing evidence:

> The Mafia and its worldwide criminal organization live and die by this code. Under it has grown up and flourished a supergovernment of crime that is more powerful than any formally constituted government on earth, because it is invulnerable. A treasure of billions is at the disposal of members of the inner council of the Mafia, men who have come up through the ranks of crime. The high priests of the Mafia are, without exception, Sicilian or of Sicilian origin. Every continent on earth has a governing board of Mafia members who rule all *organized* criminals, listen to their arguments and dispense justice, which may take the form of a grant of money or a sentence of death. The power of the Mafia is not entirely in its wealth but in its ability to kill anyone, anywhere at any time.[12]

If a putatively factual work of investigative reporting can lapse into paranoiac hysteria reminiscent of the "Protocols of the Elders of Zion" when dealing with the subject of organized crime, it is not surprising that a recent work of fiction, Ovid Demaris's *The Overlord*, would go all the way and compare the power of the masters of organized crime to that of God:

> "There are television cameras and microphones hidden everywhere in this place," she said. "He sees and hears everything."
> "Everything," I said dumbly.
> "Yes, like God, he's everywhere: sees all, hears all, knows all. And forgives nothing."[13]

One more example will indicate the near-hysteria of this current fascination with the boundless power of organized crime. In Richard Condon's recent novel *Mile High* (1969), the central figure, Edward West, is the son of a political boss who becomes the chief organizer and master of the Syndicate in America. Condon's story shows how most of the major historical events of the twentieth century—Prohibition, the stock market crash, the Second World War—are created and manipulated by this master criminal and his great organization. For example, West becomes a leading organizer of the Anti-Saloon League in order to bring about national Prohibition, which he sees as an opportunity to make enormous profits and to build up an invincible criminal organization. I should say on Condon's behalf that his novel should probably be read as an ironic allegory of the runaway American quest for wealth and power. Still, that Condon chooses to construct his allegory around the imagined power of organized crime indicates the extent to which this is a pervasive and compelling theme.

Puzo is more subtle in his treatment of the exercise of criminal power; yet, as we noted earlier, this theme pervades *The Godfather*. Puzo also makes frequent use of religious symbolism in conjunction with the definition of authority in the family. The book's very title ironically echoes the phrase "God the father," while the social institution of a godfather is intimately connected with the Catholic tradition and involves religious as well as secular duties. At the climax of the story, particularly as it was presented in the film, Michael actually stands in a church as godfather of his sister's child at the very time his assassins are destroying the rival leaders. Finally, at various points in the novel, the language chosen by Puzo makes the association between Godfather and God quite explicit:

> My Old Man. The Godfather. If a bolt of lightning hit a friend of his the old man would take it personal. He took my going into the Marines personal. That's what makes him great. The Great Don. He takes everything personal. Like God. He knows every feather that falls from the tail of a sparrow or however the hell it goes. Right? And you know something? Accidents don't happen to people who take accidents as a personal insult." [Also:] "I knew you wouldn't do it without orders from the Don. But you can't get sore at him. It's like getting sore at God."[14]

In sum, one central characteristic of the current cultural mythology of crime is a fascination with criminal organizations such as Puzo's Corleone "family" and their special kind of power. Contemporary crime literature feeds upon the image of a hidden criminal organization, so closely knit that even to reveal its existence is certain death for the informer. The members of this organization are bound together by a code of secrecy, a blood ritual, ties of kinship and cultural loyalty, and a long historical tradition dating back to medieval Italy. Because of its secrecy, its willingness to use any means to achieve its ends, its power of life and death, and its enormous wealth and hidden political power, this organization has almost boundless power. The authority of its leaders and their power over the rest of society is nearly divine or godlike. This fantasy of the "organization" looms mysteriously and ominously from the pages of senatorial investigations, popular novels, and films about crime since the 1950s, but until Puzo's novel it was rare that this ghostly presence was given a fleshly solidity and vitality. Such will, I suspect, turn out to be Puzo's major contribution to the new mythology of crime: through his own rich and complex knowledge of the Sicilian ethnic background, he has been able to give a "local habitation and a name" to the fantasy of the all-powerful criminal organization and thereby to make the fantasy even more plausible and persuasive. Indeed, so compellingly attractive is Puzo's vision of the criminal family that, though he invented it entirely out of books and his imagination, professional criminals have been reported as complimenting Puzo on his remarkable inside knowledge. An imaginative vision so profoundly satisfying to those as much in need of a myth as criminals themselves seems certain to be vitally compelling to society as a whole.

Elements of the New Formula

From this central interest in the special character of the criminal "family" and its power, three major elements of the new mythology of crime are derived. These are (1) the character of the organization leader, the Don or Godfather, as Puzo calls him; (2) the central figure of the specialized professional criminal, highly trained and talented in his vocation and ruthless in his dedication to it—let us call this figure the Enforcer from the fact that one of the most popular versions of the character is the professional assassin; and (3) the type of narrative structure that is organized around the careful preparation and execution of a complex criminal act, the caper. The most important new crime formula involves elaborate capers that have either a Don or an Enforcer as the protagonist. It implies a significant archetypal shift, from the melodrama with the gangster as punished protagonist to the adventure story with the gangster as hero.

The Don is, in many respects, a new figure in the annals of crime. Though he has an obvious resemblance to the master criminal of earlier formulaic traditions—e.g., Professor Moriarty, Fu Manchu, or Goldfinger—there are important differences in the way the Don is represented, just as there are basic differences between Puzo's "family" and more traditional images of criminal conspiracy. For one thing, the traditional master criminal is basically a large entrepreneur of crime who has an employer-employee relationship with his minions. His authority derives from his money and from fear of his ruthlessness. Frequently his corps of criminals do not respect or admire him. They are enslaved by fear and greed. No matter how powerful it may be, the traditional criminal organization is represented as based on the vices and weaknesses of its members. Consequently, it usually turns out to be quite simple for the hero to defeat the master criminal. The

Don, on the other hand, is a figure of considerable moral authority that is derived from his wisdom and responsibility as well as his shrewd ruthlessness. Like a father, the relationship between him and the members of his organization depends on his exemplification of a style of life and a moral code. He is a center of value as well as of money and power for his adherents. His authority transcends the appeal to fear and greed and partakes, as we have seen, of a touch of the godlike. Thus, the Don serves as the supreme model and guardian of the special way of life that the criminal organization as "family" represents. This way of life is usually represented as growing out of the Sicilian immigrant tradition, an aspect of the new mythology that Puzo has developed with particular vividness. I think it might also be said that the Don and his authority represent an image of organization that can be seen in opposition to those aspects of contemporary social institutions commonly perceived as signs of failure: the impersonality of the modern corporation on the one hand and the declining authority of the family on the other. Where the corporation executive is cold and impersonal, responsible only for the functional efficiency of his subordinates, the Don is warm and emotional, considering himself involved in every aspect of the life and death of the members of his organization. There is a tribal closeness about the criminal organization as it is portrayed in *The Godfather*, and the Don is its theocratic center. He is not only boss, but king, judge, and priest. Unlike the modern American family with its generational conflicts, its confused sexual roles, its absent fathers, neurotic mothers, and nuclear isolation, the tribe-family ruled by the Don is a patriarchy with absolutely clear roles and lines of authority. Women are women and men are men. There is a clear code of value and sexual roles with masculine dominance and strength at the center. Within this organization the individual is part of a larger kinship or tribal group with massive power against external enemies. The individual does not have to divide himself into diverse and conflicting social roles because the family is a totality for him.

Mario Puzo's central character, Don Vito Corleone, is unquestionably the most powerful and compelling version of the Don yet created. Though Puzo must be credited with the most articulate and effective development of the figure of the Don, it is also clear that the outlines of this figure had already begun to take shape in the imaginations of a number of other writers. In most earlier versions of the criminal leader, certain characteristics of the Don are still inextricably mixed up with the diabolical image of the master criminal. Thus in an earlier novel like Ira Wolfert's *Tucker's People*, though the criminal organization has many of the same qualities as Puzo's "family," the boss is still the evil entrepreneur of crime of the prewar criminal formulas. A character much closer to Puzo's Don appears in Leslie Waller's *The Family*, which was published a year earlier than *The Godfather*. To see a figure who is still closer to Puzo's Don, we must turn to nonfiction. Mike Royko's *Boss*, a recent study of Chicago's Mayor Daley, is a highly critical account of Mayor Daley's administration of the city of Chicago. Yet, in his presentation of the character of the mayor and his description of the organization that serves as the basis of his power, Royko comes interestingly close to the same compelling portrayal of a quasi-tribal family within the larger society ruled by a man of combined ruthlessness and moral force that Puzo develops in *The Godfather*.

Since the Don is a figure who has just emerged in the literature of crime, it is difficult to be sure how important a role he will play in future crime formulas. A second figure has been fully developed as protagonist in a substantial number of books and films. I have labeled this figure the Enforcer, though he might also be called the professional. The Enforcer is most commonly an assassin, though in some cases he is a professional thief. His central characteristic is a ruthless and brilliant professionalism. He is the master of his craft, and his whole way of life and code of values revolve around the skillful performance of his assignments. Usually there is a basic paradox in the Enforcer's character that is an important source of his dramatic effectiveness. He is a man who applies the cool and detached rationalism of the professional specialist to matters of extreme violence and illegality. In this respect, he resembles the combination found in James Bond and his imitators—the bureaucratic killer, the man with an official number that gives him license to kill. The Enforcer is also clearly in the American tradition of the western and hard-boiled detective heroes. Like the western hero, the Enforcer is often involved in vengeance plots. Or, like the aging gunfighter, he may find himself forced to reexamine the meaning of his life. And like both gunfighter and hard-boiled detective the Enforcer lives by a code that is deeply rooted in his profession and in the maintenance of his honor as a man of supreme skill and dedication to his role.

The Enforcer is a specialist in an illegal and conventionally immoral profession, but he is not necessarily on the side of organized crime. At least four current pulp series ("Executioner," "Destroyer," "The Man with No Face," and "Butcher") deal with the exploits of an Enforcer against organized crime. In all of these series, the hero is an absolutely ruthless killer who uses his skill to assassinate the leaders of organized crime who have come to dominate society. In the case of the "Executioner," the hero is a former Vietnam soldier who has returned home to find that his father and sister have been driven to ruin and suicide by the Mafia. He embarks on a one man crusade of vengeance and extermination using his great combat skills. The "Butcher," on the other hand, is a former chief Mafia hit man who now works against organized crime for a secret government intelligence agency. These characters show a kinship to Mickey Spillane's Mike Hammer, one of the hard-boiled progenitors of the Enforcer. The melodramatic moralism of their quests, the particular combination of sex and violence that surrounds their activities, and the crude, comic-book-like style in which they are written are clearly modeled on the writings of the master. Two important additions to the earlier Spillane pattern mark these more recent creations as figures in a new formula. First, there is the focus on the protagonist's professional skills in his trade. Mike Hammer was a man of raw violence who succeeded by courage and endurance rather than through special skills. He was no karate specialist or expert in booby traps and complex weaponry like the Executioner and the Butcher. Second, though he often found himself in conflict with the law, Mike was never entirely outside it, never actually involved with a criminal organization. Though he usually killed the villains without bringing them to trial, he was forced to do so in self-defense. The Enforcer heroes, on the other hand, are completely outside the law and their purpose from the beginning is assassination. Spillane, himself, has obviously been alert to this shifting popular interest in the definition of the violent hero. After developing the character of Mike Hammer in the fifties, he turned to a spy hero, Tiger Mann, with whom he was considerably less successful. Now in a recent novel, *The Erector Set*, he has developed a version of the Enforcer. Throughout most of the novel his hero appears to be a former syndicate operator involved in a large drug-smuggling plot. Only at the end of the book does it turn out that he has been an undercover agent for a secret government agency throughout his criminal career.

These characters are all crude and ultimately moralistic versions of the Enforcer figure. Their basic gambit is the turning of the criminal organization's boundless power against the criminals, thereby bringing about true justice where the law is helpless. They are, in effect, modern urban versions of the Lone Ranger.

The Enforcer figure has been developed in a much more complex and sophisticated fashion in a number of other works. He appears, of course, in *The Godfather* as the character of Luca Brasi. Other characters also frequently take on the role of the Enforcer, most notably Michael Corleone in his assassination of Virgil Sollozo and Captain McCluskey. In his earlier days, Don Vito himself was an Enforcer and used his skill in this role to build up his organization. As Puzo develops his story, we see that the Enforcer and the Don appear as two phases of the fully developed power of the family. The Enforcer represents the ultimate violence on which the family's power is based, while the Don is a figure of wisdom and responsibility who has learned how to use power to preserve and expand the family strength.

Most of the contemporary versions of the Enforcer deal with this figure as an individual involved with a group only for the purposes of a particular action or caper. The most artistically interesting series of works based on the figure of the Enforcer are the "Parker" novels created by the writer Donald E. Westlake under the penname Richard Stark. Parker is a highly skilled professional thief for whom the planning and execution of large-scale robberies is not only a means of livelihood but a way of life. As this character is presented to us through his own consciousness, we come to understand and sympathize with his illegal activities as a normal mode of life, and to share with him his pride in the combination of daring and skill with which he carries out his "scores." Because he is commonly betrayed into situations of great personal danger by the cupidity or incompetence of other members of the gang who participate in the robberies, we find ourselves involved with Parker's ruthless attempts to extricate himself and are gratified when he succeeds, even though this often involves the killing of policemen or other representatives of conventional social order. Of course, Stark generally portrays those policemen whom Parker is forced to kill as corrupt. Yet it is clear that even despite this our basic sympathies are with the criminal protagonist.

Several reasons why Stark is able to make us sympathize with the moral perspective of the Enforcer also apply in large measure to Puzo's ability to engage us in the criminal activities of the Corleone family. First of all, in the tradition of the hard-boiled detective story, Stark presents the modern urban world as a jungle of corruption and injustice. Criminal activity is simply another form of business enterprise, and the criminal syndicate is indistinguishable from any other large corporation. In his novel *Point Blank*, which was made into a film by the young director John Boorman, the story begins with Parker betrayed into prison by members of the criminal syndicate that set up a robbery in which he participated. Escaping from prison, Parker determines to get back from the syndicate his share of the loot, but as he tracks down those responsible for his betrayal, he finds himself in a bureaucratic maze of criminal executives who are indistinguishable from respectable businessmen. In the midst of this corporate miasma he alone stands out as a man of principle and honor, with the courage and skill to demand and achieve his personal goals. This is another important source of our sympathy for the Enforcer. Like the hard-boiled detective, but in a more extreme form, he is a man of honor and courage in a corrupt and hypocritical society. He knows what he is and what he wants, and he is willing to risk his life for his rights. There is an almost Kafkaesque quality about the world of Stark's novels, a quality that was effectively brought out in the film version of *Point Blank*. Urban America is absurd and life is dominated by a mysterious authority that continually threatens the individual with betrayal and meaningless death. Parker, however, is a Joseph K. who refuses to accept the indictment and attacks his judges. Another important source of our vicarious involvement with Parker, despite his frank criminality, is his life-style. Because he usually makes off with a large sum of money, Parker is able to live very well, while really working only one or two days each year; and his work is full of excitement and stimulating danger. Just as Puzo's image of the "family" can be seen as a fantasy of a social organization that has many qualities more attractive than modern industrial social organizations, so the Enforcer's mode of work is the antithesis of a routine job in a large bureaucratic organization. Finally, along with this fantasy of infrequent but fulfilling work, the Enforcer has an elaborate life of leisure. In between jobs, Parker lives in great comfort with an understanding and devoted mistress who never tries to interfere with or judge his work.

The Enforcer's leisure often centers upon a special place or retreat that he has furnished with all the equipment and artifacts necessary to a fulfilling life of relaxation and pleasure. The importance of the "pad" to the Enforcer's life-style is less central than his professional abilities and his involvement in capers, but nonetheless usually appears at the beginning and end of Enforcer stories, somewhat analogous to the Baker Street rooms of Sherlock Holmes or the office of the hard-boiled detective. Perhaps the most elaborately developed example of the "pad" occurs in the Travis McGee stories of John D. Macdonald. McGee lives in Florida on a beautifully furnished houseboat called *The Busted Flush* from which he emerges to embark upon his capers. Though he is not, like Parker, a professional criminal, and is therefore considerably closer to the traditional hard-boiled detective, McGee nonethe-less manifests two basic characteristics that differentiate the Enforcer from the detective. First, his stories are capers outside the law from the very outset rather than mysteries whose solution may force the detective to behave in an illegal fashion. McGee's central occupation is the restoration of property to victims who have had it taken away under a cloak of legality and thus have no recourse to police or the courts. In order to get this property back, McGee must invariably employ his own illegal skills of violence, burglary, and fraud. This is the second major difference between McGee and the traditional detective. McGee possesses and ruthlessly uses a wide variety of professional criminal skills, and he is a master of violence. The traditional hard-boiled detective, on the other hand, was almost never shown using criminal techniques any more complex than the occasional picking of a lock with a piece of plastic and was as often on the receiving end of violence as he was its instigator.

Another striking recent instance of the elaboration of the Enforcer figure is a series of crime films with black heroes. The considerable success of *Shaft* was followed by a sequel, *Shaft's Big Score*, and by a variety of similar adventures including *Trouble Man*, and *Super-Fly*. These are almost pure Enforcer films, though in the latter two the figure is slightly influenced by the black tradition of the hustler. Except for the fact that they are black, the protagonists of these films would not be in the least out of place in the imaginary worlds of Stark and Macdonald. Like Parker and McGee, Shaft, Super-Fly, and Mr. T. are enormously skilled professionals who use their talent to achieve ends that are, if not explicitly illegal, impossible to gain through lawful means.

The figure of the Enforcer is not unique to our times to the extent that the Don is. I have already mentioned his relationship to the hard-boiled detective and the western gunfighter. In certain obvious respects, he also harks back to Robin Hood, to the romantic outlaws of nineteenth-century melodrama, and to the gentleman crooks, e.g., Raffles and the Saint, who were popular in earlier periods. In much the same way as Robin Hood rejected the evil rule of King John in order to affirm the true authority of Richard, Mack Bolan, the "Executioner," needs to feel that his violent assassinations of criminal leaders has some higher moral purpose:

Shortly before his entry into Chicago, he penned this thought in his personal journal: ". . . it's going to be a wipe-out . . . them or me. I have lost the ability to judge the value of all this. But I'm convinced that it matters, somewhere, which side wins. It matters to the universe. I consign my fate to the needs of the universe."[15]

Despite this conventional appeal to a higher morality, the threat of meaninglessness, the fear that there is no ultimate higher purpose, perplexes the "Executioner" in a way that it never would have an earlier heroic crime-fighter:

A man moves, steadily, he knew, from the womb to the grave. It mattered little where he entered the world or where he left it. What counted was that route between the two. And Mack Bolan's only route lay in the jungle. It was the place where he lived. One day it would be the place for him to die. This was both his character and his fate. The Executioner accepted both . . . as a heritage. He would move forever along the wipe-out trail, until the final decision was rendered. Somewhere, somehow, the whole savage and bloody thing mattered. It was not a senseless game from which a guy could just disengage any time the going became a little rough.[16]

There seems to be some connection between the extreme ruthlessness and violence usually exercised by the Enforcer and this ambiguity about the moral meaning of his killings. The Lone Ranger never actually killed any of the criminals he rounded up. At most he shot the guns out of their hands and turned them over to the sheriff. Nor was there any doubt that his actions, though performed under the guise of an outlaw, were directly related to the higher moral purpose of bringing law and order to the West. In the case of the Enforcer, however, crime and corruption are so endemic to society that it is by no means clear that the destruction of a few crooks will bring about the establishment of a new order. The society in which the Enforcer operates is one of totally evil cities:

If New York had been a nightmare, then Chicago must surely be the grim awakening, the model city for The Thing of All Things, *Cosa di tutti Cosa*, the Thing already come to pass. For Mack Bolan, Chicago was the inevitable next scene of confrontation with the mob. Certainly he was knowledgeable regarding that triumvirate of power described by best-selling author Ovid Demaris in his masterful work on Chicago, *Captive City*:
"Today it is nearly impossible to differentiate among the partners—the businessman is a politician, the politician is a gangster, and the gangster is a businessman."[17]

With ultimate moral significance in doubt, and society dominated by total corruption, the only satisfaction for those who feel themselves victimized or trapped by a meaningless world lies in the fantasy of destruction. Thus, in his cruder form, the Enforcer is an avenging angel whose primary action is the

violent destruction of as many criminals as possible, not in order to purge
society of its evil elements, but simply to assuage the raging frustration and
anxiety generated by a crooked and uncontrollable world.

In more sophisticated versions, the Enforcer has come to terms with the
meaninglessness of the world and learned to exist by a code of personal
survival, sometimes qualified by a system of loyalties to another person or a
small group or clan within which he can find the protection and meaningfulness society cannot provide.

Like the "Executioner," Travis McGee has a vision of America as urban
chaos and breakdown:

> New York is where it is going to begin, I think. You can see it coming. The
> insect experts have learned how it works with locusts. Until this locust
> population reaches a certain density, they all act like any grasshoppers.
> When the critical point is reached, they turn savage and swarm, and try to
> eat the world. We're nearing a critical point. One day soon two strangers
> will bump into each other at high noon in the middle of New York. But this
> time they won't snarl and go on. They will stop and stare and then leap at
> each other's throats in a dreadful silence. The infection will spread outward
> from that point. Old ladies will crack skulls with their deadly handbags.
> Cars will plunge down the crowded sidewalks. Drivers will be torn out of
> their cars and stomped. It will spread to all the huge cities of the world, and
> by dawn of the next day there will be a horrid silence of sprawled
> bodies and tumbled vehicles, gutted buildings and a few wisps of smoke.
> And through that silence will prowl a few, a very few of the most powerful
> ones, ragged and bloody, slowly tracking each other down.[18]

Though McGee's world does not include the image of a gigantic international
criminal syndicate, such as the organization the "Executioner" has been
assiduously trying to wipe out through some twenty volumes, McGee usually
does find himself uncovering a conspiracy in which wealth, crime, and
politics are inextricably enmeshed. Moreover, McGee's adventures almost
invariably end with the violent destruction of the major leaders of this
conspiracy. Though far less reactionary and infinitely more interesting and
gifted as a writer than the potboilers who turn out the "Executioner" and its
like, John D. Macdonald works out of a fundamentally similar formula of the
Enforcer against a world of almost total corruption and amorality. Where the
"Executioner" works out the anxiety and hatred of this despairing vision in a
fantasy of savage killing, McGee attempts to construct little temporary oases
of meaning in the urban jungle. His "pad," an appropriately symbolic
floating houseboat, is the locus of these efforts, which revolve around his
friendship with a quixotic economist with a similar code and his temporary
but significant relationships with the women who invariably play an
important role in his adventures. For a character who is represented as a
savage realist and a ruthless exploiter of his prey's weaknesses, McGee is
surprisingly complex, tender, and determined to experience meaningful
emotions in his sexual relationships. His reflections on sex are full of the most

advanced popular psychology and frequently sound like a manual in human relationships written by a "Death of God" theologian. Like McGee, Richard Stark's Parker has rejected conventional social morality, yet he struggles somewhat ambiguously to find some sense of significance in his relationship with his mistress, to whom he returns after each crime.

The Enforcer's code is in many respects an extension of the tough-guy ethic already enunciated by Dashiell Hammett and other writers in the 1930s. It is probably ultimately derived from the stoic naturalism of Ernest Hemingway, whose great stories of the 1920s can certainly be seen as the initial creative statement of the vision underlying the Enforcer formula. Two major developments have transformed Hemingway's original invention into a new crime formula. First of all, the tough-guy ethic has been more broadly popularized and turned into the formula of the Enforcer story. Second, in the process of this transformation, Hemingway's tragic protagonist has been romanticized into the figure of the heroic but ruthless professional criminal. This process of development can be seen in capsule form in the successive film versions of Hemingway's story "The Killers." The original story, published in 1927, was a powerfully tragic account of a doomed boxer and a young boy's discovery of the irrational violence of life. In the 1946 film version, produced by Mark Hellinger and directed by Robert Siodmak, the young boy had almost entirely disappeared and the protagonist's role was taken over by a hard-boiled insurance investigator who eventually brought the boxer's killers and their employers to justice. The 1964 version of *The Killers*, produced and directed by Don Siegel, was clearly an Enforcer story. In this film, the protagonist is one of the killers, played by Lee Marvin who has recently made something of a specialty of the Enforcer role (cf. his performances in *Point Blank* and *Prime Cut*). Marvin plays a professional killer who has accepted an anonymous contract to assassinate a former racing driver (the analogue to Hemingway's boxer). He is puzzled by the fact that his victim seems so eager to die. Looking into his background, Marvin discovers a complex plot of corruption and betrayal growing out of a large robbery. Hoping to profit from the situation himself, Marvin tracks down the crooked businessman and his mistress who had originally planned the robbery, used the racing car driver, and then contracted for his killing in order to cover their tracks. Unlike the 1946 version, however, there is no ostensible moral purpose in Marvin's pursuit and eventual destruction of the two betrayers, since he is only interested in getting the loot for himself. Yet, despite his savagery and ruthlessness, it is clear that the Enforcer is the hero of this story, and there is at least a suggestion of heroic accomplishment when he is killed while destroying the crooked businessman. The basis of our admiration for the Enforcer in this case, as in that of Parker, lies in our response to his professionalism, his lack of hypocrisy, and his willingness to risk everything to achieve his ends. It is also important that we respond to his affection and loyalty for the young killer who is his partner. Their loyalty and comradeship in danger stand out against the complex deceit and

betrayal that characterizes most other characters in the film and thus
becomes an expression of the Enforcer's code.

The Enforcer's ruthlessness and his attempt to erect an area of meaning and
security in a corrupt and deceitful society through personal loyalties gains a
new dimension when Puzo develops it as a central theme of *The Godfather*.
In Michael's final justification to Kay of the life of his father, the family is
presented as the focus of those personal loyalties that alone can provide
security and power in a hostile society:

> My father is a businessman trying to provide for his wife and children and
> those friends he might need someday in a time of trouble. He doesn't accept
> the rules of the society we live in because those rules would have con-
> demned him to a life not suitable to a man like himself, a man of extraor-
> dinary force and character.... He refuses to live by rules set up by others,
> rules which condemn him to a defeated life. But his ultimate aim is to enter
> that society with a certain power since society doesn't really protect its
> members who do not have their own individual power. In the meantime he
> operates on a code of ethics he considers far superior to the legal structures
> of society.... I believe in you and the family we may have. I don't trust
> society to protect us. I have no intention of placing my fate in the hands of
> men whose only qualification is that they managed to con a block of
> people to vote for them.... I take care of myself, individual. Govern-
> ments don't really do much for their people, that's what it comes down to,
> but that's not it really. All I can say, I have to help my father, I have to be
> on his side.[19]

The pattern of action in which the Enforcer characteristically manifests
himself is the caper. The caper is a special sort of action in which an
individual or a group undertakes a particularly difficult feat than can only be
accomplished through a stratagem of considerable subtlety and complexity.
The usual structure for telling the story of a caper is by following the process
of the caper itself. In many cases, the plan of the caper is revealed to the
audience, followed by a suspenseful representation of the action itself, the
feeling of suspense being intensified by two uncertainties: whether the caper
will be discovered in process, or whether one of the complex details of the
plan will go awry and ruin the whole plot. Usually the feat that the caper
seeks to accomplish is a robbery or an assassination, though it may also be a
variety of other actions: a kidnapping, a commando raid, an escape, an
ambush, a capture. As a literary or cinematic structure, the caper is rather
different in its characteristics from some of the other major organizing
patterns in the literature of crime. It is quite different from the detective's
investigation of a mystery, the hero's pursuit and destruction of the master
criminal, or the gangster's rise and fall. Though an entire work may be
structured around a caper, this type of action can be developed on a smaller
scale as one or more episodes in a large work. While *The Godfather*'s overall
structure is not a caper, many of its most important episodes take this
form—for example, the attempted assassination of Don Vito, Michael's

killing of Sollozo and McCluskey, the murder of Sonny Corleone, and the series of assassinations that restore the Corleone family's power.

The caper is a narrative and dramatic form of great antiquity that has always been primarily associated with two major forms of human endeavor, warfare and crime. Our first great model for the caper is the story of the Trojan Horse, which encapsulates almost all the devices that will dominate this pattern of action for the following twenty-five hundred years: a very clever stratagem involving a carefully trained group of men and a major piece of equipment in a skillfully coordinated sequence of actions, subject to the dangers of discovery and mistake, but, when successful, resulting in a feat of great importance that had earlier seemed impossible. Though the caper has always been an important literary device, it is only in the last couple of decades that it has become one of the dominant forms of popular culture, particularly in the literature of crime. As I have noted, the major crime films of the thirties and forties dealt with the rise and fall of individual gangsters. In the late 1940s and early 1950s, an increasing emphasis on the caper becomes apparent in gangster films. For example, Raoul Walsh's *White Heat* (1949), though a classic gangster film in that it narrates the rise and fall of Cody Jarret (James Cagney), sets an elaborately detailed robbery of the payroll of an oil refinery at the climactic point of the film. In 1950, John Huston's *Asphalt Jungle* was one of the first major crime films to be completely structured around a single caper. Since that time the caper structure has proliferated in film, television, and literature. A majority of the most popular crime films of the late 1960s and early 1970s have depended on the caper structure, a prime example being *The French Connection*. On television, *Mission: Impossible*, each episode of which consists of an elaborately developed caper, has been one of the most successful series of the past several years. Finally, in literary crime, younger writers have more and more turned away from an emphasis on the investigation of mystery to tracing the process of the crime. In Britain, the work of Julian Symons, and in America that of Donald Westlake (Richard Stark), John D. Macdonald, and the several writers of such series as "Executioner" are instances of this development.

One reason for this development is the special characteristic of visual media like film and television in which the elaborately interrelated series of actions that constitute a caper can be represented with special effectiveness. The fact that the caper has also become a dominant structure in prose fiction and nonfiction where the medium is less obviously exploitable for this purpose suggests that there are thematic reasons for its popularity as well. As it appears in the new crime formula, the caper is a study in the exercise of power by a secret organization, and it usually involves a complex use of technology as well as the most elaborate planning and coordination. The caper is most often carried out against a large organization that has its own complex routines and technology. The ultimate aim of the caper is an exchange of power either through the acquisition of some form of wealth or through the destruction of important leaders of the opposing organization. Thus the narrative structure of the caper brings us back to those major concerns with organization outside the law and the exercise of power that we also saw as the underlying fascination of Mario Puzo's narrative of the history of the Corleone family.

The new formula of the Enforcer's caper is already very clearly defined and has served as the basis of a wide variety of stories and films from the crudest sort of post-Spillane avengers like the "Executioner" to fairly sophisticated and serious films like *Point Blank, The Asphalt Jungle,* and Stanley Kubrick's *The Killing.* Archetypally, these are all basically hero-tales—sometimes rather ironic in tone—with dangerous capers substituted for the traditional dragon and the skillful professional killer or assassin taking the place of the knight. The Enforcer can be either a criminal himself or an extralegal opponent of the syndicate. The popularity of this narrative formula is not evidence of any great upsurge in public acceptance of support for crime, for the fact that people like to read about criminal capers does not mean that they are any more in favor of crime than they ever were. The same thing is probably true of the myth of the "family" as manifested in *The Godfather.* With its central figure of the Don and its concern with the criminal organization's internal authority and external power, the myth of the "family" has not yet clearly evolved into a formula, though in the wake of *The Godfather's* success it almost surely will. The public's fascination with the Corleone family can certainly not be taken as an endorsement of organized crime, for the same public that has made *The Godfather* one of the best-selling novels and films of all time has clearly indicated in other ways its deep concern about a rising crime rate.

The Cultural Function of Popular Crime Formulas

The new formula of the Enforcer's caper and the emergent pattern of the Don and the criminal "family" are significant transformations of such earlier popular formulas as the classical and hard-boiled detective stories and the saga of the gangster's rise and fall. Changing cultural mythologies about crime such as the new fascination with large-scale criminal conspiracies, and changing social attitudes such as the increasing concern with the corruption of governmental and corporate power and the failure of modern organizations to provide a sense of security and fulfillment for the individual, have probably led to the increasing popularity of a formula that transforms the traditionally melodramatic gangster protagonist into a heroic figure and gives him the role of striking out against the brutality of the large organization and the general disorder, corruption, and injustice of society. Yet I doubt that the function of crime stories has undergone much change since the early nineteenth century. Looking back over the history of crime in literature, I see the same ambiguous mixture of horror and fascination, of attraction and repulsion, consistently at work. What has changed is the kind of crime that is the center of interest. Throughout its long-lasting tradition, literary crime serves as an ambiguous mirror of social values, reflecting both our overt commitments to certain principles of morality and order and our hidden resentments and animosity against these principles. In nineteenth-century England and America, the focal point of conceptions of morality and social authority was the domestic circle. At the same time, the literature of crime and the actual crimes that most fascinated the public were primarily murders of relatives—husbands poisoning wives, nephews murdering wealthy aunts, cousins doing away with cousins. These were the staples of the classical detective story and of the great Victorian murder trials. This suggests that the public's ambiguous fascination with such crimes was a way of vicariously working out feelings of hatred and frustration imposed by the intensity of the family situation. It may also account for the predominance of mystery as the central archetype for stories of crime in the later nineteenth and earlier twentieth centuries. As we shall see in the next chapter, the classical detective story with its focus on the investigation of mystery showed a particular fascination with the hidden secrets and guilts that lay within the family circle. The very structure of that formula tended to move around a group of intimates, with the finger of suspicion pointing at each in turn, until the guilt was finally projected onto someone on the edge or outside the magic circle.

The emergence of the gangster hero in the 1920s and the 1930s signaled the evolution, particularly in America, of a new constellation of values. The family circle, never as strong in America as in England, had increasingly lost its moral authority while the ideology of individual success and rising in society became the prevailing ethos. Overtly, the classic gangster film and the hard-boiled detective story portrayed the downfall of an individual who had sought wealth and power by immoral and illegal means. Yet beneath the moralistic surface of the story the gangster film expressed a burning resentment against respectable society and a fascination with the untrammeled and amoral aggressiveness of a Little Caesar or a Scarface. Similarly, the hard-boiled detective story presented a hero who not only acted outside the law to bring about true justice, but had turned his back on the ideal of success. In both these formulas, the treatment of crime enabled writers to express latent doubts about the ideal of success, while still insisting on the basic moral proposition that crime does not pay.

The new crime formula ambiguously mirrors a world in which the individualistic ethos no longer satisfactorily explains and orders society for most members of the public. The new center of value is the large organization and its collective power. The drama of the criminal gang has become a kind of allegory of the corporation and the corporate society. When the "Executioner" and his fellow enforcers are exterminating the Syndicate they are, on the surface, purging the evil corporation so that the good ones can flourish. But, covertly, the "Executioner" is engaged in a violent individualist revolution against an alienating and corrupting bureaucratic society. The attack on Syndicate bigwigs is a thinly disguised assault on the managerial elite who hold the reins of corporate power and use it for their own benefit. To express such feelings openly would presumably require a drastic transformation of the political and social perspective of many readers. The disguised allegory of the Enforcer story permits indulgence in a feeling of hatred against controlling organizations without requiring a new perception of society.

Puzo and other more sophisticated exponents of the new mythology of crime also treat the criminal organization as a symbolic mirror of the business corporation, but in a more complex way. In *The Godfather*, the surface story is a tragic drama of responsibility. Michael Corleone must give up his earlier dreams and aspirations and assume the role of Godfather, a position that not only makes him the leader of the "family" but also implicates him in deeds of murder and betrayal that contradict his previous scheme of values. But this is only the surface story. Covertly, Puzo's novel is a celebration of the "family." Michael's becoming Godfather, far from the destruction of his original hopes, is the true fulfillment of his destiny as an exceptional man. The "family" is a fantasy of tribal belongingness that protects and supports the individual as opposed to the coldness and indifference of the modern business or government bureaucracy. *The Godfather* and other related works permit us to enjoy vicariously the fantasy of an organization with boundless power and a true concern for the welfare of its members, just as the solid nineteenth-century family man could participate imaginatively in a nice bit of domestic homicide, thereby projecting his latent feelings toward his spouse onto a fictional or actual criminal.

Thus the Enforcer's caper and the incipient formula of the "family" use our perennial fascination with criminal activity to work out in stories the tension between traditional values and our sense of the decline of security, significance, and order in corporate society. The image of the "family" with its closely knit traditional authority and its power to protect the interests of its members has a powerful fascination in a period when the authority and power of the institutions that have traditionally provided direction and protection for individuals—the family, the church, the informal structures of closely knit neighborhood groups, the well-ordered career lines of the American middle class, and the ideology of success—seem to be threatened by social change and upheaval. Another contemporary cultural factor that is probably reflected in the new mythology of crime is our increasing concern about the unlimited power of the government that was so strongly intensified by our disturbing course of action in Vietnam. I suspect there is a definite relation between the fascination with limitless criminal power in the new crime formulas and the public's reluctant awareness of the uncontrollable power of violence in the hands of the government. Perhaps there is some reas-

surance in the vision of unlimited extralegal violence being used in responsible and meaningful ways by men with whose purposes we sympathize, as in
The Godfather.

But whatever the specific cultural sources of the new mythology of crime,
it seems clear to me that it expresses a deep uncertainty about the adequacy of
our traditional social institutions to meet the needs of individuals for
security, for justice, for a sense of significance. The fact that these concerns
are reflected through the dark mirror of crime indicates that most members of
the public are not prepared fully to confront and acknowledge the extent of
their despair. Here, as we have seen in the case of earlier crime formulas, the
use of crime as a subject enables the public to give some expression to its
latent hostility and frustration while still maintaining an overt stance of
affirmation of the conventional morality. The new crime stories generally
affirm a traditional view of the immorality of crime, at least to the extent of
differentiating between crime and legality, but the facade of morality and
legality often appears to be so shaky and rotten that one becomes more and
more aware of the disturbing vision that lies behind it: the dark message that
America is a society of criminals, or the still more disturbing irony that a
"family" of criminals might be more humanly interesting and morally satisfactory than a society of empty routines, irresponsibly powerful organizations, widespread corruption, and meaningless violence.

Four

The Formula of the
Classical Detective Story

The changing cultural mythology of crime has given rise to many different popular formulas. Some of these have been essentially adventure stories or melodramas, but one of the most striking embodies the cultural mythology of detectives, criminals, police, and suspects in an archetypal form that is almost pure mystery. The classical or ratiocinative detective story was first clearly articulated by Edgar Allan Poe in the 1840s, but it did not become a widely popular genre until the end of the nineteenth century. Its period of greatest popularity was initiated by the enormous success of Conan Doyle's Sherlock Holmes stories, and it flourished in the first four decades of the twentieth century. Since World War II, other formulas that include some elements of the mystery archetype, but are also stories of adventure or melodrama—the hard-boiled detective story, the spy story, the police procedural tale, the gangster saga, and the Enforcer's caper—have become increasingly popular. Few ratiocinative writers have followed in the footsteps of such creators as Agatha Christie, Dorothy Sayers, John Dickson Carr, Josephine Tey, Ngaio Marsh, and Michael Innes, though these earlier writers continue to have their dedicated fans. It seems clear that the classical formula is related to a distinctive historical period and reflects attitudes and interests that are no longer as widespread as they were.

Patterns of the Formula

The formula of the classical detective story can be described as a conventional way of defining and developing a particular kind of situation or situations, a pattern of action or development of this situation, a certain group of characters and the relations between them, and a setting or type of setting appropriate to the characters and action. In "The Murders in the Rue Morgue" and "The Purloined Letter," Poe defined these four aspects of the detective story formula so sharply and effectively that, until the emergence of the hard-boiled story with its different patterns, detective story writers largely based their work on Poe's inventions.

1. *Situation.* The classical detective story begins with an unsolved crime and moves toward the elucidation of its mystery. As Poe discovered in his two stories, the mystery may center upon the identity and motive of the criminal,

as in the case of "Rue Morgue," or, with the criminal and his purposes known, the problem may be to determine the means or to establish clear evidence of the criminal's deed, as in the case of "The Purloined Letter" where the detective must determine where the Minister D. has concealed the letter. Poe also defined two major types of crime on which much detective literature bases itself: murder, frequently with sexual or grotesque overtones, and crimes associated with political intrigue. From a formal point of view it is not difficult to see why these should be the favorite crimes of detective story writers. First of all, the significance of these crimes is proportionate to the elaborate parade of mystification and inquiry that the detective story must generate. Though Poe begins with crimes that are self-evidently important, he does not really make the significance of the crimes a major part of his story. We find out very little about the specific political issues and consequences that cluster around the theft of the queen's letter. Nor are we invited to reflect at any length upon the complex human tragedy of the sudden and horrible death of Mme L'Espanaye and her daughter. Instead, in "Rue Morgue," Poe carefully selects as his victims a rather obscure and colorless pair of people in order to keep our minds away from the human implications of their death. This seems to be an important general rule of the detective story situation. The crime must be a major one with the potential for complex ramifications, but the victim cannot really be mourned or the possible complexities of the situation allowed to draw our attention away from the detective and his investigation. A similar rule governs the detective's position in the situation. Poe tells us that Dupin has a personal reason for his involvement in the investigation. In "Rue Morgue" Poe obscurely hints at some prior friendship between Dupin and the prime suspect, Adolph Le Bon, while in "The Purloined Letter" we are offhandedly informed that Dupin is a partisan of the queen. Neither of these motives amounts to anything in comparison to what continually stands out as Dupin's major interest: delight in the game of analysis and deduction. The classical detective usually has little real personal interest in the crime he is investigating.[1] Instead, he is a detached, gentlemanly amateur. William Aydelotte suggests that this careful detachment of the detective story situation from the complexities of human life is a fundamental architectonic principle of the formula:

> In place of the complex issues of modern existence, people in a detective story have very simple problems. Life goes along well except for the single point that some crime, usually, in modern stories, a murder, has been committed. . . . From this act follow most of the troubles. Troubles are objectively caused by an external circumstance, the murder, which can and will be resolved, whereupon the troubles will disappear. . . . The mess, confusion, and frustration of life have been reduced to a simple issue between good and evil.[2]

2. *Pattern of action.* As Poe defined it, the detective story formula centers upon the detective's investigation and solution of the crime. Both "Rue Morgue" and "The Purloined Letter" exemplify the six main phases of this

pattern: (a) introduction of the detective; (b) crime and clues; (c) investigation; (d) announcement of the solution; (e) explanation of the solution; (f) denouement. These parts do not always appear in sequence and are sometimes collapsed into each other, but it is difficult to conceive of a classical story without them. Sometimes, the story begins with the introduction of the detective through a minor episode that demonstrates his skill at deduction. This is the case in "Rue Morgue," where after a brief characterization of the detective and the narrator we see Dupin "reading" his narrator-friend's mind. Then Dupin explains that he has followed the narrator's train of thought by deducing it from his expressions and gestures. Doyle later developed this initial proof of the detective's skill to a standard convention of the Sherlock Holmes stories. Not only did Doyle try to improve on Dupin's mind-reading trick in Holmes's adventure of "The Resident Patient," but he devised a great variety of such opening proofs of Holmes's miraculous powers: Holmes tells where Watson has been by examining the color of the mud on his trousers; he deduces a complete biography of Watson's unfortunate brother from a watch; he reveals men's occupations by observing the calluses on their thumbs or the characteristic wrinkles in their clothes. These initial tests of the hero are common in many forms of popular literature. The western hero rides a dangerous horse or accomplishes a particularly difficult shooting feat at his first appearance; James Bond often begins his adventures by outwitting the villain in a game, as he defeats Goldfinger at golf and Sir Hugo Drax at bridge. These episodes establish the hero's special competence and give the reader confidence that, however great the obstacles and dangers, the hero will be capable of overcoming them.

"The Purloined Letter" deployed a second way of introducing the detective hero that Doyle also made an important part of the Holmes stories. The narrator is "enjoying the twofold luxury of meditation and a meerschaum in company with my friend C. Auguste Dupin, in his little back library, or book-closet, au troisième, No. 33, Rue Dunôt, Faubourg St. Germain," when the placid calm is suddenly broken by the entry of the Prefect G. from the "gusty evening" outside.[3] This intrusion of the outside world on the serene and reflective calm of the detective's bachelor establishment was elaborated by Conan Doyle into the memorable opening scenes at 221B Baker Street. As he did with many of Poe's inventions, Doyle transformed Dupin's back library into a complex and highly developed scene whose eccentric inventory—tobacco in a Persian slipper, bullet holes in the wall spelling V.R., hypodermic syringe in its neat morocco case—forms an important part of the Holmesian ambience. This same device, though not universal, became one of the standard opening gambits of the classical detective story. One thinks immediately of Dr. Thorndyke's secluded laboratory, Dr. Fell's study, and the house of Nero Wolfe. Even the hard-boiled story has taken over this convention of the detective's retreat, transformed in this case into the shabby offices of Sam Spade and Philip Marlowe. Two considerations probably account for the effectiveness of this kind of introduction to the detective story. First, the sudden disruption of the quiet and secluded retreat is an effective emotional rhythm. The peaceful beginning in the detective's retreat establishes a point of departure and return for the story. The crime symbolizes not only an infraction of the law but a disruption of the normal order of society. It is something extraordinary that must be solved in order to restore the harmonious mood of that charming scene by the blazing fireplace. This manner of introduction also emphasizes the detachment of the detective, his lack of moral or personal involvement in the crime he is called on to investigate. The crime represents a disorder outside the confines of his personal existence, which thrusts itself upon him for resolution. Nero Wolfe goes so far as to refuse to leave his retreat at all, solving the crimes from reports brought to him by his assistant.

Another aspect of the classical detective's detachment appears in Poe's two stories. Dupin stands apart from us and the workings of his mind remain an essential mystery because the story is told from another point of view, that of his devoted but far less brilliant friend. Following Doyle's development of Poe's anonymous narrator into the unforgettable Dr. Watson, this device became a standard feature of the classical detective story. Though sometimes told by an objective narrator who sees partly into the detective's mind, the narrator is often a Watson-figure or a character involved in the story who has an excuse for being close to the detective but cannot follow or understand his line of investigation. There are a number of structural reasons for this practice. First, by narrating the story from a point of view that sees the detective's actions but does not participate in his perceptions or process of reasoning, the writer can more easily misdirect the reader's attention and thereby keep him from prematurely solving the crime. If he uses the detective's point of view, the writer has trouble keeping the mystery a secret without creating unnatural and arbitrary limits on what is shown to us of the detective's reasoning processes. This problem does not arise in the case of the hard-boiled detective because he is not presented as a man of transcendent intelligence or intuition and does not solve the crime primarily by ratiocinative processes. Giving us continual insight into his mental processes does not reveal the solution, for the hard-boiled detective is usually as befuddled as the reader until the end of the story. In the classical story, however, it seems to be important that the detective solve the crime or at least get on the right track from the beginning. In story after story, when the solution is finally revealed to us, we find that the detective immediately established the right line of investigation by making a correct inference from the conflicting and confusing testimony that had baffled everybody else. Of course, if this convention is to be maintained, the writer simply cannot afford to give us any direct insight into the detective's mind. If he decides to drop the device of the Watsonian narrator, the writer must either use a detached and anonymous narrator who sees the detective's actions but does not have any knowledge of his mental processes, or he must make the crime one that cannot be solved by the normal assumptions and methods of the detective.

There are other reasons for the particular narrative pattern of the detective story: by keeping us away from the detective's point of view, the writer can make the moment of solution an extremely dramatic and surprising climax since we have no clear indication when it will arrive. In addition, the Watsonian narrator provides us with an admiring perspective and commentary on the detective's activity. By using a narrator other than the detective, the writer can manipulate our sympathies and antipathies for the various suspects without forcing a revealing commitment on the detective himself. Moreover, the classical story's narrative method does not encourage an identification between the reader and the detective because the latter's feellings and perceptions remain largely hidden. Instead, the reader is encouraged to relate himself to the Watson figure and to the various suspects. The contrast between this pattern and that of the hard-boiled story is striking. In the Sam Spade and Philip Marlowe type of story, the action is almost invariably narrated from the detective's emotional and perceptual relation to the inquiry.

There is another important narrative tradition within the classical detective story that derives less from Poe than from Wilkie Collins's *The Moonstone* (1868). In this tradition, the story is told by a number of narrators, each of whom moves a step closer to the solution of the crime. Memorable in its few successful examples such as Carr's *The Arabian Nights Mystery* or Innes's *Lament for a Maker*, this technique is very difficult to handle, and most detective writers do not use it. The problem it poses, aside from the obvious difficulties of creating a convincing variety of points of view and coordinating their account of the action, lies in the way it necessarily fragments the process of investigation and the role of the detective.

The second major element in the classical detective story's pattern of action is the crime. In Poe's stories, and usually in Doyle's as well, the description of the crime immediately follows the introduction of the detective. Later writers, observing that this exact sequence was not necessary, found that in some instances it was desirable to present the crime first and then introduce the detective. This practice particularly relates to the use of one of the suspects' point of view as an alternative to the Watsonian narrator. In stories using this device the narrator's involvement with the crime leads to his encounter with the detective. This change in the sequence of the pattern also tends to place greater emphasis on the puzzle of the crime and less on the character of the detective than in the Poe-Doyle treatment of the introductory sequence. In general the classical detective story evolves in this direction, giving increasing importance to the intricacy of the puzzle surrounding the crime and less prominence to the detective's initiative in the investigation.

The effectiveness of the crime itself depends upon two main characteristics with a paradoxical relationship to each other. First, the crime must be surrounded by a number of tangible clues that make it absolutely clear that some agency is responsible for it, and, second, it must appear to be insoluble. With his lucidity and sense of structure Poe created this paradoxical combination with dazzling simplicity in "The Purloined Letter." We have the most tangible physical evidence that Minister D. stole the letter, for the person from whom he stole it saw him. We also know, by equally tangible evidence, that the minister still has the letter, for the catastrophic political consequences certain to follow from its leaving his possession have not appeared. Yet at the same time we have equally certain clues that the letter is not in his possession. The minister's person has been searched several times. His house has been ransacked with microscopes and long, thin needles by the Parisian police. It is certain that the letter is not concealed anywhere. A crime has evidently taken place, and yet it appears to be absolutely insoluble. This is the ideal paradigm of the detective story crime, for it poses a problem really worthy of the detective. Unfortunately, strokes as brilliantly economical as this are rare. The treatment of the crime in "The Murders in the Rue Morgue" is more typical of detective story literature. Here we find a large number of tangible clues that are confusing and obscure but do not reach the ultimate paradox of "The Purloined Letter." The "Rue Morgue" clues, like those of so many other detective stories, combine evidence that some agency has performed the deed with seeming indications that it cannot have been any person we can imagine being involved. The mutilated condition of the bodies, the way things in the room have been scattered about, the evidence of the voices heard by witnesses, make it clear that some person or persons have been involved in the murder, but other clues—the locked window, the apparently superhuman force involved in the murder, the confusion about the language spoken by the second voice—make it impossible to see how any known agent could have been involved. Thus, in the initial formulation of the problem, it is certain that a crime has taken place, but the identity of the criminal remains in doubt. The mystery is not as paradoxical as in the case of "The Purloined Letter" and the solution, when Poe drags in an orangoutan to account for the confusion of clues, is correspondingly less satisfying because it seems a way of solving the impasse by introducing a new element into the story. Later writers have generally tried to avoid this necessity by discovering ways to make the paradox of clues eventually point back to one of the initial characters.[4]

The "crime and clues" section of Poe's stories is followed by the parade of witnesses, suspects, and false solutions, which constitutes the investigation as it is presented to the reader. In "Rue Morgue" this section is brief, a sign that Poe had not quite fully articulated the classical detective form as he would in "The Purloined Letter." Nevertheless, Poe did invent two central conventions of this section: the parade of witnesses presented in quasi-documentary fashion and the "red herring" that in "Rue Morgue" takes the form of the obscure clerk Adolphe Le Bon. Remarkably, Poe even seems to have had an inkling of the desirability of having the finger of suspicion point at a character with whom the reader can identify or sympathize. Though Le Bon is too briefly treated to arouse much interest, his name, as Richard Wilbur points out, hints at an implicit moral symbolism. Moreover, we are told that Dupin feels an obligation to Le Bon who "once rendered me a service for which I am not ungrateful." The combined structural and emotional functions of the investigation section are more clearly if not more extensively articulated in "The Purloined Letter." There the emotional import of the investigation is provided by the personal and political jeopardy of the queen, which has much more impact than the fate of the obscure M. Le Bon. In addition, through the prefect's account, Poe is able to create that sense of an exhaustive examination of all the material evidence and possible suspects (in this case not people but possible hiding places), which leaves the situation more mysterious than before, thereby paving the way for the brilliant intervention of the detective.

Poe's stories at least partially developed the two major characteristics of the investigation section. Just as the crime and clues must pose a paradox, the parade of witnesses, suspects, and possible solutions, while seemingly moving toward the clarification of the mystery, must really further obfuscate it so that we finally arrive at a total impasse where the reader feels lost in a murky and impenetrable bog of evidence and counterevidence; when this point is reached, the detective is ready to step in. By means of his transcendent intuition, he has been working clearly and rationally toward a solution while the reader sinks into confusion. Second, the investigation usually threatens to uncover or expose the guilt of a character or characters with whom the reader has been encouraged to sympathize or identify, so that the detective's final solution is not only a clarification of the mystery but a rescue of characters we wish to see free from suspicion and danger. The elaboration and expansion of this section of the pattern of action was a major trend in the development of the classical detective story after Poe.

In Poe's stories, the dark confusion and uncertainty reached after the examination of clues and witnesses is suddenly and dramatically superseded by Dupin's announcement that he has solved the crime. Poe evidently took much delight in the staging of these triumphant and surprising revelations, and, as usual, he was particularly successful in "The Purloined Letter" where Dupin responds to the prefect's offer of a check for 50,000 francs to anyone who can help find the queen's letter with the calm statement that the letter is in his desk. It should also be noted that the announcement of the solution is not necessarily coincident with the actual apprehension of the criminal, which I will call the denouement. In "Rue Morgue," Dupin's sudden revelation that "the facility with which I shall arrive, or have arrived, at the solution of this mystery, is in the direct ratio to its apparent insolubility in the eyes of the police" does not lead immediately to the production of the criminal but to the immortal announcement, "I am now awaiting a person who, although perhaps not the perpetrator of these butcheries, must have been in some measure implicated in their perpetration."[5] Then, only after Dupin's explanation of how he has arrived at the solution does Poe finally introduce the mysterious sailor whose orangoutan is actually responsible for the crime.

The announcement of the solution is as important as, perhaps in some instances more important than, the actual apprehension and punishment of the criminal. Like Poe, most classical writers make a strikingly dramatic moment out of the detective's revelation that he has solved the mystery. To give just one example, think of that moment in *The Hound of the Baskervilles* where Watson, at the zenith of his confusion, enters the mysterious prehistoric dwelling on the moor to await in darkness the return of the mysterious figure he believes to be the criminal. While he sits there clutching his revolver, he hears footsteps approaching. A shadow falls across the opening of the hut and then: "'It is a lovely evening, my dear Watson,' said a well-known voice. 'I really think that you will be more comfortable outside than in.'"[6] In the ensuing conversation Holmes calmly reveals that he has worked out the whole thing. This is a paradigm of such scenes: the frantic narrator who is hopelessly lost in the maze of clues and testimony and the supremely calm detective who now takes the action into his hands. We find the same contrast between the desperate prefect who has just about given up the possibility of finding the missing letter and the serenely ironic Dupin who leisurely goes to his desk and takes it out. Naturally, since the action of the classical story focuses on the investigation of a mystery, the detective's calm announcement that he has arrived at the solution is a climactic moment. This is also the turning point of the story in another way. As indicated earlier, the reader has been forced to follow the action from the confused and limited point of view of the narrator. From this point of view investigation leads only to obfuscation. But when the solution is announced, though technically the point of view does not change, in actuality we now see the action from the detective's perspective. As he explains the situation, what had seemed chaotic and confused is revealed as clear and logical. In addition, this is the point at which the detective usually assumes the initiative against the criminal. Throughout the main part of the story the narrator appears to be surrounded by the plots of a mysterious criminal. After the announcement of the solution, the reader joins the detective in his superior position, assuming the role of spider to the criminal fly. Finally, the special importance of the moment of solution presents the classical writer with the opportunity of having two major climaxes or peaks of tension, the moment of solution and the eventual denouement when the criminal is actually captured.

These reflections help to account for the special interest of the next section in the classical pattern: the explanation. Here the detective discourses at length on the reasoning that led him to the solution and reveals just how and why the crime was carried out. To a superficial view it might seem that the explanation section risks being drearily anti-climactic, but I think that most detective story readers will testify that while they are frequently bored by an unimaginative or too detailed handling of the parade of clues, testimony, and suspects, the explanation, despite its involved and intricate reasoning, is usually a high point of interest. Indeed, many stories that get almost intolerably bogged down during the investigation become suddenly fraught with tension and excitement when the detective begins his explanation. Obviously, the explanation is important because in completing the investigation it represents the goal toward which the story has been moving. It also reflects the pleasure we feel when we are told the solution of a puzzle or a riddle. This is a combination of several factors. We are interested because we ourselves have been involved in the explanation and interpretation of the clues presented in the course of the investigation. Therefore a certain fascination hovers about the detective's explanation as we measure our own perception and interpretation of the chain of events against his. How far were we able to go along the road in the right direction? Where did we get off the track? The most exciting and successful detective stories seem to me neither those where the reader solves the crime before the detective announces his solution nor those where he is totally surprised and bamboozled by the solution that the detective arrives at. When the reader feels confident that he understands the mystery before the detective, the story loses interest. Since many stories are fairly easy to solve, I suspect that most confirmed readers develop an ability to put a premature solution out of their minds so that the story is not spoiled for them. On the other hand, if the detective's solution is a total surprise, that too seems less than satisfactory and the reader feels cheated, because it appears that his earlier participation in the story has been completely irrelevant. When Dupin reveals that the murderer in "Rue Morgue" has been an animal and that he has withheld one essential clue, a tuft of hair from the orangoutan, the explanation is far less effective than the brilliant and thoroughly satisfying account of Dupin's recovery of the purloined letter. In that story, the explanation as in the case of all good riddles requires not so much working one's way through a mass of evidence as being able to see the problem from a different angle. Once the new angle or perspective has been grasped, the solution is simple and obvious. When Dupin intuitively recognizes that Minister D. conceived the problem of concealment of the letter not as hiding it in or behind something but as making it too obvious to be seen, his act was like the change of perspective required to solve the old riddle "What's black and white and red [read] all over," where the solution is impossible as long as the guesser interprets the sound "red" as a color. Similarly, the reader of "The Purloined Letter" is unlikely to think of concealment in other than its ordinary meaning of hiding, yet the failure of the prefect makes the reader at least half aware that a new angle of vision is necessary. When the detective supplies the alternative perspective, the reader's feeling, as in the case of a good riddle, is not one of having been cheated and tricked but one of surprise and admiration at the wit of the detective and pleasure and delight at being confronted with a new way of seeing things. Finally, the puzzle or riddle aspect of the detective story depends less upon the reader's own ability to solve the mystery than on giving him enough participation in it to enable him better to appreciate the wit of the detective and to understand the new perspective on which the explanation depends.

Beyond its riddling dimension, the explanation has other sources of interest. One of its special pleasures comes from the satisfaction of seeing a sequence of events not only shaped from a different perspective, but given a different kind of order. In a very broad sense there is an analogy between this aspect of the detective story and certain contemporary novels that, like Faulkner's *The Sound and the Fury*, are constructed around the presentation of the same series of incidents from several different points of view. In Faulkner's novel the story grows as we witness the condition and history of the Compson family first from the point of view of the idiot younger brother Benjy, then as seen by his two older brothers Quentin and Jason, and finally from the perspective of an objective narrator. The sections of Benjy and Quentin, one an idiot and the other a manic young man on the verge of committing suicide, are extremely fragmentary, discontinuous, and full of distortions of "normal" spatial and temporal order. The final section is a more or less straightforward chronological narrative that is quite easy to follow. The effect of the sequence of these sections is one of a growing sense of clarity and order. The relation between the investigation and explanation section of a good detective story is similar. Clues are initially presented in the wrong order. They are wrenched out of their proper context in space and their place in a chronological sequence. The explanations section sets these events back into their logical position in a sequence of action. It provides the pleasure of seeing a clear and meaningful order emerge out of what seemed to be random and chaotic events. Watching the detective is like watching a skillful artist who is able to take a few odd patches of color and wiggly lines and make a face or a landscape emerge from them. Even though superficially similar, the difference between a detective story and the multiple perspectives of a twentieth-century novel remains basic. In the detective story, when we arrive at the detective's solution, we have arrived at the truth, the single right perspective and ordering of events. But in *The Sound and the Fury*, the omniscient narrative of the final section, though it may be clearer in some ways, does not claim a higher level of reality or meaning than the more discontinuous and fragmentary perspectives of the earlier sections. Instead of satisfying us that things are now placed in their proper positions, the final section of *The Sound and the Fury* actually reveals that the events are too complex to be understood from a single unified point of view. To use a related example, that of Joyce's *Ulysses*, Molly Bloom's internal monologue, which is the final section, does not synthesize and supersede the preceding perspectives of Leopold Bloom and Stephen Dedalus. Instead, it further intensifies the inexhaustible mystery of human relationships and character by presenting still another different but equally valid revelation of the relationship of Leopold and Molly Bloom. One might almost say that it is just this kind of revelation that the detective story is designed to prevent, for the detective's explanation is precisely a denial of mystery and a revelation that human motivation and action can be exactly specified and understood.

This brings us to the final source of pleasure in the detective's explanation, the sense of relief that accompanies the detective's precise definition and externalization of guilt. It is here that we participate in the culmination of what Northrop Frye calls "a ritual drama in which a wavering finger of social condemnation passes over a group of 'suspects' and finally settles on one."[7] The parade of false suspects and solutions brings under initial suspicion characters with whom the reader is encouraged to sympathize or identify, thereby exciting a fear that one of them will be shown to be guilty. The reader, in other words, is metaphorically threatened with exposure and shame. Then the detective proves that the sympathetic characters cannot be guilty, or if they are, he establishes by careful explanation that their crime was justified and that they are not guilty in a moral sense. The most popular convention is to externalize and objectify guilt onto the "least-likely person" who is "proved" to be the guilty one. In part, the development of the "least-likely person" as the favorite criminal in the classical detective story was a result of the necessity of displacing the reader's attention during the investigation and thereby keeping him from recognizing the solution. But, in my view, the need to make the criminal a person with whom the reader develops no sympathy or identification is a more important reason for the "least-likely person" convention. For this character is the one who has been kept in the shadow throughout the story, the one to whom relatively little thought has been given. No bonds have been built between him and the reader, and consequently he can serve his role as the personification of guilt without involving the reader's feelings. The relief that accompanies the explanation reflects the reader's pleasure at seeing his favorites and projections clearly and finally exonerated and the guilt thrust beyond question onto a person who has remained largely outside his sphere of interest.

Usually the final section in the pattern of the classical detective story involves the actual apprehension and confession of the criminal. The denouement bears a close relationship to the other climactic moment in the pattern, the announcement that the detective has reached the solution. Sometimes denouement and solution are combined. In many of the Nero Wolfe stories, for example, the solution is announced by means of a trap that both reveals the criminal and apprehends him at the same moment. An alternative treatment of the problem is found in "Rue Morgue" where solution and denouement are distinctly separated. Dupin announces that he has solved the crime and explains it to his dazzled friend before the sailor appears in response to his advertisement. In such cases the denouement serves more as corroboration of the detective's solution and explanation than as a focus of interest and suspense in its own right. In fact, as Poe demonstrated in "The Purloined Letter," the actual representation of the denouement is not essential to the detective story. In that story, Dupin sets a trap for Minister D. by leaving him a false copy of the letter. The reader is assured that this is certain to lead him into a catastrophic political blunder. Poe evidently did not feel it necessary or desirable to stage the scene, perhaps because the elaborate treatment necessary to present such a denouement would have completely taken our attention away from Dupin and made the predicament of Minister D. the real center of the story. Most classical stories do represent the capture and confession of the criminal, but they tend to follow Poe's example by making this section too brief to permit the criminal to upstage the detective. Even in a story like Doyle's *The Hound of the Baskervilles,* where the denouement is full of suspense and excitement, the focus is not on the criminal Stapleton but on the terrible hound that was the means of his crimes. The tendency to make the denouement simply bear out the detective's solution rather than give the reader a more complex interest in the criminal's predicament points to an observation we have already made: the classical story is more concerned with the isolation and specification of guilt than with the punishment of the criminal.

This completes our account of the pattern of action formulated by Poe and followed by the tradition of the classical detective story. All classical detective stories contain these main elements, though not always in the exact sequence given: introduction of the detective, crime and clues, suspects and false solutions, announcement of solution, explanation, and denouement.

3. *Characters and relationships.* As Poe defined it, the classical detective story required four main roles: (*a*) the victim; (*b*) the criminal; (*c*) the detective; and (*d*) those threatened by the crime but incapable of solving it. Later writers have elaborated on these roles and in some cases have mixed them up, but on the whole it seems safe to say that without the relations implicit in these roles it is not possible to create a detective story.

Doing the victim right is a delicate problem for the creator of classical detective tales. If the reader is given too much information about the victim or if he seems a character of great importance, the story's focus around the process of investigation will be blurred. Moreover, its emotional effect will move toward tragedy or pathos, disrupting the relative serenity and detachment of the classical detective formula. On the other hand, if the victim seems insignificant and the reader has no information about him, interest in the inquiry and suspense about its outcome will be minimal. Poe invented two extremely effective ways of striking a balance between the disturbing flow of pity and fear that accompanies tragedy and an indifference to the victim that would keep the reader from caring at all about the investigation of his fate. His first approach as exemplified in "The Murders in the Rue Morgue" was to make his victims obscure, ordinary, and colorless people who meet a grotesque and mystifying end. Consequently their characters do not engage the reader's interest or sympathies, but the nature of their end does. In other words, while Poe tells us nothing about Mme L'Espanaye and her daughter that would make us feel one way or another about what happens to them, he makes the circumstances of their demise so strange and terrifying that we feel a great interest in discovering just what happened to them. In "The Purloined Letter," however, Poe created a victim of considerable importance but kept her almost entirely out of the story, telling us only enough about her predicament to make it clear that Dupin's investigation is relevant. In both instances Poe succeeded in keeping the reader from being too deeply involved in the victim's fate while at the same time providing ample justification and suspense for the detective's inquiry. Detective story writers have tended to follow him in this practice. It is another of the paradoxes of the detective story formula that the victim, who is supposedly responsible for all the activity, is usually the character of least interest.

The criminal also poses a problem of structural focus for, if the writer becomes too interested in his motives and character, he risks the emergence of an emotional and thematic complexity that could break up the formula. The goal of the detective story is a clear and certain establishment of guilt for a specific crime. If we become too concerned with the motives of the criminal, his guilt is likely to seem increasingly ambiguous and difficult to define. It is possible for a detective story writer to create a complex and interesting criminal as Poe did in Minister D., or Doyle in Professor Moriarty, or Michael Innes in the Ranald Guthrie of Lament for a Maker, but there must never be any serious question about either the specific guilt or the evil motives of these characters. In short, their motives may be complex and their actions interesting, but they must always be definable as bad.

With the invention of Minister D.—the fascinating but supremely evil master criminal—Poe discovered a way of creating a significant and complex character without permitting him to take over the limelight from the detective. First of all, Minister D. cannot upstage Dupin because the two characters are, in many respects, mirror images of each other. Both brilliant, aristocratic, eccentric, both poets and men of the sharpest reasoning powers; there are even suggestions of an association between the two that goes back many years, to mention just a few of the structural parallels. I cannot help being persuaded by Richard Wilbur's suggestion that in some fashion these characters symbolize two parts of the same soul.[8] The same kind of relationship, though less profoundly resonant of inner allegory, exists between Sherlock Holmes and Professor Moriarty.

The master criminal is rather exceptional in the tradition of the detective story simply because he is too fascinating, too surrounded with ambiguous fantasies, and therefore extremely difficult to keep subordinated to the detective. One of my students once remarked that the most surprising thing about Sherlock Holmes is that he decided to be a detective rather than a master criminal, a remark that may shed some light on the psychological currents that led Doyle to invent Professor Moriarty as the appropriate means of disposing of a detective in whom his creator had lost interest. Further evidence of the great fascination of the master criminal appears in that type of popular literature where he is an indispensable ingredient, the spy story. Saxe Rohmer's Fu Manchu, the secret international organizations of John Buchan, and the super villains of Ian Fleming, lineal descendants of Minister D. and Professor Moriarty, so dominate the spy story's pattern of action with their extraordinary talents and their ambiguous combination of evil and attractiveness that they disrupt the classical pattern of investigation and solution and require a different kind of archetypal structure.

Poe's other solution to the treatment of the criminal established the convention of the least-likely person, which we have already discussed. In "Rue Morgue" Poe rather crudely kept the criminal from engaging the reader's attention by keeping him out of the story until the last moment and then revealing him as an agency the reader was unlikely to expect, an animal. Since the witnesses all testify that they heard voices in the room at the time of the murder, the reader assumes that the criminal was a human being. When it turns out to be an orangoutan, the switch seems a bit sudden. Succeeding writers developed the principle of the unanticipated agent into the person who is present throughout the story, but in a very marginal way. As we have seen, this convention has a double structural advantage: it keeps the reader from identifying the criminal before the detective produces the solution and by keeping the person who is to become the embodiment of guilt on the sidelines it prevents the reader from developing much sympathy for him.

Treating victim and criminal as figures without much emotional interest or complexity places the detective story's primary emphasis on those characters who are investigating the crime, the most important of which is the detective. Of all Poe's contributions to the formula of the classical detective story, his invention of the character of Dupin—with his aristocratic detachment, his brilliance and eccentricity, his synthesis of the poet's intuitive insight with the scientist's power of inductive reasoning, and his capacity for psychological analysis—was certainly the most crucial. This was essentially the same combination of qualities that Doyle built into Sherlock Holmes. With minor differences of emphasis, they have remained the distinguishing characteristics of twentieth-century classical detectives like Hercule Poirot, Dr.Gideon Fell, Mr. Campion, Lord Peter Wimsey, Nero Wolfe, and many others.

Poe introduces Dupin as a man detached not only from society but from the ordinary patterns of human experience. Though "of an illustrious family" Dupin had suffered reverses that reduced him to poverty. Instead of trying to recover his position, Dupin has "ceased to bestir himself in the world, or to care for the retrieval of his fortunes." In contemporary slang, he has dropped out. And not only has Dupin detached himself from the quest for wealth and status, he has rejected the ordinary man's pattern of living—"enamored of the Night," he has rejected the day altogether:

> At the first dawn of the morning, we closed all the massy shutters of our old building: lighted a couple of tapers, which, strongly perfumed, threw out only the ghastliest and feeblest of rays. By the aid of these we then busied our souls in dreams ... until warned by the clock of the advent of the true Darkness. Then we sallied forth into the streets, arm in arm, continuing the topics of the day, or roaming far and wide until a late hour, seeking, amid the wild lights and shadows of the populous city, that infinity of mental excitement which quiet observation can afford.[9]

This detachment from the ordinary world is a sign of the detective's eccentricity and decadence and of his particular analytic brilliance and insight, which above all takes the form of an ability to read the hidden motives of men.

> At such times I could not help remarking and admiring ... a peculiar analytic ability in Dupin. He seemed, too, to take an eager delight in its exercise.... He boasted to me, with low chuckling laugh, that most men, in respect to himself, wore windows in their bosoms, and was wont to follow up such assertions by direct and very startling proofs of his intimate knowledge of my own.[10]

There follows immediately upon this introduction the first recorded deduction of a fictional detective. After walking in silence for some minutes, Dupin suddenly breaks into the narrator's chain of thought with a comment immediately responsive to the latter's thoughts. The narrator's sudden and terrified reaction demonstrates the particular aura of psychological potency that hovers around this central ability of the detective:

> "Tell me, for Heaven's sake," I exclaimed, "the method—if method there is—by which you have been enabled to fathom my soul in this matter." In fact I was even more startled that I could have been willing to express.[11]

To the enormous relief of the narrator, Dupin explains that he has not actually been able to read his friend's thoughts but only to deduce them from his overt acts and gestures. This incident sums up the detective's essential role in the story. He is a brilliant and rather ambiguous figure who appears to have an almost magical power to expose and lay bare the deepest secrets. But he chooses to use these powers not to threaten but to amuse us and to relieve our tensions by exposing the guilt of a character with whom we have the most minimal ties of interest and sympathy. It is for this reason, I think, that there are such suggestive similarities between Poe's Dupin and Doyle's Holmes and two other characters with whom one would not at first think to associate them: the fictional figure of the gothic villain and the real character of Dr. Sigmund Freud, particularly as that character was articulated in the role of interpreter of dreams and items of neurotic behavior.

When one thinks about it, the close resemblance between Dupin and the gothic villain is immediately clear. Both are demonically brilliant, night-loving figures, and both are involved in plotting out elaborate and complex stratagems. One might interpret Poe's invention of the detective as a means of bringing the terrifying potency of the gothic villain under the control of rationality and thereby directing it to beneficial ends.

Though it has long been common to interpret popular formulas in Freudian terms, the odd analogies between the figure of the detective and that of Dr. Freud himself are rather fascinating and have often been noted, most recently in Meyer's delightful *The Seven-Percent Solution*.[12] There is even an odd resemblance between the names sometimes given by Freud to the dreams he discusses and the titles of the cases of Dupin and Holmes, for example "The Dream of the Botanical Monograph" as compared to the case of "The Purloined Letter" or "The Adventure of the Second Stain." The curious analogy between the process of dream interpretation and that of detection as represented in the classical formula can be summarized as follows: a brilliant investigator (Dupin, Freud) is confronted with a series of material clues (footprints, tufts of hair, dream symbols, slips of the tongue) that if properly interpreted are signs of a deeply hidden and disturbing truth. By a combination of method and insight, the investigator overcomes the confusion that attends these clues (the criminal's plot, psychological displacement) and reveals the hidden truth (solves the crime, interprets the dream). The great difference is that where the detective's solution always projects the guilt onto an external character, Freud's method exposes the conflicting motives in our own minds. These analogies between psychoanalysis and the detective story suggest to me a common concern with hidden secrets and guilts that may reflect a cultural pattern of the period. Where the detective story resolved this concern by pretending to find the hidden secret in someone else's mind, psychoanalysis went directly to the root of the problem by exposing and confronting the individual's own inner tension and anxiety.

The detective's terrifying ability to expose hidden secrets also relates to the convention of aristocratic and eccentric detachment from the ordinary concerns of human life. Because his skill threatens to uncover some secret guilt on the part of a character with whom the reader identifies, it is reassuring that, despite this terrifying superiority, the detective is a detached eccentric with no worldly stake in the outcome of the action. Ultimately he uses his powers not to threaten but to uphold the reader's self-esteem by proving the guilt of a specific individual rather than exposing some general guilt in which the reader might be implicated. Thus, the detective story stands in marked contrast to those important late nineteenth- and early twentieth-century novels that explored the lower depths of society and of the individual psyche and returned from their quests with a general indictment of the guilt of the respectable middle classes for their indifference and exploitation of the poor and their illicit and hidden dreams of sex and aggression. The detective may be a reflection of the new nineteenth-century cultural type of intellectual. But instead of laying bare the hidden guilt of bourgeois society the detective-intellectual uses his demonic powers to project the general guilt onto specific and overt acts of particular individuals, thus restoring the serenity of the middle-class social order. Both Freud and Sherlock Holmes are intellectual investigators of the illicit secrets of middle-class society. But where Freud and other social and psychological critics such as Marx and his followers discovered everyone's guilts, Holmes and the other classical detectives absolved society by exposing the least-likely person or the master criminal.

In this perspective the role of the fourth main group of characters in the classical detective story emerges more clearly. This consists of those characters who are involved with the crime but need the detective's aid to solve it. It includes three main types: the offshoots of Poe's narrator, the friends or assistants of the detective who frequently chronicle his exploits; the bungling and inefficient members of the official police, descendants of Poe's prefect; and, finally, the collection of false suspects, generally sympathetic but weak people who require the detective's intervention to exonerate them, the manifold progeny of Poe's Adolphe Le Bon. These characters are usually decent, respectable people who suddenly find themselves in a situation where their ordinarily secure status is no protection against the danger of being charged with a crime and where the police are as likely to arrest the innocent as the guilty. This fourth group of characters represents the norm of middle-class society suddenly disrupted by the abnormality of crime. The special drama of crime in the classical detective story lies in the way it threatens the serene domestic circles of bourgeois life with anarchy and chaos. The official guardians of this order, the police, turn out to be inefficient bunglers, and the finger of suspicion points to everybody. The ordered rationality of society momentarily seems a flimsy surface over a seething pit of guilt and disorder. Then the detective intervenes and proves that the general suspicion is false. He proves the social order is not responsible for the crime because it was the act of a particular individual with his own private motives. Through his treatment of the fourth group of characters, the classical detective writer arouses our fears that sympathetic characters are guilty, then releases that fear when the detective proves that the guilt can be attributed to a specific individual. The importance of this aspect of the classical story is probably the main reason why the criminal and the victim are frequently the least developed characters. It is not the confrontation of detective and criminal so much as the detective's rescue of the false suspects and the police that constitutes the dramatic nexus of the classical formula.

4. *Setting*. In devising the setting for his stories Poe again set the pattern for the classical detective story. Both "Rue Morgue" and "The Purloined Letter" take place in two isolated settings clearly marked off from the rest of the world: Dupin's apartment and the room in which the crime takes place. Around these two curiously delimited and fixed spaces swirls the teeming city of Paris. How often this combination of the isolated place and the bustling

world outside is repeated in the classical detective story: the locked room in the midst of the city, the isolated country house in the middle of the strange and frightening moors, the walled-in college quadrangle, or the lonely villa in the suburban town. Mystery after mystery takes us back and forth between the detective's apartment or office and the isolated room full of clues. We are always aware of the threatening chaos of the outside world, but it erupts only rarely into the story, usually at the most suspenseful times, the moment of the crime, and then again at the solution and denouement.

This setting performs many functions. First of all, it furnishes a limited and controlled backdrop against which the clues and suspects so central to the story can be silhouetted. It abstracts the story from the complexity and confusion of the larger social world and provides a rationale for avoiding the consideration of those more complex problems of social injustice and group conflict that form the basis of much contemporary realistic fiction. The isolated setting also fosters that special kind of suspense that has long been associated with places apart from the busy stream of human affairs. In this respect the classical detective story setting is a direct descendant of the isolated castle or abbey where all those mysterious goings on took place in the gothic novels of Mrs. Radcliffe, "Monk" Lewis, and their followers. But most important, the contrast between the locked room or the lonely country house and the outside world constitutes a symbolic representation of the relation between order and chaos, between surface rationality and hidden depths of guilt. We begin in the serene and rational order of the detective's apartment or in the pleasant warmth and social graces of the country house before the murder. Then we are suddenly transported to the locked room, a mirror image of the detective's apartment disrupted by the chaotic outer world that has penetrated the quiet order and left behind those mysterious clues suggesting the presence of a hidden guilt. By solving the secret of the locked room, the detective brings the threatening external world under control so that he and his assistant can return to the peaceful serenity of his library, or can restore the pleasant social order of the country house.

The isolated setting has remained popular with classical detective story writers for another reason. It establishes a framework for the treatment of manners and local color in a fashion often reminiscent of the great Victorian novelists. Though this tendency is minimal in Poe, it is nonetheless present in his interest in the variety of occupations and responses of the parade of witnesses in "Rue Morgue." Doyle developed this concern into richly atmospheric sketches of Baker Street and its "Irregulars," the London slums, and the English countryside, while in many twentieth-century classical stories local color almost takes over the tale. In Dorothy Sayers's *Nine Tailors* a rural society out of Thomas Hardy by Trollope shares the spotlight with an elaborate discussion of the art of campanology, and Michael Innes enacts an almost Dickensian social panorama in stories like *Appleby's End*. These pageants of local color provide both an air of verisimilitude and an added source of interest to the main theme of investigation. In addition, they symbolize the normally peaceful and serene order of society disrupted by the anomaly of crime and restored when the detective isolates the guilty individual. Many twentieth-century writers of classical detective stories reflect the nineteenth-century novel in their treatment of society in the form of nostalgic fantasies of a more peaceful and harmonious social order associated with the traditional rural society of England.

Cultural Background of the Formula

In my analysis of the basic patterns of the classical detective story, I have already speculated about some of the functions these patterns perform, particularly in connection with such artistic imperatives as the creation of suspense. It remains to attempt some tentative generalizations about the cultural significance of these patterns. What cultural values or beliefs do these patterns affirm, what tensions do they seek to resolve, what underlying or latent feelings seek expression in this particular formula? These questions are not easy to answer, or perhaps we should say they are too easy to answer. A great many interpretations have been offered of the appeal of the detective story, ranging from Haycraft's suggestion that it embodies a democratic respect for law to the psychoanalytic view that our fascination with mystery represents unresolved feelings about the primal scene. Is there any way in which we can sift through the profusion of possible answers and arrive at some reasoned hypotheses? There is at least one line of reasoning that I find persuasive. Our hypotheses must clearly account for the distinctive charac- teristics of the classical detective story and must show some fairly clear connection or relation between these characteristics and the period in which this formula flourished. Otherwise our interpretation, whatever validity it may have for us, will not account very persuasively for the relation between the formula and the culture that created it. The Freudian "primal scene" interpretation does not offer us any particular connection with the later nineteenth century, since it refers to a characteristic of the human psyche that transcends a particular epoch. The fascination of the primal scene may well account for the human fascination with mystery stories in all epochs, but it does not help us to account for the particular shape of the detective story. The same thing is true of Dorothy Sayers's suggestion that the detective story, in representing the solution of a mystery, makes us feel good because it is a kind of reassurance that the ultimate mystery of life and death will be solved for us.[13] Again, this may help account for the persistence of the arche- typal story pattern of the mystery, but it does little to reveal the particular relation between the classical detective story and its period. Haycraft's theory of the detective story as an affirmation of the democratic ideal of legal process does offer a relation to a specific historical period, but the time span of democratic societies is considerably larger than that of the general popularity of the classical detective story.[14] Moreover, the idea of democracy seems somewhat at odds with the rather snobbish upper-class settings that so often characterize the classical detective story.

In order to arrive at a more precise and reasoned speculation about the appeal of the classical detective formula we must first attempt to differentiate it from the mystery formulas characteristic of other periods. By determining what is unique to the classical detective formula as well as what is common between it and other mystery formulas, we should be on firmer ground in relating the formula to its period. For the unique characteristics of the classical detective formula should be related to other distinctive cultural patterns in the same approximate period.

In the preceding chapter, I suggested that a consideration of shifting patterns in the literary portrayal of crime reveals two basic qualities differentiating the classical detective story from crime formulas that flourished earlier and from a number of the newer literary patterns in which the mythology of crime has more recently become embodied. The first of these general characteristics is the transformation of crime into a game or puzzle, the aestheticizing of crime. The second is the special emphasis in the classical detective formula on domestic crimes or crimes within the family circle, as opposed to political or social crimes. Whatever our explanation of the cultural meaning of the classical detective formula, it must account above all for the emergence of these two distinctive characteristics.

In this respect, Poe is an interesting transitional figure, for his version of the classical detective story moves strongly toward the aestheticizing of crime but does not really develop the middle-class family circle as the basic milieu of crime. Perhaps because of this the detective story did not become immediately popular after Poe invented it. Rather, it had to wait until the later nineteenth century and the enormous success of Sherlock Holmes, for it is in Doyle's work that the relation between crime and the family circle is fully elaborated. By comparing Poe's work with the type of mystery that was most popular in his day, we can begin to see some of the factors underlying the emergence of the classical detective formula. Poe's conception of mystery fiction derived most centrally from one predominant model, the gothic fantasy of his day. Though he frequently derided the formlessness, the utter illogicality, the rampant sensationalism, hackneyed situations, and stylistic mannerisms of much of this fiction, Poe apparently never questioned its essential ingredients. For him it was not a question of whether violence, terror, and mystery, with their attendant symbolism of strange houses, graves, madness, and murder, were the appropriate elements of fiction, but how these elements ought to be put together. Indeed, many of Poe's stories, including such masterpieces as "The Fall of the House of Usher," fit completely into the gothic tradition. Poe wrought a number of major changes in the formal structure of gothic fiction. First of all, he took the rambling and diffuse narrative and gave it a remarkably clear and unified form. Without eliminating the sense of terror and mystery, he brought it under a firm aesthetic control by such transformations as shifting the narrative point of view from that of the confused and terrified victim, the favorite narrative center of the traditional gothic story, to that of the more detached observer who watches in mounting perplexity the decline of Roderick Usher.

The gothic novel frequently centered upon the attempts of a mysterious and diabolic villain to seduce or murder a confused and bewildered victim. In "The Fall of the House of Usher," Poe transformed the central action from an external conflict between villain and victim into a psychological struggle within the mind of Roderick Usher. This new focus on the internal action of the mind is reflected in the way in which Poe used the traditional image of the mysterious castle in his story. In the earlier gothic narrative, the reader often found himself lost in the maze of rooms, secret passages, and underground chambers that formed the locale of the villain's devious plots and stratagems. The house of Usher, however, is less significant as a locale of action than as a symbol of the mind of its master. From the beginning of the story with its view of eyeless windows over an infernally deep and black tarn, through Usher's poem of "The Haunted Palace" that symbolically expresses the conquest of the mind by hidden and uncontrollable evil, to the ultimate catastrophe in which the terrible destruction of Roderick Usher is reflected in the collapse of his house, the house exists as the projection of an inner truth about the central character, an external symbol by which we can trace Roderick Usher's internal turmoil and collapse.

In the case of "The Fall of the House of Usher," the hidden depths of man's mind impose themselves on the world of matter and lead to catastrophe. The terrifying guilt and corruption of the human soul breaks forth in the apocalypse of terror and collapse which ends that story. But suppose this extraordinary mental power could be used for beneficial purposes, to exorcise guilt and to restore the reign of reason and order? It is along some such line that we move from the dastardly and corrupt villains of Mrs. Radcliffe and "Monk" Lewis with their external stratagems, through the tragic inner struggle and climactic self-destruction of Roderick Usher, to the demonic but benevolent C. Auguste Dupin whose intimate contact with the depths of night is metamorphosed into the brilliant light of intuitive reason and used to penetrate and exorcise the dark secrets of the mysterious room with its seemingly incomprehensible clues. In both "The Fall of the House of Usher" and "The Murders in the Rue Morgue," the story moves toward the increasing imposition of the internal processes of the mind on the exterior material world. But where this internal process reveals itself as one of chaos and corruption in "The Fall of the House of Usher," Dupin imposes the supreme clarity of his mind on the apparent chaos of the outer world. As Edward Davidson defines it, "the ratiocinative exercise of the detective is simply an allegory of how the mind may impose its interior logic on exterior circumstance. Dupin is the supreme artistic ego: everything external to himself can be made to fit the theoretical, the ideal logic."[15] Davidson's formulation does not account for the basic purpose behind this exercise of reason: to bring the mysterious forces that threaten to disrupt the harmonious order of the psyche under control. Dupin performs an act of transcendent reason which in turn makes possible a specific tangible act—the capture of the orangoutan, or the recapture of the letter—which identifies, isolates, and exorcises the disruptive force. In Poe's stories, particularly in "The Purloined Letter," the disruptive force is symbolically related to the detective in many ways. Dupin resembles Roderick Usher in his romantic demonism, his affection for the bizarre, his commitment to the night, his obsession with psychology, and his combination of poetic brilliance and ratiocinative powers. Moreover, the way in which Dupin's own qualities are reflected in Minister D., the very embodiment of the disruptive force, has already been suggested. "The Purloined Letter," then, can be seen as a benevolent inversion of "The Fall of the House of Usher." The conflict of inner forces within the psyche that eventually destroys Roderick Usher is conquered and brought under control in "The Purloined Letter." It is this pattern of restoring rational order to a psyche threatened with disruption that is transformed in later classical detective stories into a more externalized and simplified social allegory in which the detective restores serenity to a traditional image of middle-class social order by proving that the disruptive force is not in the social order itself but in the particular individual motives of a relatively marginal, "least-likely" person.

We are now in a position to offer a tentative hypothesis about the cultural pattern that seems to be projected in the classical detective formula and to try to account for the formula's emergence and persistence. I suggest that much of the fascination of the gothic story for the early nineteenth-century middle-class reading public derived from the complex of feelings surrounding the breakup of long-established social and spiritual hierarchies in Europe. The authority of the church and the nobility had been weakened by political and economic change to the point where they no longer exercised unquestioned sway over the mind. In the place of these traditional centers of authority, the ethos of individualism, the ideal of the Christian family circle, and scientific rationalism were becoming dominant centers of value and feeling. Yet, the long-established institutions of social and spiritual authority still retained a special potency, particularly disturbing to the middle class, both in revolt against them and attracted by their traditional ascendancy. For example, a common career pattern of middle-class entrepreneurs shows an initial struggle against the social and ecclesiastical tradition in their business activities, followed by the purchase of a country estate and an attempt to settle down into a feudal way of life. For such a public, the symbols of church and aristocracy had a complex psychological ambiguity. Transformed into those two favorite gothic villains, the corrupt monk and the decadent and scheming lord of the mysterious castle, and set in motion against that chaste and marriageable young woman who often symbolized the cultural and social aspirations of the mobile middle classes, the potency of these symbols and the fictional representation of an escape from their machinations could be a source of pleasurable shivers and delightful terrors.

As the nineteenth century progressed, these symbols of traditional authority lost most of their remaining potency. This change was already reflected in the more avant-garde intellectual wing of gothic fantasy near the beginning of the century. Where the hero of William Godwin's *Caleb Williams* still suffered from the plots of a version of the aristocratic gothic villain, Godwin's pioneering daughter, Mary Shelley, even in the heyday of *The Monk,* developed a wholly different vein of terror in her fantasy *Frankenstein,* where the aristocrat is replaced by a scientist, the gothic castle by a laboratory and the supernatural by the wonders of technology. The transformation of gothic symbolism was almost complete when Bram Stoker added vampirism to his gothic villain, Count Dracula. The success of Stoker's fantasy in a period when the traditional gothic was in decline indicates that the old motives of monkish lust and feudal dynasty and revenge were no longer sufficiently potent to arouse the public's fascination. Vampirism, which combined the interest in folkish superstition with a fascination for the image of the hidden beast under the elegant and genteel surface, partially revitalized the fading impotent gothic villain. From that time on, the gothic tradition in literature tended to specialize in vampires, werewolves, and other beast-men, or, on a more sophisticated level, in hidden psychological terrors as in the ghost stories of Henry James. Poe, as we have seen, was fully attuned to this transformation. His presentation of Roderick Usher displaced the center of gothic fantasy from the struggle between aristocratic villain and middle-class victim to an internalized conflict between the reasoning and ordered consciousness and the hidden dynamism and anarchy in the depths of the mind.

Poe's new version of the gothic fantasy shared with his detective stories the theme of hidden guilt. Both coincided culturally with the decline of the old regime and the rise of the middle class to social and cultural dominance. Once the force of church and nobility had been weakened beyond the possibility of restoration, even in literary fantasy, the middle class encountered two new threats: the political emergence of the lower classes, and a new concern with psychological urges toward aggression and sexuality that were in sharp conflict with the ideal of the family circle. Both socially and psychologically, this new threat manifested itself as a revolt from within. In the period of revolution and reform of the late eighteenth and early nineteenth centuries, the middle classes had seen themselves as the leaders of the people in opposition to the established regime, but by the mid-nineteenth century the lower classes had begun to define themselves and their interests in terms of socialist and collectivist demands alien to the entrepreneurial capitalistic spirit of the middle classes. But the curious thing about the emergence of these lower-class reform movements is that they were greatly stimulated and even led by members of the middle classes feeling a sense of guilt at the misery of the poor. Thus, the rise of lower-class movements not only represented the challenge of another social group to middle-class hegemony but also symbolized a guilty inner tension within the middle class. Moreover, though middle-class domestic values emphasized the repression of aggressive and erotic drives that had been given a fuller expression in the chivalric and erotic codes of the aristocracy, the nineteenth century also evolved a growing interest in the psychological investigation of human sexual and aggressive instincts. One result of this investigation was the invention of the concept of hidden layers of the mind. These explorations and discoveries culminated in Freud's system of Eros and Thanatos, the two basic drives toward sex and death, and his full articulation of the idea of the unconscious.

These two paradoxes reflect the tension between confidence and guilt, so frequently encountered in the middle-class cultures of western Europe and America in the nineteenth and early twentieth centuries. For example, this is the period of cycles of reform, that rhythm of public complacency, awakening, guilt and concern, pressure for reform, the passage of a few major legislative acts, and then the sinking back into disinterest and complacency again, which can so often be observed in nineteenth-century England and America. It is worth noting parenthetically that this rhythm has a certain resemblance to the pattern of the detective story, the legislative act being analogous to the externalization of guilt when the detective identifies the criminal. Another instance is the paradox of middle-class confidence in its moral and cultural superiority combined with its fascinated interest in works of literature and social criticism that exposed the moral hypocrisy and corruption of bourgeois values.

This tension between confidence and guilt lay at the heart of middle-class values and techniques of child-training and was intensified by the closeness of the family circle. The ethic of individual achievement in a production-oriented society led parents to instill in their children an inner drive to succeed along with the entrepreneurial qualities of aggressive confidence and innovation.[16] Middle-class parents trained their children to become as free as possible from the pressures and constrictions of social and cultural tradition by replacing the psychological force of tradition with an internalized set of motives and values. From the earliest years a high standard of achievement, independence, and self-reliance was set up for the child who was held to this standard by a threatened withdrawal of parental affection. By this system of psychological rewards and punishments, the middle-class child was encouraged very early in his life to take into his own psyche the parental standard of achievement and independence. Because the goal of success and achievement was essentially intangible, a spur to continued effort and mobility rather than a clear conception of a specific status or accomplishment to be attained, the middle-class individual could never completely come to terms with his inner demand for achievement. Measured against the infinite demands of the internalized parental norms, the individual's actual accomplishments never seemed fully satisfactory, never quite enough. Instead, aggressive confidence and independence were driven on by a sense of guilt, a nagging fear that the individual could not live up to his own inner demands. If this guilt became extreme it could lead to a paralyzing fear that beneath the surface of the disciplined achievement-oriented ego lay a hidden self that could rise to the surface, overthrow rational control, and reveal the deep resentment against the internalized parental standards that had festered in the secret places of the mind since childhood. This was one of the central patterns of psychological disability articulated by Freud, but the pattern had been laid bare in fictional symbols early in the nineteenth century. The surfacing of the psyche's hidden secrets was the drama not only of Poe's "The Fall of the House of Usher," but also of Hawthorne's Dimmesdale, whose public achievement as a successful minister was terrifyingly threatened by the awful scarlet letter growing within his breast. If stories like these dramatize the surfacing of secret guilt and the consequent collapse of rational order and psychological self-control, Poe's Dupin stories explored the terms in which the secret depths might be brought under control and the sense of hidden guilt and insecurity overcome. Poe's solution was the figure of the detached, brilliant, eccentric detective who combined moral and intellectual superiority with enough of a flavor of detachment and decadence to indicate that he has voluntarily rejected the ethic of success and somehow has been able to harmonize the hidden cravings of the mind (Dupin's love for night, Holmes's drugs and anomie, Wimsey's luxuriousness and effeminacy, Nero Wolfe's sybaritic passion for orchids, to cite a few examples) with tremendous rational order and self-discipline. With this combination of qualities the detective could plunge into the lower depths of society and the mind and emerge triumphant, having demonstrated that there was not after all a secret guilt. Instead, he proves that it was someone else all along. His action is as if Roderick Usher had discovered that the death of Madeline was actually a plot on the part of that scruffy and suspicious doctor whom the narrator sees hanging around, ending the story with the arrest of the doctor instead of the fall of the house of Usher. Or to put it in psychological terms, it is as if the psychoanalyst instead of leading the patient to recognize and accept his own secret desires were to prove beyond doubt that the patient's mother or father was solely responsible for his illness.

The connection between the highly formalized and ordered character of the classical detective formula and its concentration on crime within the family circle can be seen, then, not only as a pleasing artistic form but as a response to certain cultural tensions of the late nineteenth and early twentieth centuries. Readers of classical detective stories, we hypothesize, shared a need for a temporary release from doubt and guilt, generated at least in part by the decline of traditional moral and spiritual authorities, and the rise of new social and intellectual movements that emphasized the hypocrisy and guilt of respectable middle-class society. For those committed to middle-class values of individual achievement and the ideal family, and yet dissatisfied by the restrictions of the family circle, the classical detective story offered a temporary release from doubt. First, it affirmed the basic principle that crime was strictly a matter of individual motivations and thus reaffirmed the validity of the existing social order. Second, by reducing crime to a puzzle, a game, and a highly formalized set of literary conventions, it transformed an increasingly serious moral and social problem into an entertaining pastime, thereby enabling a comic metamorphosis of the materials of crime: something potentially dangerous and disturbing was transformed into something completely under control. Finally, the classical detective story enabled readers to entertain some very powerful latent feelings generated by the repressiveness of the family circle by treating in fantasy a domestic murder, but in such a way as to negate any feelings of implication or guilt on the part of the reader. The particular combination of cultural factors, which generated this combination of needs—such factors as the decline in traditional religion, the growth of uncertainty about the social order, together with a general acceptance of the ideals of individual achievement and the family circle— were most evident at precisely the time the classical detective formula reached its widest general popularity, the early twentieth century. Furthermore, I would guess that these factors were strongest among that group who were apparently the most enthusiastic devotees and even addicts of the formula—successful, highly educated professional people whose backgrounds were most firmly in the middle-class tradition. It would follow from this line of reasoning that the classical formula would be less popular among working-class readers and those members of the middle class who had risen from a lower class, as in the case of self-made businessmen, since in these cases the combination of cultural and psychological factors would be quite different. Random observation tends to bear out this hypothesis, since those who have most enthusiastically testified to their love of classical detective stories have been middle-class professionals and, in particular, academics.

The increasing popularity since the 1930s of two quite different crime formulas—the hard-boiled detective story and the gangster melodrama— offers further evidence of the relation between the classical detective formula and the combination of cultural and psychological factors outlined above. I have indicated some of the central differences between these formulas in the preceding chapter and will deal in greater detail with the contrast between the classical and hard-boiled detective formulas in one of the following chapters. In the next chapter, however, I turn to another dimension of the classical formula, its unique artistic potential. While the appeal of any popular formula partly rests on its way of resolving certain cultural and psychological tensions, it also depends on the fact that certain skilled artists have seized upon the artistic possibilities of the formula and created effective and memorable works. Thus, the topic of my next chapter is what might be called the aesthetic of the classical detective story.

Five

The Art of the Classical Detective Story

Central Artistic Problems of the Genre

In the preceding chapter, I defined the formulaic pattern of the classical detective story and offered some tentative explanations of the psychological and cultural forces that have made this genre fascinating to so many Europeans and Americans in the later nineteenth and twentieth centuries. But another important problem cannot be dealt with solely in these terms: what kind of artfulness is possible within the boundaries of the formula? An account of the psychological and cultural needs fullfilled by a formula gives us—insofar as it is correct—only some of the factors responsible for its widespread popularity. Perhaps it is primarily a matter of psychology that addicts of a particular formula find some pleasure in any rendition of it, no matter how dully written or hackneyed. But even when trying simply to define the patterns of the classical detective story, I found myself frequently drawn to comment on relatively "effective" or "ineffective" ways of carrying out the formulaic imperatives. To some extent the "effectiveness" to which I referred was a comment on the way in which a writer like Poe or Doyle engaged underlying psychological or cultural tensions, but it also related to an artistic craftsmanship that can be consciously and rationally appreciated. Even the most addicted reader of classical detective stories probably derives greater pleasure from a first-rate Agatha Christie than from one of her more plodding improvisations. Moreover, the fact that writers like Christie and Dorothy Sayers remain popular while the majority of mystery stories lapse into obscurity suggest that there are many levels of art within the formulaic type. Though a fine Hercule Poirot tale can hardly be distinguished from a thousand plodding imitations in terms of such traditional literary criteria as universality, plausibility of character and action, or breadth and significance of theme, most readers would agree that there is all the difference in the world within the boundaries of the type.

In general, the classical story involves, like any successful literary formula, a combination of interests of a rather divergent sort. In the preceding chapter, I described the combination of situations, characters, settings, and themes characteristic of this formula as they relate to certain cultural and psychological needs. These needs can be generalized as the fantasy projection of guilt away from the reader. This aspect of the classical formula is more a matter of psychology than of art.

This basic function can be carried out with varying degrees of power and imagination and can in turn give rise to other interests that a talented and skillful writer can exploit. One such opportunity arises in the construction and deployment of the detection plot. Is the problem of sufficient complexity to seriously challenge the ratiocinative powers of the reader? Are the deductions from clues necessary to the solution reasonable and plausible? Is the writer fair to the reader in presenting the appropriate clues for inspection? This emphasis on the rational element of detection in the classic story usually looms large in reader's comments, the observation of reviewers, and the sets of rules for the genre occasionally constructed by practitioners and critics.[1]

The element of ratiocination must play an important part in any reader's enjoyment of the classic detective story or he would choose some other formula. Nonetheless, there are probably many different levels of intensity at which readers involve themselves with detection. Judging from his evaluations and comments on individual works in *The Catalogue of Crime*, detection and reasoning are of the highest priority for Jacques Barzun. In my own case, however, I put much less mental energy into the chain of deductions involved in a detection plot and am generally satisfied if they have the air of complicated but correct reasoning about them. Does this mean then that readers like myself are less capable of appreciating the art of the classic detective story than acute and demanding logicians like Professor Barzun? We are certainly less likely to appreciate fully the writer's skill and responsibility in puzzle making. Why then do we—who don't care as much about the details of the puzzle—read such stories at all? There are apparently other interests complementary to the detection element. A successful detective tale of this sort must not only be solved, it must mystify, and to effectively serve the basic psychological functions of the classic formula, it must mystify in a particular way: we must truly be able to suspect persons whom we do not wish to be proved guilty before, finally, the crime is brought home to some person with whom our identification is minimal. These two interests—ratiocination and mystification—stand in a tense and difficult relationship to each other. If either one is overstressed, the story will be less effective. Thus, the first artistic problem of the classical detective writer is to establish the proper balance between reasoning and mystification.

A second major problem of balance in the detection tale is the proportion of inquiry to action. The heart of the classical story is the examination of clues and the questioning of suspects. Insofar as the writer is serious about keeping the apparatus of deduction and mystery at the center of the reader's attention, he must present a large number of scenes where various witnesses and suspects are interviewed. Yet, it must be confessed that interminable questions about where everybody was at nine o'clock the preceding evening when Sir John Fortescue was stabbed with a New Zealand assegai quickly pall. The writer must necessarily use all his ingenuity and imagination to invent ways of staging the parade of clues and suspects in such a way that it will generate some human excitement without at the same time distracting from the basic interplay of investigation and mystification. Skillful writers have devised a number of ways to do this, but it remains a major difficulty. Raymond Chandler even suggests that this balance is so difficult to achieve that the pure ratiocinative detective story is really an impossible genre:

> I suppose the principal dilemma of the traditional or classic or straight-deductive or logic-and-deduction novel of detection is that for any approach to perfection it demands a combination of qualities not found in the same mind. The fellow who can write you a vivid and colorful prose simply won't be bothered with the coolie labor of breaking unbreakable alibis.[2]

The balance between inquiry and action is the most immediate expression of a larger and more general problem of proportion in the classical formula that derives from a fundamental tension in the structure of the story. On the one hand, the formula emphasizes clarity, order, and logic, not only in the presentation of the investigation and rational solution of a problem, but in the ritual conventionality of its patterns. The formula also deals extensively with crime, violence, and death together with the terrible human motives and feelings that lead to such consequences. The psychological dynamic of guilt projection links these two aspects of the classical formula, but, in the context of artistic considerations, the tension between violence and order raises basic problems of tone and form. If there is not enough violence and danger lurking in the story, the order achieved will seem trivial and inconsequential. But, if the elements of threat and chaos become too strong or dominant, the resolution into order will appear artificial and implausible. This may be one reason why, as George Grella so perceptively observes, the classical detective story bears a greater resemblance to the traditional genre of comedy than to those of romance or tragedy.[3] A basically comic literary universe in which characters and action are so constructed as to continually reassure us that things will ultimately work out happily can encompass a considerable degree of disorder and danger without destroying our basic sense of security. This is exactly the kind of thing the classical detective story sets out to do. Yet, dependent as it is on comic elements, the classical detective story is apparently not a comedy because the detective protagonist is not really a comic hero. He may have many comic elements in his makeup—he may be comically vain about his appearance like Hercule Poirot, or eccentric in many of his habits like Nero Wolfe or Dr. Fell, or even extravagantly arrogant about his abilities like Sherlock Holmes—but when it comes to his central action, the investigation and solution of a crime, there is nothing comically limited or distorted about him.

The exception that proves the rule are those few detective stories with a bumbling and inefficient hero who solves the crime by inadvertence or mistake. No work of this sort can be called a significant achievement of the art, and there is good reason for this. If the detective's ability as a crime-solver is comically limited, the whole structure of deduction and mystification falls into chaos and the basic order of this stylized literary universe is overthrown. Therefore, the major art of the classical detective writer is to achieve the appropriate relation between comedy and seriousness, between rational order and the threat of disruption of either a comic or a tragic sort.

Because these balances between ratiocination and mystification, between inquiry and action, and between formal order and the threat of disruption, are very delicate and difficult to achieve, many of the major masterpieces of the genre are in the form of short stories. Certainly no writer working within the boundaries of the classical formula has accomplished better work than Poe's two major stories, or the best of Doyle's Sherlock Holmes tales. Many other writers have created good short stories of detection. This has led some critics to feel that the detective novel is a degenerate and inappropriate format for this type of literary structure. This is, in my opinion, an incorrect judgment. The detective novel probably developed for a number of reasons, but surely one of them had to do with the very artistic potentialities of the genre. While the balance between different interests can be effectively realized in shorter form, it must be at the sacrifice of complexity in the development of mystifying suspects and clues. There is simply not time to develop a very elaborate murder plot with several possible suspects within the boundaries of a short story. Therefore, many of the best short stories deal with the finding of a lost or stolen object or with the explanation of a curious circumstance in which the focus of the inquiry is more on material clues than on the backgrounds and motives of a group of suspects. Since a certain degree of complexity is obviously of value in a genre where the complementary relationship of ratiocination and mystification is a central artistic tension, it is not surprising that writers and readers quickly developed an interest in the longer as well as the shorter formats for the detective tale. But with the emergence of the longer format, the problem of balancing the central focus of investigation with other sources of interest became intensified. While it was possible to construct a short story around nothing but the examination of clues, a long novel with no greater variety of action soon exceeds the patience of all but the most addicted lover of detection. Even the old master Conan Doyle had a good deal of trouble with the longer form. His initial solution was the story within a story that he employed in three of his four longer works, *A Study in Scarlet*, *The Sign of Four*, and *The Valley of Fear*. Each of these novels develops a story of detection leading up to the detective's solution of the mystery. At this point the culprit's own narrative of his background and the events leading up to the crime takes over. After this narrative, a fairly brief denouement attempts to link the detective's action with that of the culprit and to bring both to some kind of conclusion. Though the inner narrative in *The Valley of Fear* is quite a story in its own right, it is not really integrated with the outer framework of detection any more effectively than in the case of the other two longer tales. The trouble is that once the detection has reached its goal, the story is effectively over. Even though the inner narrative ostensibly provides a fuller explanation of the crime, it remains structurally tangential, an elaborate and frustrating digression from the main center of interest.

Doyle was much more successful with *The Hound of the Baskervilles* in which he possibly took his cue from Wilkie Collins's *The Moonstone* by developing a more complex detective action through a variety of narrative perspectives. The story opens with Dr. Watson narrating present incidents, shifts to his reports to the absent Holmes, then to diary-like entries, and finally back to the narrative present again. Though some of these devices seem a bit arbitrary, they work rather well and do resolve one of the basic problems of the longer detective story: how to protract the process of the detective's investigation without casting doubt on his brilliance. By keeping Holmes off the scene and letting Watson do much of the detecting, Doyle manages to develop an effectively complicated group of characters and a richly mysterious atmosphere before he brings his detective back into the forefront of the story.

But such a gambit was too restricted to work for every detective story. Therefore, writers who chose to develop longer and more complex stories had to find a number of ways of resolving the inevitable tension between the detection-mystification structure with the detective at the center and the variety of other interests—character, action, setting, local color, or assorted bits of information—that were necessary to flesh out and add variety to the bare bones of the inquiry structure. The major artistic problem of the longer classical detective story is how to develop additional narrative interests without dissipating the central line of the action. Or, to put the problem in reverse, how effectively does the writer construct a structure of detection-mystification that is strong and capacious enough to accommodate a variety of other interests? We might say, for example, that the more completely our attention becomes concentrated on the unique inner life of one of the characters involved in the tale, the more we are likely to be distracted from the detection element. On the other hand, if the characters are not interesting enough to involve us in their fates, the mystery structure will seem like a sterile and desiccated skeleton and to that extent fail to sustain our involvement.

Georges Simenon is certainly the best at developing and sustaining this fruitful balance of detection and other interests, and therefore he stands so far as master of the longer classical detective formula just as Poe and Doyle remain the high points of the shorter format. Because Simenon's skill is so rich and subtle, I will attempt to give some specificity to these generalizations about the art of the genre by examining first some examples of two excellent if not transcendent practitioners of the genre, Agatha Christie and Dorothy Sayers.

Artistic Failures and Successes:
Christie and Sayers

Agatha Christie has deservedly earned the title of Queen of the Detective Story, not only through her sustained productivity over six decades, but through the remarkable ingenuity of her structures of detection and mystification. Because many of her tales employ nearly identical structures of this sort it is possible to get a better appreciation of the various aspects of art within the classical formula by comparing instances where the same basic strategy of mystification has been developed with greater or lesser success. Here is one such structure:

> A rich and powerful man has secured his great position in life by committing a crime at an earlier period. With the aid of a female accomplice he has been able to prevent this crime from becoming known and has risen to a situation of great responsibility and influence. His accomplice has continued to be faithful to him and together they have been able to deceive all their present acquaintances about their past crime and their actual relation to each other. The mystery plot commences when a person who knew the culprit or his accomplice at an earlier period comes into the present situation and endangers it by the threat of exposure. This witness from the past accidentally or purposely reveals the situation to an unscrupulous blackmailer who threatens the culprit and his accomplice. They determine to murder the witness and the blackmailer, constructing an ingenious scheme that makes full use of the female accomplice's capacity for impersonation. To insure that they will not be caught for the murder the culprit and his accomplice not only skillfully frame an innocent scapegoat, but do their best to make it appear that one of them is among the intended victims of the murderer. In addition, because of the culprit's important position there are hints that the situation involves some form of espionage or international politics. The murders are skillfully accomplished without the slightest suspicion falling on the culprits. The scapegoat is nearly convicted of the crime before Poirot finally arrives at the proper solution.

The ingenuity of this structure is considerable, for it not only provides a suitable machinery for the crime (impersonation) and a lavish possibility of red herrings, it also, even more importantly, allows for the kind of basic reversal in assumption so important to a truly effective scheme of mystification. We are not simply confronted with the question of which suspect nipped into the bedroom and slipped the prussic acid to dear old Aunt Penelope but are led from the beginning to make the wrong assumptions about just who was murdered and why. This well-constructed set of false assumptions is a more elaborate analogy to what Poe accomplished so brilliantly in "The Purloined Letter" with his revelation that one can hide most effectively by not concealing. If well handled, this structure makes possible not only one big reversal of expectations when the guilty person is unmasked but a progression of incidents through which the reader continually faces a new series of deductions from the basic clues only to find himself mystified once more. Agatha Christie's ability to work out stratagems of this sort is preeminent.

But, as we have seen, the ingenious scheme of detection and mystification is only one aspect of the art of the classical detective story. The selection or invention of a good detective stratagem does not guarantee that it will be effectively deployed in a story. Here, Christie's own example is illuminating for she employed the same structure of detection and mystification in two works, one of which is her finest and the other one of her biggest failures. The novels I refer to are *An Overdose of Death* (originally *The Patriotic Murders* [1940]) and *Third Girl* (1967). What accounts for the enormous difference in effectiveness between these two embodiments of the same stratagem of mystification?

Essentially, in one novel Christie finds specific embodiments for her ingenious system of crime and inquiry that establish an effective balance between the major elements held by the detective formula in tension, while, in the other, some of the elements get out of control and destroy the delicate formal equilibrium so essential to the genre. Let us look first at the basic balance between detection and mystification. This depends on the relationship the writer establishes between the crime, the detective's pattern of inquiry, and the way in which the inquiry is presented to the reader. The crime is essentially the same in both *An Overdose of Death* and *Third Girl*. But when we come to the two related patterns of detective and reader inquiry we find a very different treatment in the two books. In *Overdose* a crime at the beginning of the story draws both Poirot and the reader into the inquiry. From that point on, the reader is present with Poirot at every significant event, interview, or examination of clues. Throughout most of the first two-thirds of the book the reader shares to a considerable extent in Poirot's perception of things and is thus able to follow the course of events with clarity and interest. Only at the end of chapter 6 (out of a total of ten) does it become evident that Poirot has been able to draw major deductions about the case, a fact that Christie carefully announces to the reader, thus indicating quite clearly the terms on which the reader's and the detective's structure of inquiry must either significantly change or diverge. This announcement is a striking one. It is set off by a biblical quotation and ends up with a clearly formulated challenge to the reader's powers of deduction:

Hercule Poirot essayed a hesitant baritone.
" 'The proud have laid a snare for me,' " he sang " 'and spread a net with cords: yea, and set traps in my way.' "
His mouth remained open.
He saw it—saw clearly the trap into which he has so nearly fallen! . . .
He was in a daze—a glorious daze where isolated facts spun wildly round before settling neatly into their appointed places. It was like a kaleidoscope—shoe buckles, size nine stockings, a damaged face, the low tastes in

literature of Alfred the page boy, the activities of Mr. Amberiotis, and the part played by the late Mr. Morley, all rose up and whirled and settled themselves down into a coherent pattern.

For the first time, Hercule Poirot was looking at the case *the right way up*.[4]

This is the moment at which Poirot grasps the basic structure of the crime, namely that the man who had been assumed to be the victim was actually the culprit and that all the prime suspects heretofore presented to the reader and to Poirot have actually been victims. In fact, all the clues mentioned in the quoted passage do play an important part in the deduction as one recognizes in retrospect after Poirot explains it all. Even the dullest reader is probably able to make some kind of inference from one or more of these clues. Yet it seems to me that the important thing from an artistic point of view is not Christie's vaunted fairness to the reader—of which this is an unusually full example—but her successful accomplishment of the effect of combined rationality and mystification. The striking clarity of this announcement of the solution assures us that these seemingly unconnected fragments have a perfectly rational relation if we can understand the meaning of "looking at the case *the right way up*." For most readers, however, the crimes and the characters have been skillfully enough presented that the right set of deductions is impossible. The end result is a more suspenseful mystification that enables Christie to develop another narrative interest in the remainder of the tale. Now, in addition to the attempt to figure out the crime, we are also confronted with the puzzle of the detective's activity. Since Poirot has come to understand what is going on, his actions in testing his hypothesis and entrapping the criminal become further clues for the reader to chew on. In the final phase of the story all three lines of the structure of detection and mystification become separated as the reader tries to figure out not only who the culprit is but the logic behind Poirot's actions. This tension between the activity of the criminal, the detective, and the reader leads to a very satisfying climax when the explanation finally arrives.

Before turning to the confusions of *Third Girl*, let us look more fully at two of the ways in which Christie makes it nearly impossible for the reader to break through the pattern of mystification while at the same time she keeps him deeply interested in the effort to do so. Characterization in *An Overdose of Death* is well calculated to perform its necessary function in the structure of mystification. The culprit is a fine example of the least likely person in both senses of the term. First of all, he is presented to us throughout the story not as a suspect but as a victim. Moreover, despite his importance as a possible motive for the crimes, the culprit remains a rather marginal figure in the inquiry until he is unmasked at the very end. Other characters talk a good deal about him, but he himself appears only briefly in a couple of scenes. In the most important of these, he actually urges Poirot on to discover the missing Miss Sainsbury Seale and insists that the idea of a plot against him cannot be true, two items that further suggest his innocence, unless of course we are familiar with Christie's habit of making her culprits play this kind of role in the inquiry. But even the reader's wariness of such devious narrative practices tends to be lulled by a nicely imagined stroke of character. The culprit is made a prime exponent of reason, order, and responsibility in a social universe that seems dangerously on the verge of chaos. The most likely suspects presented to us, on the other hand, are embodiments of loutishness, irrationality, and anarchy. Thus Christie makes the deeper emotional structure of the classical formula, with its emphasis on the restoration of order, function as a means of distracting the reader's attention from the true culprit.

The crime in *An Overdose of Death* is also designed with remarkable ingenuity, not only in the sense that it is complex and difficult, but also in the way it establishes a balance of inquiry and action throughout the story. In general, there seem to be six main ways in which a reader can be effectively misled about a fictional crime: he can be deceived as to the person, the motive, the means of the crime, the time at which it is committed, the place where it occurs, and, finally, whether it is a crime or not. In this case, Christie manages to work all these modes of mystification into her pattern. The first crime is the apparent suicide of Poirot's dentist. Actually, this is a murder, the key to which lies in the fact that its motive is hidden and that it takes place at an earlier time than the evidence leads one to believe. The handling of this crime is a nice example of how to involve the reader effectively in attempts at detection that lead only to further mystification. Though Morley's, the dentist's, death is officially accounted a suicide by the police, Christie makes it clear to the reader that this cannot be true by both logical and narrative means. One of the most unshakable conventions of the classical detective story is that every crime must have a rationally comprehensible motive, and there appears to be no such motive for Morley's suicide. Then, in her presentation of the brief conversation between Poirot and his dentist, not long before Morley's mysterious suicide, Christie carefully inserts a tantalizing remark. Morley says: " 'I don't remember names, but it's remarkable the way I never forget a face. One of my patients the other day, for instance—I've seen that patient before.' "[5] Actually this remark is not simply a narrative trick; it later turns out to be a significant clue. At this point, it serves primarily to warn the reader that some kind of plot is afoot. On both the grounds of physical evidence and this bit of dialogue the reader cannot accept the conclusion that Morley's death is suicide. In fact, this situation is so firmly based on formulaic conventions that one of the most striking possible solutions at the end of the tale would have been a demonstration that Morley had in fact committed suicide.

Christie does not choose to develop things in this way. Instead, she introduces a second murder, which is first thought to be an accidental death. This is the mysterious Amberiotis who dies of an overdose of dental anesthetic after a visit to Morley. The police theory is the obvious deduction:

having recognized that he had accidentally given his client a lethal dose of anesthetic, Morley commits suicide in despair. Again the reader is challenged and drawn further into the tale by a conclusion that is patently superficial and inconclusive. The reader is certain that this explanation is unsatisfactory when a second dental client mysteriously disappears. Here, as throughout the story, a phase of inquiry leads to an action that stimulates further deductions. Because of the ingenious structure of the crime, however, these deductions can only produce further mystification. After rejecting the superficial inference offered by the police, the reader is first led to seek out some explanation for the murder of Morley on the assumption that his death is the primary crime. This is, of course, the reverse of the truth. In fact, Morley's death is secondary; the real targets of the culprit are Amberiotis and Miss Sainsbury Seale. In addition, we are skillfully misled as to the order of the murders (Miss Seale's death actually occurs first; the person we see in the dentist's office is one of the culprits dressed as Miss Seale) and to their time (the dentist is killed almost an hour earlier than we have been made to believe).

Christie seems to be well aware that most readers confronted by a fruitless detection situation such as that just outlined will soon lose interest. Thus another red herring appears and we are offered another possible line of inquiry with the introduction of Alastair Blunt—the actual culprit—as the most logical intended victim. Blunt, too, had been a patient of Morley on that crowded morning. A further complication is added when the corpse of the real Miss Sainsbury Seale turns up and is identified by her teeth as Mrs. Chapman, wife of a mysterious secret agent, thus adding force to the hypothesis that Alastair Blunt is the victim of some international plot.

By this time the reader is more mystified than when he began, drowned in a mass of tantalizing clues, none of which seem to fit with the possible explanations that have been offered. Then, in still another twist of the story, a young man who has been sullenly lurking around the edges of the story is caught in what appears to be an attempt on Alastair Blunt's life. This actually is the scapegoat that the culprits have cunningly prepared. The reader, of course, is encouraged to suspect that something is wrong here. As she often does, Christie plays one of the unwritten conventions of the detective story against what appears to be a palpable fact. We seemingly see Frank Carter attempt to murder Alastair Blunt, but we know that he cannot be the real culprit because he has been such an obvious suspect all along. Moreover, a moment's reflection shows that this character could not have planned a crime so elaborate and ingenious as we have come to understand this sequence of deaths to be.

It is just at this point that the story takes another twist. Poirot announces that he has finally seen the crime the right side up. We enter the final phase of the story in which our mystification about Poirot's doings is added to our bewilderment about the crime itself. The climax when Poirot unmasks Blunt and his mistress and explains the incredibly elaborate motive and method of the crime becomes a fully satisfying reversal and release from the cognitive and emotional tension.

Thus, as this ingenious and artful narrative structure unrolls itself before us, we are confronted at each moment with a new twist that at first seems to lead to a more likely possibility of solution but that in fact drives us deeper and deeper into mystification. It is important to note that this is not the mystification of the thriller or the ghost story, because we never lose our certainty that the right chain of reasoning will explain everything. *An Overdose of Death* illustrates the classical detective formula in its most concentrated and purest form. Character and atmosphere are reduced to the barest minimum and function only as necessary embodiments to the structure of detection and mystification. Actions have little interest in their own right; they exist solely to enable the introduction of a new line of inquiry.

It is instructive, then, to look at one of Christie's relative failures. *Third Girl* is, as I have indicated earlier, a variation of the same ingenious criminal plot. But where *An Overdose of Death* is taut, clear, and continuously engrossing, *Third Girl* is messy, turgid, and almost completely lacking in the twists and turns of deduction and mystification that the former develops so brilliantly.

Let us compare the way in which the same basic plot is deployed in *Third Girl* and *An Overdose of Death*. In the latter book we begin with the curious death of the dentist. This is followed quickly by the death of one of his clients and the mysterious disappearance of another. As we have seen, each of these events encourages a chain of deductions that lead to mystification until the next twist sets off another chain. In *Third Girl*, however, the tale begins with an obviously confused young girl who appears at Poirot's apartment in a daze and says that she needs help in determining whether or not she has murdered someone. But before she can say anything more she tells Poirot he is too old and rushes out without even leaving her name. This opening incident produces puzzlement, but does not suggest even the most minimal line of rational inquiry. The second chapter produces a little more information through the rather fortuitous introduction of Mrs. Ariadne Oliver—Christie's comic surrogate—who often undertakes a Watson-like role in her later tales. By chance Mrs. Oliver has met the mysterious young woman and is able to provide Poirot with her name. Wondering whether in fact a crime has taken place, Poirot and Mrs. Oliver make further investigations; Poirot even engages the services of a detective agency to follow the young lady and report on her activities. These inquiries introduce us to various people in the young lady's life; her father and stepmother, her roommates, and her boy friend, but these encounters do not constitute enough of a coherent chain either to stimulate hypotheses or to destroy them. The ostensible source of mystification is not a particular crime, but whether a crime has taken place, and secondarily whether the mysterious young lady was its perpetrator. And yet the method that Christie employs to develop the inquiry is so confused, strained, and lacking in effective clues that the reader remains simply bemused.

First, since this is a detective story, there is an overwhelming presumption that a crime has taken place. If Christie wanted to create some significant interest around this point, she should have planted some evidence casting doubt on this presumption. Instead, she introduces a ridiculous incident in which Ariadne Oliver, following the young girl's boy friend, is knocked on the head by some party unknown. Aside from the fact that such an incident creates serious problems of tone (after all, Mrs. Oliver is no Philip Marlowe with an ironclad skull), it actually increases the presumption that a crime has taken place, thereby producing mystification, but no deductive activity. Finally, this little event is so marginal to the actual plot that Christie experiences great difficulty in having Poirot account for it afterward. When we do finally discover that a crime has been committed (structurally analogous to the murder of Miss Sainsbury Seale in *An Overdose of Death*), it is a pale shadow of the ingenious and complex murder plot in the earlier book. In fact, the whole mystery depends on such hoary and clumsy devices as the drugging of the young girl in order to make her think she has committed a murder. Even the least-likely person gambit is rather mis-handled in this book. The culprit turns out to be a master criminal who is masquerading as the young girl's father, aided by his wife who in turn leads a double life as one of her roommates. The weakness of this version of the elegantly ingenious criminal plot of *An Overdose of Death* is twofold. First, this complex of impersonations is too far-fetched to be the subject of rational detection. Even after it is explained by Poirot, it remains incredible. Second, the portrayal of the culprit is such that one is inclined to suspect him from the beginning simply because his behavior and background are so peculiar. Thus the reader more or less identifies the culprit early on in the story, but without rational evidence, and when the reasoning is finally produced, it is too strained to resolve the mystery.

Third Girl nicely illustrates one major type of artistic failure in the classical detective genre, a basic weakness of construction in which the narrative presentation does not maintain a balance between detection and mystifi-cation. Instead, the reader is simply kept in a continuous state of puzzlement and uncertainty. While this might be appropriate to a good spy thriller or gothic romance where other interests are developed, the patterns of the classical detective formula are so exclusively centered on the interplay of deduction and mystification that it is very difficult to create alternative sources of suspense and excitement without destroying the basic fabric of the tale.

Another kind of artistic problem seems to plague Christie in *Third Girl*. Despite the fact that the classical detective formula seems easiest to work out in a very stable and restricted setting such as an English village or a university college, Christie has, to her credit, never been satisfied simply to imitate herself over and over again. Her earliest successes such as *The Mysterious Affair at Styles* or *The Murder of Roger Ackroyd* were indeed of the "Murder at the Vicarage" or "Mayhem Parva" school, and the country house or village has remained an important convention throughout much of her career, most notably of late in her Jane Marple stories. But Christie has by no means limited herself to this background. Her later tales have explored the modern scene in London, Europe, and even Egypt. One of her more successful mysteries, *Death on the Nile*, reaches its climax on a Nile steamer. But no matter how up to date the time or how far away from the English countryside the setting may be, Christie usually brings a traditional cast of characters along with her and succeeds best when working with the familar stereotypes of English drawing-room comedy of the 1920s: the tyrannical aunt or mother, the weak but handsome young man, the girl with a past, the shallow but amorous servant girl, the high-toned but rather suspicious butler, the prim, straitlaced spinster, the Colonel Blimpish rich uncle and so on. While these characters are not exactly dazzling in their originality or deeply moving in their human complexity, they are superbly adapted to function as least likely persons, red herrings, and suspects who will eventually be cleared. In fact, the characteristic that all these stereotypes seem to share is a mixture of attractive and suspicious traits: tyrannical but kindly, weak but handsome, dubious but elegant, rich but unhappy. Because of this basic and simple mixture of qualities, the Christie character interests the reader but does not draw him into the sort of deep and disturbing involvement where he might begin to care more about the individual person than the plot.

In recent years, Christie has occasionally tried to enroll some different and more complex characters in her masques. Most often, these are young people about whom, like everyone else these days, Christie seems to be deeply concerned and perplexed. Similarly, in her more recent tales, she is evidently trying to understand the contemporary scene, or at least to fit it into her well-established scheme of human motivation and action. Unfortunately, this attempt to represent contemporary young people has a rather deleterious effect on the delicate balance between the mystery and other narrative interests. Thus, in *Third Girl*, Norma Restarick, the young lady whose peculiar behavior involves Poirot in the investigation, is an attempt to portray the confused, alienated, and deeply disturbed youth of the 1960s. In fact, this character is immediately reminiscent of those desperate young ladies who so often form the center of the American detective stories of Ross Macdonald. But Macdonald is not only working within a different set of formulaic patterns, he has developed his own unique mystery structure in which complexity of character and richly lyrical portrayal of the contemporary scene do not come into conflict with an elaborate system of detection and mystification. In *Third Girl*, as a consequence, we find Hercule Poirot rather uncomfortably impersonating Lew Archer in his brooding concern over the desperate plight of the people he is investigating, while at the same time he is still the same old Hercule Poirot chattering on about the little grey cells and throwing out enigmatic hints about clues and their significance. Finally, in order to neatly resolve the crime in her traditional fashion, Christie must conveniently arrange for Norma to be cured and to leave the scene happily normal and engaged to the young doctor who has miraculously solved her psychological problems in little more than a week!

Third Girl is a fascinating instance of a failure of formulaic art brought on by a disproportion among character, setting, and mystery. Such imbalances are particularly noticeable when they occur in the work of a writer who, like Agatha Christie, tends to lay particular emphasis on complexity and ingenuity in the development of her basic structure of detection and mystification.

I would guess that it is Christie's ability to design an unusually complex and well-balanced detection-mystification structure and to set it forth with enough character and atmosphere to give it some flesh but not enough to distract from the chain of inquiry that has made her the most successful living writer of the classical detective formula. She gives us the pure, concentrated essence of the classical art with just enough flavoring to keep it from becoming tasteless and sterile. While there are other writers in the tradition who have constructed more elaborate and complex puzzles, and who have depended even more on pure rational processes, Christie has most success-fully combined complex detection with a highly functional approach to character and atmosphere. Except when they lose this balance of appeals, as in occasional slip-ups like *Third Girl*, Christie's stories almost infallibly engross the reader who enjoys the game of detection and mystification above all.

For many readers this will always be the most important aspect of the classical detective genre and they will tend to reject stories that allow other sources of interest to encroach on the centrality of the detection-mystification structure. I quite agree with this contention insofar as it asserts that a story which is not structured around a puzzling inquiry cannot be a good detective story, whatever its other merits. And yet it does seem to me that many superb detective tales, in effect, reverse the Christie balance of character-atmosphere and mystery by using the mystery structure as a means of giving us a certain special angle on the world. The work of Dorothy Sayers is an excellent example.

Dorothy Sayers is often cited in the same breath with Agatha Christie because they do have so many things in common. The English setting—frequently of the "Mayhem Parva" school—the eccentric detective, the social comedy cast of characters, the domestic crime with its elaborate and ingenious problems of scheduling, motives, means, all these formulaic elements seem fundamentally similar in the Sayers-Christie canon. I would even go so far as to say that Sayers sometimes does her best to construct a tale that has the same Christiesque emphasis on the fantastically ingenious crime and the game between reader and detective. I find these stories much less successful than Christie at her best because Sayers is not as skillful as

Christie in constructing a cast of characters and a situation that will effectively dramatize the twists and turns of the detection-mystification structure. A work like *Five Red Herrings*, perhaps the most complicated and ingenious of Sayers's crime plots, is finally boring to read because it bogs down in the interminable examination of clues and schedules without Christie's little touches of character and changing situations to dramatize the process of inquiry. When Sayers involves the presentation of mystery with the evocation of a set of characters and a social atmosphere, she is in my opinion a far richer and more complex artist than Christie.

Sayers's best work, *The Nine Tailors*, uses the classical detective story structure to embody a vision of the mysteries of divine providence. This moral and religious aspect of the story by no means prevents it from having an effective and complex structure of detection and mystification, but this structure relates to the other interests of character, atmosphere, and theme in a very different way than is typical of Christie. For one thing, to a considerable extent we experience the inquiry as Lord Peter Wimsey does. Indeed, he remains mystified about the central crime in much the same way that we do and the way in which he finally arrives at the true solution is shown to us in much the same light as it appears to him. In other words, the detective and the reader do not part company two-thirds of the way through the tale but share in the process of discovery throughout. Character, also, assumes a kind of prominence in the story that is almost unknown to Christie. While the cast of characters is much the same as one would expect to find in a Christie story and has a decided stereotypical quality, they are not simply functional adjuncts of the detection-mystification structure. For instance, there are a number of characters who are never presented to us as possible suspects and who yet play important parts in the story. This is almost never the case with Christie, except in her less successful tales. Finally, there is a great deal of material that characterizes or explains important aspects of the social setting without significantly contributing to the development of the mystery. The most notorious instance of this is Sayers's elaborate treatment of the art and ritual of change-ringing. While the bells do have an important role in the mystery, it was obviously not necessary to present a treatise on campanology in order to account for that circumstance.

Thus *Nine Tailors* is an example of a classical detective tale in which alternative narrative interests in character, social setting, and thematic significance have been interwoven into the structure of a mystery. At this point one might reasonably ask why bother with the mystery structure at all? If Sayers really wanted to write a novel about English rural society combining piquant touches of local color with traditional religious themes, why did she not simply do so? In fact, some critics of Sayers have argued that these other elements in *The Nine Tailors* interfere with the effectiveness of the detection-mystification structure just as the necessities of mystification limit and weaken the development of character and theme. I would like to argue, however, that in this case these various aspects of the tale are successfully integrated, that the nature of this particular mystery required this kind of treatment, and that Sayers's religious and social vision was perhaps most effectively expressed through the format of a classical detective story.

The background of the mystery is as follows:

> About fifteen years before the story opens a very expensive emerald necklace belonging to a guest at the Thorpe mansion in Fenchurch St. Paul was stolen. Though the thief, Jeff Deacon, a servant in the Thorpe house, was identified by his London confederate, one Nobby Cranton, the emeralds were never found because they had been hidden in a church by Deacon who had kept a paper in cipher to remind himself of the location. Deacon and Cranton were both given extensive prison sentences, while the Thorpe family was reduced to considerably straitened circumstances by Sir Henry Thorpe's insistence on paying his guest for the missing emeralds. After serving four years of his term, Deacon escaped from prison and was thought to have been killed while fleeing the police, though in fact he escaped to France during the confusion of the First World War. There he had taken up a new identity while waiting for a chance to return and secure the hidden emeralds. In the meantime, back at Fenchurch St. Paul, Deacon's former wife had remarried a local man named Will Thoday.
>
> Shortly before the opening of the book, Deacon returns to Fenchurch St. Paul where he is found prowling around the church by Will Thoday. Deacon threatens to reveal Mary Thoday's bigamy. Will agrees to hide him and to give him money to get out of the country. Will ties Deacon up in the bell chamber of the church until he can arrange for the money, but before he can do so, Will falls deliriously ill of the flu, barely managing to confide his problem to his visiting brother Jim. It happens that the very evening Deacon is tied in the bell chamber, the local rector has arranged for an all night change-ringing. The terrible noise of the bells kills Deacon, and the next morning he is found by Jim Thoday. Jim concludes that Will has killed Deacon and hides the body in a newly dug grave, which happens to be that of Lady Thorpe. He then returns to his ship and leaves the country.

Looked at in this way, the mystery of *The Nine Tailors* is an incredible tissue of improbability, coincidence, and turgid sensationalism. Compared to the relative clarity and plausibility of the Christie mystery plot outlined above, this tale of dark doings and complex betrayals in deepest rural England sounds like a fiction by some demented follower of Thomas Hardy. Indeed, *The Nine Tailors* with its atmospheric treatment of the Fen country, its climactic natural catastrophe, and its theme of the tragic reappearance of a former villager bears more than a little resemblance to *The Return of the Native*. What is most striking, however, is the transformation of this garish melodrama by its integration into the inquiry structure of the classical detective story. By doing so, Sayers transforms the incredible tissue of coincidence into a ritual allegory of providential action with the detective as priest, uncovering and expounding the mysterious ways of God to the bewildered participants in the action. With the actual structure of the crime in mind, let us now briefly summarize the pattern of the inquiry:

The story begins with an accident. Lord Peter Wimsey has been driving through the Fen country on a dark New Year's Eve when his car runs into a ditch near Fenchurch St. Paul. Going to the nearby vicarage for help, Lord Peter discovers the rector, Mr. Venables, in a considerable state. He has scheduled an epic ring of changes to celebrate the New Year, but one of his ringers, Will Thoday, has become prostrated with illness. Lord Peter agrees to take his place, and the change-ringing goes on as scheduled. As he leaves the next day, Lord Peter encounters on the road a suspicious looking older man who asks the way to Fenchurch St. Paul.

Some months later, at Easter time, Lord Peter receives a letter from Rector Venables inviting him to inquire into the mysterious appearance of a corpse in the graveyard, discovered when Lady Thorpe's grave was opened to bury the recently deceased Sir Henry Thorpe. Wimsey is intrigued with the situation, and, having heard of the earlier theft of emeralds from the Thorpe mansion, assumes there is some connection between the mysterious body and the earlier crime. Of course, at this stage Wimsey (and the reader) believe that Deacon is dead; therefore, the proper inferences about the body cannot be arrived at. After inquiries based on clues connected with the body, Wimsey does succeed in tracing the dead man to France where he has been living for several years under what is obviously an assumed name.

At this point attention shifts from the dead man to a strange paper which had been found at Easter time by Miss Hilary Thorpe, the attractive daughter of the unfortunate Thorpes. The paper, which reads like the apocalyptic vision of a lunatic, turns out on examination by Wimsey to be a cipher revealing the hiding place of the missing necklace. Lord Peter retrieves the necklace from its place of concealment among the gilded angels in the church ceiling. The discovery of the emeralds only leaves the mystery of the dead body still more in the dark.

It is at this point of complete mystification that Lord Peter has the insight which seems to unravel most of the mystery; by inferring that the dead body is actually the long-dead Jeff Deacon he is able to understand and explain the role of Will Thoday and his brother. When confronted, the two brothers explain everything, but claim in a plausible way that neither one has actually killed Deacon. In fact, neither Wimsey nor the police are able to establish with any certainty the manner of Deacon's death. Thus, though we seem to know every person involved and understand the whys and wherefores of Deacon's movements, the cause of his death remains still more mysterious than ever.

More time passes. Wimsey decides to spend Christmas at Fenchurch St. Paul. As he drives toward the village on Christmas Eve he notices the waters ominously rising in the canals and sluices. A few days later the sluice gates break and a flood spreads over the land forcing all the inhabitants to cluster at the high ground of the church for safety. While the alarm bell is ringing to warn the people around, Lord Peter happens to climb into the bell tower and narrowly escapes being killed himself by the sound. Finally he realizes how and in what manner Jeff Deacon has met with his death: that Deacon has been investigated, tried, and given judgment by a higher power. Will Thoday drowns trying to save a friend, and the whole area is, one might say, purged and cleaned out by the rising and receding flood waters.

Miss Sayers's powers of invention, organization, mystification, and style seem to have reached a peak in *The Nine Tailors* perhaps because this story embodied more deeply than most not only some of her own deepest social and religious feelings, but also her sense of what was most basic about the detective story. In the introduction to her *Omnibus of Crime* published just six years before *The Nine Tailors* Sayers offered her own speculations about the fundamental human appeal of puzzles and mysteries:

> It may be that in them [man] finds a sort of catharsis or purging of his fears and self-questionings. These mysteries made only to be solved, these horrors which he knows to be mere figments of the creative brain, comfort him by subtly persuading that life is a mystery which death will solve, and whose horrors will pass away a tale that is told.[6]

Whether or not this statement fully explains the detective story genre, it is a rich insight into the special vision of *The Nine Tailors*, for in that work Sayers does work with a kind of catharsis both with the developing events of her story and with the kind of mystery that they reveal. This special kind of feeling is enhanced by the ritual and ceremonial symbolism that Sayers employs in so many ways throughout the book. The entire story is wrapped in the formal symbolism of change-ringing, each chapter title being derived from some aspect of campanology; the action takes place around a church, and its major events occur at the main points of the ritual year: New Year's, Easter, and Christmas; biblical rhetoric and symbology are encountered at every point, and the climax arrives with a flood that does unto the microcosmic village of Fenchurch St. Paul what Noah's Flood did to the world.

While some readers may find something mildly blasphemous or perhaps even comically incongruous in this deployment of the great tradition of the Church of England in order to enliven the rhetoric of a detective story, a more sympathetic reader might think of all this as rather "metaphysical" in homage to the great seventeenth-century poets whose love of puzzles, wit, and incongruous stretched-out metaphors did not seem to conflict with their sincere religious feeling or their high artistry. The process of the inquiry in *The Nine Tailors* is carefully organized in such a way that human reason resolves minor mysteries, but only realization of the hand of God can solve the ultimate mystery of life and death. The sense of providential action is built up most skillfully and consistently throughout the story. Wimsey enters the inquiry through an accident, which turns out to be providential in the sense that only he has the capacity to explain the mystery. Deacon's death has the same pattern, though of larger magnitude. He dies because coincidentally with his temporary incarceration in the bell chamber the saintly Rector Venables had decided to ring a record peal of Kent Treble Bob to celebrate the New Year, and because the one man aware of Deacon's situation was helplessly ill and delirious. The emeralds are discovered only because the piece of paper accidentally dropped by Deacon is picked up by Hilary Thorpe, whose parents' lives had been ruined by the original theft. Throughout the text references to providence, humorous and serious, abound and serve as clues in the structure of detection and mystification that confronts the reader. These seemingly random comments have a clearly articulated order of development. Early in the story, even before the Eastertide resurrection of Deacon's corpse, the following colloquy occurs between Rector Venables and one of his parishioners:

> "We mustn't question the ways of Providence," said the Rector.
> "Providence?" said the old woman. "Don't yew talk to me about Providence. First he took my husband, and then he took my 'taters, but there's one above as'll teach him to mind his manners, if he don't look out."[7]

Though one first reads this as a bit of colorful local humor, it turns out in the light of later events to have more than one serious implication. The frequent presence of passages like this makes *The Nine Tailors* unusually rewarding on rereading. Later, after the discovery of Deacon's body, the sexton suggests that the ironically appropriate hymn "God moves in a mysterious way" be sung at the graveside. Finally, when the truth of Deacon's death is accidentally revealed during the flood, Rector Venables makes explicit in a serious statement the theme of providential agency:

> "There have always been," he said, "legends about Batty Thomas [one of the bells]. She has slain two other men in times past, and Hezekiah will tell you that the bells are said to be jealous of the presence of evil. Perhaps God speaks through those mouths of inarticulate metal. He is a righteous judge, strong and patient and is provoked every day."[8]

Thus, in *The Nine Tailors*, Dorothy Sayers effectively integrates the formulaic structure of the classical detective story with the additional narrative interests of religious theme and social setting. The mixture works effectively in this case without breaking the bounds of the formula because the mystery and the structure of inquiry through which it is presented are unified with the central theme of the mystery of God's providential action. Though this is a high accomplishment in the art of the classical detective story, some of its limitations become immediately apparent if we place *The Nine Tailors* in comparison with some of the great novels that deal with the religious aspects of murder, such as *Crime and Punishment* or *The Brothers Karamazov*. In *The Nine Tailors* God's will rather too comfortably aligns itself with a noticeably limited vision of English class justice. Compared with Dostoevsky's treatment of the purging and redemption of Raskolnikov one becomes too easily aware that in Sayers's English village evil seems to be defined more in terms of nasty, aggressive members of the lower classes trying to punch their way up the social scale than as the more universally meaningful sense of mystery and evil that Dostoevsky so powerfully delineates. To enjoy fully and be moved by *The Nine Tailors* one must be able temporarily to accept the snobbish, class-ridden, provincial world of Fenchurch St. Paul as a microcosm of the world; otherwise one will inevitably agree with those readers who find the religious symbolism of the book pretentious and inappropriate. Whether these limitations of vision represent the attitudes of Miss Sayers or the formulaic boundaries of the classical detective story—and they are probably a combination of both—does not greatly matter. The fact that Sayers was able to work comfortably within the basic patterns of the classical formula suggests that her own religious commitments made sense in this way. Nonetheless, those who are willing to accept the stringent limitations of this fictional universe for the sake of such curious pleasures as the final twist by which it becomes apparent that God is the least likely person, are grateful to Dorothy Sayers for this embodiment of her art.

The Art of Simenon

Christie and Sayers exemplify two possibilities for art within the formula of the classical detective story: the first combines a pure ingenuity of ratiocination and mystification with other narrative interests—character, setting, theme—completely subordinated to their role in this structure, and the second uses the classical formula's pattern to body forth a variety of other narrative interests, in this case a vision of justice and society embedded in an allegory of the mystery of divine providence. Sayers's *The Nine Tailors* is an unusually complex example of this mode of subordinating the structure of mystery to the interests of theme, character, and setting. Nevertheless, many of the finest stories in the classical formula achieve their effectiveness primarily because the patterns of detective inquiry give the writer a structure within which to present a dramatically intensified vision of some social microcosm or to create a situation of tension in which some atmosphere or theme will manifest itself. The circumstances of mystery—murder and the search for its perpetrator—create extreme situations in which characters can be shown in a particularly lurid and intense light and in which certain ultimate qualities of society and background can be revealed. Some writers use this potentiality of the formula for comic purposes as is the case with the American ladies who write under the name of Emma Lathen. In Lathen's books, each of the murders presents the amateur detective with a different social microcosm usually based on a particular institution—an investment firm, a dog show, a diocesan school. A crime that disrupts this microcosm casts a gently satiric and ironic light on its elements. On the other hand, the Australian detective novelist Arthur W. Upfield uses the eruption of crime

into the particular social atmosphere of the Australian outback for melodramatic or tragic effects. His best novels, such as *Death of a Lake*, usually
parallel some highly dramatic natural phenomenon, such as the periodic
drying up of a lake, with the detective's search and exposure of the criminal.
The way in which mystery and background intensify each other can be quite
stunning.

On the other hand, the kind of art exemplified by Agatha Christie is also
evident in the "challenge to the reader" stories of writers like John Dickson
Carr and Ellery Queen. Here the central focus is on complication and
ingenuity in constructing the crime in the first place and in the devious
stratagems involved in presenting the inquiry in such a way that the reader is
deeply engrossed in trying to figure out the mystery. In between the extremes
of a dominantly atmospheric writer like Upfield and a master of detection
and mystification like Christie there have been many different kinds of
balance struck between the contending interests of the classical detective tale,
but no writer has worked with more artistic skill within the limits of the
formula than Georges Simenon. Most critics would agree about the high
quality of Simenon's writing, but many would seriously question the
assertion that he is working within the same genre as Christie and Sayers.
Two supposed points of difference are most often noted. First, it is argued
that the Maigret books do not really concern themselves with detection.
Maigret's skills as a detective, these critics argue, are not ratiocinative but a
result of tireless energy and irrational intuition.[9] These critics believe that the
Simenon tales are either inferior to the great monuments of deduction or
belong to a different genre entirely. Second, many critics class Maigret with
what they see as either a different genre of detection or a subgenre of the
classical story: the police procedural tale.

To take the second point first, there is, I think, a subgenre of the classical
story that can be called the procedural tale. Though it often involves a
policeman or some unit of the police force as detective protagonist, it is
misleading to call this the *police* procedural tale because the basic structural
characteristics of the subgenre do not require a police detective. Also, there
are many examples of police detectives functioning as protagonists in the
regular type of classical detective tale. What distinguishes the procedural
subgenre is a matter of emphasis in the narrative. The mark of the regular
detective story is that our attention is focused on the mystery of who
committed the crime and how and why it was done. In the procedural
subgenre, however, excitement and suspense are primarily generated by our
involvement with the process by which the crime or crimes are dealt with. An
early example of this subformula was the so-called inverted story pioneered
by R. Austin Freeman in which the reader is first shown the crime and then
how the detective used his scientific and deductive skills to solve it. There is
no mystery in the inverted tale about who killed the victim and how; the
mystery is whether the detective will be able to solve the crime. The
procedural story does not have to be inverted. As long as the writer

emphasizes the details of the detective's inquiry and, most importantly, lets us in on all the main deductions he makes, the story will tend to emphasize process rather than mystery, and will be better understood as an example of the procedural subgenre. Agatha Christie's stories are almost totally non-procedural, since the detective's thought processes are largely hidden from us except in tantalizing and mystifying hints. Sayers's tales have more of a procedural cast, but, as Lord Peter is usually at least two or three steps ahead of the reader, do not become fully procedural. On the other hand, Freeman Wills Croft relentlessly exposes us to Inspector French's tiniest insight at the moment it occurs. His novels become almost purely procedural, the reader almost losing sight of the mystery altogether in his involvement in the detective's complex attempts to solve it.

Another trend of increasing importance in the procedural subgenre has been an almost novelistic emphasis on the personal lives or professional situations of the detective investigator insofar as these impinge on the process of investigation. Thus John Creasy in his Gideon series shows us the complex of personalities and backstairs rivalries as these play a role in the police investigation of a series of crimes. Like the Gideon series, Ed McBain's 87th Precinct stories sometimes deal with a number of crimes investigated by a variety of policemen. Because the emphasis in the procedural subformula is on the process of investigation, it is possible for the writer to present a group of detectives rather than a single investigator, and even to deal with a number of unrelated crimes, without losing the central unifying thread of the story. It seems clear that this latter tendency does involve a movement away from the classical detective formula by giving a disproportionate emphasis to the development of character and social background. Some of the most success-ful recent works that have employed many of the formulaic patterns of the procedural story have in fact moved beyond the limits of the formula to become full-scale novels like Thorp's *The Detective* and Wambaugh's *The New Centurions*.

The Maigret stories do develop some of the patterns of the procedural subgenre. Simenon gives us a much richer sense of Maigret as a human being than most other detective writers do by showing Maigret in a variety of different relationships—with his wife, with his staff of inspectors, with his counterparts in the French judicial bureaucracy, even with some of the criminals he has arrested. In addition, a typical Maigret novel, though technically narrated by an objective third-person author, is actually much like an interior monologue by Maigret. The flow of the narrative is largely confined to the flow of Maigret's perceptions, observations, and feelings. Therefore, we see what happens just as Maigret does, and in addition we are privy to many of the inferences and deductions he draws from the clues. This sort of emphasis on the process of the detective's inquiry, and his relationship with other members of the judicial bureaucracy in the course of the investigation, is characteristic of the procedural type of story. But there is one crucial way in which Simenon's tales do not pass over into the procedural vein and that is in the emphasis on mystery. One of the central aspects of Simenon's art is his ability to make a human drama of the process of inquiry without undercutting the power of the mystery that lies at the end. Even the best tales of Agatha Christie have, I think, their somewhat attenuated moments in which the necessarily complex exposition of particular clues gives a thin, bloodless character to the narrative. In Simenon, such moments almost never occur, partly because of his skill in making a human drama of the inquiry and partly because of the rich interest and subtlety of his mysteries.

In most classical detective story writers, the mysteries are focused upon material circumstances. Our knowledge of "whodunit" depends essentially on the discovery of how, why, when, and where it was done. Though the motivation of the crime is usually important as a means of accounting for the circumstances and firmly establishing the guilt of the culprit, the motives themselves are usually quite simple: greed, self-protection, jealousy, hate. The mystification in a story by Christie or Sayers is not a reflection of complexities and ambiguities of character, but of complications in the scheduling and methods of the crime. For Simenon, however, the central mystery is that of character, and to solve the crime Maigret and the reader must make complex inferences about the character of the suspects and about the social background that has caused them to act as they do. Physical clues play a much smaller role in the Maigret investigations than in those of Poirot, Lord Peter Wimsey, and other classical detective stories. This does not mean, as some critics have argued, that deduction is not important in the Maigret stories, or that Simenon does not build up an effective structure of detection and mystification. In fact, because his mystifications are rooted in the complexities of human character, Simenon's tales of detection bring the various interests of the classical formula into a highly effective unity.

We can best see the way in which Simenon unites the structure of detection and mystification with the alternative interests of character and atmosphere by considering a specific example. In *Maigret and the Reluctant Witnesses* (*Maigret et les témoins récalcitrants* [1959]) the substructure of criminal action is as follows:

> For several generations the Lachaume family has operated a large bakery making cookies and wafers that once were sold throughout France. The family has come to conceive of itself as a great bourgeois dynasty that must be perpetuated. In the last few decades, however, the ancient factory and antiquated business methods of the family have not been able to keep up with new competition and the business has been losing money. First, it has eaten up what remained of the family fortune and then began to depend on the fortunes brought into the family by the wives of the two sons, Armand and Leonard. Both sons have married the well-to-do daughters of self-made men who have seen marriage into the long-established Lachaume family as a means of assuring social respectability for their offspring. Leonard's wife has died some time before and her

money has been almost entirely used up. Now the family in its decaying old mansion near the broken-down factory has become almost totally dependent on the money of Armand's young wife, Paulette. Not long before the story begins, Leonard Lachaume discovers that Paulette has become involved with a lover and that she is determined to divorce Armand Lachaume and marry her lover. If Paulette leaves the family and takes her money with her, the Lachaume *biscuiterie* will soon be forced to close down. Leonard decides to murder Paulette, after breaking a window and placing a ladder by the wall of the house to make it appear as if the killings has been done by a burglar. As he bends over Paulette's bed and prepares to hit her with a wrench, Paulette suddenly awakens and shoots Leonard with a gun given her by her lover. The family then attempts to rearrange things so that it will look as if Leonard has been killed by a burglar, taking advantage of the material clues already spread around. This is the situation that confronts Maigret when he arrives on the scene.

In narrative structure, *Maigret and the Reluctant Witnesses* is not very different from a standard Agatha Christie. The detective is called in; he confronts an enigmatic situation in which there are a number of confusing physical clues and a group of witnesses who initially refuse to speak at all. When they do, they all claim no knowledge of the murder. As the story develops, Simenon creates the same sort of detection and mystification for the reader that we find in Christie and Sayers. The first phase involves the burglary clues. These are almost immediately deduced to be false clues, yet this deduction only produces a further puzzle: why did the murderer plant such clumsy and obviously false clues? The second phase is based on the assumption that some member of the family must be responsible for the murder. Yet the further examination of each person and their circumstances leads only to the conclusion that the possible suspects lacked either the capacity or the motive to commit the crime. Maigret's further investigations reveal the existence of Paulette Lachaume's lover and her intention to divorce Armand Lachaume, but this discovery only creates further mystification about a possible motive for the murder of Leonard Lachaume. There certainly seems to be no reason for Paulette Lachaume to murder Leonard if she was on the verge of leaving the Lachaume household. The final revelation of the truth involves a reversal not dissimilar in form to those of Agatha Christie. We have been seeing the case in the wrong way by proceeding on the assumption that Leonard Lachaume was the intended victim. Actually, it was Paulette who was supposed to be murdered by Leonard. Instead, she has killed him in self-defense, while the whole Lachaume family has cooperated in covering up the crime, ironically trying to use the false clues planted by Leonard to conceal his own intended murder.

Thus Simenon creates an effective structure of detection and mystification with the final revelation held until the very end. Though this structure is less intricate and clearly marked by overt challenges to the reader than in Christie and Sayers, it is in many ways more engrossing because it becomes an inquiry into human complexities and ambiguities. The most important deductions are not explanations of material clues but inferences about how human character and social background interact to create a certain chain of behavior. Poirot arrives at a solution to the mystery when he has grasped the way in which the particular clues point unerringly to a specific culprit, but Maigret's solutions reflect the capacity to make his intuitive immersion in the social atmosphere of a crime and the characters involved yield a moment of rational and moral illumination. Thus the chief power of Simenon's artfulness in the classical detective genre is his practically unique ability to make us share Maigret's synthesis of intellectual and moral perceptions, his discovery not only of the culprit but of the moral significance of the crime. Even in the most complex story by Agatha Christie, the culprit remains an evil person who has committed a particularly ingenious bad deed. The same is largely true of Sayers. Jeff Deacon, the source of the trouble in *The Nine Tailors*, is purely and simply an evil person. Will Thoday, who is inadvertently responsible for the murder of Deacon, is a slightly more complex person, more like a Simenon culprit in some ways. Yet the inquiry does not lead the reader to a fuller involvement with Thoday's situation because he is simply a piece in the larger allegory of guilt, innocence, and providence that interests Sayers. But for Simenon, the individual beings of murderer and victim, the mysterious combination of individual psychology, social background, and human relationship that inevitably resulted in murder are revealed and dramatized in the process of the inquiry. Maigret's own personal attitudes, his particular moral scruples, his conflict with the impersonal legal machinery of the French judicial bureaucracy, even our glimpses of his relationship with Mme Maigret, are part of Simenon's dramatization of the mystery of individual destinies. In *Maigret and the Reluctant Witnesses*, for example, Maigret must work with the young examining magistrate Angelot:

> This fellow Angelot, so fresh and brisk, he'd only just left college. Either he was an exceptional fellow, one of the few in each generation, whom you could count on your fingers, or else he was being backed by people in high places; otherwise, instead of getting a job in Paris, he'd have been sent to kick his heels for years in some sub-prefecture magistrate's court.[10]

Angelot's self-confidence, his upper middle-class rectitude and concern for the letter of the law keep intruding into the investigation. Unlike some of the other examining magistrates, Angelot insists on looking over Maigret's shoulder throughout his inquiry. He is obviously concerned that Maigret will fail to treat this distinguished bourgeois family with due respect. Since the Lachaume family's obsessive concern for respectability and tradition is the social motivation underlying the crime, Magistrate Angelot's own character reflects the same upper-bourgeois ideals that have helped to shape the catastrophe.

Simenon's version of the classical detective formula may not be quite as striking in its suspenseful manipulations of the reader and its reversals of expectation as Christie's best works, but it does possess nuances of insight into people and society that cannot be achieved with the more abstract emphasis on the twists and turns of mystification favored by Christie and her followers. Because of these qualities, Simenon's influence has been a very important one for most of the gifted younger mystery writers—Julian Symons in Britain, Nicholas Freeling in Holland, Ross Macdonald in America, and Sjovall and Wahloo in Sweden, for example. Like Simenon, each of these writers uses the traditional structure of the detective mystery in order to cast light on individual character in its environment. Simenon's work and its important influence on a young generation of writers raises two further questions important to our fuller understanding of the classical detective formula as an artistic genre: first, why have Simenon and these other writers chosen the form of the mystery story to pursue ends that are close to those of the "serious" novel, i.e., the realistic representation of character and social background; and second, if the mystery formula can be developed for such purposes, just what are the boundaries of the formula? How does a novel differ from a detective story?

Detective Stories and Detection as an Element in Other Literary Genres

Ross Macdonald in a fascinating essay, "The Writer as Detective Hero," gives us, I believe, considerable insight into how the structure of the detective story makes possible a kind of art that might not otherwise be possible for certain writers and readers. Macdonald suggests that the detective story's formula of transforming human situations of death and horror into problems perceived by a more or less detached investigator makes it possible for writer and reader to confront and try to understand aspects of life that may be too painful or disturbing to confront without this mediating structure. Of his own detective, Lew Archer, Macdonald says:

> He can be self-forgetful, almost transparent at times, and concentrate, as good detectives (and good writers) do, on the people whose problems he is investigating. These other people are for me the main thing: they are often more intimately related to me and my life than Lew Archer is. He is the obvious self-projection which holds the eye (my eye as well as the reader's) while more secret selves creep out of the woodwork behind the locked door. Remember how the reassuring presence of Dupin permitted Poe's mind to face the nightmare of the homicidal ape and the two dead women.[11]

In the same way, I think the deeply feeling but ultimately detached perspective of Maigret enables Simenon to uncover secret terrors of the human soul without being overpowered by the dark tides of unreason, despair, and anguish. Such explorations are perhaps implicit in writers like Agatha Christie but remain masked by the skillful ratiocinative legerdemain that focuses our attention on clues and circumstances rather than on character and the complexities of human motive. In Christie and in Simenon we find different uses of the classical detective formula. For Christie, the structure of detection and mystification works brilliantly to develop the moral fantasy that human actions have a simple and rational explanation and that guilt is specific and not ambiguous. In Simenon, however, the formula is a means of struggling to bring under rational and emotional control an awareness of human ambiguity that is painful to face directly.

There is a considerable range and depth of artistry possible within the limits of the classical detective formula. At the same time, I think its basic characteristics can be clearly differentiated from other mystery and adventure formulas such as the hard-boiled detective story and the gangster saga on the one hand, and from the nonformulaic novel on the other. While one can list a number of different situations, actions, characters, and settings that are likely to appear in a classical detective story, there are three minimal conditions for the formula. If a work does not meet these conditions, it is something else: (1) there must be a mystery, i.e., certain basic past facts about the situation and/or a number of the central characters must be concealed from the reader and from the protagonist until the end, or, as in the case of the inverted procedural story the reader must understand that such facts have been concealed from the protagonist; (2) the story must be structured around an inquiry into these concealed facts with the inquirer as protagonist and his investigation as the central action; however, the concealed facts must not be about the protagonist himself; (3) the concealed facts must be made known at the end. Only when these rudimentary conditions are present will a story be able to generate the particular interests and satisfactions of the detective story genre.

With these considerations in mind, we can see that it is quite possible to create a detective story without a character who is a detective, as long as that character performs the role of successful inquirer. For instance, the Emma Lathen stories in which a Wall Street banker, John Putnam Thatcher, is the protagonist are clearly detective stories because they represent Thatcher solving mysteries. On the other hand, there are a number of novels that have criminals and detectives as central characters but are not at all in the detective genre. Perhaps the most important work is Dostoevsky's *Crime and Punishment*, much of which does center upon the police detective Profiry Petrovich's investigation of the brutal murder of an old pawnbroker and her sister, a situation not unlike that which confronts C. Auguste Dupin in Poe's "Murders in the Rue Morgue." The reader knows from the outset that Raskolnikov has committed the murders because the narrator not only shows him in the act, but also explores deeply the development of his motives and state of mind. Moreover, *Crime and Punishment* is not structured around the inquiry, but around the change in the murderer's soul. What remains concealed from the reader and the protagonist is not any particular set of past facts but whether or not the protagonist will come to feel the necessity of confessing his crime and accepting his punishment. Though it employs all the basic elements of the detective story—a crime, a murderer, a detective, an inquiry, the apprehension of the criminal—*Crime and Punishment* does not fulfill a single one of the basic structural conditions of the classical detective formula. It is a completely different, nonformulaic, arrangement of this material.

Sophocles' *Oedipus* poses a more striking problem of differentiation, at least in the structure of the work, for it would seem to fulfill almost all the basic conditions of the detective story—something is concealed; the form of the play is an inquiry; and the end of the play is a revelation of the hidden truth. Of course, the cultural materials in which this structure is embodied are quite different from those we associate with the classical detective story formula, and this highlights the point I have already made that formulas are combinations of specific cultural materials and more universal story archetypes. Even if we allow for this aspect of the story and think of *Oedipus* as a kind of historical detective story, I still find myself a bit uncomfortable about the association.[12]

There are two fundamental patterns in *Oedipus* that ultimately make the play more like the antidetective stories of Borges and Robbe-Grillet than like the classical formula. First of all, the inquirer himself turns out to be the culprit, since his past crimes are uncovered by the inquiry. While one is momentarily tempted to suggest an analogy between this situation and Agatha Christie's notorious *Murder of Roger Ackroyd* where the narrator turns out to be the murderer, the analogy quickly breaks down. In Christie's story, the narrator and the detective are separate persons; it is the relatively detached Hercule Poirot who conducts the inquiry, not the culprit-narrator. Oedipus' situation is more analogus to that of the detective in Robbe-Grillet's *The Erasers* whose inquiries lead him to commit a crime, or the central figure of Borges's "Death and the Compass" whose investigation lures him into becoming the victim of a murder. Another crucial structural difference between *Oedipus* and the classical detective formula lies in the relation between audience, detective-protagonist, and the concealed facts. In a skillfully written detective story, the protagonist discovers the truth while the reader is still floundering around in mystery. Thus there is little possibility of the tragic irony for which Sophocles is justly famous. In *Oedipus*, even if we discount the audience's prior knowledge of the myth, the play itself reveals the truth long before the inquiring protagonist becomes aware of it. Not only does Tiresias correctly identify the murderer near the beginning of the play; Sophocles carefully structures the presentation of clues and inferences in such a way as to give the audience almost certain knowledge, thus enabling us to have the terrible experience of witnessing Oedipus in the process of pursuing his fate while he thinks he is averting it. This harrowing of the soul is of course a very different thing from the experience of the detective story. Even

in the more darkly serious stories of Georges Simenon we are insulated from
the tragic experience by our identification with the detached intermediary
agency of Inspector Maigret.

Despite these differences, there is an important connection between the
compelling fascination of the drama of *Oedipus* and the interest of the
detective story; both depend on our fascination with the uncovering of
hidden guilt or secrets. Some psychoanalysts have theorized that this
attraction arises from unresolved infantile feelings about the primal scene
leading to an adult compulsion to repeat the experience in the disguise of
fantasy.[13] If so, *Oedipus* deals with the primal scene fascination in a more
direct and explicit way, while the detective story disguises the experience in
symbolic form, as might be expected from a literary type designed primarily
for purposes of relaxation and escape.

William Faulkner's *Intruder in the Dust*, another novel that makes use of
elements similar to the detective story, indicates another boundary of the
classical formula. In Faulkner's novel, unlike either *Oedipus* or *Crime and
Punishment*, there is a mystery that is kept from the reader until the book is
nearly finished. Also, the inquiring protagonist is never himself suspected of
the murder. Therefore, he does have something of the detached position of
the classical detective. Like many writers, Faulkner was evidently fascinated
by detection and its literary possibilities and even wrote a few more or less
straight detective stories himself.[14] In the case of *Intruder in the Dust*,
however, the structure of detection and mystification is an element in the
novel, but does not constitute the main action. Instead, the mystery situation
functions as an occasion for the development of another central situation, the
young protagonist Chick Mallison's complex initiation into the meaning of
such values as responsibility, moral courage, and honor. While the events of
the story center upon Chick's search for evidence to prove Lucas Beauchamp's
innocence of murder, the way in which Faulkner tells the story really
concentrates attention on the series of discoveries that Chick makes about his
relationship to his community and tradition. Detective inquiry is in effect the
stimulus for another kind of investigation in a way that would not be the case
in a detective story.

To conclude this discussion of the boundaries of the classical detective
formula, I would like to call attention to a fairly complex novel which,
though it develops a great variety of other elements, remains essentially
within the limits of the detective story. The work I have in mind is Wilkie
Collins's *The Moonstone*, which was historically a precursor of the great
body of detective fiction, and yet, like Poe's stories, is properly judged as one
of the major creations of the classical genre. *The Moonstone* has many
elaborate complications and a scale of time and space much larger than the
majority of the works that have succeeded it. It has a variety of narrators and
a number of inquiring protagonists who play the role of detective at various
phases of the inquiry. In addition, the hidden secret that is finally uncovered

at the end does concern the guilt or innocence of the most important of the inquiring protagonists. These characteristics indicate the degree to which *The Moonstone* is at some point on the line of development between the nineteenth-century novel of sensation and the twentieth-century classical detective story. Despite all its complications, however, the central narrative line of Collins's novel is the inquiry into the missing moonstone and correlatively into the guilt or innocence of Franklin Blake. As in the classical detective genre, the novel moves from detection to mystification with one reversal piled upon another until the solution is finally reached. Though that final revelation does concern the fate of the inquiring protagonist, the fact that he is a basically sympathetic, romantic character whose innocence is finally established makes a very important structural difference. I would argue that the romantic conventions of true love triumphant and the way in which we are associated through narrative method with the fate of Franklin Blake reassure us that somehow the circumstantial evidence against him will be disproved. With this reassurance we are able to concentrate on the pleasures of detection and mystification without having to spend emotional energy preparing ourselves for a possible catastrophe to a character about whose situation we have increasingly come to care. In addition, *The Moonstone* presents a professional detective—one of the first in literature—as a central figure. Though Sergeant Cuff is not exactly a protagonist in the fashion of the fully developed classical formula, and though he initially arrives at an incorrect solution to the crime, his presence suggests the extent to which Collins foresaw the fascination of the detective-mystification structure. In sum, I would say that the difference between *The Moonstone* and the classical detective is not so much a matter of kind as of degree. A little more emphasis on Sergeant Cuff and a more external treatment of a complex romantic relation between Franklin Blake and Rachel Verinder, and *The Moonstone* would be indistinguishable in structure from a work by Agatha Christie or Dorothy Sayers. Because of its affinity to the emphasis on detection and mystification in the classical detective genre, it is not surprising that it is considered by some to be one of the most perfectly plotted works in English literature:

> Certainly no English novel shows a structure and proportions, or contrives a narrative tempo, better adapted to its end: that of lending variety and amplitude to a story the mainspring of which has to be a sustained interest in the elucidation of a single mysterious event.[15]

In contrast to *The Moonstone*, Collins's contemporary and friend Charles Dickens also made frequent use of the materials of mystery, as did many nineteenth-century novelists and melodramatists. Only in the unfinished *Mystery of Edwin Drood* did Dickens approach the classical detective formula, and even there it is difficult to determine whether the novel would have become something like a detective story because it is not certain just how Dickens intended to develop it. In *Bleak House*, for example, there is a hidden crime and a detective, Inspector Bucket, who is a still earlier precursor of the modern literary detective. And yet, the element of investigation of the mystery is so completely subordinated to other narrative interests in this novel that *Bleak House* is no more a detective story than *Crime and Punishment*.

The Future of the Classical Detective Story

What is the future of the classical detective genre? Historians and critics seem generally agreed that the "golden age of detection" is past and that a new generation of writers and readers are no longer satisfied with the kind of formula employed in the heyday of the classical story by writers like Agatha Christie, Dorothy Sayers, John Dickson Carr, Josephine Tey, Ngaio Marsh, R. Austin Freeman, and many others.[16] Of course, Agatha Christie goes right on being a best-seller, though most of her recent novels have shown a tendency to cultivate other narrative interests in addition to detection. Still, these epitaphs may be a bit premature. Many of the finest classical stories of the golden age were not examples of pure detection and mystification, as we noted in our analysis of Dorothy Sayers, and today writers like the Americans Emma Lathen and Amanda Cross are still writing first-rate tales with almost the identical proportion of detection-mystification, comedy of manners, and social vision found in Sayers.

Nevertheless, the classical detective formula does not seem at the moment to be a major stimulus to creativity. The most interesting younger writers have either followed in the footsteps of Simenon by giving greater emphasis to the complex psychological interplay between detective, criminals, and society (Nicholas Freeling, Peter Dickinson, Ross Macdonald, Ed McBain) or have turned away from the investigator to a study of the criminal and the crime (Julian Symons, Colin Watson, and Donald Westlake ["Richard Stark"]). In addition, the classical detective formula has never been as acceptable to the media of film and television as the more action-oriented, hard-boiled detective and crime formulas. Moreover, to a period inclined to be distrustful of rationality and ambiguously suspicious of the value of social authority, the classical formula's emphasis on deduction and the detective's role as protector of the social order seem to embody a quaintly antiquated view of the world, a fantasy that is almost too far-fetched to be believed in, even for a moment.

Paradoxically, perhaps the most important influence of the classical detective story since World War II has been on the new "postmodern" novel. Michael Holquist has recently argued that "What the structural and philosophical presupposition of myth and depth psychology were to Modernism (Mann, Joyce, Woolf, etc.) the detective story is to Post-Modernism (Robbe-Grillet, Borges, Nabokov, etc.)."[17] As Holquist sees it, the postwar literary reaction against the psychological complexities and large myth-making of modern literature found in the detective story a model of antiliterary expression:

> If, as such figures as Robbe-Grillet and Borges have been, you are interested in disestablishing the mythic and psychological tendencies of the tradition you are defining yourself against, what better way for doing so could recommend itself than that of exploiting what had already become the polar opposite of that tradition in its own time. Detective stories had always been recognized as escape literature. But escape from what? Among other things, escape from *literature itself*, as we emphasized above in the dichotomy between the detective story with its exterior simplicities and modernism with its interior complexities. Thus, when after World War II Robbe-Grillet was searching for ways to overcome the literary tradition of the novel he so naturally turned to the detective story as a mode. . . . The possibilities for symbolic action and depth psychology which Homer provides for James Joyce are replaced in the later period by the ambiguous events and the psychologically flat and therefore mysterious world which Holmes and Poirot make available to Robbe-Grillet and Borges.[18]

But the "detective" stories constructed by Robbe-Grillet, Borges, and Nabokov are really antidetective stories, which drastically undercut the formulaic expectations associated with the genre:

> The most common expectation, based on reading classical detective stories, which Post Modernism defeats is that of syllogistic *order*. Like Poe, Robbe-Grillet and Borges have a deep sense of the chaos of the world, but unlike Poe, they cannot assuage that sense by turning to the mechanical certainty, the hyper-logic of the classical detective story. Post-Modernists use as a foil the assumption of detective fiction that the mind can solve all: by twisting the details just the opposite becomes the case.[19]

Because the classical detective formula is perhaps the most effective fictional structure yet devised for creating the illusion of rational control over the mysteries of life, it has served such varied purposes as intellectual play and witty escapism in the puzzles of Agatha Christie, of controlled exploration of human beings in situations of obsession and desperation as in the stories of Georges Simenon, and as a set of conventional expectations to be disturbingly undercut and shattered in the antinovels of Robbe-Grillet and the labyrinthine stories of Borges. Robbe-Grillet, Borges, and Nabokov use the classical detective formula like a distorting fun-house mirror to reflect more sharply the ambiguity, irrationality, and mystery of the world. Mysteries are created rather than solved in their works. Thus they become not only anti- but backward or inverted detective stories, a transcendence or rupturing of the formula.

That modern European and American cultures can produce and enjoy both the straight detective story and its ironic, absurd inversion is either a sign of profound cultural splits and tensions or of rich and diverse creativity or perhaps of both. Whether the classical detective formula will be able to assimilate its antithesis and still generate a new kind of mystery formula remains to be seen.

Six

The Hard-Boiled Detective Story

Hard-Boiled and Classical Detective Stories

In the early 1920s there emerged a detective story formula so different from the classical genre that it constituted a distinctive type. This formula was created by many authors, particularly those who wrote for the pulp magazine *Black Mask*. Dashiell Hammett, the most important, gave definite expression to the new formula in a series of novels published between 1929 and 1932. Since that time many detective story writers, good and bad, have followed what can best be labeled the hard-boiled formula. In mass popularity the hard-boiled story has far outstripped its classical predecessor. Of the major classical detective writers of the 1930s and 1940s, only Agatha Christie has regularly appeared on the best-seller lists, while Mickey Spillane has written several of the best-selling books of the twentieth century. The most prolific and successful of twentieth-century American mystery story writers, Erle Stanley Gardner, began his career by writing hard-boiled pulps for magazines like *Black Mask* and has reached an immense audience by combining important features of both classical and hard-boiled formulas in his Perry Mason and D. A. stories, while in his Donald Lam–Bertha Cool series he has created a more genteel and humorous form of the hard-boiled story. Other writers like Frederick Prather, Carter Brown, and Brett Halliday have sold millions of copies of straight hard-boiled adventure. And in the novels of Ross Macdonald the hard-boiled genre has reached a high level of artistic quality.

Few of the classical detectives have been successfully translated into radio, the movies, or television. Yet in the 1940s Hammett's *The Maltese Falcon* and *The Thin Man* and Chandler's *The Big Sleep* and *Farewell, My Lovely* were made into films of considerable artistic merit as well as box-office success. The detective heroes of these novels, Sam Spade, Nick Charles, and Philip Marlowe, also figured in successful radio dramas. When television developed, the hard-boiled hero was ready and waiting. In programs like "Peter Gunn," "77 Sunset Strip," and "Call Surfside 666," and more recently in "Cannon," "Barnaby Jones," and others, the hard-boiled formula proved that it could work with a very large public. Only the ever-popular western has kept pace with the hard-boiled formula in the suspense–adventure stakes.

Recently the private eye's popularity has been challenged by the spy, but it is obvious that contemporary spy adventures, as distinguished from the earlier thrillers of English writers like Buchan, Oppenheim, and Yates, have been strongly influenced by the hard-boiled tradition. Moreover, despite the success of James Bond, the novels of Mickey Spillane and his various imitators still sell in the millions. Hollywood continues to make private-eye films, some of which, like Jack Smight's *Harper*, Robert Altman's *The Long Goodbye*, and Roman Polanski's *Chinatown*, are comparable to the best hard-boiled films of the 1940s.

One of the most important aspects of the hard-boiled formula is the special role of the modern city as background. The importance of the city as a milieu for the detective story has been apparent from the very beginning when Poe's C. Auguste Dupin and his narrator-friend "sallied forth into the streets, arm in arm, continuing the topics of the day, or roaming far and wide until a late hour, seeking, amid the wild lights and shadows of the populous city that infinity of mental excitement which quiet observation can afford."[1] One can hardly imagine Doyle's Sherlock Holmes far from his famous lodgings at 221B Baker Street in late-Victorian London, surrounded by hansoms, fogs, the Baker Street Irregulars, and the varied and ever enchanting mysteries of a great urban area. True, the great detective and his later disciples in the works of writers like Dorothy Sayers, Margery Allingham, John Dickson Carr, Agatha Christie, and Michael Innes were occasionally lured out to isolated country mansions to contemplate a peculiarly strange and puzzling murder, but they themselves remained distinctly urban types, always bringing a touch of the city into sleepy little villages and desolate moors. Even in hot pursuit of the hound of the Baskervilles, Holmes, "in his tweed suit and cap . . . looked like any other tourist on the moor, and he had contrived, with that catlike love of personal cleanliness which was one of his characteristics, that his chin should be as smooth and his linen as perfect as if he were in Baker Street."[2] The relation between the detective story and the city was early noted by one of the formula's most brilliant practitioners, G. K. Chesterton, who argued that the most important reason for the detective story's cultural significance was its poetic treatment of the city:

> The first essential value of the detective story lies in this, that it is the earliest and only form of popular literature in which is expressed some sense of the poetry of modern life. Men lived among mighty mountains and eternal forests for ages before they realized that they were poetical; it may reasonably be inferred that some of our descendants may see the chimney-pots as rich a purple as the mountain-peaks, and find the lamp-posts as old and natural as the trees. Of this realization of a great city itself as something wild and obvious the detective story is certainly the "Iliad." No one can have failed to notice that in these stories the hero or the investigator crosses London with something of the loneliness and liberty of a prince in a tale of elfland, that in the course of that incalculable journey,

the casual omnibus assumes the primal colours of a fairy ship. The lights of the city begin to glow like innumerable goblin eyes, since they are the guardians of some secret, however crude, which the writer knows and the reader does not. Every twist of the road is like a finger pointing to it; every fantastic skyline of chimney-pots seems wildly and derisively signalling the meaning of the mystery.[3]

In many ways, this fantasy of the modern city as a place of exotic and romantic adventure, as the appropriate setting for a new version of the Arabian nights, permeates the classical detective story, particularly in its earlier phases in the later nineteenth century. We find it in the theme of the Asian conspiracy brought to the modern city that informs some of the great nineteenth-century tales of crime and detection such as Wilkie Collins's *Moonstone* and Doyle's *The Sign of Four*. The same theme, treated in a more sensational fashion, became the basis of one of the twentieth century's long-lived popular series of crime and detection, the Fu Manchu stories of Saxe Rohmer, first appearing in 1913. From Robert Louis Stevenson's *The New Arabian Nights* (1882) to John Dickson Carr's *The Arabian Nights Murder* (1936), this transformation of the city from a modern center of commerce, industry, and science into a place of enchantment and mystery where symbolic figures from the heroic past and the exotic East walk abroad has been one important aspect of the English or classical detective story.

When we step from the world of the classical detective formula into the milieu of the American hard-boiled story, the vision of the city is almost reversed. Instead of the new Arabian nights, we find empty modernity, corruption, and death. A gleaming and deceptive facade hides a world of exploitation and criminality in which enchantment and significance must usually be sought elsewhere, in what remains of the natural world still unspoiled by the pervasive spread of the city. Compare the following passage in which Raymond Chandler's hero Philip Marlowe describes a trip across the city with Chesterton's evocation of the investigator's journey across the city in which "the casual omnibus assumes the primal colours of a fairy ship."

We curved through the bright mile or two of the strip, past the antique shops with famous screen names on them, past the windows full of point lace and ancient pewter, past the gleaming new night clubs with famous chefs and equally famous gambling rooms, run by polished graduates of the Purple Gang, past the Georgian-Colonial vogue, now old hat, past the handsome modernistic buildings in which the Hollywood flesh-peddlers never stop talking money, past a drive-in lunch which somehow didn't belong, even though the girls wore white silk blouses and drum majorettes' shakos and nothing below the hips but glazed kid Hessian boots. Past all this and down a wide smooth curve to the bridle path of Beverly Hills and lights to the south, all colors of the spectrum and crystal clear in an evening without fog, past the shadowed mansions up on the hills to the north, past

Beverly Hills altogether and up into the twisting foothill boulevard and the sudden cool dusk and the drift of wind from the sea.[4]

It is interesting to note that some traces of the new Arabian nights fantasy still recur from time to time, but the following quotation will show how different even this theme has become in the American detective story:

> The bitch city is something different on Saturday night, sophisticated in black, scented and powdered, but somehow not as unassailable, shiveringly beautiful in a dazzle of blinking lights. Reds and oranges, electric blues and vibrant greens assault the eye incessantly, and the resultant turn-on is as sweet as a quick sharp fix in a penthouse pad, a liquid cool that conjures dreams of towering glass spires and enameled minarets. There is excitement in this city on Saturday night, but it is tempered by romantic expectancy, She is not a bitch, this city. Not on Saturday night.[5]

There is an Arabian enchantment here all right, but it is shot through with the undertones of assault, betrayal, and danger.

But, in order to reach a fuller understanding of the hard-boiled formula, we must search beyond the explicit characterizations of the urban milieu and try to analyze the whole complex of action, character, and setting that defines the narrative pattern. Most significantly, the creation of the hard-boiled pattern involved a shift in the underlying archetype of the detective story from the pattern of mystery to that of heroic adventure. Of course, some elements of the mystery archetype remained since the hero was still a detective solving crimes. To see how the archetypal pattern has been transformed we must compare the treatment of such major elements as the detective, the crime, the criminal, and the pattern of the action in the classical and hard-boiled formulas.

Patterns of the Formula

The hard-boiled formula resembles the main outlines of the classical detective story's pattern of action. It, too, moves from the introduction of the detective and the presentation of the crime, through the investigation, to a solution and apprehension of the criminal. Significant differences appear in the way this pattern is worked out in the hard-boiled story. Two are particularly important: the subordination of the drama of solution to the detective's quest for the discovery and accomplishment of justice; and the substitution of a pattern of intimidation and temptation of the hero for the elaborate development in the classical story of what Northrop Frye calls "the wavering finger of suspicion" passing across a series of potential suspects.

The hard-boiled detective sets out to investigate a crime but invariably finds that he must go beyond the solution to some kind of personal choice or action. While the classical writer typically treats the actual apprehension of the criminal as a less significant matter than the explanation of the crime, the hard-boiled story usually ends with a confrontation between detective and criminal. Sometimes this is a violent encounter similar to the climactic shootdown of many westerns. This difference in endings results from a greater personal involvement on the part of the hard-boiled detective. Since he becomes emotionally and morally committed to some of the persons involved, or because the crime poses some basic crisis in his image of himself, the hard-boiled detective remains unfulfilled until he has taken a personal moral stance toward the criminal. In simpler hard-boiled stories like those of Spillane, the detective, having solved the crime, acts out the role of judge and executioner. In the more complex stories of Raymond Chandler and Dashiell Hammett, the confrontation between detective and criminal is less violent and more psychological. In both cases we find the detective forced to define his own concept of morality and justice, frequently in conflict with the social authority of the police. Where the classical detective's role was to use his superior intellect and psychological insight to reveal the hidden guilt that the police seemed unable to discover, the hard-boiled detective metes out the just punishment that the law is too mechanical, unwieldy, or corrupt to achieve. As Mike Hammer puts it in his forthright way:

> By Christ, I'm not letting the killer go through the tedious process of the law. You know what happens, damn it. They get the best lawyer there is and screw up the whole thing and wind up a hero! . . . No, damn it. A jury is cold and impartial like they're supposed to be, while some snotty lawyer makes them pour tears as he tells how his client was insane at the moment or had to shoot in self-defense. Swell. The law is fine. But this time I'm the law and I'm not going to be cold and impartial.[6]

Chandler's Philip Marlowe, a bit more subtly, also views the law as an impediment to the accomplishment of true justice:

> Let the law enforcement people do their own dirty work. Let the lawyers work it out. They write the laws for other lawyers to dissect in front of other lawyers called judges so that other judges can say the first judges were wrong and the Supreme Court can say the second lot were wrong. Sure there's such a thing as law. We're up to our necks in it. About all it does is make business for lawyers.[7]

Because the hard-boiled detective embodies the threat of judgment and execution as well as exposure, the pressure against his investigation is invariably more violent than in the classical story. Philip Marlowe, Sam Spade, Mike Hammer, and the rest are threatened by physical violence to a degree unknown to the classical detective whose activities are largely confined to the examination of clues, the taking of testimony, and the reconstruction of the crime. The hard-boiled detective faces assault, capture, drugging, blackjacking, and attempted assassination as a regular feature of his investigations. Moreover, he is frequently threatened with loss of his license or tempted with bribes of various kinds to halt his investigations, for the criminal is commonly a person of considerable political and social influence. Inevitably there comes a point in the hard-boiled detective's investigation when he can lament with Philip Marlowe: "I get it from the law, I get it from the hoodlum element, I get it from the carriage trade. The words change, but the meaning is the same. Lay off."[8]

These two differences of emphasis—the detective becoming judge as well as investigator, and the intimidation and temptation of the detective—shape the pattern of action in the hard-boiled story into a formula different in many respects from its classical counterpart. Like the classical story, we usually begin with the introduction of the detective, but instead of the charming bachelor apartment of Holmes and Watson, or the elegant establishment of Lord Peter Wimsey, the hard-boiled detective belongs to the dusty and sordid atmosphere of an office located in a broken-down building on the margin of the city's business district. Sometimes the story begins in this office but, more often, the detective is already in motion to the scene of the crime, on his way to visit a client, or, like Philip Marlowe in the opening to *Farewell, My Lovely*, simply sucked violently in:

> The doors swung back outwards and almost settled to a stop. Before they had entirely stopped moving they opened again, violently, outwards. Something sailed across the sidewalk and landed in the gutter between two parked cars. . . . A hand I could have sat in came out of the dimness and took hold of my shoulder and squashed it to a pulp. Then the hand moved me through the doors and casually lifted me up a step. . . . The big man stared at me solemnly and went on wrecking my shoulder with his hand.[9]

Sometimes instead of plunging the hero immediately into violence, the story opens in a context of decadent wealth. *The Big Sleep* begins with Marlowe visiting rich old General Sternwood in a hothouse atmosphere redolent of corruption and death:

> The air was thick, wet, steamy and larded with the cloying smell of tropical orchids in bloom. The glass walls and roof were heavily misted and big drops of moisture splashed down on the plants. The light had an unreal greenish color, like light filtered through an aquarium tank. The plants filled the place, a forest of them, with nasty meaty leaves and stalks like the newly washed fingers of dead men.[10]

These opening scenes immediately establish a number of the central motifs of the hard-boiled story. We see the detective as a marginal professional carrying on his business from the kind of office associated with unsuccessful dentists, small mail-order businesses, and shyster lawyers. However, we soon realize that he has chosen this milieu. His way of life may look like failure, but actually it is a form of rebellion, a rejection of the ordinary concepts of success and respectability:

> The other part of me wanted to get out and stay out, but this was the part I never listened to. Because if I ever had I would have stayed in the town where I was born and worked in the hardware store and married the boss's

daughter and had five kids and read them the funny paper on Sunday morning and smacked their heads when they got out of line and squabbled with the wife about how much spending money they were to get and what programs they could have on the radio and TV set. I might even have got rich—small town rich, an eight-room house, two cars in the garage, chicken every Sunday and the Reader's Digest on the living room table, the wife with a cast-iron permanent and me with a brain like a sack of Portland cement. You take it, friend.[11]

Or as Shell Scott puts it:

I suppose I should be—oh, more orthodox. Nose to the old grindstone, up at the croak of dawn, charge around with an expression of severe pain on my face. Like right now, for example. But that wouldn't be *me*, and if I lost me, where would I be.[12]

The beginning of the hard-boiled story usually represents both this marginal, rebellious aspect of the hero and his capacity to function effectively in a world of wealth, corruption, and violence. Since his office is scruffy and his salary and mode of life that of the lower middle class we see the detective not as a brilliant eccentric with transcendent powers of ratiocination but as an ordinary man. At the same time the opening incidents reveal that his commonness is a mask for uncommon qualities. For this antihero, this seemingly frustrated and cynical failure knows how to handle himself in the midst of violence. The rich, the powerful, and the beautiful desperately need his help with their problems.

As the pattern of action develops, the rich, the powerful, and the beautiful attempt to draw the detective into their world and to use him for their own corrupt purposes. He in turn finds that the process of solving the crime involves him in the violence, deceit, and corruption that lies beneath the surface of the respectable world. Lew Archer enters on his investigation in *The Doomsters* with a typical hard-boiled reflection on what he knows will come of his quest:

We passed a small-boat harbor, gleaming white on blue, and a long pier draped with fishermen. Everything was as pretty as a postcard. The trouble with you, I said to myself: you're always turning over the postcards and reading the message on the underside. Written in invisible ink, in blood, in tears with a black border around them, with postage due, unsigned, or signed with a thumbprint.[13]

As in the classical story, the introduction of the hard-boiled detective leads immediately to the presentation of the crime, but substantial differences in the treatment of the crime give it rather different implications. The classical detective generally faces a *fait accompli*. The crime has left behind its mysterious clues. The detective is called to the quarantined site and challenged to expose the hidden guilt. This proceeding emphasizes the abnormality and isolation of the crime, its detachment from the detective and the reader. The hard-boiled story, on the other hand, typically implicates the detective in the crime from the very beginning. In many hard-boiled stories, the detective is given a mission—usually a deceptive one—which seemingly has little to do with murder and violence. Pursuing this mission, the detective happens upon the first of a series of murders that gradually reveal to him the true nature of his quest. In this way, the hard-boiled detective's investigation becomes not simply a matter of determining who the guilty person is but of defining his own moral position. For example, Sam Spade in *The Maltese Falcon* is asked by a beautiful young lady to investigate the disappearance of her sister. While pursuing this investigation, Spade's partner is mysteriously murdered. Then Sam himself is confronted by a mysterious Levantine who first asks him puzzling questions about a bird and then attempts to hold him up and search his office. Gradually events accumulate, more murders take place, and additional mysterious characters are introduced. The shape of Sam's mission keeps changing from the search for the client's sister, to the investigation of his partner's death, to the hunt for the falcon until finally it turns out that his real problem is not to find the killer but what to do about a woman he has fallen in love with and who has turned out to be a murderess. A similarly shifting definition of the detective's mission occurs in many Mike Hammer stories. In *The Body Lovers*, Mike undertakes to locate the sister of a convict. His investigations lead to a ring of rich and powerful sadists who get their kicks from torture-murders. But with this discovery the problem changes, for the sadist group is largely made up of UN diplomats from the Middle East who have "diplomatic immunity" and therefore cannot be punished by the police. Finally, Mike must take up his usually climactic role of personal judge and executioner and work out some way of blowing up the dirty foreigners. It only remains to be added that in a fashion almost invariable to Spillane but common to the hard-boiled story, Mike discovers that the beautiful and fashionable woman who has thrown herself at his feet is actually the procuress for the sadist ring. In the end, like Sam Spade, Mike faces a personal moral and emotional decision: must he destroy the woman he loves but who has turned out to be a vicious killer? That Mike has so little trouble with such decisions suggests some of the more disturbing psychological undercurrents of the hard-boiled story.

Thus, while the classical detective's investigation typically passes over a variety of possible suspects until it lights at last on the least-likely person, his hard-boiled counterpart becomes emotionally involved in a complex process of changing implications. Everything changes its meaning: the initial mission turns out to be a smoke screen for another, more devious plot; the supposed victim turns out to be a villain; the lover ends up as the murderess and the faithful friend as a rotten betrayer; the police and the distict attorney and often even the client keep trying to halt the investigation; and all the seemingly respectable and succesful people turn out to be members of the gang. While all these discoveries of the villainy of the seemingly innocent, the duplicity of the seemingly faithful, and the corruption of the seemingly respectable do not occur in every hard-boiled story, what can be called the rhythm of exposure is almost invariable in one form or another. In many ways this rhythm is the antithesis of the classical story where the detective always shows that the corruption is isolated and specific rather than general and endemic to the social world of the story.

Like the classical story, the hard-boiled formula develops four main character roles: (a) the victim or victims; (b) the criminal; (c) the detective; and (d) those involved in the crime but incapable of resolving the problems it poses, a group involving police, suspects, and so on—in effect, the set of characters who represent society in the story. To this set of relationships, the hard-boiled formula very often adds one central role, that of the female betrayer.

I have already noted the characteristic multiplicity of victims in the hard-boiled story. While the classical story typically maintains an emotional detachment from the victim by making him relatively obscure and by stressing the complicated and exotic circumstances surrounding his death instead of its brutality and violence, the hard-boiled story more often encourages readers to feel strongly about the crimes by eliminating most of the complex machinery of clues. Often, the initial victim is a friend of the detective or some other person whose death seems not simply mysterious but regrettable. For example, in *The Maltese Falcon* the first victim is the detective's partner; in *The Big Sleep* he is a noble and handsome son-in-law much loved by the detective's client; in *I, the Jury* he is the detective's best friend. In many stories, the emotion roused by the sympathetic victim is intensified by a threat to the detective or one of his friends. Mike Hammer's beautiful secretary Velda commonly faces a horrible fate at the hands of the criminal before she is rescued by the opportune appearance of her boss. (The criminal here nearly succeeds in carrying out what the detective can never quite steel himself to perform: violation of the ideal and chaste sweetheart and companion.)

The sympathetic victim and the threat to the detective stimulate the reader's feelings of hostility toward the criminal and his wish for the detective to pass beyond solutions and attributions of guilt to the judgment and execution of the criminal. In contrast to the classical pattern of making the criminal a relatively obscure, marginal figure, a "least-likely" person, the hard-boiled criminal usually plays a central role, sometimes *the* central role after the detective. Since Dashiell Hammett first created the pattern in *The Maltese Falcon*, one hard-boiled detective after another has found himself romantically or sexually involved with the murderess. In other hard-boiled stories, the criminal turns out to be a close friend of the detective, as in *The Dain Curse*, where the criminal has been in a Watson-like association with the detective throughout the story. In this respect the pattern of the hard-boiled story is almost antithetical to the classical formula. In Agatha

Christie, Dorothy Sayers, and their fellow writers, sympathetically interesting or romantic characters frequently appear to be guilty in the middle of the story but are invariably shown to be innocent when the detective finally unveils the solution. (The great prototype of all such stories is Wilkie Collins's *The Moonstone* where the two lovers are successively suspected and exonerated of the crime.) In Dorothy Sayers's *Strong Poison*, for example, Harriet Vane, with whom Lord Peter Wimsey falls in love (a gesture rather uncharacteristic of the classical detective), is thought to be guilty of a murder. The action of the story focuses on Lord Peter's successful demonstration of her innocence. The exact opposite is the case in *I, the Jury*, where the detective's romantic object is the one character who appears to be innocent throughout most of the story but who is finally revealed as the killer.

Thus the hard-boiled criminal plays a complex and ambiguous role while the classical villain remains an object of pursuit hiding behind a screen of mysterious clues until the detective finally reveals his identity. The hard-boiled villain is frequently disguised as a friend or lover, adding to the crimes an attempted betrayal of the detective's loyalty and love; when revealed, this treachery becomes the climax of that pattern of threat and temptation noted earlier. To support this pattern of threatened betrayal, the hard-boiled criminal is often characterized as particularly vicious, perverse, or depraved, and, in a striking number of instances as a woman of unusual sexual attractiveness. Facing such a criminal, the detective's role changes from classical ratiocination to self-protection against the various threats, temptations, and betrayals posed by the criminal.

A second important characteristic of the hard-boiled culprit is his involvement with the criminal underworld. Rarely is the classical criminal more than a single individual with a rational and specific motive to commit a particular crime. The hard-boiled criminal, on the other hand, usually has some connection with a larger criminal organization. Sometimes, as in Dashiell Hammett's *Red Harvest*, the detective's mission is to battle a criminal syndicate that has taken over a town. More characteristically, the criminal is a highly respectable member of society whose perverse acts have involved him with the underworld. In *The Big Sleep*, Carmen, the daughter of the wealthy General Sternwood, has killed Rusty Regan in a pathological sexual rage. Her sister has called on a local racketeer to help dispose of the body and to cover up the crime. By the time Marlowe enters the story, the racketeer has moved in to blackmail the Sternwood family. Marlowe finds that he must cope not only with Carmen's perversities but with the threats and attacks of a gang of racketeers somehow connected with the wealthy and respectable Sternwoods. This, as we have seen, is the typical hard-boiled pattern of action: the detective is called in to investigate a seemingly simple thing, like a disappearance; his investigation comes up against a web of conspiracy that reflects the presence of a hidden criminal organization; finally, the track leads back to the rich and respectable levels of society and exposes the corrupt relationship between the pillars of the community and the criminal underground.

What sort of a hero confronts, exposes, and destroys this web of conspiracy and perversion? Like many formula heroes, the hard-boiled detective is a synthesis of antithetical traits. Where the classical detective combined scientific ratiocination with poetic intuition, the hard-boiled detective's character paradoxically mixes cynicism and honor, brutality and sentimentality, failure and success. The hard-boiled detective is first and foremost a tough guy. He can dish it out and he can take it. Accustomed to a world of physical violence, corruption, and treachery, the detective's hard and bitter experience shows in his face:

> Samuel Spade's jaw was long and bony, his chin a jutting v under the more flexible v of his mouth. His nostrils curved back to make another, smaller, v. His yellow-grey eyes were horizontal. The v *motif* was picked up again by thickish brows rising outward from twin creases above a hooked nose, and his pale brown hair grew down—from high flat temples—in a point on his forehead. He looked rather pleasantly like a blond satan.[14]

Even an exotic costume cannot hide the rugged and battered look of a later avatar of Sam Spade like Shell Scott:

> The effect of sheer beauty was perhaps marred only by the bent-down-at-the-ends inverted-V eyebrows over my gray eyes, since those brows were also obtrusively white.... And naturally, nothing could be done about my twice-broken and still bent nose, the bullet-clipped ear top, the fine scar over my right eye, and the general impression of recent catastrophe I've been told I sometimes present.[15]

Behind this face, the detective's mind has become knowing about the persuasive corruption of society. Unlike the classical detective, for whom evil is an abnormal disruption of an essentially benevolent social order caused by a specific set of criminal motives, the hard-boiled detective has learned through long experience that evil is endemic to the social order:

> "When I went into police work in 1935, I believed that evil was a quality some people were born with, like a harelip. A cop's job was to find those people and put them away. But evil isn't so simple. Everybody has it in him, and whether it comes out in his actions depends on a number of things...."
> "Do you judge people?"
> "Everybody I meet. The graduates of the police schools make a big thing of scientific detection, and that has its place. But most of my work is watching people, and judging them."
> "And you find evil in everybody?"
> "Just about. Either I'm getting sharper or people are getting worse. And that could be. War and inflation always raise a crop of stinkers, and a lot of them have settled in California."[16]

Philip Marlowe explains the inescapable relation between crime and society:

> "Crime isn't a disease. It's a symptom. We're a big rough rich wild people
> and crime is the price we pay for it, and organized crime is the price we pay
> for organization. We'll have it with us a long time. Organized crime is just
> the dirty side of the sharp dollar."
> "What's the clean side?"
> "I never saw it."[17]

In this respect, Mike Hammer's world is much the same. As one of his news-
paperman friends puts it, "in every man's past there's some dirt."[18]

Though his sense of an all-pervasive evil and violence is similar, a writer
with right-wing political leanings like Mickey Spillane dramatizes the cause
of the corruption as the worldwide Communist conspiracy, with its American dupes. More recently, with the improvement of Soviet-American relationships, Spillane seems to have shifted his animus to other foreign sources.
His 1967 *The Body Lovers* projected corruption onto a group of middle
eastern sadist-diplomats centered at the UN. But whatever the specific foreign
source, the evil encountered by Mike Hammer most frequently manifests
itself in that same group of internationalist-minded, upper-class, intellectual
easterners that Senator Joseph McCarthy and his disciples used to attack. A
more liberal writer like Raymond Chandler ascribes the evil to American
materialism and greed, rather than to some foreign source of corruption.
Dashiell Hammett, despite his radical political leanings, implies a more
philosophical basis for the detective's sense of a world full of evil in a
pessimistic vision of the universe that goes beyond the parochial political
animosities and frustrations of Spillane. But whether his vision of evil is
political or metaphysical, the hard-boiled detective has rejected the ordinary
social and ethical pieties and faces a world that he has learned to understand
as fundamentally corrupt, violent, and hostile. To put it more abstractly, he
is a man who has accepted up to a point the naturalistic view of society and
the universe and whose general attitude toward society and God resembles
that alienation so often and fashionably described as the predicament of
"modern man."

As R. V. Cassil suggests, modern democratic man "uses the fiction of
violence for its purgative effect [but] what needs to be noted is that whatever
his brow level, he doesn't really want to be purged very hard. Not really
scoured . . ."[19] So, the hard-boiled detective, below his surface of alienated
skepticism and toughness, tends to be as soft as they come. No one has
asserted the essential sentimentality as well as the power of the conception of
the hard-boiled detective more eloquently than Raymond Chandler, one of
his major creators:

> Down these mean streets a man must go who is not himself mean, who is
> neither tarnished nor afraid. The detective in this kind of story must be
> such a man. He is the hero, he is everything. He must be a complete man

and a common man and yet an unusual man. He must be, to use a rather weathered phrase, a man of honor, . . ."[20]

Chandler's characterization suggests that though the hard-boiled detective's world bears some resemblance to the bitter, godless universe of writers like Crane, Dreiser, and Hemingway, his personal qualities also bear more than a little resemblance to the chivalrous knights of Sir Walter Scott. Not above seducing, beating, and even, on occasion, shooting members of the opposite sex, he saves this treatment for those who have gone bad. Toward good girls his attitude is as chaste as a Victorian father. The very thought of anyone touching his virginal secretary Velda reduces Mike Hammer to a gibbering homicidal mania. Such knightly attitudes determine much of the hard-boiled detective's behavior: he is an instinctive protector of the weak, a defender of the innocent, an avenger of the wronged, the one loyal, honest, truly moral man in a corrupt and ambiguous world.[21]

Despite his involvement in the contemporary urban metropolis, the hard-boiled detective's ethical attitudes and modes of judgment usually evoke some earlier era, most commonly the chivalric code of the feudal past, though sometimes, as in the case of Mickey Spillane, a more primitive tribal ethos of vendetta. In this respect, the hard-boiled detective greatly resembles the western hero whose moral code also transcends the existing social order. Like the western hero, the tough-guy detective's action-oriented code of honor enables him to act in a violent world without losing his moral purity and force. Though the hard-boiled detective remains a marginal man, a loner, who must end his cases by returning to his dusty office in the broken-down office building—an act analogous to the cowboy hero's departure back into the desert—his unsullied isolation and failure maintain the purity of his stance as a man of honor in a false society:

> If being in revolt against a corrupt society constitutes being immature, then Philip Marlowe is immature. If seeing dirt where there is dirt constitutes an inadequate social adjustment, then Philip Marlowe has inadequate social adjustment. Of course Marlowe is a failure and usually he knows it . . . . But a lot of very good men have been failures because their particular talents did not suit their time and place.[22]

The intensely moral stance that lies behind the facade of toughness and cynicism accounts for many of the characteristic differences in method between the hard-boiled and classical detectives. For the hard-boiled detective, a case is not merely a problem; it can become a crusade to root out and destroy the evils that have corrupted the urban world.

> I've been almost anxious to get to some of the rats that make up the section of humanity that prey on people. People. How incredibly stupid they could be sometimes. A trial by law for a killer. A loophole in the phrasing that lets a killer crawl out. But in the end the people have their justice.

> They get it through guys like me once in a while. They crack down on
> society and I crack down on them. I shoot them like the mad dogs they are
> and society drags me to court to explain the whys and wherefores of the
> extermination.[23]

Mike Hammer's vigilante ideal of justice is, as usual, a flat-footed, simple-
minded statement of the hard-boiled detective's mission that would probably
disgust more subtle and humane detectives like Philip Marlowe and Lew
Archer who are both more reluctant about their causes and not motivated by
Mike's pathological blood-lust. Yet, though more ironically treated, their
actions also take on the shape of a personal crusade against evil. After telling
off the county sheriff ("Something that looks like law and talks like law but
doesn't smell like law. Not in my nostrils. It smells like zombie meat. A
zombie that takes the public's money and sits behind a courthouse desk
pretending to be an officer") and having his wounds sewn up, Lew Archer
remarks:

> When I left his office, I had a powerful impulse to climb into my car and
> drive away from Las Cruces and never come back. I couldn't think of a
> single solid reason for staying. So I drove across town to the courthouse,
> accompanied by my Messianic complex.[24]

In short, the hard-boiled detective is a traditional man of virtue in an
amoral and corrupt world. His toughness and cynicism form a protective
coloration protecting the essence of his character, which is honorable and
noble. In a world where the law is inefficient and susceptible to corruption,
where the recognized social elite is too decadent and selfish to accomplish
justice and protect the innocent, the private detective is forced to take over
the basic moral functions of exposure, protection, judgment, and execution.

In the classical detective story, most of the minor characters function as
suspects who are eventually exonerated from guilt when the true criminal is
revealed. These characters play a different role in the hard-boiled story. Here,
since the detective is engaged in a crusade as well as an investigation, the
minor characters must be either for him or against him. Two groups emerge.
The first consists of those who seem respectable at first, but turn out to be
involved in the pervasive corruption of society if not directly in the crime
itself. These characters confront the detective with the various threats and
temptations to "lay off" that he must resist in order to carry out his mission.
Much of the drama of the story consists in the detective's eventual putting
down or exposing these characters. The other group of minor characters
function as friends or allies. They help the detective to solve the crime and
certify his worth by judging him a good man despite his facade of brutality
and amorality. The cynical but honest reporter is a favorite figure for this
role of friend and confidant to the detective, because he can be presented as a
man who has seen the sordid side of life and is frustrated by his inability to do
anything about it. The honest ex-policeman who has been fired for trying to
do his job and even the noble racketeer, a male version of the respectable

prostitute, also turn up on occasion as allies. Whatever the type, the essential characteristic of the detective's allies is their disgust with society's corruption and their recognition of the inherent virtue under the detective's cynical exterior.

Sometimes even the police can serve as the detective's allies. In the relationship between Mike Hammer and police lieutenant Pat Chambers, Pat upholds the legal method of dealing with criminals and tries to persuade Mike to modify his methods. But, though individual policemen may befriend the detective, the police as an institution are presented as incapable of dealing with the pervasive evil, because the law is too decadent to mete out true justice. The hard-boiled detective's relationship to the police is inevitably competitive and hostile. Sometimes the classical detective had his problems with the police, but more often than not their differences are ironed out once the detective shows that he intends to do the same thing as the police in a more efficient manner: to determine the identity of the hidden criminal. Contrarily, the hard-boiled detective soon finds out that his aims do not coincide with those of the police. He seeks justice. The police, by insisting on the tortuous routines of legality, cannot achieve justice in a society pervaded by evil. Occasionally the corruption of the police manifests itself in a literal way. In Macdonald's *Find a Victim* or Chandler's *Lady in the Lake*, the police officer tries to prevent the detective from solving the crime because, as it turns out, the policeman's wife or girl friend is the murderess. More often, the police represent symbolically the limitations, inadequacies, and subtle corruption of the institutions of law and order:

> A man named Nulty got the case, a lean-jawed sourpuss with long yellow hands which he kept folded over his kneecaps most of the time he talked to me. He was a detective-lieutenant attached to the 77th Street Division and we talked in a bare room with two small desks against opposite walls and room to move between them, if two people didn't try it at once. Dirty brown linoleum covered the floor and the smell of old cigar butts hung in the air. Nulty's shirt was frayed and his coat sleeves had been turned in at the cuffs. He looked poor enough to be honest, but he didn't look like a man who could deal with Moose Malloy.[25]

A most striking difference between the character patterns of classical and hard-boiled detective formulas comes from the role of women in the latter type. As I have noted, the classical detective rarely becomes romantically or sexually involved. Sexual attractiveness, however, is one of the key characteristics of the private eye, and there are few stories in which he does not play either seducer or seduced. But sex tends to be represented in a double-edged way in the hard-boiled story. It is an object of pleasure, yet it also has a disturbing tendency to become a temptation, a trap, and a betrayal. Two important aspects of the portrayal of women in the hard-boiled novel appear to be connected with this paradoxical combination of attraction and fear. First of all, the desirable and disturbing female is usually presented as blonde and big-breasted, or rather I should say aggressive-breasted, since the favorite metaphorical description has the woman's large breasts thrusting against her clothing. "She threatened him with her pointed breasts," as Mike Shayne's creator put it.[26] This combination of qualities inevitably suggests a latent symbolism that combines the images of virginity (the chaste woman in the nineteenth-century novel was commonly portrayed as blonde in opposition to the more lubricious and sexually active brunette) and motherhood (large, thrusting breasts). This may sound like overreading, but such symbolism is consistent with the combination of pleasure and threat that hovers around the hard-boiled detective's sexual relationships. The second theme in the presentation of women is a fear of feminine aggression and domination (again those aggressive breasts), which often manifests itself in the plot in the form of the terrifying female murderess but also appears in such smaller details as Mike Hammer's description of the office of a woman's fashion magazine:

> The two harried little men I saw scuttled around like mice in a house full of cats, forcing badgered smiles at the dominant females who wore their hats like crowns, performing their insignificant tasks meticulously, gratefully acknowledging the curt nods of their overlords with abundant thank you's. What was missing were the whips on the wall. The damn place was a harem and they were eunuchs. One looked at me as if I were a peddler who came to the front door of the mansion, was about to ask me my business when he caught the reproving eye of the receptionist and drifted off without a word.[27]

The evident passion behind this description, so much more intense than most of Spillane's rather wooden prose, and the curious combination of harem and mansion connotations suggest that the intense masculinity of the hard-boiled detective is in part a symbolic denial and protective coloration against complex sexual and status anxieties focusing on women. The function of the woman in the hard-boiled formula then is not simply that of appropriate sexual consort to the dashing hero; she also poses certain basic challenges to the detective's physical and psychological security. These challenges frequently serve as the climax to the pattern of temptation, threat, and bribery I have already defined and thereby lead to the most brutal violence of the story.

The setting of the hard-boiled detective story resembles nothing so much as a world born out of a curious marriage between the muckraking of Lincoln Steffens and the lyrical sterility and sordidness of T. S. Eliot's "Waste Land," shading off at times into the glamorous high life of *Playboy* or its earlier avatar, *Esquire*. It is a world of lurking dangers but also a fast-moving, frenetic scene appropriate to the furious pace for which most hard-boiled writers strive. In case after case, the private eye is on the move without respite from the beginning to the end. It is almost invariably an urban world, particularly the kind of swinging, sprawling, rapidly changing, disorganized but glamorous American city epitomized by Los Angeles, though a few hard-boiled detectives continue to operate out of New York and one of them centers his activities on Miami. Only such cities represent the combination of corruption and glamour necessary to produce the situations and set the tempo that seem indispensable to the hard-boiled detective story.

That this modern urban world is profoundly decadent and that the key to its decadence is a link between crime and respectability seem articles of faith for most hard-boiled writers. Thus at the same time that their stories celebrate a tough and brutal hero whose native milieu is the twentieth-century American city, they anatomize and condemn that city's endemic violence and cynicism. Indeed, the hard-boiled writers frequently sound like disciples of Lincoln Steffens excoriating *The Shame of Our Cities* and exposing the unholy alliance between business, politics, and organized crime:

> The realist in murder writes of a world in which gangsters can rule nations and almost rule cities, in which hotels and apartment houses and celebrated restaurants are owned by men who make their money out of brothels, in which a screen star can be the fingerman for a mob, and the nice man down the hall is a boss of the numbers racket; a world where a judge with a cellar full of bootleg liquor can send a man to jail for having a pint in his pocket, where the mayor of your town may have condoned murder as an instrument of money-making, where no man can walk down a dark street in safety because law and order are things we talk about but refrain from practicing.[28]

The city as wasteland, as a man-made desert or cavern of lost humanity, is a major theme in the landscape of the hard-boiled detective story:

> The morning was colored a New York gray, damp with river fog that held in suspension the powdered grime and acid grit the city seemed to exhale with its breathing process. It came from deep inside as its belly rumbled with early life, and from the open wounds in its surface where antlike people rebuilt its surface. Everyone seemed oblivious to the noise, never distinguishing between the pain sounds and the pleasure sounds. They simply followed a pattern, their own feet wearing ruts that grew deeper and deeper until there was no way they could get out of the trap they had laid for themselves.[29]

Yet, for all its sterility, this landscape has its moments of glamour, though even these tend to be a bit uncomfortable, subtly hostile, or somehow misleading and out of place. In the following description of an exotic new hotel in the desert outside of Los Angeles, the theme of disturbingly aggressive and ambiguous feminine sexuality becomes inextricably associated with the untrustworthy glamour of the city:

> First I saw the huge central dome, as smooth and sensually rounded as a woman's breast, then a few tall and subtly phallic spires almost but not quite like Indian minarets. And green all around it—green of grass, of

trees, of feathery palm fronds and large-leafed plants. It was truly a beautiful sign, but strangely jarring. After the modern streets of Palm Springs, the smart shops and almost futuristic buildings, this looked like something slipped from a warp in time, unreal in the California desert.[30]

At its best, the hard-boiled detective story is as brilliantly atmospheric as the gothic novel. But the symbols of terror have undergone a major shift. Instead of the gothic castle, lair of a diabolical, aristocratic, and masculine villain, danger and betrayal emanate from the city and are most often manifested in an ambiguously attractive and dangerous woman who sets out to seduce the hero in order to prevent him from discovering that she is the murderess. Two aspects of this change are worth noting. First, the location of the gothic villain in an isolated castle or monastery and his connection with aristocracy or church suggests that evil lies outside of the ordinary patterns of society. Evil represents the threat of transcendent diabolical forces of or traditional aristocracy to an essentially harmonious and benevolent bourgeois society. In the hard-boiled detective story, however, evil has become endemic and pervasive; it has begun to crumble the very pillars of middle-class society, respectable citizens, the modern metropolis, and the institutions of law and order. Indeed, evil seems particularly embodied in one of the central phenomena of the bougeois revolution, the new woman. This transformation of symbols, by the way, has not been limited to the hard-boiled detective story. Contemporary gothic fiction even shows its influence. The recent best-seller *Rosemary's Baby* is a good example. Instead of a mysterious castle in the Apennines, the action takes place in an old apartment house in New York City, one of those symbols of Victorian bourgeois elegance now in decay. And the villains, though they represent a transcendent Satanic evil, are seemingly the most ordinary middle-aged midwesterners, not unlike those retired farmers or small-towners from Iowa who turn up on the West Coast in Chandler's or Macdonald's hard-boiled stories.

The second aspect that stands out from the comparison of gothic and hard-boiled stories is the transformation of woman from victim to villain. While there are female villains in the gothic novel and male murderers in the hard-boiled story, the contrary is more usually the case. There can be no question that the figure whose honor is at stake in the hard-boiled story is not some palpitating female but the detective himself, and the character who threatens that honor by distracting the detective's attention from the quest for justice, even when she does not turn out to be the murderess, is the woman.

Cultural Background of the Formula

The urban world of the hard-boiled detective story is, then, a surface of specious and ambiguous glamour hiding depths of corruption. It is ruled by a secret alliance between the rich and respectable and the criminal underworld.

Insofar as the police are honest and decent, they are helpless to attack the real criminals. The city is also a place of strong sexual temptation and excitement, but this very sexuality, embodied in stunningly attractive and seemingly approachable women, is a source of betrayal and of fundamental attacks on masculinity. The hero who confronts this nightmare world is a figure whose basic characteristics identify him with the lower middle class, those condemned by their lack of economic mobility to inhabit the decaying center of this urban society. He is a marginal professional with a smattering of culture, but on the whole his tastes and attitudes are ordinary. He is surrounded by continual threats to his safety and even his status. His sexual identity and masculine certitude is constantly being put on the line and threatened with betrayal and destruction. Yet the hard-boiled hero is potent and courageous. Though he must continually face the fears of loneliness and isolation, of status uncertainty and of sexual betrayal, he is the kind of man who can fight his way to the source of the pervasive evil and, meeting violence with violence, destroy it. In the process of his quest, he also lays bare the widespread corruption of the social order, thereby proving and maintaining his own moral integrity.

The hard-boiled detective has chosen this way of life because honor and integrity mean more to him than fame and fortune. This insistence upon honor dominates both the nature of his quest and his relationship with his employers. The private eye resists the temptation to perform lucrative investigative work in favor of the lonely and personal quest for justice. Philip Marlowe, for example, refuses to do divorce work and he is never so happy as when he is acting not for an employer but for himself. The hard-boiled detective usually has an employer, but in the long run he refuses to let the client shape either the goals or the methods of his investigation. Telling the boss off is as important to the private eye as exposing the corruption of the rich and respectable, and many hard-boiled novels have central scenes in which the confrontation of employer and hero results in the putting down of the client. In such actions, the hero indicates his rejection of the drive for success by refusing to conform to the employer's authority. In effect, the hard-boiled detective refuses to become a successful but conformist executive. Instead, he demonstrates that those who have achieved wealth and status are weak, dishonorable, and corrupt.

We must be careful not to take the hero's rejection of success too seriously. Despite his attack on the authority of the rich and respectable, the private eye always wins. His exploits are written up in the newspaper, his bravery is applauded by an admiring female companion, and he usually receives a solid fee for his services. In this sense, the hard-boiled story also affirms the basic success ideology. The private eye's quest seems not so much a criticism of success as a means of resolving the anxieties of the success ethic by imagining a model character whose actions demonstrate that the successful are corrupt, while at the same time he achieves the rewards of success by maintaining his honor and integrity. For individuals who feel frustrated and anxious that they have not succeeded and yet are unable to transcend the basic imperatives of the success ethic, the attractions of this model for fantasy seem clear.

The real hostility of the hard-boiled story is directed toward women and the rich. Moreover, the animosity generated by these objects is ambiguously mixed with attraction and desire. In the fourth chapter I suggested that the emphasis on the externalization and specification of guilt in the classical story created an escape formula that temporarily resolved the pressure of guilt feelings in a personality dominated by an internalized standard of personal achievement. The hostility toward women and the rich with its mixture of attraction and repulsion in the hard-boiled story seems to reflect a tension more characteristic of what David Riesman calls the other-directed personality type.

As Riesman defines it, other-directed personalities are marked by a much greater sensitivity to the attitudes and values of others:

> Under these newer [other-directed] patterns the peer-group (the group of one's associates of the same age and class) becomes much more important to the child, while the parents make him feel guilty not so much about violation of inner standards as about failure to be popular or otherwise to manage his relations with these other children. Moreover, the pressures of the school and the peer-group are reinforced and continued ... by the mass media: movies, radio, comics, and popular culture media generally.[31]

This learned sensitivity to peer-group opinions, this internal radar system as Riesman characterizes it, means that the other-directed personality has no clear and fixed pattern of values. Instead, he feels himself pressured to shift his attitudes and values each time he encounters a new group in the process of his life.

> The goals toward which the other-directed person strives shift with that guidance: it is only the process of striving itself and the process of paying close attention to the signals from others that remain unaltered throughout life. This mode of keeping in touch with others permits a close behavioral conformity, not through drill in behavior itself, as in the tradition-directed character, but rather through an exceptional sensitivity to the actions and wishes of others.[32]

For the person who succeeds in responding to the cues and conforming to the demands of his various peer-groups the rewards are considerable: popularity and success, the sense of status and belonging. But anxiety still drives the other-directed character. He fears he will not continue to live up to the elusive demands of the group. This anxiety brings resentment that is intensified by the feeling of continual pressure to shift goals and values. Thus the other-directed person often feels that the pressures of conformity have somehow seduced or corrupted his inner integrity, that he has, as a favorite twentieth-century American phrase puts it, lost his identity. To compensate for this perpetual anxiety the other-directed person frequently develops a bitter cynicism and hostility toward the others whose expectations and judgments he fears. Since he feels that his own behavior and attitudes are forced upon him by social pressures to conform that he cannot escape, he is continually aware of a discrepancy between what he imagines as his true inner desires (to tell the boss to go to hell; to beat up his wife) and his actual behavior (deference to the boss and adjustment to his wife). This emotion is intensified when the other-directed individual believes that he is not gaining a full share of the rewards of the social system in terms of popularity, esteem, and consumption. To escape from this inner tension, the other-directed person projects his own sense of corruption and phoniness onto others, particularly onto those who control the central symbols of esteem and status in his world: the rich and successful who possess the power to consume with impunity; and women, whose sexual and emotional deference symbolize popularity and esteem. Projecting his own tension between desire and conformity he becomes what Riesman calls an inside-dopester, a believer in the basic hypocrisy and corruption of society. Since the successful have gained the goals of esteem and power to consume, they must be even more phony and corrupt than he is. Yet, at the same time, those who have made it control the goals he has been trained to seek and he admires their success. Thus, toward these representatives of success the other-directed person feels an irresolvable tension between desire and hostility.

This tension is further complicated by the new status of woman as economic and social competitor as well as object of sexual desire and symbol of popularity. For the other-directed personality, success with women is a crucial index of status, and "making-out" one of the few tangible measures of the elusive goal of group esteem and popularity. The more economically and socially independent of masculine domination women become, the more male esteem and status are threatened. The only possible resolution to the insecurity caused by the conflict between the need for women as sexual and social fulfillment and the threat of feminine independence and domination is the simultaneous possession and destruction of the female, a goal that can hardly be achieved except in fantasy. Mickey Spillane represents exactly this fantasy in the famous final confrontation of I, the Jury when Mike Hammer faces the beautiful, rich, and successful psychiatrist Charlotte Manning, who represents both sexual desirability and the new woman's threat to male status (note the symbolic significance of the name Manning). This complex object of desire and fear strips seductively before the hero, a supreme act of feminine submission. Mike realizes that this seduction is a stratagem that will eventually lead to his death, since Charlotte has a gun concealed where she can reach it while making love. Mike waits until she has completely stripped and as she offers her naked charms to him, he shoots her. Thus possession and destruction reach a simultaneous climax. Doubtless, it is Spillane's ability to create images that embody these symbolic tensions and resolutions in the most simplified fashion that accounts for his extraordinary popularity.

Thus the hard-boiled formula resolves the tension between admiration and hostility for the symbols of success and esteem in a society where the individual feels the strongest pressure to achieve the elusive esteem of the social groups to which he belongs. The marginal social position, the ambiguous relationship to the social elite, and the mood of failure and frustration that characterize the hard-boiled detective bear enough resemblance to feelings many contemporary Americans can identify with. Strong reader-identification is further encouraged by the structural device of narrating the story from the detective's point of view. Other important characteristics of the detective, his masculinity and courage, his integrity and sense of honor, his great sexual attractiveness, reflect other common fantasies: the desire to escape from the anxious tension between conformity and resentment; the desire to replace the sense of inner corruption and insecurity and to avenge oneself upon the successful by physical force; the desire to completely dominate women and thereby overcome their sexual and social challenge. In its pattern of action, the hard-boiled formula also resolves the characteristic social and psychological tensions of the other-directed character. When the story opens, the hero's marginal position is made fully clear. He is a relatively unsuccessful, lower-middle-class entrepreneur with a grubby office and he leads a life of constant risk and tension. He is lonely and isolated, except for the lovely secretary who is both sexually and socially subordinate to him. The secretary, who represents an older image of middle-class femininity—chaste, domestic, and deferent to masculine authority—cannot really satisfy the detective's (and presumably the reader's) psychological needs, precisely because she is too idealized a figure to represent his real feelings about women. Only when the secretary is captured by the criminals and thus becomes associated with a real threat to the detective does he become truly interested in her. In most stories, however, the secretary is left behind as the hero becomes involved with a woman of ambiguous character who both desires and threatens him. In similar fashion, the detective becomes involved with characters who embody the ideals of status, esteem, and success to the highest degree. It turns out that, despite their power and success, these people need the hero, and, needing him, they seek to corrupt him, to overpower him with their demands, to threaten him with their social authority, and to make him lose his own sense of justice and honor by corrupting him with their bribes. But, unlike the other-directed man, the hard-boiled detective is impervious to demands, threats, and bribes. Instead of being used by the others, he exposes their corruption and phoniness, revealing that the respectable are criminals and that the sexually attractive female is a perverted villain. Exposing the inefficiency and corruption of legally constituted social authorities like the police, the hard-boiled detective pursues his mission until he has defined its moral implications in such a way as to satisfy his own sense of honor and integrity. Finally, in a moment of climactic and justified violence, he relieves his pent-up hostility and aggression in an act that combines the possession and destruction of the values that have been so ambiguously tormenting him throughout the story. In this process of eliminating the anxiety associated with social and sexual goals, the reader momentarily resolves his ambiguous feelings about the central symbols of success.

On a more philosophical or theological level, the hard-boiled formula constitutes an escape from the full implications of the modern naturalistic moral universe. Like the heroes of Ernest Hemingway, who must be considered a major literary influence on the genre, the hard-boiled detective finds himself up against a corrupt and violent society that threatens to destroy him. He, too, is tempted, betrayed, and wounded by that society to the point where he realizes that to preserve his integrity he must reject the public ideals and values of the society and seek to create his own personal code of ethics and his own set of values. It is precisely at this point that the Hemingway hero and the private eye part company. When Jake Barnes and Frederick Henry reject the corrupt and hypocritical ideals of their world and set out to make a separate peace, they find that the price they must pay is tragically high. For Jake Barnes, integrity and a relative degree of serenity also mean impotence and despair. Frederick Henry must pay for his brief period of happiness by facing the tragic death of his love. To these heroes comes an inescapable realization of the tragic limitations of human life. The hard-boiled story moves in just the opposite direction. When its detective-hero is hit on the head, the wound doesn't face him with death; it symbolizes his toughness and ability to survive. When his love dies it is not the inscrutable and inescapable force of human mortality, but a sign that he has escaped the fatal trap of love. Finally, what the hard-boiled hero uncovers in his investigation is not the cosmic limitation of death, but the corruption and perversion of society. In the end, the hard-boiled story represents an escape from the naturalistic consciousness of determinism and meaningless death just as it embodies a flight from the other-directed anxiety about success and conformity. And it achieves this escape with minimal cost and maximal pleasure. In fact, in the least interesting and most formulaic of the hard-boiled stories the hero is eventually rewarded in the very terms he has been exposing as treacherous and degrading throughout the story: money and girls. Jake Barnes's insight and integrity, his freedom from false values, were forced upon him by his wound. He is as much victim of the world as voluntary rebel. The hard-boiled detective has a few scratches, but no deep wounds spoil his function as a fantasy hero. He is the man who has been able to say the hell with it and yet to retain the world's most important benefits—self-esteem, popularity, and respect.

Seven

Hammett, Chandler, and Spillane

Any successful formula is likely to inspire individual work on many levels of quality. This is certainly true of the hard-boiled detective story. Two of its major creators, Dashiell Hammett and Raymond Chandler, hold a high place on most lists of the finest writers of mystery fiction. Some critics consider them important literary figures worthy of being ranked with contemporaries like John O'Hara and John Steinbeck. Even in dismissing the whole of classical detective fiction as beneath serious attention, Edmund Wilson exempted Raymond Chandler from his anathemas. On the other hand, the most popular writer of hard-boiled stories, Mickey Spillane, is a favorite literary villain, everybody's supreme embodiment of the tasteless, vulgar, obsessive, sadistic, and unredeemable dregs of popular formula literature. The purpose of this chapter is to examine some of the central differences between these writers and to define more fully their individual characteristics and artistic significance.

Dashiell Hammett

In contrast to most hard-boiled detective writers who tend to employ the same detective and the same essential story over and over, Dashiell Hammett's work is extremely various. Each of his novels presents a different kind of problem and pattern of action. His first two full-length books, *Red Harvest* and *The Dain Curse*, feature an anonymous professional detective known as the Continental Op, who is also the central figure of most of Hammett's short stories. Though they share the same detective, these two novels are nonetheless very different in character. *Red Harvest* is westernlike in its setting and in its violent and chaotic narrative of gang warfare. *The Dain Curse* resembles a gothic novel with its eerie atmosphere of family curses, drugs, strange religious cults, and twisted motives. Hammett's third novel, *The Maltese Falcon*, develops a new detective, Sam Spade, who bears some resemblance to the Continental Op but is younger, wittier, and more of a ladies' man than his predecessor. His story too is different, shaped like a classical detective story complete with complex mystery and hidden treasure. *The Glass Key* goes beyond the detective story altogether to become a study in political power and corruption. Finally, in *The Thin Man*, Hammett invents still another detective, the private investigator Nick Charles, newly married to an heiress and transformed into a socialite and successful businessman but still capable of a good bit of detection between parties. Despite this manifold inventiveness, a distinctive Hammett quality pervades all his works. Most critics have summarized this characteristic as the importation into the detective story of a new "realism." Raymond Chandler, for example, argued that

> Hammett gave murder back to the kind of people that commit it for reasons, not just to provide a corpse; and with the means at hand, not with handwrought duelling pistols, curare, and tropical fish. He put these people down on paper as they are, and he made them talk and think in the language they customarily used for these purposes.[1]

That there was a new quality in Hammett's detective stories is certainly the case. Hammett, more than any other person, invented the hard-boiled detective. It is true that there were action-filled, tough-guy detective stories before Hammett came on the scene; in fact, the origins of the formula are lost in the obscurity of early twentieth-century western and action-detective pulps. Several hard-boiled writers emerged more or less simultaneously with Hammett in the pages of *Black Mask Magazine* during the twenties, but Hammett was the most important. It was he who licked the new story into shape, gave it much of its distinctive style and atmosphere, developed its urban setting, invented many of its most effective plot patterns, and, above all, articulated the hard-boiled hero, creating that special mixture of toughness and sentimentality, of cynical understatement and eloquence that would remain the stamp of the hard-boiled detective, even in his cruder avatars.

The claim that Hammett's contribution to the detective story was primarily a new kind of truth or accuracy about people who commit murders and the individuals who find them out is dubious on two counts. First, Hammett's stories are not that much more realistic than many classical detective stories and, second, Hammett's power as a writer does not lie in his greater fidelity to the realistic details of crime and punishment but in his capacity to embody a powerful vision of life in the hard-boiled detective formula.

Actually, Chandler's insistence that Hammett is primarily a "realist in murder" must be seen in its context as a defense of the hard-boiled story against the classical genre of complex puzzles and clues. The main ground of Chandler's defense is that the classical story lost contact with reality in its development of intriguing and mystifying puzzles solved by a gentlemanly amateur detective whom, as Chandler puts it, "the English police seem to endure ... with their customary stoicism; but I shudder to think of what the boys down at the Homicide Bureau in my city would do to him."[2] But is it really the case that a Hammett novel like *The Maltese Falcon*, which revolves around a mysterious age-old treasure, eccentric villains, and complex webs of intrigue, is more "realistic" than the detective novels of Dorothy Sayers with their ordinary settings, their relatively plausible motivations, and their rich texture of manners and local color? Such an assertion surely exemplifies that American literary tendency to identify the "real" with the violent, the sordid, and the brutal aspects of life. As Lionel Trilling points out in his analysis of this tendency in Theodore Dreiser and Vernon Parrington, such an identification can be just as arbitrary and limited a view of "reality" as the more philosophical or genteel perspectives it set out to attack.[3] If one approaches the Hammett canon without accepting the premise that toughness and violence are supremely real, the fantastic nature of most of his stories becomes clear. The Continental Op creates and controls a revolution in a mysterious Balkan country in a story tougher in style but no more plausible in incident than the popular Graustarkian romances of the early twentieth century. A criminal genius named Pappadoupolous (but clearly a Hammett version of Doyle's Professor Moriarty) brings an army of gangsters to San Francisco, pulls off a bank robbery that involves a pitched battle with the entire city police force, and then succeeds in killing off the great majority of his henchmen before he is finally brought to bay by the Op. The Op becomes involved in the tangled affairs of the Leggett family, which are so bizarre that they even involve a family curse. In one of the climactic moments of this story the Op confronts a maddened prophet who is about to sacrifice the heroine on the altar of his temple, a setting as gothic as anything out of *The Mysteries of Udolpho*. To say that such characters, actions, and settings are more realistic than the advertising agencies, country villages, or university quadrangles of Dorothy Sayers cannot withstand serious scrutiny.

Far from being a straightforward realist who rescued the detective story from sterile littérateurs and gave it back to the actual world, Hammett was an extremely literary writer. His work shows both an awareness of earlier literary models and a continual interest in such literary effects as irony and paradox. One of his earliest published works, "Memoirs of a Private Detective," though based on Hammett's own experiences as a Pinkerton operative, implies a perspective shaped as much by the elegant, fin-de-siècle cynicism of writers like Ambrose Bierce as by the direct perception of life. Though Hammett probably had more practical experiences as a detective than any other writer of mystery novels, his presentation of his own career takes the form of brief, delicately turned paradoxes that have a flavor something between *The Devil's Dictionary* and an O. Henry story.

> Wishing to get some information from members of the W.C.T.U. in an Oregon city, I introduced myself as the secretary of the Butte City Purity League. One of them read me a long discourse on the erotic effects of cigarettes upon young girls. Subsequent experiments proved this trip worthless.[4]

As he developed as a writer, Hammett lost some of the aroma of the *décadence*, not so much because his attention focused more directly on life, but because his literary models changed. Hammett's early stories grew directly out of the pulp tradition and many of them, like *Red Harvest*, resemble westerns as much as they do detective stories. Even at this time Hammett occasionally experimented with the transformation of other traditional literary types into his own hard-boiled mode. This became a standard practice in his later novels. Thus, *The Dain Curse* makes use of a wide variety of gothic traditions—the family curse, the mysterious temple with its secret passages and ghosts, religious maniacs, the tragedy on the beetling cliffs— while *The Maltese Falcon* reflects the great tradition of stories of hidden treasure like "The Gold-Bug" and *Treasure Island* with Cairo and Gutman playing the role of Long John Silver. *The Thin Man* embodies a more contemporaneous literary tradition, the novel of high society and urban sophistication. The quality of its dialogue, setting, and general tone of breezy hauteur suggests that it was at least partly modeled on the novels and stories of F. Scott Fitzgerald.

In part Hammett may have felt that his employment of the hard-boiled detective in stories that owed so much to established literary traditions added respectability and dignity to the saga of the tough-guy hero in such a way as to make his adventures more acceptable to a cultivated, middle-class reading public. It would not be the first time that a pulp writer had tried to add tone to his creations by wrapping them in a literary toga. Hammett's contemporary Max Brand (Frederick Faust) even went so far as to construct an entire western called *Hired Guns* using the plot and characters of the *Iliad* in cowboy costumes (a ten-year range war between two families that started in an argument over a young lady named Ellen). But this is only part of the story. Hammett's use of these traditional literary materials is more often ironic than straightforward, satirical rather than serious. Hammett continually builds up conventional literary moods and then punctures them with the flat, rasping cynicism of the private eye who has seen it all before and knows it is phony. In the famous climax of *The Maltese Falcon*, Sam Spade unmasks Brigid O'Shaughnessy as the killer, accusing her of having used him to save her neck. Brigid, however, still hopes to capitalize on the romance that has grown up between the two:

> "Yes, but—oh, sweetheart!—it wasn't only that. I would have come back to you sooner or later. From the first instant I saw you I knew—
> Spade said tenderly: "You angel! Well, if you get a good break you'll be out of San Quentin in twenty years and you can come back to me then."
> She took her cheek away from his, drawing her head far back to stare up without comprehension at him. He was pale. He said tenderly: "I hope to God they don't hang you, precious, by that sweet neck." He slid his hands up to caress her throat.[5]

Sam's flat refusal—"I won't play the sap for you"—shatters the world of romantic illusion that Brigid has woven about the attraction between herself and Sam and dissipates the haze of dashing adventure with which she has cloaked the sordid reality of her pursuit of the falcon. This sort of ironic contrast between romantic fantasies and real violence and ugliness permeates *The Maltese Falcon* as it does much of Hammett's work. We see it in the way Cairo and Gutman's exotic elegance has an underside of petty and sordid ruthlessness, or in the way Spade refuses to accept any of the noble motives that various characters seek to ascribe to him; for example, though Sam insists on tracking down the killer of his partner, Miles Archer, he makes it clear that he does so not out of affection or loyalty, but as a matter of good business: "When one of your organization gets killed it's bad business to let the killer get away with it. It's bad all around—bad for that one organization, bad for every detective everywhere." Perhaps, most powerfully of all, Hammett's pervasively flat, hard-edged, and laconic vernacular style with its denial of the lyrical effects cultivated by vernacular stylists like Hemingway or, in a different way, by Hammett's fellow hard-boiled writer Raymond Chandler, runs against the breathless excitement of his stories. Even the most fantastic episodes retain the solid, cold, slightly tired tone in which Hammett's detectives narrate their adventures. Everything is calmly weighed and measured:

> It was a diamond all right, shining in the grass half a dozen feet from the blue brick walk. It was small, not more than a quarter of a carat in weight, and unmounted. I put it in my pocket and began searching the lawn as closely as I could without going at it on all fours.[6]

> He came in, looking and acting as if I were St. Peter letting him into Heaven. I closed the door and led him through the lobby, down the main corridor. So far as we could see we had the joint to ourselves. And then we didn't. Gabrielle Leggett came around a corner just ahead of us. She was barefooted. Her only clothing was a yellow silk nightgown that was splashed with dark stains. In both hands, held out in front of her as she walked, she carried a large dagger, almost a sword. It was red and wet. Her hands and bare arms were red and wet. There was a dab of blood on one of her cheeks. Her eyes were clear, bright, and calm. Her small forehead was smooth, her mouth and chin firmly set. She walked up to me, her untroubled gaze holding my probably troubled one, and said evenly, just as if she had expected to find me there, had come there to find me: "Take it. It is evidence. I killed him."
> I said: "Huh?"[7]

The stylistic combination that these passages exemplify—utterly fantastic incidents described in nearly emotionless, lucidly descriptive vernacular prose—has a surrealistic flavor, like those paintings by Dali where flaming giraffes and melting watches are rendered with the most carefully drawn "realistic" detail. This interweaving of flat realism and wild fantasy seems to grow out of Hammett's basic sense of life: the vision of an irrational cosmos, in which all the rules, all the seeming solidity of matter, routine, and custom can be overturned in a moment, pervades his work from beginning to end. Even the early "Memoirs of a Private Detective" continually reflects this utterly paradoxical sense of the world:

A man whom I was shadowing went out into the country for a walk one Sunday afternoon and lost his bearing completely. I had to direct him back to the city.

I was once falsely accused of perjury and had to perjure myself to escape arrest.

I knew a detective who once attempted to disguise himself thoroughly. The first policeman he met took him into custody.

I knew a man who once stole a Ferris-wheel.[8]

By the time he wrote *The Maltese Falcon* several years later, Hammett's whimsical, fin-de-siècle cynicism had developed into a starker vision of cosmic treachery. Early in *The Maltese Falcon* Sam Spade tells Brigid O'Shaughnessy the story of Flitcraft, a successful businessman in Tacoma who had suddenly disappeared, leaving behind his wife and children. When Sam finally met Flitcraft five years later in Spokane, he was again a successful businessman, had remarried, and settled down to a life identical in all respects to that he had left. Flitcraft gladly explains to Sam the reason for his strange behavior.

One day, walking down the street, he had been nearly killed by a falling beam. This made him realize that life was not fundamentally neat and orderly, but that men "lived only while blind chance spared them." He felt a need to adjust to this new vision of life and so he went away. But in moving to Seattle, Flitcraft had gradually drifted into the same life pattern he had known before. Sam is obviously fascinated by this story. He tells Brigid that Flitcraft

wasn't sorry for what he had done. It seemed reasonable enough to him. I don't think he even knew he had settled back naturally into the same groove he had jumped out of in Tacoma. But that's the part of it I always liked. He adjusted himself to beams falling, and then no more beams fell, and he adjusted himself to them not falling."[9]

In the context of the novel, the Flitcraft story is a kind of warning to Brigid that Sam has adjusted himself to a world that is likely to betray him at any time. As it turns out, Sam needs all his cynical equanimity, for Brigid conceals a devastating treachery behind a facade of beauty and romance. In the end it is only Sam's total disillusionment that saves him from destruction.

Yet the moral of both stories—that of Flitcraft and of Sam Spade— is more than a little ambiguous. It is true that Flitcraft and Spade manage to survive the falling beam, but for what? Flitcraft goes back to the same respectable middle-class life that he had so suddenly awakened from; Spade returns to his shabby office, having sent the woman he loves off to prison. The price of survival would seem to be a terrible emptiness, a restriction of human possibilities, a cynical rejection of deeper emotion and commitment. Though some critics have suggested that the Flitcraft story is an existentialist parable, it implies something more ambiguous to me. The existentialist believes that recognizing the irrationality and absurdity of the universe can be the prelude to a new spiritual depth. Through such a realization man can pass beyond despair to a freely chosen moral responsibility that gives meaning to an otherwise ridiculous and empty existence. The Flitcraft parable seems to come out at the other end. Only a rejection of all emotional and moral ties can help man survive in a treacherous world.

Instead, the job is the source of value and meaning for Hammett's hard-boiled hero. When the beautiful Russian Princess Zhukovski offers him money and her body not to turn her in, the Continental Op replies:

> "We'll disregard whatever honesty I happen to have, sense of loyalty to employers, and so on. You might doubt them, so we'll throw them out. Now I'm a detective because I happen to like the work. It pays me a fair salary, but I could find other jobs that would pay more.... Now I pass up about twenty-five or thirty thousand of honest gain because I like being a detective, like the work. And liking work makes you want to do it as well as you can. Otherwise there'd be no sense to it. That's the fix I am in. I don't know anything else, don't enjoy anything else, don't want to know or enjoy anything else. You can't weigh that against any sum of money. Money is good stuff. I haven't anything against it. But in the past eighteen years I've been getting my fun out of chasing crooks and tackling puzzles, my satisfaction out of catching crooks and solving riddles. It's the only kind of sport I know anything about, and I can't imagine a pleasanter future than twenty-some years more of it. I'm not going to blow that up."[10]

Sam Spade exposes Brigid, the woman he thinks he loves, as a murderess because "when one of your organization gets killed it's bad business to let the killer get away with it.... It doesn't make any difference what you thought of him." The Hammett hero has little of the quixotic knight-errantry or complex inner reluctance of Raymond Chandler's Philip Marlowe. He is capable of helping young ladies in trouble or of suppressing evidence so that relatively innocent persons will not be hurt, but his major dedication is to being a good detective and not letting either romantic illusions or the irrational forces of chance catch him off guard. As one of the girls he helps tells him, he is "a monster. A nice one, an especially nice one to have around when you're in trouble, but a monster just the same, without any human foolishness like love in him."

Hammett's first full-length novel, *Red Harvest*, presents the confrontation of the Hammett hero with a world of crazy, irrational violence that nearly catches him up in an orgy of destruction. Only his common sense, his brutal cynicism and disillusion, and his technical skills as a manhunter save him from the torrent of chaos unleashed in the town of Personville by his own investigations. *Red Harvest* is a prime example of that rhythm of exposure and temptation that was designated in the preceding chapter as one of the major characteristics of the hard-boiled formula. The Op is called to Personville—known as Poisonville to many—by a newspaper editor, Donald Willson. Before the Op can even see his client, Willson is murdered. The Op soon discovers that Willson had sent for a detective in connection with a newspaper crusade he planned to launch against the rampant corruption in Personville. At the center of this corruption lies Willson's own father, the violent old mining baron Elihu Willson. The older Willson had run the town of Personville like a little kingdom of his own until challenged by the IWW. To break the power of organized labor, Willson had brought in criminal-dominated gangs of strike-breakers. But, as a former labor leader tells the Op,

> old Elihu didn't know his Italian history. He won the strike, but he lost his hold on the city and the state. To beat the miners he had to let his hired thugs run wild. When the fight was over he couldn't get rid of them. He had given his city to them and he wasn't strong enough to take it away from them.[11]

Finding his city dominated by such disreputable characters as "Whisper" Thaler, Pete the Finn, and Lew Yard, old Willson gives his idealistic son the *Morning Herald* in the belief that a newspaper crusade against crime will help him to regain his old power. Willson's gangster allies, suspecting his intentions, have apparently murdered his son to stop the crusade. Old Elihu doesn't show much interest in the connection between his son's murder and Personville's rampant corruption until, the next evening, a gangster named Yakima Shorty breaks into his home. At this point, Willson decides that his former gangster allies are determined to kill him as well. He commissions the Op to clean up Personville.

The Op proceeds to apply the principle of divide and conquer. With information provided by a woman named Dinah Brand who has been the mistress of several of the men involved in Personville's gangs, the Op splits the various forces and brings them to a state of open war against each other. Explaining his technique to Dinah, the Op reveals the kind of stoical self-reliance that marks the Hammett hero:

> "The closest I've got to an idea is to dig up any and all the dirty work I can that might implicate the others, and run it out. Maybe I'll advertise—*Crime Wanted—Male or Female*. If they're as crooked as I think they are I shouldn't have a lot of trouble finding a job or two that I can hang on them." . . .
> "So that's the way you scientific detectives work. My God! for a fat, middle-aged, hard-boiled, pig-headed guy, you've got the vaguest way of doing things I ever heard of."
> "Plans are all right sometimes," I said. "And sometimes just stirring things up is all right—if you're tough enough to survive, and keep your eyes open so you'll see what you want when it comes to the top."[12]

The Op's stirring-up technique works beautifully at first. As he hears shooting break out all over the city, the Op purrs with satisfaction:

> Off to the north some guns popped.
> A group of three men passed me, shifty-eyed, walking pigeon-toed.

A little farther along, another man moved all the way over to the curb to give me plenty of room to pass. I didn't know him and didn't suppose he knew me.

A lone shot sounded not far away.

As I reached the hotel, a battered black touring car went down the street, hitting fifty at least, crammed to the curtains with men.

I grinned after it. Poisonville was beginning to boil out under the lid, and I felt so much like a native that even the memory of my very un-nice part in the boiling didn't keep me from getting twelve solid end-to-end hours of sleep.[13]

If this represented the Op's final attitude toward the Personville situation, only Hammett's style would differentiate his hero from a bloodthirsty manhunter like Mickey Spillane's Mike Hammer. But legitimating brutal aggression in the name of justice is not exactly Hammett's intention. Instead, as the violence in Personville mounts, driven on by his own machinations, the Op himself begins to lose his grip, caught up in the bloodlust.

"This damned burg's getting me. If I don't get away soon I'll be going blood-simple like the natives. There's been what? A dozen and a half murders since I've been here. . . . I've arranged a killing or two in my time, when they were necessary. But this is the first time I've ever got the fever. . . . Play with murder enough and it gets you one of two ways. It makes you sick, or you get to like it."[14]

Additional ironies compound the ambivalence of the Op's position. It turns out that the killing of Donald Willson, which initiated the slaughter, was committed by a bank clerk, jealous of Willson's attentions to Dinah Brand. Thus it had nothing to do with underworld intrigue. When Elihu Willson realizes this, he attempts to call the Op off the case. Moreover, the gangsters soon discover that internecine warfare can only lead to ruin. All parties concerned would like to bury the hatchet. The Op arranges a "peace conference" at old Willson's house where he plays so effectively on the fears and jealousies of the assembled gangsters that a new orgy of violence breaks out almost before the meeting is over. Unlike most of the hard-boiled writers, Hammett does not ignore or evade the vicious implications of his hero's actions. The Op senses that he, too, is becoming a murderer. Speaking to Dinah Brand, who has become his ally, the Op bitterly explains the significance of what he did at the "peace conference."

"I could have gone to [Elihu Willson] this afternoon and showed him that I had them ruined. He'd have listened to reason. He'd have come over to my side, have given me the support I needed to swing the play legally. I could have done that. But it's easier to have them killed off, easier and surer, and, now that I'm feeling this way, more satisfying. I don't know how I'm to come out with the agency. The Old Man will boil me in oil if he ever finds out what I've been doing. It's this damned town. Poisonville is right. It's poisoned me."

"Look. I sat at Willson's table tonight and played him like you'd play trout, and got just as much fun out of it. I looked at Noonan and knew he hadn't a chance in a thousand of living another day because of what I had done to him, and I laughed, and felt warm and happy inside. That's not me. I've got hard skin all over what's left of my soul, and after twenty years of messing around with crime I can look at any sort of a murder without seeing anything in it but my bread and butter, the day's work. But this getting a rear out of planning deaths is not natural to me. It's what this place has done to me."[15]

The Op's personal immersion in violence reaches its climax in a drunken party with Dinah Brand. Trying to escape the emotional tension between his hatred of Personville and his doubts about the bloodlust into which his personal crusade to clean up the city has fallen, the Op gets drunker and drunker. Finally, he asks Dinah for a drink of laudanum and falls into a nightmarish semiconsciousness in which he dreams that he is hunting through a strange city for a man he hates. When he finds the man, he is on the roof of a tall building. The ending of the dream symbolizes the Op's own destruction in the violence he has sought.

His shoulder slid out of my fingers. My hand knocked his sombrero off, and closed on his head. It was a smooth hard round head no larger than a large egg. My fingers went all the way around it. Squeezing his head in one hand, I tried to bring the knife out of my pocket with the other—and realized that I had gone off the edge of the roof with him. We dropped giddily down toward the millions of upturned faces in the plaza, miles down.[16]

When the Op awakes in the morning, he finds that he is holding an ice pick in his right hand and that the pick's "six-inch needle-sharp blade" is thrust into Dinah Brand's breast. But, instead of being devastated by the realization that he has killed a woman for whom he had begun to feel a real comradeship and affection, the Op becomes once again the detached and cynical professional with a job to do.

I knelt beside the dead girl and used my handkerchief to wipe the ice pick handle clean of any prints my fingers had left on it. I did the same to glasses, bottles, doors, light buttons, and the pieces of furniture I touched or was likely to have touched.
Then I washed my hands, examined my clothes for blood, made sure I was leaving none of my property behind, and went to the front door. I opened it, wiped the inner knob, closed it behind me, wiped the outer knob, and went away.[17]

At this point in the story, Hammett shifts the narrative focus from the Op as hunter to the Op as hunted. Instead of manipulator of forces and puppet-master of violence, the Op himself becomes a wanted man as the town explodes into a final chaos of violence. Such a shift is necessary to resolve the moral ambiguities of the Op's role without directly confronting the meaning of violence in such a way as to take *Red Harvest* out of the moral fantasy of heroic adventure and make it a mimetic action. To remain within the limitations of the hard-boiled formula, Hammett must somehow pull his hero out of the moral dilemma created by his immersion in violence, thus freeing him from the devastating awareness of personal guilt. He does this by a device that has been well prepared for in the course of the novel and, as we saw in a previous chapter, became one of the foundations of the hard-boiled detective formula: the violence and corruption are finally attributed to the city itself, to Poisonville. Through this means, the Op is exonerated, his causal role in so many murders being legitimated as an act of purification. Finally, the Op tracks down the one surviving gang leader, now mortally wounded. This gangster makes a dying confession to the murder of Dinah Brand. With the elimination of the underworld elite and a final clean-up by the National Guard, the Op is able to leave the devastated city. "Personville, under martial law, was developing into a sweet-smelling and thornless bed of roses."[18]

Though he finally brings about the exoneration of his hero and the legitimation of his role as agent of destruction and purifying violence, Hammett ironically undercuts this resolution in several ways. All the murder and destruction accomplish very little. As the Op himself realizes, the eventual result of his terrible crusade to purify Poisonville is that the city will be handed back to Elihu Willson, "all nice and clean and ready to go to the dogs again." Purification through violence only prepares the way for another "red harvest." Moreover, as the orgy of murder reaches its climax, even the Op loses control over the process and the National Guard has to be called in to stand watch over the shambles of a city. This final scene brings to mind the conclusion of Akira Kurosawa's movie "Yojimbo," a Japanese analogue of *Red Harvest*. In the film's last scene, the samurai hero stands among the smoking ruins and scattered bodies of the town he has cleaned up. Turning to the old man who had originally begged him to break the power of the town's rival gangs, he says with bitter irony, "Well, old man. You'll have lots of peace and quiet now." Though the Op does finally discover that Dinah Brand was murdered by the gangster Reno Starkey, his essential guilt can hardly be escaped. Not only did his determination to purify Poisonville by setting the rival gangs against each other establish the motive for Dinah's murder, his own actions directly caused the killing. As Starkey tells the Op, he had come to Dinah's house the night of the murder in order to trap "Whisper" Thaler, but was suspicious that the trap might be for himself:

> "I'm leary that I've walked into something, knowing her. I think I'll take hold of her and slap the truth out of her. I try it, and she grabs the pick and screams. When she squawks, I heard man's feet hitting the floor. The trap's sprung, I think. . . . I don't mean to be the only one that's hurt. I twist the

pick out of her hand and stick it in her. You gallop out, coked to the edges, charging at the whole world with both eyes shut. She tumbles into you. You go down, roll around till your hand hits the butt of the pick. Holding on to that, you go to sleep, peaceful as she is."[19]

Though he may not literally have struck the blow, the Op's hand held the weapon. Like Sam Spade in *The Maltese Falcon*, the conclusion of the Op's case requires the destruction of a woman who has offered him a wider range of emotion and fulfillment than the bleak and rigid rituals of the job. And the final irony is that there is not much sense of heroic completion to the Op's crusade. The final curtain of *Red Harvest* comes down to the tune of the Op's boss roasting him for his illegal tactics in Personville: "I might just as well have saved the labor and sweat I had put into trying to make my reports harmless. They didn't fool the Old Man. He gave me merry hell."[20]

In Hammett's hands what later became the hard-boiled story was a bitter and ironic parable of universal corruption and irrational violence. *Red Harvest* might be interpreted as a political parable—Personville being a symbol of the exploitative capitalistic society that has reached the point where its internal contradictions keep it in a state of perpetual corruption and chaos. Such a reading might fit the details of the novel and our knowledge of Hammett's personal ideological commitments, but it seems basically irrelevant to *Red Harvest*. Instead, the book suggests that underneath his radicalism Hammett was a bleak and stoical pessimist with no more real faith in a revolutionary utopia to come than in existing societies. Though *Red Harvest* distantly resembles other "proletarian" novels in which the clash of capital and labor in a gang-ridden company town leads to violence, there is no surge of optimistic hope for the future at the end. Proletarian novels usually ended with the conversion of the protagonist to a vision of the proletariat on the march, but *Red Harvest* leaves us with a bitter, fat, aging, and tired detective who has survived the holocaust only because he is harder and tougher and doesn't ask much out of life. The enemy that Hammett's bitter fictions found beneath the decadent facade of twentieth-century capitalist society was the universe itself. More than any other hard-boiled writer, Hammett's work reflects the vision of a godless naturalistic cosmos ruled by chance, violence, and death that dominates such major twentieth-century writers as Conrad, Crane, and Hemingway. Though his work is shaped by the formulaic imperatives of mystery, suspense, and the victorious protagonist, Hammett's stories have a philosophical power and seriousness beyond most other writers of hard-boiled detective stories. Like the greater works of Conrad, Crane, and Hemingway, his stories are essentially about the discovery that the comforting pieties of the past—belief in a benevolent universe, in progress, in romantic love—are illusions and that man is alone in a meaningless universe.

Raymond Chandler

Hammett's style is lean, cool, and objective. Its impact derives not from figurative and emotional language but from the collision between flat, emotionally empty, but extremely lucid prose and the striking events and characters it describes. The following is perhaps the most emotionally intense and grotesque scene in *The Dain Curse*, but, with the exception of a few rather austere adjectives, the language is almost purely descriptive with little metaphorical embellishment and almost nothing to indicate the reactions and feelings of the narrator. The scene is powerful enough, but it gains its power through the direct presentation of colors, light, action, and situation:

> The altar was glaring white, crystal, and silver in an immense beam of blue-white light that slanted down from an edge of the roof. At one end of the altar Gabrielle crouched, her face turned up into the beam of light. Her face was ghastly white and expressionless in the harsh light. Aaronia Haldorn lay on the altar step where Riese had lain. There was a dark bruise on her forehead. Her hands and feet were tied with broad white bands of cloth, her arms tied to her body. Most of her clothes had been torn off. Joseph, white-robed, stood in front of the altar, and of his wife. He stood with both arms held high and widespread, his back and neck bent so that his bearded face was lifted to the sky. In his right hand he held an ordinary horn-handled knife with a long curved blade.[21]

Compare this with the following passage from Chandler's *The Big Sleep*, describing Philip Marlowe's climactic encounter with the psychopathic killer Carmen Sternwood:

> The gun pointed at my chest. Her hand seemed to be quite steady. The hissing sound grew louder and her face had the scraped bone look. Aged, deteriorated, become animal, and not a nice animal.
> I laughed at her. I started to walk towards her. I saw her small finger tighten on the trigger and grow white at the tip. I was about six feet away when she started to shoot. The sound of the gun made a sharp slap, without body, a brittle crack in the sunlight. I didn't see any smoke. I stopped again and grinned at her.
> She fired twice more, very quickly. I don't think any of the shots would have missed. There were five in the little gun. She had fired four. I rushed her.
> I didn't want the last one in my face so I swerved to one side. She gave it to me quite carefully not worried at all. I think I felt the hot breath of the powder blast a little.
> I straightened up. "My, but you're cute," I said.
> Her hand holding the empty gun began to shake violently. The gun fell out of it. Her mouth began to shake. Her whole face went to pieces. Then her head screwed up toward her left ear and froth showed on her lips. Her breath made a whining sound. She swayed.[22]

In both these scenes the detective-hero confronts a mad killer. Both exemplify the taut vernacular cultivated by hard-boiled writers with its short, staccato sentences, rhythmic repetitions, and rapid pace. Chandler's language has a figurative and emotionally charged quality that is quite absent from the Hammett passage despite the grotesque intensity of the scene itself. Chandler's style is elaborately metaphorical. The killer's face has a "scraped bone look," the gun makes a "sharp slap" and a "brittle crack in the sunlight." The killer is seen as undergoing a striking series of metamorphoses, from a woman, into a snake ("the hissing sound"), into an animal, and then finally into some totally distorted figure like a cubist painting ("Her whole face went to pieces. Then her head screwed up toward her left ear"). The language intensifies our impression of the strange and incomprehensible involvement of the narrator in the scene; he is being shot at, but he laughs and grins and then finally calls his assailant cute. In comparison, Hammett's description of his detective's physical involvement in the scene that immediately follows the static tableau quoted above seems lucid and objective:

> I was fighting. When the knife, shining over our heads, started down, I went in under it, bending my right forearm against his knife-arm, driving the dagger in my left hand at his throat. I drove the heavy blade into his throat, in till the hilt's cross stopped it. Then I was through.[23]

When Chandler's Marlowe fights, the scene is described with the same subjectivity that characterizes his confrontation with Carmen Sternwood:

> The door jumped open. I was flat against the wall on the opening side. He had the sap out this time, a nice little tool about five inches long, covered with woven brown leather. His eyes popped at the stripped bed and then began to swing around.
> I giggled and socked him. I laid the coil spring on the side of his head and he stumbled forward. I followed him down to his knees. I hit him twice more. He made a moaning sound. I took the sap out of his limp hand. He whined.
> I used my knee on his face. It hurt my knee. He didn't tell me whether it hurt his face. While he was still groaning I knocked him cold with the sap.[24]

Like his style, the world of Chandler's books has little of the lucid impenetrable objectivity of Hammett's vision. Instead, it is permeated with the bitter, lonely, neurotic, but humorous imagination of Philip Marlowe.

Marlowe's characteristic stylistic device is the slangy, hyperbolic simile:

> Even on Central Avenue, not the quietest dressed street in the world, he looked about as inconspicuous as a tarantula on a slice of angel food.[25]
> She approached me with enough sex appeal to stampede a business men's lunch.[26]
> The subject was as easy to spot as a kangaroo in a dinner jacket.[27]
> His smile was as faint as a fat lady at a fireman's ball.[28]
> The eighty-five cent dinner tasted like a discarded mail bag and was served to me by a waiter who looked as if he would slug me for a quarter, cut my

throat for six bits, and bury me at sea in a barrel of concrete for a dollar and a half, plus sales tax.²⁹

These similes are sometimes sharply pointed and effectively witty; occasionally they degenerate into a mannerism. In general they are an effective means of stylistic characterization, reflecting Marlowe's personal style of perception and response. By contrasting such exaggerated comparisons with the understatement and lack of explicit emotion that also characterize Marlowe's narration, Chandler gives us a continual sense of Marlowe's complexity of attitude and character: he is intensely sensitive, yet carries a shield of cynical apathy; he is disturbed to a point of near-hysteria by the moral decay he encounters, yet always affects a wise-guy coolness and wit; he is bitter, exasperated, and lonely, behind a veneer of taut self-control, sarcasm, and indifference.

Marlowe's bitter sensitivity is mirrored by the bleakness and desolation of the urban landscape he prowls. Where Hammett's descriptions measure things coolly by size, weight, color, and shape, Marlowe's perceptions are charged with strained and blocked emotion. Objects manifest themselves by their impact on the narrator's oversensitive nerves:

> The poinsettia shoots tap-tapped dully against the front wall. The clothes line creaked vaguely at the side of the house. The ice cream peddler went by ringing his bell. The big new handsome radio in the corner whispered of dancing and love with a deep soft throbbing note like the catch in a torch singer's voice.
>
> Then from the back of the house there were various types of crashing sounds. A chair seemed to fall over backwards, a bureau drawer was pulled out too far and crashed to the floor, there was fumbling and thudding and muttered thick language. Then the slow click of a lock and the squeak of a trunk top going up. More fumbling and banging. A tray landed on the floor.³⁰

Though he lacks Hammett's clarity, vigor, and philosophical depth, Chandler created a hero whose personal qualities have had a considerable impact on the development of the private eye. Chandler was unable to accept Hammett's bleak pessimism. He saw the corruption and violence of the modern city, not as an inescapable human condition, but as the result of American materialism and greed. He sought to create a hero who could encounter this pervasive corruption, protect the innocent, and maintain his honor. Marlowe is not a cynical organization detective who feels that doing a good job of detective work is the one thing that can give meaning to a capricious and valueless universe, but a lone ranger who somehow redeems the world by his bravery and decency:

> But down these mean streets a man must go who is not himself mean, who is neither tarnished nor afraid.³¹

At the same time, Chandler was enough of a realist to want his hero to be a plausible contemporary figure with some of the frustrations and difficulties of the twentieth-century antihero. Thus Marlowe became a reluctant and ambiguous knight engaged in an obscure quest for a grail whose value he could never completely articulate. As Richard Schickel puts it, Marlowe is a "moral man, who refuses to play the game of life in a conventionally immoral or amoral way," and he consequently is doomed to an isolation and loneliness that he hides "behind a protective set of tough-guy mannerisms." Chandler himself summed up Marlowe's character in a letter to a friend:

> I think he will always have a fairly shabby office, a lonely house, a number of affairs but no permanent connection. I think he will always be awakened at some inconvenient hour by some inconvenient person to do some inconvenient job. It seems to be that that is his destiny—possibly not the best destiny in the world, but it belongs to him. No one will ever make him rich, because he is destined to be poor. But somehow, I think he would not have it otherwise.... I see him always in a lonely street, in lonely rooms, puzzled, but never quite defeated.[32]

In one of Chandler's best books, *Farewell, My Lovely*, the pattern of the hard-boiled formula becomes the complicated and enigmatic story of Marlowe's quest for justice. As in most of the novels where he appears, Marlowe becomes initially involved in one line of investigation that seems to lead to a dead end. He then takes up another problem that at first appears to have no connection with the original situation. When the story reaches its climax, however, the solution is seen to lie in the intersection of the two lines of investigation. In part, this plot structure is a technique of obfuscation aimed at keeping the reader from solving the mystery. As Chandler once explained:

> It often seems to this particular writer that the only reasonably honest and effective method of fooling the reader that remains is to make the reader exercise his mind about the wrong problem, to make him, as it were, solve a mystery (since he is almost sure to solve something) which will land him in a bypath because it is only tangential to the central problem.[33]

But the device is also appropriate to Marlowe's character in that it sets the detective on a quest that becomes increasingly ambiguous and exasperating, forcing him to seek not only for the factual solution to the various mysteries he confronts, but for a moral stance toward the events in which he has become enmeshed. *Farewell, My Lovely* begins with Marlowe's random involvement in the affairs of one Moose Malloy, a former bank robber who has just been released from eight years in prison. In fact, Marlowe is literally plucked off the street by Malloy, a man of gigantic stature and strength.

> He lifted me up two more steps. I wrenched myself loose and tried for a little elbow room. I wasn't wearing a gun. Looking for Dimitrios Aleidis hadn't seemed to require it. I doubted if it would do me any good. The big man would probably take it away from me and eat it.[34]

Malloy, in a perfectly friendly though somewhat bewildered way, wants Marlowe to accompany him to a nearby bar where his girl friend, Little

Velma, had formerly worked. When they arrive at the bar, Moose and Marlowe discover that it has become a black establishment and that nobody there has ever heard of Little Velma. Moose gets into a fight with the bar's owner and kills him. Moose then disappears. After reporting to the police, Marlowe makes a desultory attempt to track him further. When Marlowe talks to an old woman, Mrs. Florian, who had known Moose and Velma in earlier days, she tells him that Velma is dead. He gives up the chase.

At this point Marlowe becomes involved in what seems to be a completely new line of action. A certain Lindsay Marriott tells Marlowe a complicated and dubious story about having to pay ransom for a fabulous jade necklace and hires the detective to act as his bodyguard during the payoff. When they drive to the deserted road supposedly designated by the jewel thieves, Marlowe is knocked out and Marriott is murdered. Marlowe is left with a bitter sense of having failed in his job. He investigates further and discovers that the jade necklace belongs to the wealthy Mrs. Lewin Lockridge Grayle. Marlowe calls on Mrs. Grayle, who tells him another story about her jade necklace and then makes a date to meet him at a night club. In the meantime, examining some marijuana cigarettes found on Marriott's body, Marlowe finds a card with the name "Jules Amthor, Psychic Consultant" printed on it. Amthor turns out to be a Hollywood spiritualist with an establishment similar to that of the Haldorn's in Hammett's *The Dain Curse*. When he approaches Amthor, however, Marlowe comes out second. He is beaten up by Amthor and a huge Hollywood Indian named Second Planting, and then turned over to two crooked policemen from neighboring Bay City. The two policemen deposit Marlowe in a clandestine hospital where the corrupt Dr. Sonderberg injects him with drugs. Waking from his drug-induced stupor, Marlowe escapes from Sonderberg's "hospital." In the process he discovers that Moose Malloy has been hiding out there. When he tells his story to the police, Marlowe is warned to stay off the case and to let the police handle the rest of the investigation. By this time it is fairly obscure just who and what are being investigated.

The next phase of the action begins when Marlowe and the police discover that Mrs. Florian, with whom Marlowe had talked earlier, has been violently murdered, apparently by Moose Malloy. Marlowe returns to Bay City and discovers that Moose Malloy is probably hiding out on a gambling ship anchored off shore. With the assistance of an honest former policeman he meets on the waterfront, Marlowe manages to board the gambling ship secretly and to persuade its owner, the racketeer Laird Brunette, to deliver a message to Moose. By this time, the reader, like Marlowe, has probably realized that the wealthy and beautiful Mrs. Grayle is actually Moose's former sweetheart who has married an elderly millionaire during Moose's long stretch in prison. The climax of the novel is a confrontation between Moose and Mrs. Grayle-Velma in Marlowe's apartment. The culmination of this meeting is worth quoting as an example of the taut, emotionally charged, but understated narrative that is one of Chandler's most effective stylistic qualities:

> He didn't look at me at all. He looked at Mrs. Lewin Lockridge Grayle. He leaned forward and his mouth smiled at her and he spoke to her softly. "I thought I knew the voice," he said. "I listened to that voice for eight years—all I could remember of it. I kind of liked your hair red, though. Hiya, babe. Long time no see."
> She turned the gun.
> "Get away from me, you son of a bitch," she said.
> He stopped dead and dropped the gun to his side. He was still a couple of feet from her. His breath labored.
> "I never thought," he said quietly. "It just came to me out of the blue. *You* turned me in to the cops. *You*, Little Velma."
> I threw a pillow, but it was too slow. She shot him five times in the stomach. The bullets made no more sound than fingers going into a glove.[35]

Velma escapes, and Moose dies. This is the end of Marlowe's direct involvement with the case. We are told, however, that, three months later, in Baltimore, a detective recognizes Velma singing in a night club. When he corners her, Velma shoots the detective and then herself.

Needless to say, it is not clarity of plot or the suspenseful intensity of a straightforward line of action that accounts for the particular power of *Farewell, My Lovely*. Chandler's plot is both fantastically intricate and lacking in suspense, at least as far as the mystery itself is concerned, for it requires little penetration to see that the key to the mystery lies in the identity of Mrs. Grayle. The central problem of *Farewell, My Lovely* is not who did the murders but why Philip Marlowe goes to so much trouble and runs so many risks to arrange the final confrontation between Moose Malloy and his Little Velma. The whodunit answer to this question is that after the death of Mrs. Florian only Moose can identify the wealthy Mrs. Grayle as Little Velma and thereby implicate her in the murder of Lindsay Marriott. But this motive seems disproportionate to the trouble and risk Marlowe takes to bring Moose and Velma together. His actions clearly imply that Marlowe has come to feel that Moose and Velma have earned the right to confront each other without interference. When Moose lets Velma shoot him down, Marlowe recognizes that Moose has made his choice, and sympathizes with him. Later, the doctor tells him that Moose has a chance to survive the shooting, and Marlowe's laconic judgment is, "He wouldn't want it."

Though Moose Malloy is a brutal killer, he is a man of epic proportions whose motives derive from the simple code he lives by and from his love for Velma. He is an Ajax anachronistically thrust into the antiheroic twentieth-century city, a gargantuan Romeo whose innocent passion is betrayed and who is eventually murdered in cold blood by his Juliet. Yet there is a kind of grandeur about him and his situation that, for Marlowe, places him beyond the sterility and corruption of the city and earns him the right to confront his Velma. "Because the big sap loved her—and still does. That's what makes it funny, tragic-funny," Marlowe comments toward the end of the story as he struggles to articulate his reaction to the final confrontation. Even when Moose kills, he does so in the innocence of his epic strength, reminding one of the feeble-minded Lennie in John Steinbeck's *Of Mice and Men,*

> "You killed a woman," I said. "Jessie Florian. That was a mistake."
> He thought. Then he nodded. "I'd drop that one," he said quietly.
> "But that queered it," I said. "I'm not afraid of you. You're no killer. You didn't mean to kill her. The other one—over on Central—you could have squeezed out of. But not out of beating a woman's head on a bedpost until her brains were on her face."
> "You take some awful chances, brother," he said softly.
> "The way I've been handled," I said, "I don't know the difference any more. You didn't mean to kill her—did you?"
> His eyes were restless. His head was cocked in a listening attitude.
> "It's about time you learned your own strength," I said.
> "It's too late," he said.[36]

Both Marlowe as reluctant knight and Moose Malloy as epic bandit live by codes of behavior that contrast with the sordid routines of the city. Consequently there is a mutual attraction from the moment that Marlowe sees Moose dressed like a parody of a romantic dandy in the middle of tawdry Central Avenue "looking up at the dusty windows with a sort of ecstatic fixity of expression." Moose, as Marlowe initially observes,

> was worth looking at. He wore a shaggy borsalino hat, a rough gray sports coat with white golf balls on it for buttons, a brown shirt, a yellow tie, pleated gray flannel slacks and alligator shoes with white explosions on the toes. From his outer breast pocket cascaded a show handkerchief of the same brilliant yellow as his tie. There were a couple of colored feathers tucked into the band of his hat, but he didn't really need them. Even on Central Avenue, not the quietest dressed street in the world, he looked about as inconspicuous as a tarantula on a slice of angel food.[37]

Once Marlowe realizes that this epic figure is engaged in an enterprise at once so innocent and absurd as seeking to find the woman he loves right where he had left her eight years ago, he becomes increasingly sympathetic to the ferocious bandit. Even though he knows Moose is a killer, he comes to feel that Moose's quest is somehow authentic:

> "It didn't matter to him that she hadn't written to him in six years or ever gone to see him while he was in jail. It didn't matter to him that she had turned him in for a reward. He just bought some fine clothes and started to look for her the first thing when he got out. So she pumped five bullets into him, by way of saying hello. He had killed two people himself, but he was in love with her. What a world."[38]

Moose's romantic illusions partly resemble those of Fitzgerald's Gatsby.

Like Gatsby, Moose cherishes the memory of an earlier love and he dreams of turning the clock back to the time of this romance. When he discovers that this is impossible, he dies instead of living on in a world of shattered illusions. Needless to say, Fitzgerald's characters are more humanly plausible and their actions more moving and tragic than in Chandler's story. For example, the relationship between Daisy and Gatsby is deeply and richly treated by Fitzgerald in all of its phases, while the Moose-Velma relationship remains largely on the level of simple illusion and betrayal. Similarly when Nick Carraway, who plays the role of "detective" in *The Great Gatsby*, gradually comes to understand Gatsby's motives and significance, it is a deeply shattering and maturing experience for him. Marlowe, on the other hand, is not fundamentally changed by his encounter with Moose and Velma. On the contrary, he plays the role of swashbuckling *deus ex machina* and final judge who shapes life in the image of his own sense of rightness rather than coming to a new recognition of the dilemmas of human life.

Though the limitations of the formula and of his own sense of life prevent Chandler from creating a work as rich as *The Great Gatsby*, he does give his characters moral implications beyond their role in the pattern of mystery, investigation, and exposure. Moose and Velma are both in quest of an elusive grail that continually eludes them. Velma (Mrs. Grayle) is the object of Moose's quest. She herself has tried to escape from the sordid reality of her origin into a life of wealth and freedom. But both these quests become destructive and corrupt. Because she will not come to terms with her past, Velma becomes a murderess. In his obsessive insistence on finding Velma, Moose not only becomes a murderer himself, but frightens Velma into murdering Lindsay Marriott. Thus the quests of Moose and Velma become sources of a kind of moral infection that spreads through the social order and involves the crooked policeman, phony spiritualists, and racketeers who try to stop Marlowe from completing his investigation. There is also a cultural allegory in Chandler's treatment of these two characters. Moose and Velma embody the dreams of youthful romance and success, which Chandler, like many writers of his period, saw as characteristic American illusions.

Marlowe is no victim of such illusions. He is armed against them by the bitter cynicism and world-weariness that are revealed in his recurrent sense of disgust and revulsion at his involvement with this corrupt society:

> A lovely old woman. I liked being with her. I liked getting her drunk for my own sordid purposes. I was a swell guy. I enjoyed being me. You find almost anything under your hand in my business, but I was beginning to be a little sick at my stomach.[39]

Yet Marlowe, too, seeks a grail, a moral justice transcending the tawdry and corrupt routines of society's legality. Thus an extremely important theme in *Farewell, My Lovely* is Marlowe's running conflict with the police, a conflict through which Chandler dramatizes the limitations of social institutions and justifies Marlowe's determination to allow Moose and Velma to confront their own destinies rather than turning them over to the police. In *Farewell, My Lovely* the police range in character from the decent but tired Nulty and the honest but too cynical Randall of the Los Angeles police to the totally corrupt officers of "Bay City." But whether honest or corrupt, the police, in Marlowe's view, are too insensitive or too limited by the necessities of politics to deal justly with a situation like that of Moose and Little Velma. Their handling of Velma is a case in point. So long as she remains the wealthy Mrs. Lewin Lockridge Grayle, the police will do everything they can to keep her from being approached or questioned by characters like Philip Marlowe. With the connivance of the police of "Bay City," Marlowe is assaulted, drugged, and imprisoned in a phony medical establishment to keep him from making further inquiries into the relationship between Mrs. Grayle and Lindsay Marriott. Once Mrs. Grayle is exposed as Velma Valento, however, she becomes simply a quarry, an object to be hunted down and made the center of a public circus. To Marlowe there is something deeply immoral about this total absorption of the individual into the public role. And it is Velma's ultimate refusal to play the degrading role that society's justice would force upon her, even though this role might save her life, that finally determines Marlowe's own judgment:

> "I'm not saying she was a saint or even a halfway nice girl. Not ever. She wouldn't kill herself until she was cornered. But what she did and the way she did it, kept her from coming back here for trial. Think that over. And who would that trial hurt most? Who would be least able to bear it? And win, lose or draw, who would pay the biggest price for the show? An old man who had loved not wisely, but too well."[40]

It should be noted that Marlowe's lapse into Shakespearean grandiloquence is immediately covered up with the private eye's patented overcoat of protective cynicism. When police lieutenant Randall rejects this analysis as sentimentality, Marlowe replies: " 'Sure. It sounded like that when I said it. Probably all a mistake anyway. So long.' "[41] But Marlowe's final comment is an eloquently ambiguous statement: "It was a cool day and very clear. You could see a long way—but not as far as Velma had gone."[42]

Thus, *Farewell, My Lovely* uses the hard-boiled detective formula to treat such contemporary moral and cultural themes as romantic illusion, destructive innocence, and the conflict between individual moral feeling and the collective routines of society. Because they embody serious themes in a quasi-allegorical fashion Chandler's characters gain richness and depth even though they remain rather artificial and melodramatic creations. One might find it a little difficult to believe in a chess-playing, Shakespeare-quoting, supremely chivalrous tough guy like Marlowe were it not that the moral dilemmas posed by the characters he encounters have a degree of serious significance and human complexity missing from most of the hard-boiled detective writers.

Mickey Spillane

By most traditional literary or artistic standards, the works of Mickey Spillane are simply atrocious. His characters and situations not only strain credulity to its limits, they frequently turn the stomach as well. Spillane's narrative technique is so "hard-hitting," as the reviewers say, that it has the expressiveness of a blackjack. His style and dialogue are awkward, stilted, and wooden. His idea of a theme consists of a primitive right-wing diatribe against some of the central principles of American democracy and English law. Yet, despite all these disadvantages (or perhaps they are advantages), Spillane's books have sold over forty million copies. Among the thirty top best-sellers from 1895 to 1965, seven were by Spillane. Only such super best-sellers as Dr. Spock, *Peyton Place*, *Gone with the Wind*, and *The Carpetbaggers* have exceeded the sales of *I, the Jury* and *The Big Kill*. Such superb hard-boiled stories as Chandler's *Farewell, My Lovely* and Hammett's *The Maltese Falcon* have sold just over a million copies, while Spillane's books average four to five million.

Spillane's immense popularity is often attributed to the unregenerate depravity and stupidity of the mass reading public. Since his closest sales competitors are hard-boiled writers like Brett Halliday and Richard Prather, prolific hacks who more or less imitate the Spillane recipe without adding much in the way of literary interest, one can easily envision mindless millions of cretins slobbering idiotically as Mike Hammer pistolwhips another naked female. But such visions are too vague and moralistic to be of much help in understanding the Spillane phenomenon. The mass audience and its motives are too complex for such simplistic generalizations to do anything but relieve the feelings of those who are distressed that such questionable works of literature should attract so wide a public.

Spillane's first and best-selling novel, *I, the Jury*, shares with Chandler's *Farewell, My Lovely* the basic characteristics of the hard-boiled formula. Both novels take the form of a personal narrative by a tough private investigator. This hero pursues an investigation that leads him ever deeper into the perversion and evil endemic to the urban setting in which he operates. In the process both Chandler's Philip Marlowe and Spillane's Mike Hammer become involved in an ambiguous relationship with the police, a relationship that reveals the limitations of the legal process in achieving "true" justice. Through this portrayal of the inefficiency and helplessness of the established authorities, the hero's own personal sense of justice and his aggressive acting out of his judgment are made emotionally necessary and morally righteous. Finally, both heroes discover that the criminal they seek is a beautiful but vicious woman who has sexually tempted them earlier in the book.

The difference between the two writers is nonetheless substantial. Chandler fleshes out this fable with fairly complex characters and a richly symbolic action, whereas Spillane operates by leaving the basic formulaic framework as simple and uncomplicated as possible. Instead of adding human complexity to the skeleton, he heightens the pattern of the formula through violence, quasi-pornography, and other devices of emotional intensification. Both the style and the larger structure of his novels manifest this kind of heightening. For example, in both *I, the Jury* and *Farewell, My Lovely* women attempt to seduce the detective-hero. In Chandler's novel, however, the seduction is described in a relatively detached and ironic fashion that emphasizes its sordidness, artificiality, and pathos, especially when, in the middle of the action, the temptress's elderly husband wanders pathetically into the scene:

> She fell softly across my lap and I bent down over her face and began to browse on it. She worked her eyelashes and made butterfly kisses on my cheeks. When I got to her mouth it was half open and burning and her tongue was a darting snake between her teeth.
> The door opened and Mr. Grayle stepped quietly into the room. I was holding her and didn't have a chance to let go. I lifted my face and looked at him. I felt cold as Finnegan's feet, the day they buried him.
> The blonde in my arms didn't move, didn't even close her lips. She had a half-dreamy, half-sarcastic expression on her face.
> Mr. Grayle cleared his throat slightly and said: "I beg your pardon, I'm sure," and went quietly out of the room. There was an infinite sadness in his eyes.[43]

When Spillane does a seduction scene, not a hint of irony or pathos enters in, except unintentionally. In its place there is a voyeuristic fascination with the woman's movements and a fantasy of male dominance as the woman extends her sexual invitation. Clearly Spillane's model here as elsewhere in his descriptions of sexual relations is not the actual encounter of men and women but the conventionalized sexual ritual of the striptease:

> Mary drew her legs up under her on the divan and turned on her side to face me. During the process the negligee fell open, but she took her time to draw it shut. Deliberately, she let my eyes feast on her lovely bosom. What I could see of her stomach was smooth parallel rows of light muscles, almost like a man's. I licked my lips. . . .
> Her eyes were blazing into mine. They were violet eyes, a wild blazing violet. Her mouth looked soft and wet, and provocative. She was making no attempt to keep the negligee on. One shoulder had slipped down and her brown skin formed an interesting contrast with the pink. I wondered how she got her tan. There were no strap marks anywhere. She uncrossed her legs deliberately and squirmed like an overgrown cat, letting the light play with the ripply muscles in her naked thighs.[44]

In comparison with the Chandler scene where sexuality is open, brutal and a direct expression of character (the woman callous but driven, the detective reluctant and ironic), in Spillane, as in pornography, it is largely divorced from character. This abstract sexuality uses repetition and a drawing out of the action to produce a heightened feeling in the reader. Interestingly enough, there is almost no description of the sexual act itself in Spillane. Indeed, in the passage cited above, Mike Hammer refuses the lady's overtures at the last minute and departs in righteous chastity. As in the case of the stripteaser, the preliminaries are more important than the goal. After the repetitive, teasing buildup of bumps and grinds, the actual moment of nakedness is an anticlimax. So Spillane has his females endlessly ripple their muscles while letting their dresses hang open provocatively. One might almost say that his novels are structured as elaborate stripteases in which Mike is increasingly tempted by a series of sexy damsels; in the end, the tease almost reaches the point of passionate sexuality, but the final teaser always turns out to be the murderess and consequently must be destroyed. In one of the central emotional rhythms in Spillane's work, sexual provocation leads to fulfillment in violence.

Violence as orgasm is a main theme of Spillane's novels. Despite the prevalence of violence in the novels of Hammett and Chandler, one must look fairly hard to find instances where the detective-hero himself either hits or shoots another character. When they do, the incident is usually treated with a neutral terseness or with the ironic detachment that marks the hero's character. I have already commented on the increasing disgust and fear that mark the Continental Op's involvement with the mounting violence of Hammett's *Red Harvest*. Only once does the Op actually shoot somebody in that novel, and there the description is cold and emotionless with no sense of fulfillment in violence:

> Across the street, burly Nick had stepped out of a doorway to pump slugs at us with both hands.
> I steadied my gun-arm on the floor. Nick's body showed over the front sight. I squeezed the gun. Nick stopped shooting. He crossed his guns on his chest and went down in a pile on the sidewalk.[45]

Nor does the Op enjoy banging people around in the manner of Spillane's Mike Hammer. The one time he actually knocks another character down, it is presented as a decent and humane act: " 'I poked him to give him back some of his self-respect. You know, treated him as I would a man instead of a down-and-outer who could be slapped around by girls.' "[46] Like Hammett's detective-hero, Chandler's Marlowe is rarely the source of violence, though on these occasions Chandler does stylistically heighten the description of violence to a greater degree than Hammett. Marlowe's ironic reluctance is still a part of the scene:

> He whirled at me. Perhaps it would have been nice to allow him another shot or two, just like a gentleman of the old school. But his gun was still up and I couldn't wait any longer. Not long enough to be a gentleman of the old school. I shot him four times, the Colt straining against my ribs. The

gun jumped out of his hand as if it had been kicked. He reached both his hands for his stomach. I could hear them smack hard against his body. He fell like that, straight forward, holding himself together with his broad hands. He fell face down in the wet gravel. And after that there wasn't a sound from him.[47]

In Spillane's novels, however, Mike Hammer is the main source of violence. His chief investigative technique consists of beating up the suspects to force confessions, and this violence is described with a detail and intensity that leaves no doubt of the great emotional catharsis it brings to the hero:

> The goddamn bastards played right into my hands. They thought they had me nice and cold and just as they were set to carve me into a raw mess of skin, I dragged out the .45 and let them look down the hole so they could see where sudden death came from.
> It was the only kind of talk they knew. The little guy stared too long. He should have been watching my face. I snapped the side of the rod across his jaw and laid the flesh open to the bone. He dropped the sap and staggered into the big boy with a scream starting to come up out of his throat only to get it cut off in the middle as I pounded his teeth back into his mouth with the end of the barrel. . . . The punk was vomiting on the floor, trying to claw his way under the sink. For laughs I gave him a taste of his own sap on the back of his hand and felt the bones go into splinters. He wasn't going to be using any tools for a long time.[48]

Spillane makes the relationship between sexual teasing and violent catharsis a part of the basic texture of his stories. In his hands, the hard-boiled structural formula of increasing involvement in a web of corruption becomes an alternating pattern of sexual provocation and orgies of shooting or beating that seem to function psychologically as a partial release of the emotional tension built up by the unconsummated sexual teasing. This structural pattern reaches its climax in the nightmarish final scenes of Spillane's novels. Spillane has a remarkable ability to imagine and visualize scenes in which the disturbing emotions aroused by the mounting tensions of sexual teasing and orgiastic violence reach culmination. The key to these scenes is a legitimated sadism that differentiates Spillane from most of the other hard-boiled writers. Three examples will indicate the way in which Spillane creates the climactic sadism of his stories. In *One Lonely Night*, Mike Hammer's chaste secretary-sweetheart Velda has been captured by Communist spies. When Mike breaks in on their secret hideout he finds that Velda has been strung up naked and is being whipped. Although Mike then shoots the Commie rats, it seems clear that one reason for his passionate destruction of her torturers is his own ambiguous delight in the flagellating of Velda.

> Then there was only beauty to the nakedness of her body. A beauty of the flesh that was more than the sensuous curve of her hips, more than the sharp curve of breast drawn high under the weight of her body, more than those long full legs, more than the ebony of her hair. There was the beauty

of the flesh that was the beauty of the soul and the guy in the pork-pie hat grimaced with hate and raised the rope to smash it down while the rest slobbered with the lust and pleasure of this example of what was yet to come, even drooled with the passion that was death made slow in the fulfillment of the philosophy that lived under a red flag.[49]

It is worth noting that Spillane frequently expresses such political or social attitudes in connection with the emotions aroused by his porno-violence. In a number of his novels "patriotic" hostility toward "communism" and foreigners serves as part of the justification for Mike's participation in the culminating orgy of sadism and destruction.

Another example of Spillane's way of bringing his two major themes of sexual provocation and violence together is the conclusion of *The Big Kill*. Marsha Lee, the beautiful actress who has been tempting Mike throughout the novel—"the soft pink tones of her body softened the metallic glitter of the nylon gown that outlined her in bronze, flowing smoothly up the roundness of her thighs"[50]—turns out to be a vicious blackmailer who is responsible for the killing of a man whose little boy Mike has been protecting. When Mike confronts Marsha, she manages to get the drop on him, but just as she is about to shoot, the little boy, who happens to be in the room, starts to play with Mike's forgotten gun. Providentially, the gun goes off and the bullet flies across the room "with a horrible vengeance that ripped all the evil from her face, turning it into a ghastly wet red mask that was really no face at all."[51] Here, as in *One Lonely Night*, the sadism is slightly disguised by attributing it to someone other than the hero, but in *I, the Jury*, the climactic scene of sadistic masculine response to sexual provocation is brutally overt. Mike confronts the beautiful blonde he has discovered to be the murdering head of a dope ring. In response to Mike's accusations, the lady slowly and provocatively strips until she stands naked and inviting before him. Then Mike shoots her. The final dialogue between the lovers is devastatingly revealing of Mike's bitter hostility toward women.

> When I heard her fall I turned around. Her eyes had pain in them now, the pain preceding death. Pain and unbelief.
> "How c-could you?" she gasped.
> I only had a moment before talking to a corpse, but I got it in.
> "It was easy," I said.[52]

Since they are built up out of this texture of sexual provocation and masculine violence climaxed by the infliction of pain and death on the sexual object, Spillane's books are an extreme embodiment of the fear, hostility, and ambiguity toward society and particularly toward women that are built into the hard-boiled detective formula. Where writers like Hammett and Chandler qualify the endemic aggression and sadism of this formula with a considerable degree of irony and complexity, Spillane's skill as a popular writer lies precisely in his ability to suppress characters and turns of plot that might confuse or enrich the essential emotional pattern, and in his capacity to invent incidents like the ritual striptease killing of *I, the Jury* that embody the central emotional themes of the hard-boiled formula with primitive and vivid directness. Even the detective-hero has highly simplified motives in the Spillane story. Instead of Marlowe's complex reluctance, or the Continental Op's stoic professionalism, Mike Hammer usually becomes involved in a case through a simple desire for revenge. In *I, the Jury* the novel begins with the murder of Mike's best friend, and the rest of Mike's actions are explicitly motivated by a desire to avenge this death. In *The Big Kill* Mike witnesses the murder of a father of a young child. He becomes temporarily the child's protector and swears to avenge the father. The action of *One Lonely Night* centers on the capture of Mike's secretary Velda by Communist agents. The story derives from Mike's violent desire to rescue Velda and/or destroy her tormentors. Once established, Mike's single dominant motive does not change in the course of the story, in contrast to Marlowe's constantly shifting attitudes and redefinitions of his mission.

One might well inquire why, if this is the central purpose of his version of the hard-boiled formula, Spillane's readers do not simply prefer straight sadistic pornography. Erwin Panofsky greatly assists us in dealing with this problem, when, in an essay on "Style and Medium in the Motion Pictures," he sums up the central characteristics of the "folk art mentality" as they become embodied in the early movies:

> They gratified—often simultaneously—first, a primitive sense of justice and decorum when virtue and industry were rewarded while vice and laziness were punished; second, plain sentimentality when "the thin trickle of a fictive love interest" took its course "through somewhat serpentine channels," or when Father, dear Father returned from the saloon to find his child dying of diphtheria; third, a primordial instinct for bloodshed and cruelty when Andreas Hoffer faced the firing squad, or when (in a film of 1893–94) the head of Mary Queen of Scots actually came off; fourth, a taste for mild pornography; and finally that crude sense of humor, graphically described as "slapstick," which feeds upon the sadistic and the pornographic instinct, either singly or in combination.[53]

The one improvement we might suggest for this fine enumeration of the characteristics of folk art is a greater emphasis on the relationship between the elements. For it is not simply the presence of sadism or pornography but their careful and inextricable relationship with sentiment and a "primitive sense of justice," that is important. Thus, Mike Hammer's orgiastic sadism is acceptable and cathartic for a mass audience because it is initiated by sentimental feelings, such as Mike's deep sorrow for a murdered friend and justified by the unpunished evil that his investigations uncover. Weighed against the individual and social evils he confronts, Mike's brutality is made to seem a necessary and even indispensable course of action. In an urban world dominated by gangsters, Communist agents, and socialite dope pushers, the only person who can bring the elites of evil to their reckoning is Spillane's lone wolf of destruction. Spillane's social paranoia with its hysterical fears of urban sophistication, foreigners, and minority groups therefore serves an important function in justifying his hero's brutality. Similarly, Spillane's sentimentality and didacticism are given greater intensity through their eventuation in violence.

This combination of sentimentality, pornography, and violence, linked by a delight in the extralegal punishment of successful evildoers and by a profound, ambiguous fear of the temptations and wickedness of the city have long been a staple of folklore, as Panofsky points out. In addition, this particular combination has been endemic to the popular literature of nineteenth- and twentieth-century England and America ranging in time (and quality) from Dickens and *Uncle Tom's Cabin* to *Peyton Place*. If we look, however, for a nineteenth-century analogue to this combination of elements, simplified and heightened in the fashion of Mickey Spillane, we find it in the immensely popular but now forgotten didactic temperance novels written by such authors as T. S. Arthur, whose *Ten Nights in a Bar Room* had the same kind of a skeletal form as Spillane's novels. Moreover, there is enough similarity of theme and attitude between these two literary types to make the comparison curious but revealing. In the temperance novel, the hero, like Spillane's detective, encounters the disturbing temptations of the sophisticated city: the corruptions of wealth, the destructive habits of tobacco and alcohol (and the dangerous seductiveness of the Scarlet Woman). Spillane, writing for a society that has accepted smoking and drinking as part of its way of life, transmutes the animus against liquor into a fear of drugs. The Scarlet Woman is a central figure in his stories. In addition, temperance novels are full of tearful children who beg their wavering daddies to set aside the fatal glass of beer and come home. Similarly, Spillane frequently arouses his reader's feelings for the plight of the innocent child by having his detective-hero protect children threatened by the surrounding corruption. The temperance novel even tends to manifest the same pattern of social hostility as Spillane: the corrupters represent sophisticated wealth on one side and non-white or non-Protestant groups on the other. For the nineteenth-century didactic novelists, popery plays the role assumed by communism in Spillane: a foreign conspiracy associated with threats to the sexual purity and moral asceticism of the American way of life. Finally, the temperance novels characteristically end with a terrible providential vengeance against the corrupters, just as Spillane's novels end with the violent death of the Scarlet Woman. While Spillane does not suggest that his Mike Hammer is an agent of divine providence, he does frequently imply that Mike is driven by forces larger than himself, that his brutality comes from a sacred frenzy against the rampant evils at large in the world. For example, at one point Mike thinks that he might give up his crusade against evil:

   I ought to get out of it. I ought to take Velda and my office and start up in
real estate in some small community where murder and guns and dames
didn't happen. Maybe I would, at that. It was wonderful to be able to think
straight again. No more crazy mad hatred that tied my insides into knots.
No more hunting the scum that stood behind a trigger and shot at the
world.[54]

But this is only a passing moment. In the next few pages Mike is at it again,
compulsively driven by his instinct for primitive justice to wipe out more
rotten gangsters and foreigners.

   This comparison with the temperance novel suggests that beyond his
capacity to simplify and emotionally heighten the basic formula of the
hard-boiled detective story, Spillane also brings to this formula something of
the fervor and passion of the popular evangelical religious tradition that has
long been a dominant element in the culture of lower-middle- and lower-class
America. It is certainly no accident that this tradition also exemplifies many
of Spillane's primary social hostilities: rural suspicion of urban sophistication; nativist hatred of racial and ethnic minorities; the ambiguous hostility
toward women of those anxious about their status and concerned about the
erosion of masculine dominance. But, above all, it is the similar intensity of
passion, growing out of a bitter, overpowering hatred of the world as a sinful
and corrupt place that unites Spillane with the popular evangelical tradition.
Spillane's own temporary involvement in the passionate millenialism of the
Jehovah's Witnesses suggests the extent to which his own view of the world is
similar to that of the evangelical tradition.

   Thus, Mickey Spillane's version of the hard-boiled detective formula has a
special quality that comes from two main sources: first, there is Spillane's
ability to construct a narrative that embodies in heightened form the pure
skeleton of the formula; Spillane has a visceral feel for the essential pattern of
action and theme that underlies the hard-boiled story and is able to express
this pattern with great simplicity and force in highly colored episodes and
images. Second, Spillane has always instinctively recognized the connection
between his narratives and the popular evangelical tradition and has been
able to tap the great passion that many Americans have invested in that
tradition by embodying its central themes of hostility toward the sinful city
with its corrupt men of wealth, its degenerate foreigners, and its Scarlet
Women. Of all the hard-boiled writers, Spillane's art is closest in its mythical
simplicity to folktale and in its passionate hatred and denunciations to the
popular revivalist sermon. It is to its combination of these qualities and not
simply to its preoccupation with sex and violence that the work of Mickey
Spillane owes its immense popularity. It is tempting to suggest that the
strained and hysterical violence of so much of his work reflects the fact that
he is a prophet of the past, that his vision of the brutal redeemer Mike
Hammer is the agonized but final outcry of the evangelistic subculture of

rural America about to be swallowed up in the pluralistic, cosmopolitan world of the cities. The cool, bureaucratic style of Mike Hammer's successors, the James Bonds and the Matt Helms, is certainly far removed from the passionate crusades of Spillane's bitter and violent hero.

Eight

The Western:
A Look at the Evolution of a Formula

In concentrating on the definition and comparison of formulaic structures, their artistic limitations and potentials, and the cultural and psychological basis of their appeals, I was not able to say very much about the historical evolution of individual formulas. Formulas do tend to change over the course of time and many different factors interact during this process of evolution: the impact of new media, the inventiveness of creators and performers, and, above all, changes in the culture. In the third chapter I showed how changing cultural attitudes toward crime influenced the creation of a number of different crime formulas. In this chapter, I will narrow my focus and concentrate on the evolution of a single formula, the western, as an illustration of how the process of formulaic development can be analyzed. The western is a particularly interesting subject for this kind of analysis since its history covers nearly one hundred and fifty years and several different media.[1] Because of this considerable length of time, and the enormous number of individual western novels, films, stories, dramas, radio programs, comic books, and Wild West spectacles, I will necessarily have to be highly selective in my treatment. Since the western tends to be as formalized in its way as the detective story, such selectivity is not inappropriate. I have attempted to hit upon the major points of variation in the formula and thereby to chart the major phases of the western's evolution.

The western formula probably came into existence when James Fenimore Cooper made a particularly felicitous combination of fictional materials dealing with the settlement of the American wilderness and the archetypal pattern of the adventure story. Cooper's first full-scale development of this material in *The Pioneers* had elements of the adventure archetype but was essentially a novel of manners with strong melodramatic overtones. By the time Cooper completed his Leatherstocking saga with *The Deerslayer*, the basic shape of the western formula had become the adventure story, and this has remained the case down to the present time. Though writers often attempt to use western materials in connection with other literary archetypes, their stories clearly differ from what we think of as the "western" in the degree that they depart from the basic form of the adventure with its apotheosis of a hero.

Unlike the detective story, the western formula is not defined by a fixed pattern of action. Where the plot of the detective story is always the same, many different plots can be used for westerns so long as they pose some basic challenge to the hero and work toward his ultimate confrontation with an antagonist. Thus many westerns employ revenge stories, while others emphasize the action of chase and pursuit, or conflicts between groups such as pioneers vs. Indians, or ranchers vs. farmers. The element that most clearly defines the western is the symbolic landscape in which it takes place and the influence this landscape has on the character and actions of the hero. This is, I think, why this particular formula has come to be known by a geographical term, the western, rather than by a characterization of the protagonist's form of action, as in the case of the detective story or the gangster saga, or by some quality of action and mood as in the case of the gothic romance or the horror story.

The symbolic landscape of the western formula is a field of action that centers upon the point of encounter between civilization and wilderness, East and West, settled society and lawless openness. The frontier settlement or group is a point both in space and in time. Geographically, it represents a group of civilizers or pioneers on the edge of a wilderness, tenuously linked to the civilized society behind them in the East by the thinnest lines of communication. These links are constantly in danger of being cut by the savages—Indians or outlaws—who roam the wilderness. Historically, the western represents a moment when the forces of civilization and wilderness life are in balance, the epic moment at which the old life and the new confront each other and individual actions may tip the balance one way or another, thus shaping the future history of the whole settlement.

This epic confrontation of forces calls forth the hero, who, whether Leatherstocking, cowboy, gunfighter, or marshal, is defined by the way he is caught between contrasting ways of life. Most commonly, the hero is a man of the wilderness who comes out of the old "lawless" way of life to which he is deeply attached both by personal inclination and by his relationship to male comrades who have shared that life with him. Thus the many cases of sheriffs whose former friends are outlaws, or of Leatherstocking-like figures whose deepest personal relationships are with Indians. Sometimes the hero is not originally tied to the old life, but in such stories—that of the dude become hero, for example—he develops skills and attitudes, or is involved in some set of circumstances, that distinctly separate him from the rest of the pioneers. For example, in Emerson Hough's *The Covered Wagon*, a false report of the hero's past actions makes the pioneers identify him as an outlaw through most of the story. But, despite his separation from the pioneers and his association with the old wilderness life, the hero finds himself cast in the role of defender of the pioneers. The way in which this commitment is brought about is one of the central variations in different versions of the western formula. Sometimes the hero becomes committed to the pioneers because he falls in love with a girl from the East; in other versions, the hero makes a moral decision in favor of the new ideals of settled life. But, whatever the reason for his situation, the western hero finds himself placed between the old life and the new with the responsibility for taking those actions that will bring about the final destruction of the old life and the establishment of settled society. The fact that this resolution almost invariably requires a transcendent and heroic violence indicates that the contending forces of civilization and wilderness reflect strongly conflicting values.

In *The Six-Gun Mystique*, I presented a more detailed analysis of the general characteristics of the western formula and indicated its many sources of appeal. The reader may wish to refer to that discussion for a fuller cataloging of the western formula's major elements of setting, character, and action. For our present purpose of analyzing some of the major changes in the formula over the course of its history, the most significant aspect of the western is its representation of the relationship between the hero and the contending forces of civilization and wilderness, for it is in the changing treatment of this conflict, so basic to American thought and feeling, that the western most clearly reflects the attitudes of its creators and audiences at different periods. Therefore, we will begin our analysis of the western's evolution with a discussion of Cooper's treatment of the dialectic between civilization and nature in his Leatherstocking saga.

Cooper and the Beginnings of the Western Formula

James Fenimore Cooper was a man of many contradictions. Since these contradictions embodied some of the major problems and paradoxes of American civilization, and because he had a talent for getting them down on paper, he became one of the chief inventors of American literature. His great creation, Nathaniel Bumppo, the Leatherstocking, became the prototype for the western hero and thus the progenitor of countless stories, novels, films, and television programs that use the formula Cooper first articulated. Cooper not only became the founder of this major popular tradition but the influence of his Leatherstocking is equally inescapable in major American writers and forms part of the background of Thoreau, Melville, Hawthorne, Twain, Faulkner, and Hemingway. From the beginning, the western intersected with the mainstream of American literature, and, though it developed in its own direction, it has never completely lost touch. One might even say that it was the popular western's function to resolve some of the unresolvable contradictions of American values that our major writers have laid bare. It was Cooper who began the process by exploring some of the central paradoxes of our culture and by establishing some of the ways in which they could be resolved in literature.

Like many of his contemporaries, Cooper was strongly torn between the traditional ideal of culture cultivated by the European aristocracy and the new conception of American democracy. In terms of his own career and background, the conflict between his commitment to a traditional social order and the fascination of a new openness and freedom shaped his life.

Though scion of an aristocratic family, Cooper became a writer of extremely popular novels who supported refined activities by appealing to a large public. Though he was a man of cultivated tastes and spent much of his life in Europe, Cooper was a dedicated patriot and the first major author to set forth a distinctive vision of the American landscape. Yet throughout his life he was dedicated to the ideal of the gentleman. In his book, paradoxically entitled *The American Democrat*, Cooper even went so far as to argue "if the laborer is indispensable to civilization, so is also the gentleman. While the one produces, the other directs his skill to those arts which raise the polished man above the barbarian. . . . Were society to be satisfied with a mere supply of the natural wants, there would be no civilization. The savage condition attains this much. All beyond it, notwithstanding, is so much progress made in the direction of the gentleman."[2] Yet this apologist for the gentry was also the great romanticizer of the primitive. His great heroes, Natty Bumppo the Leatherstocking and Chingachgook and Uncas the noble savages, were men of the wilderness.

Henry Nash Smith has suggested that these paradoxical oppositions of attitude reflected a basic ideological conflict in nineteenth-century American culture between the sense of America as a continuation of European civilization and the vision of a new and better society growing out of the more natural circumstances of the virgin wilderness. Cooper felt the opposing pulls of civilization and nature even more strongly than most of his contemporaries. In his exploration of the dialectic between advancing civilization and the free and natural life of the wilderness, and in his attempt to synthesize these forces, Cooper invented the western. His fictional medium for this exploration was the series of novels centered upon the life of the frontiersman Natty Bumppo, who was loosely modeled on the actual figure of Daniel Boone. This series, *The Pioneers* (1823), *The Last of the Mohicans* (1826), *The Prairie* (1827), *The Pathfinder* (1840), and *The Deerslayer* (1841), have become known as the Leatherstocking Tales.

Cooper's conception of the Leatherstocking saga underwent a considerable evolution. It is even tempting to say, with some oversimplification, that Cooper's transformation of his western narrative from a story of the re-establishment of the gentry in the new West, to a tale of the isolated hero whose very virtues make him flee the oncoming civilization, summarizes the evolution of the western itself from the epic of the pioneers in the nineteenth century to the ambiguous myth of the gunfighter in the 1950s, from Wister's Virginian who not only outguns the villain but becomes a successful rancher and political leader to Henry King's Jimmy Ringo who wants to escape from his gunslinging past but is pursued and destroyed by his own reputation as the fastest gun in the West. In Cooper's case it seems clear that this gradual shift of context, hero, and theme reflected an increasing tension between his aristocratic predispositions and his vision of American society. Cooper's initial hopes for American civilization were high because he felt that the new society, while undoubtedly lacking some of the brilliance of European civilization, would more than compensate for this loss by general peace, prosperity, and decorum. In his *Notions of the Americans* (1828), the key characteristic of American life was progress, and while progress had its costs, it also meant the triumph of common sense and of a "decent middling standard of life based on an expanding provision for social wants and national growth, under the firm governance of order and decorum."[3] Cooper also believed that once the earlier phases of settlement were over, a new kind of social order would develop led by an American gentry class, purified of the corruptions characteristic of European aristocracy, committed to democratic values, and supported by the voluntary deference of their fellow citizens. Under the leadership of this new gentry class, American society would synthesize democratic common sense and moral simplicity with the traditional refinement and cultivation of European civilization.

> The democratic gentleman must differ in many essential particulars, from the aristocratical gentleman, though in their ordinary habits and tastes they are virtually identical. Their principles vary; and, to a slight degree, their deportment accordingly. The democrat, recognizing the right of all to participate in power, will be more liberal in his general sentiments, a quality of superiority in itself; but, in conceding this much to his fellow men, he will proudly maintain his own independence of vulgar domination, as indispensable to his personal habits.[4]

The Pioneers, first-written of the Leatherstocking Tales, presented Cooper's vision of the development of the new American society in almost allegorical fashion. The plot is one of resolution and synthesis. The central action is divided into two lines: the dynastic misunderstanding between the Temple and Effingham families and the conflict of interest between Judge Temple, who represents law and civilization, and Natty Bumppo, who resents the impingement of legal restrictions on the freedom of the old wilderness life. At the beginning of the novel, Natty, who is an aging hunter, his equally old Indian friend Chingachgook, and the young Oliver Edwards appear in the vicinity of the new settlement of Templeton, which has been developed by Judge Temple. When Natty shoots a deer out of season, he comes into conflict with the law of the settlement. This rift is further complicated when two schemers, Hiram Doolittle and Jotham Riddle, attempt to take advantage of the law to search Natty's wilderness hut because they believe the old man has hidden some horde of wealth. Actually, Natty has been protecting old Major Effingham, who Natty and his friends believe has been cheated out of his fortune by Judge Temple. When Natty assaults the wretched Doolittle to keep him from entering the hut, Judge Temple feels that he must enforce the principles of law and order and in his capacity as judge he sentences Natty to a short term of imprisonment. After an escape from jail and a narrow escape from a forest fire, all these complications are unraveled. It turns out that Judge Temple had been keeping the Effingham fortune in trust during the Revolutionary War and has himself been looking for the heirs to the fortune.

Young Oliver Edwards is revealed as the grandson of Major Effingham, and he marries the judge's lovely daughter Elizabeth, with whom he has fallen in love. Though Natty refuses to accept the Temple-Effingham offer of a peaceful old age in the new settlement and, like Daniel Boone, heads off into the wilderness, he has made his peace with the Temple-Effingham family and he departs giving his blessing to the union of Oliver and Elizabeth.

Thus, in *The Pioneers*, the advance of American civilization is seen in generally optimistic terms. At the end of the novel, though the old hunter no longer has a role, the wilderness is rapidly on its way to becoming the ordered and harmonious society that Cooper describes at the beginning of the novel:

> Beautiful and thriving villages are found interspersed along the margins of the small lakes, or situated at those points of the streams which are favourable to manufacturing; and neat and comfortable farms, with every indication of wealth about them, are scattered profusely through the vales, and even to the mountain tops. Roads diverge in every direction, from the even and graceful bottoms of the valleys, to the most rugged and intricated passes of the hills. Academies, and minor edifices of learning, meet the eye of the stranger at every few miles, and places for the worship of God abound with that frequency which characterizes a moral and reflecting people, and with that variety of exterior and canonical govern-ment which flows from unfettered liberty of conscience. In short, the whole district is hourly exhibiting how much can be done, in even a rugged country, and with a severe climate, under the domination of mild laws, and where every man feels a direct interest in the prosperity of a commonwealth, of which he knows himself to form a part. The expedients of the pioneers who first broke ground in the settlement of this country are succeeded by the permanent improvements of the yeoman, who intends to leave his remains to moulder under the sod which he tills, or perhaps, of the son, who, born in the land, piously wishes to linger around the grave of his father. Only forty years have passed since this territory was a wilderness.[5]

I have quoted this passage at some length because it exemplifies so completely what might be called the official myth of the West, that vision that Henry Nash Smith so brilliantly analyzes, of an agrarian paradise in the interior of the United States. *The Pioneers* differs somewhat from the Jeffersonian version of the agrarian utopia in the special role assigned to an American gentry class, in this case the Temple-Effingham dynasty. In most respects, however, the world of *The Pioneers* is well on the way to becoming that serene Jeffersonian society of virtuous yeomen presided over by a natural aristocracy of talent and virtue. Cooper even goes so far as to see to the defeat and expulsion of the two major dangers to this ideal republic: the corrupt and ambitious politician and lawyer and the greedy entrepreneur, symbolized by the two figures of Hiram Doolittle and Jotham Riddle.

The Pioneers was the last of the Leatherstocking Tales in which an optimistic view of progress determined the narrative focus. In *The Last of the Mohicans*, Cooper shifted his attention from the complex problems of reestablishing social institutions in a new settlement to the theme that would dominate the rest of the series: the violence of Indian warfare and the destruction of the old wilderness life.

Violence does exist in the world of *The Pioneers*, but it is largely the result of accident, misunderstanding, or natural forces. Oliver Effingham is wounded at the beginning by a misdirected bullet from the gun of Judge Temple; the heroine, Elizabeth Temple, narrowly escapes death from a panther; a forest fire endangers many of the characters at the climax of the novel. But the landscape of *The Last of the Mohicans* mixes romantic grandeur with danger lurking behind every bush.

> The river was confined between high and cragged rocks, one of which impended above the spot where the canoe rested. As these, again, were surmounted by tall trees, which appeared to totter on the brows of the precipice, it gave the stream the appearance of running through a deep and narrow dell. All beneath the fantastic limbs and ragged tree-tops, which were, here and there, dimly painted against the starry zenith, lay alike in shadowed obscurity. Behind them, the curvature of the banks soon bounded the view, by the same dark and wooded outline; but in front, and apparently at no great distance, the water seemed piled against the heavens, whence it tumbled into caves, out of which issued those sullen sounds that had loaded the evening atmosphere. It seemed, in truth, to be a spot devoted to seclusion, and the sisters imbibed a soothing impression of security, as they gazed upon its romantic, though not unappalling beauties. A general movement among their conductors, however, soon recalled them from a contemplation of the wild charms that night had assisted to lend the place, to a painful sense of their real peril.[6]

This landscape takes on the double implication of trancendence and violence that is so typical of the western. Cooper's increasing emphasis on violence in *The Last of the Mohicans* also meant that he abandoned the fixed social setting of *The Pioneers* and placed his characters in motion across the wilderness, involving them in what became the western's characteristic rhythm of chase and pursuit. In *The Pioneers* the important action takes place in the settlement, in Judge Temple's mansion, in the law court, in the prison, and in the area just outside the town where Natty has his cabin. There is relatively little sense of the surrounding wilderness coming up to and endangering the town. In *The Last of the Mohicans*, the wilderness has erupted in the violence of the French and Indian War, the story opens with the destruction of a wilderness settlement, and the remainder of the narrative deals with the leading characters' attempts to escape from a group of Indians involved in the massacre.

Because of the new emphasis on violence, there are also important changes in the cast of characters of *The Last of the Mohicans*. These new characterizations adumbrate to a remarkable extent the future development of the western. Most important is the conception of the western hero, the extra-ordinary man whose double gifts of civilization and savagery make him able to confront and conquer the perils of the wilderness. Natty Bumppo does appear in *The Pioneers*, but in that book Cooper seems more concerned with the problem of where he fits in socially than with his extraordinary powers. In fact, there is more pathos than heroism about the old woodsman. As Natty finds himself in situation after situation with which he doesn't quite know how to cope, he can only complain in the tones of a bitter and helpless old man about the incomprehensibility of newfangled notions of law. Though something of the Natty to come breaks through occasionally, particularly in his Daniel Boone-like gesture of refusing to stay in the settlement, the last scene of *The Pioneers* places Natty right back in the traditional social order from which he seems to be fleeing. As Natty is about to go off into the wilderness, Oliver Effingham shows him the monument he has erected to the memory of old Major Effingham, whom Natty had long served and protected. The monument reads in part:

> The morning of his life was spent in honor, wealth, and power; but its evening was obscured by poverty, neglect, and disease, which were alleviated only by the tender care of his old, faithful, and upright friend and attendant, Nathaniel Bumppo. His descendants rear this stone to the virtues of the master, and to the enduring gratitude of the servant.[7]

When Natty hears this statement he replies in the tone and manner of an old family servant:

> "And did ye say it, lad? have you then got the old man's name cut in the stone, by the side of his master's? God bless ye, children! 'twas a kind thought, and kindness goes to the heart as life shortens."[8]

This presentation of Natty as faithful old retainer is not simply a matter of age. In *The Prairie* he is older still, but an aura of mystery and majesty surround him. Compare, for example, the first descriptions of the old hunter in the two novels. In *The Pioneers*, Natty is first described to us from the perspective of Elizabeth Temple, who, returning to the settlement after a long stay in the East, sees the hunter as one of the local curiosities:

> There was a peculiarity in the manner of the hunter that attracted the notice of the young female, who had been a close and interested observer of his appearance and equipments from the moment he came into view. He was tall and so meagre as to make him seem above even the six feet that he actually stood in his stockings. On his head, which was thinly covered with lank, sandy hair, he wore a cap made of foxskin.... His face was skinny and thin almost to emaciation: but it bore no signs of disease.... The cold and the exposure had, together, given it a color of uniform red. His gray eyes were glancing under a pair of shaggy brows that overhung them in long hairs of gray mingled with the natural hue; his scraggy neck was bare, and burnt to the same tint with his face.[9]

By the time we reach *The Prairie*, however, this same figure, older and presumably even more shaggy and scraggy, has been mythicized into something far more transcendent and heroic:

> The whole party was brought to a halt, by a spectacle as sudden as it was unexpected. The sun had fallen below the crest of the nearest wave of the prairie, leaving the usual rich and glowing train on its track. In the centre of this flood of fiery light a human form appeared, drawn against the gilded background as distinctly, and seeming as palpable, as though it would come within the grasp of any extended hand. The figure was colossal; the attitude musing and melancholy; and the situation directly in the route of the travellers. But imbedded, as it was, in the setting of garish light, it was impossible to distinguish its just proportions or true character.[10]

Here is the true western hero, playing that scene of man against the sky that he would later enact innumerable times for the movies. This figure, aged as he is, is that transcendent hero Cooper talks about in the later preface to the Leatherstocking Tales who, "removed from nearly all the temptation of civilized life, and favorably disposed by nature to improve such advantages ... appeared ... a fit subject to represent the better qualities of both conditions without pushing either to extremes."[11]

This figure, no longer subsumed under the existing social hierarchy but spanning both civilized and savage conditions, makes his first complete appearance in *The Last of the Mohicans*. Though Natty is still related to the social hierarchy through his services to the daughters of Colonel Munro and to the aristocratic Duncan Heyward, there are important differences. The Natty of *The Last of the Mohicans* is in the full possession of his mature strength and skill; he is on his own ground, the Indian-infested wilderness, instead of the settlement where he is inevitably an anachronism; and, finally, his service is not that of the traditional faithful retainer but is voluntary and temporary. Moreover, his commitment is essentially to the females and the nature of his assistance is that offered by a strong man to helpless women, not a matter of the service that those of lower status rightfully owe to their social superiors. The change in Natty's relationship to the social order is further indicated by the contrast between his relationship with Oliver Effingham and with Duncan Heyward, the young aristocrats who act as romantic heroes and whose marriage to their respective heroines symbolizes the dynastic continuation of the social hierarchy. In *The Pioneers* both Oliver and Elizabeth Temple are strong and competent characters who are fully in control except in a few situations of wilderness peril. But the aristocratic hero and heroine of *The Last of the Mohicans* are almost totally incompetent and dependent on Leatherstocking's help. Duncan Heyward is brave and high-spirited, but he is also the first dude or greenhorn in western literature. He invariably reacts in the wrong way to perilous situations and must be rescued by the more skillful Leatherstocking. Alice Munro, the genteel and refined ingenue, spends most of her time weeping and fainting. She is the first in a long line of eastern women who can't deal with the western experience until they have learned to accept the guidance of the hero. The Natty of *The Last of the Mohicans* is no longer the curious combination of deferent old family retainer and subversive hater of law that he is in *The Pioneers*. He has become a hero.

This increasing romanticization of the Leatherstocking hero, along with the new focus on violence as the dominant element of the frontier experience, probably reflects an increasing tension between conflicting attitudes and feelings in Cooper's mind. Divided between his belief in a traditional social hierarchy and the dream of a free, spontaneous life in nature, Cooper had originally developed the figure of Natty Bumppo in terms of two distinct aspects; first, there is the loyal servant of the great family, a man of simple Christian virtues who has no desire to challenge the traditional social order; second, there is the marginal, lonely man of the wilderness who hates the restrictions of society and who fears, above all, the operations of a social authority that he does not understand or feel he needs. In *The Pioneers* these conflicting aspects of Natty's significance pose relatively few problems; Natty's subversive impulses are controlled by his dedication to the Temple-Effingham dynasty; he remains on the periphery of the action; and, finally, the development of civilization under the benevolent and wise leadership of the American gentry is so obviously progressive that any criticism of society implicit in Natty's final rejection of the settlement is blunted.

As Cooper's own confidence in the evolution of civilization in the United States became more qualified and his views of democracy more disillusioned, his fascination with nature as an ideal became more intense. As the Leatherstocking Tales progressed, the nobility and heroism of the natural man became more idealized, the advance of the pioneers became increasingly associated with violence and anarchy, and the settlement of the wilderness connected with the loss of significant values. These trends are already evident in *The Last of the Mohicans*. Natty is younger, more heroic, and a far more central character. The situation is one of violence, and the representatives of civilization have become more effete and overrefined. In addition, the theme of the vanishing wilderness is developed far more extensively in an elegaic picture of the decline of the noble Delawares. Cooper still remains somewhat ambiguous about whether the destruction of his noble savages is to be attributed to a principle of violence in nature itself, as symbolized by the diabolical Mingos, or is the result of the advance of white settlement. In the end, he retreats to the old resolution of dynastic marriage, a resolution that in this case hardly balances the tragedy of the deaths of Uncas and Cora.

The situation becomes even more ambiguous in *The Prairie*, which is, in many ways, the darkest, most sinister, of the Leatherstocking Tales. In this novel, the conflict between Leatherstocking's natural freedom and the advance of civilization can only be resolved by the death of the hero. Moreover, the dialectic between nature and civilization is further complicated by the fact that the Bush family, a new element in the Leatherstocking Tales, represents both the advance of the pioneers and the most unconstrained violence and anarchy. The Bush family is one of Cooper's most striking creations, for they derive in part from one aspect of the original Natty of *The Pioneers*, his hatred of the law of the settlements and his insistence on a man's natural freedom to live according to his inner law. Like Natty himself, Ishmael Bush, the patriarch of the family, has turned his back on the settlements and come to the prairie in order to live by his own laws. Unlike Natty, however, Ishmael Bush knows no limits; his rejection of civilized law has become lawlessness, and his fanatical Christianity is confused with his worship of his own impulses. Thus, as Natty becomes more idealized, the antisocial impulses that were originally a part of his character are abstracted from him and embodied in pure form in another set of characters. Cooper is still not quite ready to face the possibility that the Bush family embodies the future of American civilization. He concludes the novel by engineering their departure into obscurity and tries once more to suggest that the future course of settlement lies in the hands of the genteel Duncan Middleton and the respectable beekeeper Paul Hover—a truncated representation of the orderly and peaceful society of Templeton. His final comment on the Bush family seems rather uncertain as to whether the advance of settlement will swallow up the Bushes or vice versa.

> On the following morning the teams and herds of the squatters were seen pursuing their course towards the settlements. As they approached the confines of society the train was blended among a thousand others. Though some of the numerous descendants of this peculiar pair were reclaimed from their lawless and semi-barbarous lives, the principals of the family themselves were never heard of more.[12]

When, over a decade later, Cooper returned to the Leatherstocking figure, he completed Natty's transformation into an idealized hero, who, separated from both traditional and white societies, embodied only the best qualities of both cultures. Instead of the crabbed old backwoodsman of *The Pioneers*, the Deerslayer is

> a being removed from the everyday inducements to err, which abound in civilized life, while he retains the best and simplest of his early impression; who sees God in the forest, hears Him in the winds, bows to Him in the firmament that o'er-canopies all, submits to his way in a humble belief of his justice and mercy; in a word, a being who finds the impress of the Deity in all the works of nature, without any of the blots produced by the expedients, and passion, and mistakes of man.[13]

Natty has become, in short, a new kind of pastoral hero, exemplifying the natural virtues that civilization has unfortunately lost. Against his purity and simplicity the vices of society are measured and found wanting.

The first of these new versions of the Leatherstocking was the least successful of the series. In *The Pathfinder* we have the full-fledged pastoral hero, the man of transcendent virtues based on natural simplicity, but Cooper did not devise an appropriate plot for this hero. His mistake was to attempt the portrayal of Natty as a hero of romance. Since he was dealing with a character who was, by definition, unmarried, it was necessary to make him fail in his suit. Moreover, Cooper was caught within a paradox of his own making. For the heroine to be worthy of the love of such an idealized figure as Natty, she had to be herself so relentlessly pure and genteel that it was inconceivable for her to share the wilderness way of life. Consequently *The Pathfinder* is full of confusion that tends toward the ludicrous and the pathetic. At times, Natty even reminds the reader of those moonstruck pastoral swains who lurch around after heartless shepherdesses.

Cooper largely overcame these difficulties in *The Deerslayer*. In this novel Natty is pursued by the passionate Judith Hutter rather than being himself the rejected swain. Moreover, since the worldly Judith has something of a stain on her past, Natty has all the more reason for rejecting her in favor of pure, uncorrupted nature. But, most important of all, the real center of *The Deerslayer* is not Natty's relationship with Judith but his initiation into a life of violence. The hero becomes a killer rather than a lover.

The Deerslayer, like all of Cooper's later Leatherstocking Tales, is a rather complex and rambling narrative of chases and captures, escapes and pursuits, in which the Leatherstocking finally succeeds in rescuing his companions from the threat of death or torture at the hands of savage Indians. But the novel also possesses a more unifying and effective line of action in the story of Natty's initiation into the character of Leatherstocking and the way of life it represents. This initiation has several major elements: Natty kills a man, he receives the name of a hunter and warrior, he shows his capacity for adult leadership, he demonstrates his ability to abide by the wilderness code of honor, and he rejects the worldly Judith's advances in favor of the violent masculine life of the wilderness. These elements are still important themes of the western formula. The famous chapter 7 of *The Deerslayer* in which Natty shoots his first Indian adumbrates the man-to-man confrontations of the later western, fast-draw, simultaneous shot, and all:

> The black, ferocious eyes of the savage were glancing on him, like those of the crouching tiger, through a small opening in the bushes, and the muzzle of his rifle seemed already to be opening in a line with his own body.
>
> Then, indeed the long practice of Deerslayer, as a hunter, did him good service. Accustomed to fire with the deer on the bound . . . he used the same expedients here. To cock and poise his rifle were the acts of a single moment and a single motion. . . . So rapid were his movements that both

parties discharged their pieces at the same instant, the concussions mingling in one report. The mountains indeed gave back but a single echo.[14]

Cooper's treatment of this scene gives it a very different interpretation than the twentieth-century western. In the contemporary western, the violent confrontation of the protagonist and his savage enemy represents the point at which the hero finally transcends the various uncertainties and reluctances that have prevented him from dealing with his antagonist. It is, in all but the most complex and serious westerns, a moment of supreme culmination and resolution in which good finally rises above the limitations of reality and triumphs over evil. For Cooper, however, this moment of violent action comes near the beginning of the story and it is initiation rather than culmination. Moreover, it is a moment of considerable ambiguity, for Natty's shooting of the Indian is followed by one of the most strange and haunting scenes in the history of the western. During his adversary's dying moments, Natty, in almost maternal fashion, cradles the Indian's head in his lap, assuring him that his scalp will not be taken and soothing the dying man and receiving in return his adult name, Hawkeye. Finally, with the death of the Indian, that ineffable melancholy, which is so much the sign of the older Hawkeye, settles down:

> "His spirit has fled!" said Deerslayer, in a suppressed, melancholy voice. "Ah's me! Well, to this must we all come, sooner or later; and he is happiest, let his skin be of what color it may, who is best fitted to meet it. Here lies the body of no doubt a brave warrior, and the soul is already flying toward its Heaven or Hell, whether that be a happy hunting ground, a place scant of game, regions of glory, according to Moravian doctrine, or flames of fire! So it happens, too, as regards other matters. Here have old Hutter and Hurry Harry got themselves into difficulty, if they hav'n't got themselves into torment and death, and all for a bounty that luck offers to me in what many would think a lawful and suitable manner. But not a farthing of such money shall cross my hand. White I was born and white will I die; clinging to color to the last, even though the King's majesty, his governors, and all his councils, both at home and in the Colonies, forget from what they come, and where they hope to go, and all for a little advantage in warfare. No, no—warrior, hand of mine shall never molest your scalp, and so your soul may rest in peace on the p'int of making a decent appearance when the body comes to join it, in your own land of spirits."[15]

Many ambiguities flit in and out of this passage. Natty cannot but be glad to have killed the Indian, not only because in doing so he has saved his own life, but because he has proved his ability to act like a warrior when necessary, something that has been on his mind since the beginning of the novel. Yet at the same time he feels an unmistakable sadness at the event, and we cannot but see this killing, as many critics have pointed out, as a fall from innocence, a passage on Natty's part from a simple and spontaneous way of

life in harmony with the beauty and serenity of nature into a moral universe in
which violence and death are inescapable, not only in the world but in
oneself. From this point on Natty will never really be able to enjoy his
beloved forest without knowing its dangers at the same time, just as
henceforth in order to live with his noble Indian companion, Chingachgook,
he will also have to commit himself to hatred and destruction of the savage
Mingos. The episode also thrusts into prominence the conflict of loyalties and
values that derive from Natty's position as a man between two cultures and
races. His initiation into violence immediately confronts him with the
division within himself; he is Indian enough to respect the warrior's way of
life, but he cannot bring himself to adopt the Indian ethic and religion insofar
as it contravenes Christian teachings against violence. Moreover, he knows
from experience that the white culture as represented in such men as Thomas
Hutter and Hurry Harry is even more meaninglessly violent than that of the
Indians. Faced with this web of emotional and cultural conflicts within
himself, Natty kills but finds he can take no real satisfaction in the deed. His
ambiguity of values is so great that he cannot even decide on a way in which
he can tell of the action to his dearest friend:

> "If I was Injin-born, I might tell of this, or carry in the scalp, and boast of
> the expl'ite afore the whole tribe; or, if my inimy had only been even a
> bear, 'twould have been nat'ral and proper to let everybody know what
> had happened; but I don't well see how I'm to let even Chingachgook
> into this secret, so long as it can be done only by boasting with a white
> tongue. And why should I wish to boast of it a'ter all? It's slaying a human,
> although he was a savage.[16]

Similar ambiguities cluster around Natty's other triumphs. Though he
receives the name of a warrior and proves his ability as a leader, he also
discovers his immutable alienation from his own people, without, at the same
time, being able to assimilate himself wholly into the Indian way of life. He
becomes inextricably caught between cultures, a potentially great leader
without a possible following. Natty enters on the adventures of *The
Deerslayer* in company with Hurry Harry March, the white backwoodsman,
and he leaves with his lifelong friend, the noble Indian Chingachgook, but in
the course of the action he is neither white nor Indian. For the white culture,
though it teaches Christian charity and love and sets up the imitation of
Christ as its highest virtue, is represented in actuality by the rapacious
avarice and selfishness of Hurry Harry and Tom Hutter, who spend most of
the book trying to take Indian scalps for bounty. As Natty points out, there
seems to be a basic contradiction in white society between Christianity and
violence:

> "all is contradiction in the settlements, while all is concord in the woods.
> Forts and churches almost always go together, and yet they're downright
> contradictions, churches being for peace and forts for war. No, no—give

me the strong places of the wilderness, which is the trees, and the churches, too, which are arbors raised by the hand of nature!"[17]

In *The Pioneers* white settlement had its ambiguities, but it also had its great virtues, as represented by the benevolent public spirit of the Temple-Effingham dynasty and the increasing social harmony that rewarded their efforts. In this context, Natty's rejection of the limitations of civilization seems understandable but not conclusive. Though Natty might not be able to fit comfortably into it, the benevolent and harmonious future of American civilization clearly outweighed the simple and natural virtues represented by the Leatherstocking and, as we have seen, associated with the faithful family retainer as well as the wilderness. In *The Deerslayer*, however, American civilization is represented by the rapacious and selfish violence of Hurry Harry and Tom Hutter, and by the sensual passion and materialism of Judith Hutter. The public-spirited gentry no longer lurk in the wings ready to transform the raw forces of the frontier into the peaceful and harmonious society of Templeton. In this context, Natty's rejection of a role in the new civilization takes on a more heroic, if romanticized, meaning. The personal peculiarities of *The Pioneers* have been erected into idealized ethical principles against which the dominant drives of American settlement have been measured and found wanting. Instead of the story of pioneers creating a new and better society on the American frontier, *The Deerslayer* becomes an elegy for a lost Eden. The idealized new Adam is already obsolete. Judith Hutter sums up the sense of loss that pervades *The Deerslayer* in a conversation with her sister Hetty:

"We must quit this spot, Hetty, and remove into the settlements."
"I am sorry you think so, Judith," returned Hetty, dropping her head on her bosom, and looking thoughtfully down at the spot where the funeral pile of her mother could just be seen. "I am *very* sorry to hear it. I would rather stay here, where, if I wasn't born, I've passed my life. I don't like the settlements—they are full of wickedness and heartburnings, while God dwells unoffended in these hills! I love the trees, and the mountains, and the lake, and the springs; all that His bounty has given us, and it would grieve me sorely, Judith, to be forced to quit them. You are handsome, and not at all half-witted, and one day you will marry, and then you will have a husband, and I a brother, to take care of us, if women can't really take care of themselves in such a place."
"Ah! if this *could* be so, Hetty, then, indeed, I could *now* be a thousand times happier in these woods than in the settlements! *Once* I did not feel thus, but *now* I do. Yet where is the man to turn this beautiful place into such a garden of Eden for us?"[18]

By creating an increasingly idealized Natty Bumppo, Cooper joined the European tradition of pastoral to the historical violence and darkness of the American frontier. The result was a narrative pattern that symbolized his complex feelings about the meaning of American social development. As

Cooper's own doubts about the future of American society increased, so did the wisdom and virtue of his hero until in *The Deerslayer* the young Natty talks like a natural philosopher and behaves like an incarnation of the faithful shepherd. Yet, the action of the novel stresses violence. The fact of the matter is that the sweet, gentle lover of the woods is forced by the circumstances of his life to become a killer of men. How far from the pastoral ideal is the character described by D. H. Lawrence as "a man who turns his back on white society. A man who keeps his moral integrity hard and intact. An isolate, almost selfless, stoic, enduring man, who lives by death, by killing, but who is pure white."[19]

This striking combination of pastoral innocence with deadly violence became a central theme of *The Deerslayer*. It completed the transformation of the Leatherstocking series from the saga of advancing civilization in America into a strangely ambiguous adventure story about the hero's loss of innocence. Originally Cooper had predicted that American society would progress from the primitive equalitarian society of pioneers through a chaotic phase of social competition into a stable and benevolent social hierarchy. This final stage would be a civilization less refined, but more democratic and moral, than that of Europe. American advance on the West could be seen with some reservations as progress toward this admirable social state. The happy outcome of *The Pioneers* with its dynastic marriage symbolized the hope of this new society, the Temple-Effingham family playing the role of the new American gentry. But to read the Leatherstocking series from the perspective of *The Deerslayer* is to encounter a very different view of American civilization. When we follow the series in its fictional chronology beginning with *The Deerslayer*, it is at least possible to see the pioneers as dominated by violence, destruction and senseless waste. The action of *The Deerslayer* results largely from the avarice and brutality of Harry March and Tom Hutter, two backwoodsmen who bring on a fight with the Indians primarily because they want scalps for the bounty money. Into the vortex of their violence the gentle and innocent Natty Bumppo is sucked. Through this action the pastoral hero becomes implicated with society against his will. Society's need for his skill in violence forces him into a role as participant in the destruction of the wilderness he loves. From this beginning, the rest of the Leatherstocking series can be seen as the hero's increasingly frustrated attempt to rediscover the simplicity of innocence of his lost way of life, a quest that finally turns into headlong flight from civilization. In *The Prairie* he even takes a step that he had always rejected: he symbolically accepts kinship with the Indians by adopting the Pawnee warrior Hardheart as his son. At the last he dies among the Plains Indians, totally alienated from the society he has spent his life killing for.

So it is possible to see the Leatherstocking series in two contrary ways. From one angle, it appears to be an affirmation of the benevolent progress of American civilization; from another, it is an attack on that same civilization as measured against the natural nobility of a pastoral hero. David W. Noble has suggested a most interesting way of reconciling these seemingly contrary themes. He argues that the story of Leatherstocking embodies the American myth of a new society based on nature confronted with the realities and limitations of human life. Leatherstocking's inability to marry, his life of violence, and his final flight symbolize the failure of the myth:

> For Cooper, it was here on the great plains, during Jefferson's administrations, that the myth of the frontier perished because of the penetration of the last unknown territories by human beings, who, by their very presence, destroyed the mysterious potential of the virgin land. In the words of Professor Lewis, there no longer existed "space as spaciousness, as the unbounded, the area of total possibility." And from the first moment when Deerslayer was forced to participate in the disharmony of history ⁀ooper has prepared for this moment. The five Leatherstocking novels are a sustained argument against the autonomous existence of an American Adam.[20]

Professor Noble's interpretation does not take into account the changes in theme and pattern between *The Pioneers* and *The Deerslayer* and Cooper's increasing tendency to treat his backwoods hero as an idealized figure of wisdom and virtue. I am still inclined to agree with Henry Nash Smith and others that Cooper was a writer of basic contradictions and unresolved ambiguities: a firm believer in the ultimate value of simple Christianity, yet at the same time deeply committed to refined and sophisticated civilization; a lover of the wilderness and a devotee of gentility; at once a progressive and a conservative; quite able to see in man a natural moral instinct and at the same time certain of basic human depravity; an affirmer of the freedom and lawlessness of the forest and an upholder of law and social hierarchy. His Leatherstocking hero does seem to embody a lost possibility, a myth of human potentiality that cannot be realized in any conceivable social order, and yet Cooper seems to reject both the romantic view of man and the kind of open society in which such a man might rise to a high social level. His social ideal is a very traditional conception of order based on an established gentry class. These conflicting views never really get resolved, nor does Cooper push them to the point where their basic irreconcilability becomes evident. Instead, he invents narrative patterns in which it is possible to resolve the tensions associated with conflicting values without working out the conflicts themselves. For example, Natty's flight into the wilderness averts a real showdown between the values of nature and of civilization. Another instance is the treatment of violence in *The Deerslayer*. From the beginning Natty feels divided between the pacifism of his Moravian background and the code of violence that he shares with the Indians. Cooper does not ask us to face the irreconcilability of these values. Instead, in Deerslayer's shootdown with the Indians, a reluctant but deadly hero has violence thrust upon him by a treacherous and irreconcilable adversary.

Even in the case of Natty's romance, this principle of avoiding the ultimate irreconcilability of values operates. The conflict here is between the values of domesticity—marriage, family, social respectability, and security—and the ideal of a free, unconstrained, masculine way of life. But Natty never really has to work this conflict out to a point of decision between his natural freedom and the lure of domesticity, neither in *The Pathfinder* nor *The Deerslayer*. In one case it turns out that the girl doesn't really love him, and in the other Natty does not love the girl.

Cooper's great popular success as well as his ultimate limitation as a serious writer lay in his refusal or incapacity to fully explore the dialectic of civilization and nature that his imagination generated.[21] He felt the ambiguities of the American dream of a new society more keenly than most of his contemporaries, yet his mind was too conventional and satisfied with life in general to see these ambiguities in the tragic terms in which they would be developed by Hawthorne and Melville. Thus Cooper became the creator of a dialectic of action and a type of hero that in the hands of lesser writers could serve the purposes of popular escapist fantasy, resolving in fantasy the ideal of peaceful progress toward civilization and the impulse toward lawless freedom and aggressive violence. By creating a setting and a group of plot patterns through which the irreconcilable conflicts of society and individual freedom, of peaceful civilization and uncontrolled violence, could be resolved in action, Cooper brought the western into existence. We must now examine how some of his successors used his invention.

Nick of the Woods *and the Dime Novel*

The most important early novel of western adventure in the manner of Cooper, Robert Montgomery Bird's *Nick of the Woods* (1837), supposedly presented a "realistic" picture of Indian warfare in contrast to the noble savages of Cooper. Actually, Bird's novel greatly simplified Cooper's dialectic, glossing over the complexities in Cooper's treatment of the frontier. Thus it became a step in the direction of the dime novel.

One of the most important changes Bird made in Cooper's narrative pattern was to eliminate the noble savage altogether. He transformed Cooper's complex contrast between white civilizations and the natural ethic of the wilderness into a simple opposition of good and evil: decent pioneers trying to settle the wilderness and overcome the savage Indians. With this exception, Bird's cast of characters is basically the same as *The Last of the Mohicans* and *The Prairie*: the aristocratic lovers Roland and Edith Forrester match Duncan Heyward and Alice Munro; the half-caste Telie Doe whose father lives with the Indians resembles Cora Munro; Colonel Bruce and the Kentuckians represent the good pioneers, and Roaring Ralph Stackpole symbolizes the kind of frontier anarchist Cooper portrayed in Ishmael Bush. Most important of all, the Leatherstocking figure, torn between Christian pacifism and deadly violence, appears in the role of Nathan Slaughter, the Quaker Indian-hater. The action, too, resembles Cooper with its central focus on flight and pursuit, framed by aristocratic romance and dynastic plots. Bird develops a complicated story that springs from the theft of a will. In consequence the hero is deprived of his aristocratic heritage. The villain tries to eliminate the hero and marry the heroine by using the savage Indians to accomplish his desires. Thus, being rescued from the Indians also involves the elimination of the villain and the recovery of a great inheritance, to say nothing of a happy marriage between hero and heroine.

Though his characters and plot derive from Cooper's example, Bird treats them in such a way as to resolve the ambiguities of Cooper's dialectic and to affirm clearly the virtues of American civilization. The Indians become diabolical savages without any redeeming qualities. There is no sense that natural values are being lost in the advance of civilization. As Bird says in his preface:

> The North American savage has never appeared to us the gallant and heroic personage he seems to others. The single fact that he wages war—systematic war—upon beings incapable of resistance or defence,—upon women and children, whom all other races in the world no matter how barbarous, consent to spare,—has hitherto been, and we suppose, to the end of our days will remain, a stumbling-block to our imagination: we look into the woods for the mighty warrior . . . rushing to meet his foe, and behold him retiring, laden with the scalps of miserable squaws and their babes.[22]

In addition, the aristocratic hero no longer seems, like Cooper's gentleman, vaguely incompetent in the woods. Roland Forrester, the hero of *Nick of the Woods*, possesses both an aristocratic background and the energy and adaptability of a self-made man. Bird completely avoids any ambiguous comparisons such as that between Uncas and Duncan Heyward in *The Last of the Mohicans* that might cast doubt on the capacity of his hero to be equally at home in the drawing rooms of his native Virginia or on the dark and bloody ground of the Kentucky frontier. Nor does he pose any basic questions about the relation between Christian pacifism and the war against Indians. Though his Nathan Slaughter embodies this contradiction—like Natty he has a Christian pacifist upbringing but is a committed destroyer of Indians—Bird resolves the contradiction between belief and action. Since Slaughter has been driven mad by the Indian's massacre of his family, his savage assaults on the Indians and the contradictions between his violent behavior and the pacifist beliefs he continues to assert are justified by the savagery of the Indians and Slaughter's own anguished mental state.

The dime novel carried this reduction of Cooper's dialectic of civilization and nature still further in the direction of simple moral opposition. Only a skeletal residue of Cooper's ideal of natural simplicity remains in *Seth Jones* (1860), one of the earliest successful dime novels. Though most of the male characters are presented to us as "nature's noblemen," the term has evidently ceased to mean anything other than that the character is strong, healthy, and vigorous. The idea that there is a way of life or a set of moral values associated with nature and opposed to civilization simply doesn't enter the picture. In fact, the first of the various "nature's noblemen" we encounter in *Seth Jones* is chopping down a tree and when asked why he has come out to the frontier, he replies, "Enterprise, sir; I was tired of the civilization portion of the country, and when such glorious fields were offered to the emigrant as have here spread before him, I considered it a duty to avail myself of them."[23] Such incidents suggest that nature has become identified with the gospel of success. The dialectic between civilized aristocrat and backwoodsman so important to the Leatherstocking series has been translated into the mythical terms of disguise. The central character of the book, though apparently a rough backwoodsman, continually gives hints that he is not what he seems. One such incident is surely one of the great moments in popular literature. Seth, who has been captured by Indians while trying to rescue the heroine, leaves the following message scratched on a flat stone in a brook where it is found by the girl's father and sweetheart:

> Hurry forward. There are six Indians, and they have got Ina with them. They don't suspect you are following them, and are hurrying up for village. I think we will camp two or three miles from here. Make the noise of the whippowil when you want to do the business, and I will understand.
> Yours, respectfully.
> SETH JONES[24]

Such a master of epistolary form could hardly be just a simple backwoodsman. It is no surprise when, at the end of the story, Seth is revealed as the dashing young Eugene Morton, Revolutionary War hero and scion of a distinguished New England family.

Henry Nash Smith points out that Seth Jones's disguise is "a neat maneuver for combining the picturesque appeal of the 'low' hunter with the official status of the 'straight' upper-class hero."[25] As Smith suggests, such devices undercut the Leatherstocking character's significance as a symbol of natural virtue opposed to the artificialities and constraints of civilization.

Through such developments, the dime novel moved the western away from Cooper's ambiguous examination of the discrepancy between the American dream of a new society and the reality of greed and violence on the frontier. During the heyday of the dime novel the western developed primarily as a form of adolescent escapism, complete with the simple moral conflicts and stereotyped characters and situations usually found in such literature. The western setting, instead of being the place where advanced civilization confronts the virgin wilderness, gradually developed a new set of connotations.

Edward L. Wheeler's *Deadwood Dick on Deck, or Calamity Jane, the Heroine of Whoop-up* (1878) illustrates the full-blown dime novel. The story of this novel exemplifies the common principle of pulp literature that incident takes precedence over plot, i.e., that it is more important to have a lot of exciting actions than to have them clearly related to each other. In such a narrative characters exist less for the purpose of confronting difficult moral or human problems than for getting into and out of scrapes. Thus, instead of a single line of action, *Deadwood Dick on Deck*, despite its brevity, contains at least five strands of plot that intersect at various points. The brew is further thickened by the fact that almost all the main characters are in disguises of one kind or another. The hero, Earl Beverly, of the distinguished Virginia Beverlys, has come West because he mistakenly believes himself guilty of murder and forgery. Disguised as Sandy the miner, he hopes to make a new life. He is pursued by the man who had originally led him into temptation, the rich but evil Honorable Cecil Grosvenor, who, for reasons never made too clear, still wishes to destroy Sandy. The conflict between Sandy and Cecil becomes further complicated when Sandy makes friends with a girl who has disguised herself as a man. Under the name of Dusty Dick, this young lady becomes known as Sandy's "pard." Dusty Dick, coincidentally, is also fleeing from Cecil, who had tricked her into marriage before she discovered his true character. The triangle Sandy-Dusty Dick-Cecil Grosvenor is resolved at the end when another character in disguise turns out to be a detective who has discovered that Sandy is innocent of the crimes he thought he had committed. In addition, Cecil's marriage to Dusty Dick turns out to be invalid because—second plot strand—the villain's real wife shows up to controvert him. She is Mad Marie, the highwaywoman, who flits mysteriously around the periphery of the narrative until it is time for her to play her role. The third strand involves Calamity Jane and the Danite ghoul, Arkansas Alf, a vicious outlaw and Cecil's henchman. Calamity seeks revenge against Arkansas Alf because he has committed some horrible but nameless offense against her. Fourth, we have the complex relationship between the other characters and the lady who is usually referred to as "the beautiful blonde proprietress of the Castle Garden, Madame Minnie Majilton." Madame Minnie loves Sandy, who loves Dusty Dick. Cecil lusts after Madame Minnie, but is scorned, which adds more fuel to the fires of his vengeful spirit. To wrap up all these complications requires a transcendent hero indeed. The fifth strand is, believe it or not, none other than Deadwood Dick, who, disguised as Old Bullwhacker, the "regulator," always manages to appear on the scene in time to help get the situation straightened out.

Aside from the usual perilous scrapes, flights, captures, and battles, *Deadwood Dick on Deck* places great emphasis on disguises and on an elaborate play with sexual roles. In *Deadwood Dick on Deck* disguises fly so thick and fast that in one episode we find Calamity Jane disguised as Deadwood Dick disguised as an old man. She is unmasked by Deadwood Dick himself disguised as somebody else. This play with disguises has always been a vital part of children's literature. Perhaps young people who are having social roles thrust upon them in the process of growing up find a great fascination in disguises because a disguise is a role that can be put off when it is no longer wanted. Thus such stories enable adolescent readers to participate imaginatively in the process of putting on and taking off roles at will, a kind of experimentation without commitment that may help ease some of the tensions associated with the increasing pressure on the young person to undertake a permanent social role. Such reflections seem to be borne out by the treatment of sex in these books. In one sense, there is no sex at all in the dime novels; everything is very pure, and one cannot imagine a hero being unchaste. Yet, at the same time, the hero is usually a center of female admiration. At one point beauteous blonde Madame Minnie Majilton tells Sandy:

> I mean that three women in this very town adore you—worship you as the only perfect man in the mines. First of all is Dusty Dick, who has got you into all this trouble in the eyes of your friends; secondly, ranks that eccentric daredevil girl, Calamity Jane. She probably loves you in the fiercest, most intense manner. I fill the third place myself. I am beautiful, and of a most generous, impulsive nature—the very woman suited to you. I have money, independent of yours. I have brought you in here to ask you to marry me. Earlier to-day Cecil Grosvenor proposed and I refused him. I want you, Sandy—will you take me?[26]

Unfortunately for the success of her suit, Madame Minnie forgets that no self-respecting young American hero could possibly accept such an aggressive and independent woman, particularly one who runs a dance hall. Where Madame Minnie represents an overly aggressive feminine sexuality, Calamity Jane plays the part of an overly masculine woman. It is the sweet and clinging Dusty Dick who is our hero's true and appropriate love, but, interestingly enough, she must play a transvestite before the romance can blossom. Again this seems to make sense in terms of an adolescent reader's psychological needs. A figure like Dusty Dick can be both boyish companion and sexual object, easing in fantasy the uncertainty that accompanies the adolescent's increasing awareness of girls in sexual terms. The figure of the boyish woman or the woman who takes a man's role before changing into a lover plays an important role in many later westerns.

This kind of resolution in fantasy of the sexual and status anxieties characteristic of adolescents does not, on the surface at least, have anything to do with the West. In fact, the same themes frequently appear in other forms of literature aimed primarily at adolescents, including the Alger books and the Rover boys. Certain aspects of the western setting as defined by Cooper and his followers were particularly appropriate to the presentation of these themes. The West had a mythical aura that neither the nineteenth-century city nor the small town could match. It was a setting in which transcendent heroes, disguises, and perilous scrapes could be more believably generated because it had the quality of romantic distance. Moreover, the dime novelists could characterize the West as a place where peer group relationships dominated the social order. The Wild West thus became the locus of an adolescent dream society without the complex institutions and restrictions on impulsive freedom associated with the East. In line with this development, the favorite villain was a figure associated with the corrupt institutions and artificial social roles of the East. In *Deadwood Dick on Deck*, the chief villain is an eastern politician and crooked banker while the true-blue hero has fled the East because in its corrupt society he has been branded a criminal:

> "in the eyes of the law I am a criminal—a forger, and an accused murderer. You heard Cecil Grosvenor throw it up in my face; it is the only weapon he has to brand me with. If he were in the States, where law reigns supreme, he would have me more in his power."[27]

The concept of the West as a society of comrades dimly reflects Cooper's dialectic of civilization and nature. The residual influence of Cooper's pastoral ideal can still be seen from time to time. For example, at the beginning of *Deadwood Dick on Deck*, the hero Sandy muses on the natural beauties of the West:

> "Nowhere does Nature so forcibly illustrate the power of the Divine Creator as in the mountainous regions," Sandy muttered, as he gazed dreamily off through an opening between the mountain peaks. "I sometimes wonder how it is that people do not more devoutly worship God in His works."[28]

Deadwood Dick on Deck shows not only a simplification of Cooper's dialectic but a shift away from the opposition of civilization and nature that dominated Cooper's presentation of the West. First of all, the Indians are gone. *Deadwood Dick on Deck* is set in a mining town in the Black Hills, and its characters are entirely white. This contrasts sharply with an earlier dime novel like *Seth Jones* in which escape from Indians still furnishes, as in Cooper, the primary source of the action. While many later dime novels deal with Indian warfare, the Indian has become an item of furniture rather than an opposing force. In Cooper, while the Indian is not exactly equivalent to Nature, he represents a way of life that has a natural simplicity and dignity and is therefore opposed to both the refinement of high civilization and the greed and avarice of the advancing pioneers. Cooper's version of the Indian way of life presents a significant moral alternative to white civilization. Thus, the noble Mohicans, Uncas and Chingachgook, embody a pastoral critique of the artificiality, vanity, and selfishness of white civilization. Even Cooper's Indian villains, the savage Mingos, suggest an awesome natural force. In *Seth Jones*, the only thing left to the Indians is savagery, while the later dime novel tends to eliminate even that, giving the role of savage to white outlaws.

These changes reflected a new meaning of the West. Cooper's image of the West as a place of encounter between civilization and nature gave way to the portrayal of the West as an open society where the intricacies of complex social institutions are unknown, where people are surrounded by loyal friends, where hearty individualists can give vent to their spontaneous urges, and where justice is done directly and without ambiguity. The dime novel West is also a place of excitement and color; it is, to use the current phrase, "where the action is." One major sign of this change is the fact that the frontier town becomes more important as a locus of action than the pathless forest. In *Deadwood Dick on Deck*, the story keeps coming back to the frenetic activity, exciting maskers, and transvestites of the town of Whoop-Up, which often reminds me of our contemporary vision of the "Wild West" as exemplified in the glamourous wilderness of Las Vegas:

> For a mile and a half along the only accessible shore of Canyon Creek, were strewn frame shanties and canvas tents almost without number, and the one street of the town was always full to overflowing with excited humanity. The monotonous grinding and crushing of ore-breakers, the ring of picks and hammers, the reports of heavy blasts in the rugged mountain-side, the shouts of rival stage-drivers, the sounds of music, and tipsy revelry from dance-houses and saloons; the boisterous shouts of the outdoor Cheap John, dealer in "biled shorts" and miners' furnishing golds, the occasional reports of revolver-shots, may be heard in the streets of Whoop-Up, no matter, dear reader, if it be during the day or during the night, when you pay your visit. For in this latest mining success of the country there is no suspension of bustle or business on account of night; in walking through the town you might wonder if these people never slept, because the long, thronged street is even livelier at an hour of the night when the sun trails a pathway of light along the bottom of Canyon Gulch.[29]

With the elimination of the dialectic between nature and civilization, the western lost the serious thematic significance Cooper had given it and became primarily a fictional embodiment of fantasies of transcendent heroism overcoming evil figures of authority. As suggested above, this development hinted at a new kind of thematic conflict between the free and easy way of life of the West and the overcivilized, corrupt culture of the East. To revitalize the western as a fictional formula required that someone invent a pattern of action that could give a greater degree of complexity to this incipient conflict. This was the achievement of Owen Wister.

Wister's Virginian *and the Modern Western*

Owen Wister's *The Virginian* topped best-seller lists in the year of its publication, 1902, and was 1903's fifth highest seller. Since that time it has sold at least two million copies and has inspired a number of movies and a TV series.[30] Generally, the novel is credited with beginning the twentieth-century western craze. More than any other book, it stands as the transition between the dime novel and the modern literary and cinematic western. Its characters and the chief incidents of its plot have been repeated in countless novels and films. Above all, Wister brought back to the tale of western adventure something of the thematic seriousness and complexity that had largely been absent since the works of Cooper. In short, Wister accomplished a major transformation of the western formula.

Like Cooper, Wister was a man of upper-class background who found himself in a world in which the status of his class seemed increasingly tenuous. As White has shown in *The Eastern Establishment and the Western Experience*,[31] Wister's childhood experience and cultural situation rather closely paralleled that of two friends who also became early twentieth-century apostles of the West, Frederic Remington and Theodore Roosevelt. All three men came from established eastern families, felt a sense of the loss of family position, underwent neurotic crises in their youth, and found personal regeneration in the West. Wister became the exponent of the West in fiction, Remington its artistic interpreter and the illustrator of many of Wister's books, while Roosevelt created a political symbolism that drew heavily on the western mystique. Wister dedicated his major western novel to Roosevelt.

Undoubtedly, Wister's own sense of regeneration in the West was reflected in his portrayal of a young man who has left a decaying Virginia to find a new life in Wyoming and of a New England heroine who is transformed by her western experience. Wister's new treatment of the West depended on literary precedent as well as personal experience and need. Wister's version of the West caught on with the public because it synthesized a number of important cultural trends into the archetypal form of adventure. While Wister certainly knew Cooper and probably had some awareness of the dime novel tradition, another literary development had an important influence on his portrayal of the West. Along with the dime novel, there emerged in the later nineteenth century a new kind of western literature that, unlike most of the western adventure stories, was written by men with an actual experience of the area. The humorous, satirical, sometimes sentimental sketches written by Bret Harte, Mark Twain, and Stephen Crane, and their numerous imitators embodied an image of the West far different from Cooper's romantic wilderness. This new version of the frontier was social rather than natural, and it was of a society distinctively different from that of the East, to the point that a new kind of dialectic began to operate, replacing the opposition of nature and civilization by a cultural dialectic between the East and the West. Twain's *Roughing It* satirically embodies this tension in its portrayal of the narrator as greenhorn being initiated into the new society of the West. Twain was far too familiar with his subject to make a heroic romanticization of this new society. In *Roughing It*, western life has its delights, but it is also profoundly corrupting. As the narrator becomes acclimated to its animalistic brutality, he is bitten by the get-rich-quick fever; his mad pursuit of wealth in the mining country drives all other ideas from his mind. When the bust comes, he can barely muster enough energy and interest in life to go back to work for a living:

> After a three months' absence, I found myself in San Francisco again, without a cent. When my credit was about exhausted (for I had become too mean and lazy, now, to work on a morning paper, and there were no

vacancies on the evening journals), I was created San Francisco correspondent of the *Enterprise*, and at the end of five months I was out of debt, but my interest in my work was gone; for my correspondence being a daily one without rest or respite, I got unspeakable tired of it. I wanted another change. The vagabond instinct was strong upon me.[32]

The key to the West as Twain portrayed it in *Roughing It* was not nature, but a new kind of social order in which the traditional restraints were off and the hierarchy changed every day as one man's claim played out and another struck it rich.

In the early days a poverty-stricken Mexican who lived in a canyon directly back of Virginia City had a stream of water as large as a man's wrist trickling from the hillside on his premises. The Ophir Company segregated a hundred feet of their mine and traded it to him for the stream of water. The hundred feet proved to be the richest part of the entire mine; four years after the swap its market value (including its mill) was $1,500,000.[33]

Twain himself was fascinated by this new society and the men it produced. *Roughing It* is full of humorous, colorful, fantastic, and even sometimes terrifying anecdotes about western life. Yet, at the same time that he feels its glamour and excitement, Twain cannot accept this life and its values without reservation. His ambiguity reveals itself clearly in his treatment of the very type that later western writers would so strenuously romanticize: the gunfighter. One such character, the desperado Slade, so intrigued Twain that he devoted two chapters to a discussion of the man's character. Occasionally Twain speaks of Slade in something resembling the accents of a dime novelist: "an outlaw among outlaws and yet their relentless scourge, Slade was at once the most bloody, the most dangerous, and the most valuable citizen that inhabited the savage fastnesses of the mountains."[34] But in the final evaluation of the gunfighter there is none of the haze of romance that later clustered around this character. Instead, there is the complex puzzle of human behavior and its problematic moral significance, as Twain reflects on the strangely pathetic way in which Slade faced his execution:

There is something about the desperado nature that is wholly unaccountable—at least it looks unaccountable. It is this. The true desperado is gifted with splendid courage, and yet he will take the most infamous advantage of his enemy; armed and free he will stand up before a host and fight until he is shot to pieces, and yet when he is under the gallows and helpless he will cry and plead like a child.... Many a notorious coward, many a chicken-livered poltroon, coarse, brutal, degraded, has made his dying speech with what looked like the calmest fortitude, and so we are justified in believing, from the low intellect of such a creature, that it was not *moral* courage that enabled him to do it. Then, if moral courage is not the requisite quality, what could it have been that this stout hearted Slade lacked?— this bloody, desperate, kindly-mannered, urbane gentleman, who never

hesitated to warn his most ruffianly enemies that he would kill them when-
ever or wherever he came across them next! I think it is a conundrum
worth investigating.[35]

Harte was far more sentimental than Twain in his treatment of the West,
though his basic emphasis was much the same: the West as a uniquely
colorful society in which the traditional moral and social restraints no longer
operated. But Harte was particularly fascinated with the way in which
traditional middle-class values and attitudes might reappear in such a society
among individuals who seemed to have left such virtues as domesticity,
purity, and love far behind. Thus Harte's classic situation was the appearance
in the wide-open mining camp of some symbol of traditional middle-class
ideals—a baby, an innocent maiden, a feeling of true romantic love or self-
sacrifice—and he delighted in tracing the impact of this symbol on the rough
and lawless souls who encountered it. Thus his chief stock in trade was
sentimental and, occasionally, ironic paradox. The brutal and violent miner
gives his life in an attempt to save the baby from drowning. The innocent
young girl dies in the arms of a prostitute and both are redeemed by the
experience. The dance-hall girl who has nothing but contempt for the most
handsome and virile men falls in love with a man who has been totally
paralyzed in an accident and devotes her life to service as his nurse. Thus, for
Harte, the Wild West was a place where people rediscovered and reaffirmed
the most important values of life, a quality that would be central to the
western romances of Wister and Zane Grey. Yet, despite his sentimentality,
Harte had a darker and more complex view of life than would be characteristic of the modern western. In his stories, though the characters might be
redeemed, it was usually too late. Their regeneration usually cost them their
lives. It is interesting to compare Harte's most famous story, "The Luck of
Roaring Camp," with two later westerns modeled on the same basic
situation: Wister's novel *Lin Mclean* and John Ford's film *Three Godfathers*.
All three of these works concern rough characters whose lives are changed
when they become involved with a small child. In Harte's story, one gets the
sense there is something inherently hostile to Roaring Camp's attempt to
reform itself when the prostitute, Cherokee Sal, dies while giving birth to a
child. Though the aura of the child transforms the camp from a slough of
violent outcasts into a quiet and decorous place, nature itself rises against the
experiment and camp, child, and all are swept away in a violent rainstorm.
The story ends on a note of sentimental tragedy with the most violent and
brutal of all the miners giving his life in a fruitless attempt to rescue the child.
In Wister's novel and Ford's film, the result is almost the opposite. In both
cases, responsibility for a child transforms the lawless cowboy who, after
various trials and tribulations in the attempt to live up to his new duties, will
clearly settle down into happy domesticity, having found a sweetheart to
complete his newfound family. Thus, where Harte ultimately points up the
almost irreconcilable paradox of lawless violence and the peaceful virtues of

settled domesticity, Wister and Ford synthesize the two sets of values in a redemptive conclusion.

The twentieth-century western inherited from Harte, Twain, and other local colorists a new sense of the western setting as well as elements of humor and sentiment that would persist in such stock characters as those created by movie actors like Andy Devine and Walter Brennan. But, above all, what the western needed was a new hero. As writers came to treat the West not as the embodiment of nature but as a different social environment, the Leatherstocking hero, defined by his adherence to natural values and his flight from society, was no longer very appropriate. Actually, while the Leatherstocking figure became an important protagonist in the twentieth-century nonformulaic western epics of writers like A. B. Guthrie, Frederick Manfred, and Vardis Fisher, he tended to disappear from the formula western because the kind of values that he symbolized were not associated with the West of mining towns, cattle ranches, and farms. The benevolent outlaw, so beloved of the dime novel, was somewhat more a part of the new legend of the West, but this character was so obviously mythical that he could not operate much beyond the limits of the dime novel and later western pulps. Harte, Twain, and other western writers peopled the western town and gave a distinctive shape and character to its society, but they were not primarily interested in heroes. Therefore it was, above all, Owen Wister who initiated the modern western by creating a hero type who belonged to the new image of the West but was, at the same time, in the tradition of transcendent heroism launched by Cooper. This new figure was the cowboy.

Wister certainly did not invent the cowboy-hero, but he did give this already popular figure a new thematic significance. Though the cowboy had already become an American hero through the dime novel, through newspaper stories, books, and plays about western figures like Wild Bill Hickock, Wyatt Earp, and General Custer and, above all, through the enormously popular spectacle of the Wild West Show, Wister, in *The Virginian*, created a story that related the cowboy-hero to a number of important social and cultural themes. The novel begins with the relationship between the narrator and the Virginian, the first of a number of studies in cultural contrast between East and West. The narrator, a somewhat effete easterner on his first visit to friends in the West, encounters the Virginian at the railway station of Medicine Bow when he disembarks for the long overland journey to the ranch of his friend, Judge Henry. The Virginian, a cowboy on the Henry ranch, has been delegated to meet the "tenderfoot." Their first encounter immediately establishes the basic contrast between East and West. The easterner is tired and confused. The railroad has somehow misplaced his trunk, and he feels utterly cast adrift in a savage wilderness:

I started after [the train] as it went its way to the far shores of civilization. It grew small in the unending gulf of space, until all sign of its presence was gone save a faint skein of smoke against the evening sky. And now my lost trunk came back into my thoughts, and Medicine Bow seemed a lonely spot. A sort of ship had left me marooned in a foreign ocean; the Pullman was comfortably steaming home to port, while I—how was I to find Judge Henry's ranch? Where in the unfeatured wilderness was Sunk Creek?[36]

In the midst of the narrator's despair, the Virginian politely introduces himself with a letter from Judge Henry. When the narrator adopts a condescending and familiar attitude toward this "slim young giant" who radiates an air of "splendor" despite his "shabbiness of attire," he is met by a sharp but civil wit that shakes him to the core and leads him to his first realization about the West: that this is not simply a savage wilderness but a land where the inner spirit of men counts more than the surface manners and attitudes of civilization. In such a setting a man must prove his worth by action and not by any assumed or inherited status:

> This handsome, ungrammatical son of the soil had set between us the bar of his cold and perfect civility. No polished person could have done it better. What was the matter? I looked at him and suddenly it came to me. If he had tried familiarity with me the first two minutes of our acquaintance, I should have resented it; by what right, then, had I tried it with him? It smacked of patronizing; on this occasion he had come off the better gentleman of the two. Here in flesh and blood was a truth which I had long believed in words, but never met before. The creature we call a *gentleman* lies deep in the hearts of thousands that are born without chance to muster the outward graces of the type.[37]

After this realization, the narrator soon comes to a new view of the West. Despite the appearance of wildness or squalor, this landscape is a place where deep truths of human nature and life, hidden in the East by the artifices and traditions of civilization, are being known again. Soon he begins to see the apparent chaos and emptiness of Medicine Bow in very different terms:

> I have seen and slept in many like it since. Scattered wide, they littered the frontier from the Columbia to the Rio Grande, from the Missouri to the Sierras. They lay stark, dotted over a planet of treeless dust, like soiled packs of cards. Each was similar to the next, as one old five-spot of clubs resembles another. Houses, empty bottles, and garbage, they were forever the same shapeless pattern. More forlorn they were than stale bones. They seemed to have been strewn there by the wind and to be waiting till the wind should come again and blow them away. Yet serene above their foulness swam a pure and quiet light, such as the East never sees; they might be bathing in the air of creation's first morning. Beneath sun and stars their days and nights were immaculate and wonderful.[38]

Just as the purity of the landscape redeems the seeming squalor of the town, so the inner nobility of the cowboys illumines their apparent wildness:

> Even where baseness was visible, baseness was not uppermost. Daring, laughter, endurance, these were what I saw upon the countenance of the

cowboys. And this very first day of my knowledge marks a date with me. For something about them, and the idea of them, smote my American heart, and I have never forgotten it, nor ever shall, as long as I live. In their flesh our natural passions ran tumultuous; but often in their spirit sat hidden a true nobility, and often beneath its unexpected shining their figures took a heroic stature.[39]

Wister's image of the West is dominated by the theme of moral regeneration. To some extent, his treatment of this theme reflects a primitivism not unlike Cooper's. Because civilization and its artificial traditions have not yet taken a firm hold in the West, the influence of nature is more strongly felt in that "pure and quiet light, such as the East never sees." But the influence of nature is less important for Wister than the code of the western community, a distinctive set of values and processes that is in many respects a result of the community's closeness to nature but also reflects certain basic social circumstances. Because institutional law and government have not yet fully developed in the West, the community has had to create its own methods of insuring order and achieving justice. As Judge Henry explains when the heroine is distressed by vigilante justice, the code of the west is not inimical to law. On the contrary, the vigilantes represent the community acting directly, instead of allowing its will to be distorted by complex and easily corrupted institutional machinery. Of course, Judge Henry insists this situation will change when civilization reaches the West, yet in his praise of the principle of vigilante justice, the judge intimates that the western type of direct action is not merely a necessary expedient, but a rebirth of moral vitality in the community:

In Wyoming the law has been letting our cattle-thieves go for two years. We are in a very bad way, and we are trying to make that way a little better until civilization can reach us. At present we lie beyond its pale. The courts, or rather the juries, into whose hands we have put the law, are not dealing the law. They are withered hands, or rather they are imitation hands made for show, with no life in them, no grip. They cannot hold a cattle-thief. And so when your ordinary citizen sees this, and sees that he has placed justice in a dead hand, he must take justice back into his own hands where it was once at the beginning of all things. Call this primitive, if you will. But so far from being a *defiance* of the law, it is an *assertion* of it—the fundamental assertion of self-governing men, upon whom our whole social fabric is based.[40]

As presented by Wister, the code embodies the community's moral will but it also gives full weight to the importance of individual honor. Since the fundamental principles of honor and the will of the community transcend responsibility to the official agencies of government and the codified, written law, the Virginian finds it incumbent upon him to participate both in a lynching and a duel, illegal actions according to the written law, but recognized by all his fellow western males as inescapable obligations. The

Virginian's difficulties do not come from the demands of the code. Though the actions it requires of him are dangerous, they cause him little inner conflict. His real problem is that he has fallen in love with the eastern schoolteacher, Molly Wood. Women pose a basic threat to the code, because they are the harbingers of law and order enforced by police and courts, and of the whole machinery of schools and peaceful town life. These institutions make masculine courage and strength a much less important social factor. The Virginian becomes increasingly aware of the danger his love poses to the code, and at one point his love makes him break with the code, by explaining to Molly the villainy of another man:

> Having read his sweetheart's mind very plainly, the lover now broke his dearest custom. It was his code never to speak ill of any man to any woman. Men's quarrels were not for women's ears. In his scheme, good women were to know only a fragment of men's lives. He had lived many outlaw years, and his wide knowledge of evil made innocence doubly precious to him. But to-day he must depart from his code, having read her mind well. He would speak evil of one man to one woman, because his reticence had hurt her.[41]

But if the hero's romantic interest in the schoolmarm tends to draw him away from the code, his struggle with the villain Trampas reaffirms his dedication to it and ultimately demonstrates what seems to be Wister's main thesis: that the kind of individual moral courage and community responsibility embodied in the code is a vital part of the American tradition and needs to be reawakened in modern American society. Romance and the struggle against villainy are interspersed throughout the novel. At the very beginning of the novel, the Virginian confronts Trampas over a card game and puts him down with the immortal phrase, "When you call me that, *smile!*" This supremely cool challenge, which forces on Trampas the necessity of choosing either to draw his gun or back down, illustrates an important aspect of the code—one must never shy away from violence, but at the same time never bring it on by one's own actions. Honor cannot be compromised, but the true hero, as opposed to a lawless man like Trampas, always lives within distinct moral limits. He never fights out of anger or even from a desire for glory, but only when he must preserve his own honor or enact the community's just sentence. In this initial incident, the Virginian is supremely in control of himself and no inner conflict gives him any doubt about the proper course of action. But it is not long before the snake enters this garden of honorable masculinity. Careering across the countryside in a stagecoach driven by a drunken driver, Miss Molly Stark Wood of Bennington, Vermont, descendant of revolutionary heroes, is nearly tumbled into a dangerously high creek before a dashing man on horseback rides out of nowhere and deposits her safely on the other shore. After saving her life, a gallant gentleman can hardly avoid falling in love with the lady. When they meet again, some time later, the Virginian announces his determination to make Molly love him, even though she has just finished unmercifully roasting him for his part in some masculine high jinks. Thus begins the conflict between the masculine code of the West and the genteel ideas of civility that Molly carries with her from the East.

Wister develops the Virginian's courtship of Molly and his conflict with Trampas in counterpoint until the two lines of action intersect and the Virginian must choose between his two commitments. Molly is at first quite resistant to the Virginian's courtship. Her eastern manners and beliefs make her recoil at what seems to be the Virginian's crudity, childishness, and lack of civility. When she discovers that, despite his lack of formal education and social graces, the Virginian has an instinctive gentility as well as a strong native intelligence, she begins to become interested in him. We have already seen the narrator of the book go through a similar process. Molly's eastern prejudices against the West and her inability to conceive of the idea that a Wood of Bennington, Vermont, might marry a cowboy still defend her against the Virginian's love until a dramatic incident completely changes her attitude. On his way to a rendezvous with Molly, the Virginian is attacked and left for dead by a marauding band of Indians. (Note how in Wister, as in many later dime novels, the Indian has become a narrative convenience rather than a central element of the story.) When the Virginian does not appear at the rendezvous, Molly rides out along the trail and finds him seriously wounded. Wister represents this as a great moment of truth for Molly. Casting off her demure gentility, she summons up the courage and daring of her revolutionary ancestors, rescues the Virginian, and nurses him back to health in her cabin. This experience is the first real step in the westernizing of Molly, which Wister sees as a kind of atavistic return to the spirit of her ancestors. In this way, Wister suggests that the West is not entirely a new cultural experience, but a rebirth of the revolutionary generation's vigor.

Along with this awakening of the deeper instincts in her blood, Molly's love for the Virginian blossoms and she agrees to marry him. Now the story moves toward the final confrontation between Molly's eastern scheme of values and the code of the West. Trampas increasingly menaces the good community of the ranch. When he tries to persuade the ranch crew to go off hunting gold, he is outwitted by the Virginian. In response, he leaves the ranch and turns rustler, carrying along two of the Virginian's former friends to be members of his gang. The code of the West swings into action against the rustlers. Judge Henry, the ranch owner, makes the Virginian leader of a posse charged with the capture and execution of the rustlers. The Virginian must reluctantly join in the lynching of his former friend Steve, while Trampas escapes and succeeds in eluding further pursuit. Finally, Trampas returns to town and the Virginian prepares to meet his challenge to individual combat. Molly insists that the Virginian refuse to fight Trampas or she will break off their engagement and return to the East. Caught in this conflict of love, duty, and honor, the Virginian does not hesitate. He explains to Molly why the code of masculine honor must always take precedence over other obligations:

"Can't yu' see how it must be about a man? It's not for their benefit, friends or enemies, that I have got this thing to do. If any man happened to say I was a thief and I heard about it, would I let him go on spreadin' such a thing of me? Don't I owe my own honesty something better than that? Would I sit down in a corner rubbin' my honesty and whisperin' to it, 'There! there! I know you ain't a thief'? No, seh; not a little bit! What men say about my nature is not just merely an outside thing. For the fact that I let 'em keep on sayin' it is a proof I don't value my nature enough to shield it from their slander and give them their punishment. And that's being a poor sort of a jay."⁴²

So the Virginian confronts Trampas, believing that his defense of his honor will lose him the woman he loves. But, of course, it doesn't work out that way. Once Molly sees her sweetheart in danger, she realizes that her love for him transcends all her moral compunctions. Their reunion follows:

The Virginian walked to the hotel, and stood on the threshold of his sweetheart's room. She had heard his step and was upon her feet. Her lips were parted, and her eyes fixed on him, nor did she move, or speak.
"Yu' have to know it," said he. "I have killed Trampas." "Oh. thank God!" she said; and he found her in his arms. Long they embraced without speaking, and what they whispered then with their kisses matters not.
Thus did her New England conscience battle to the end, and, in the end, capitulated to love. And the next day, with the bishop's blessing, and Mrs. Taylor's broadest smile, the Virginian departed with his bride into the mountains.⁴³

The fourth main plot line of The Virginian is the story of his success. Like some grown-up Alger hero, the Virginian, beginning as a poor cowboy, is soon appointed foreman of Judge Henry's ranch. In that post, he meets the challenge of leadership and demonstrates his aspiration to rise in life by investing his wages in land so that he can become a rancher himself. At the end of the novel, we are assured that the Virginian will continue to rise and in due course become one of Wyoming's leading citizens.

What Wister did with his story of the Virginian was to synthesize Cooper's opposition of nature and civilization with the gospel of success and progress, thus making his hero both an exponent of natural law and of the major ideals of American society. This shift is particularly evident in Wister's treatment of the code of the West, which, as we have seen, is based on both the individual's sense of personal honor and the moral will of the community. In the final conflict with Trampas, the hero not only maintains the purity of his individual image but acts in the true interest of the community. Cooper was never quite able to resolve the conflict between Leatherstocking's commitment to the wilderness life and the advance of civilization. In one of his later novels, The Oak Openings, he attempted to create a protagonist who, like the Virginian, would pass from the wilderness into society and become a success. But two things prevented Cooper from arriving at the kind of happy synthesis that Wister pulled off in *The Virginian*: first, Cooper could not imagine that the qualities that made a Leatherstocking so effective in the wilderness would also lead him to social success. Second, Cooper's view of civilization was still strongly enough permeated by traditional aristocratic assumptions that he did not consider it appropriate or even possible for a man to rise from the status of a frontiersman to that of a leading citizen in a single lifetime. Consequently, he made the protagonist of *The Oak Openings* a bee-hunter rather than an Indian fighter like Natty. Ben Boden's involvement in the wilderness is a matter of accumulating capital rather than a commitment to the life of nature. Once he has acquired enough of a stake to become a merchant, he turns his back on the wilderness. Cooper makes it clear that Ben is only the founder of a genteel family. At the end of the novel we are assured that it will take another generation for the rough edges to wear off before the Boden family will take its place with the gentry.

For Wister, however, the western hero possesses qualities that civilized society badly needs. It is not his lack of refinement that prevents the Virginian from assuming his rightful place as a social leader, but the shallow prejudices of an overrefined and effete society that has lost contact with its own most significant values. When the Virginian goes east to meet Molly's family, it is Molly's great aunt, the one closest to the family's revolutionary heritage, who understands and fully appreciates the Virginian's qualities. This representative of an earlier order sees the basic resemblance between the Virginian and General Stark, the founder of the family. Because of this she understands that the West is not a barbarous land, but a place where the original American traits of individual vigor, courage, and enterprise have been reborn: "'There he is,' she said, showing the family portrait. 'And a rough time he must have had of it now and then. New Hampshire was full of fine young men in those days. But nowadays most of them have gone away to seek their fortunes in the West.'"[44]

Thus Wister resolved the old ambiguity between nature and civilization by presenting the West not as a set of natural values basically antithetical to civilization, but as a social environment in which the American dream could be born again. As Wister summed up the message of his book in the "Rededication and Preface" that he wrote for a new edition:

If this book be anything more than an American story, it is an expression of American faith. Our Democracy has many enemies, both in Wall Street and in the Labor Unions; but as those in Wall Street have by their excesses created those in the Unions, they are the worst; if the pillars of our house fall, it is they who will have been the cause thereof. But I believe the pillars will not fall, and that, with mistakes at times, but with wisdom in the main, we people will prove ourselves equal to the severest test to which political man has yet subjected himself—the test of Democracy.[45]

There are many similarities between Wister's view of the West and Frederick Jackson Turner's frontier hypothesis, for the two men were near contemporaries. Like Wister, Turner characterized frontier society in terms of revitalization. He argued that America's recurrent frontier experience was the source of many of the values and institutions of democracy, just as Wister, in *The Virginian*, portrayed the West as a place of social and cultural regeneration, where the vigor and enterprise of revolutionary America might be rediscovered. Turner saw the closing of the frontier and the growth of large industrial corporations, labor organizations, and governmental bureaucracies as signs that American culture was entering a new phase of development. Because he believed that the most important aspects of American democracy had depended on the open frontier, he feared that in the new institutional context these values might be lost. Similarly, Wister represented the East as an environment of decaying values and the West as a source of social and moral regeneration. His comments in the 1911 "Rededication" quoted above even suggest Turner's view of the danger of large organizations in the absence of an open frontier.

In actuality, however, Turner and Wister's views of the frontier were quite different. That one can find so much surface similarity between them suggests the extent to which both reflected certain widespread cultural preoccupations at the end of the nineteenth century: the final settlement of the continental United States, the growing awareness of the changes wrought by industrialism, the sense of moral decay in American life, the realization that America was changing from a predominantly rural to an urban society, and the search for some sense of reassurance and regeneration. We find the same preoccupations and the same fascination with America's frontier experience in individuals as diverse as Wister's dedicatee Theodore Roosevelt, who made the quest for national regeneration a basic topic of his political rhetoric, and in the sentimental religious novelist Harold Bell Wright, who wrote best-seller after best-seller by sending his jaded urban protagonists to the Ozark Mountains or the West in search of redemption. Turner, who stimulated American historical interest in the western experience, and Wister, who created the modern western romance, shared these preoccupations, but if we look more closely at their versions of the West we discover fundamental differences. For Turner, the most important aspect of the West was the way in which it maintained social fluidity and equality of opportunity, and because of this, transformed the mass of men into free individuals with hope and idealism for the future:

> Most important of all has been the fact that an area of free land has continually lain on the western border of the settled area of the United States. Whenever social conditions tended to crystallize in the East, whenever Capital tended to press upon labor or political restraints to impede the freedom of the mass, there was this gate of escape to the free conditions of the frontier. These free lands promoted individualism, economic equality,

freedom to rise, democracy.... In a word, then, free lands meant free opportunities. Their existence has differentiated the American democracy from the democracies which have preceded it, because ever, as democracy in the East took the form of highly specialized and complicated industrial society, in the West it kept in touch with primitive conditions.[46]

For Wister, however, the real significance of the West lay not in the way western social conditions transformed the mass of men, but in the revitalization of aristocracy. For him the rise of the Virginian symbolized the emergence of a new kind of elite capable of providing the vigorous and moral political leadership that America desperately needed. America, as Wister saw it, was as much a class society as any other country; the difference lay in the fact that the American elite was not determined by family status or traditional prerogative, but by inner worth tested in the competition between men.

There can be no doubt of this:—
All America is divided into two classes,—the quality and the equality. The latter will always recognize the former when mistaken for it. Both will be with us until our women bear nothing but kings.
It was through the Declaration of Independence that we Americans acknowledged the *eternal inequality* of man. For by it we abolished a cut-and-dried aristocracy. We had seen little men artificially held down in low places, and our own justice-loving hearts abhorred the violence to human nature. Therefore, we decreed that every man should thenceforth have equal liberty to find his own level. By this very decree we acknowledged and gave freedom to true aristocracy, saying "Let the best man win, whoever he is." Let the best man win! That is America's word. That is true democracy. And true democracy and true aristocracy are one and the same thing. If anybody cannot see this, so much the worse for his eyesight.[47]

Turner's West was that of a liberal progressive, and he laid considerable stress on the necessity for social action to "conserve democratic institutions and ideas" in a period when the natural safety-valve of free land would no longer operate to prevent the formation of rigid classes:

In the later period of its development, Western democracy has been gaining experience in the problem of social control. It has steadily enlarged the sphere of its action and the instruments for its perpetuation. By its system of public schools, from the grades to the graduate work of the great universities, the West has created a larger single body of intelligent plain people than can be found elsewhere in the world. Its political tendencies, whether we consider Democracy, Populism, or Republicanism, are distinctly in the direction of greater social control and the conservation of the old democratic ideals.[48]

Wister's view of the future of western politics reveals a very different perspective:

When the thieves prevailed at length, as they did forcing cattle owners to leave the country or be ruined, the Virginian had forestalled this crash. The herds were driven away to Montana. Then, in 1892, came the cattle war, when after putting their men in office, and coming to own some of the newspapers, the thieves brought ruin on themselves as well. For in a broken country there is nothing left to steal.[49]

If we ask how the same West that could produce the heroic Virginian and revitalize the eastern narrator and heroine could also be taken over by a gang of thieves, we see, I think, the essential conservatism of Wister's point of view. Where Turner sees the West as playing a fundamental role in the ongoing evolution of American democracy, Wister sees it essentially as a return to the true American aristocracy, a return that is threatened rather than enhanced by further social evolution. Wister admired the early stages of western development. He hoped the new elite, revitalized by their contact with the primitive strength and honor of the code of the West, would return and reform the corrupted East. His friend and hero, Theodore Roosevelt, seemed to be playing this role; though offspring of an aristocratic family, Roosevelt had lived in the West and had proved himself a man of courage and honor by western standards. Enormously vigorous and projecting a high sense of honor and morality, Theodore Roosevelt seemed able to articulate and embody the moral will of the people. Indeed, Roosevelt's career might be interpreted as a national embodiment of the same kind of democratic aristocracy that the Virginian symbolized in western terms. Yet it remained an open question for Wister whether the Virginian could overcome the "thieves" just as he was not sure whether Theodore Roosevelt could roll back the "political darkness" that "still lay dense upon every State in the Union [when] this book was dedicated to the greatest benefactor we people have known since Lincoln." Despite the success of his hero, there still remained an edge of the elegaic tone with which Cooper orchestrated his Leatherstocking series. For the society that had begun to evolve in the West after the disappearance of the cowboy looked ominously like that new American society that Cooper, too, hoped would be only a passing phase. All the romance and excitement and honor seemed to be gone:

What is become of the horseman, the cowpuncher, the last romantic figure upon our soil? For he was a romantic. Whatever he did, he did with his might. . . . The cowpuncher's ungoverned hours did not unman him. If he gave his word, he kept it. Wall Street would have found him behind the times. Nor did he talk lewdly to women; Newport would have thought him old-fashioned. He and his brief epoch make a complete picture, for in themselves they were as complete as the pioneers of the land or the explorers of the sea. A transition has followed the horseman of the plains; a shapeless state, a condition of men and manners unlovely as that bald moment in the year when winter is gone and spring not come, and the face of Nature is ugly. I shall not dwell upon it here. Those who have seen it

know well what I mean. Such transition was inevitable. Let us give thanks
that it is but a transition, and not a finality.⁵⁰

But the elegaic tone is muted in Wister. Generally, the note of triumph and
synthesis rings clear, and it is to this that Wister probably owed the great
success of his book and its capacity to spawn so immense a progeny. *The
Virginian* brings together in harmony a number of conflicting forces or
principles in American life and this synthesis and resolution of conflicting
values is a literary exemplification of the principle of having your cake and
eating it too. Wister's characters, actions, and setting have a surface verisimilitude, but it is moral fantasy that shapes character and action. Thus a
reader can enjoy a world in which things work out just as he wishes them to
without any sense that this world is overly artificial or contrived. This
principle so permeates the book that we can find examples at every level from
particulars of style to the overall pattern of the action. Two passages quoted
earlier, one of which describes the jerry-built ugliness of the western town
against the serene and uplifting beauty of the landscape and the other the
cowboy's inner nobility of spirit lying under his rude and seemingly amoral
exterior, are good examples of the basic stylistic level. In just this fashion
Wister constantly represents characters and setting through a synthesis of
seeming commonness, ugliness, or violence with transcendent beauty and
morality. On a larger scale, the character of the Virginian neatly combines
verisimilitude and fantasy. In one sense the Virginian is the opposite of a
traditional romantic hero. His origin is obscure, he has to work for a living,
he likes to horse around and play practical jokes. He is far from chaste and
pure, and in one of the first episodes in the novel Wister even suggests his
involvement in an adulterous love affair. Yet, the Virginian is also a shining
knight, a man of supreme integrity and purity, a chevalier without fear and
without reproach. Such a combination is inescapably attractive and has been
the delight of readers since 1902. Even today I find that cynical and
sophisticated students are more often than not charmed by *The Virginian*,
rather delighted, I expect, that its verisimilitude about little things allows
them to accept a fantasy that otherwise they would feel compelled to reject.

The Virginian also synthesized a number of other cultural conflicts. Just as
Conan Doyle created a character of great fascination by bringing together in
a single figure the diverging cultural symbols of the romantic artist and the
scientist, Wister combined in the Virginian several conflicting images of
American life: the Virginian is a new self-made man, but he is also a
throwback to heroic types of the past like the medieval knight; he is a
nascent entrepreneur and he marries a New England schoolteacher, but he is
also a son of the old South and carries in his demeanor the chivalric ideals of
the antebellum South; thus he represents a synthesis of the conflicting
stereotypes of Cavalier and Yankee; he is a tough, fearless killer, skilled in
violence, and a gentle lover and friend; and, finally, he is a supreme
individualist of unstained honor, and yet a dedicated agent of the commu-

nity. In *The Virginian*, Cooper's problematic antithesis between nature and the claims of civilization was annealed and harmonized.

Zane Grey and W. S. Hart: The Romantic Western of the 1920s

The publication of *The Virginian* coincided with another event of tremendous importance in the history of the western formula, the production of Edwin S. Porter's *The Great Train Robbery* (1903), the first significant western on film. Porter's film certainly did not revolutionize the content of the western since it consisted of a loosely episodic presentation of a train robbery followed by pursuit of the outlaws on horseback and a final shootout. In fact, the film made little attempt to generate character or plot beyond what was necessary for the basic situation. What *The Great Train Robbery* did demonstrate in an unmistakable way was that the western spectacle which had already been cheered by the enthusiastic audiences of the Wild West Show could be effectively presented on film. Moreover, film added to the effectiveness of costumes, horses, guns, riding, roping, and shooting by making it possible to use as background the extraordinary western landscape, the drama and beauty of which had been discovered through the work of painters like Bierstadt, Remington, and Russell, and the new medium of photography. For its development in the twentieth century, the western film was able to call on three major popular traditions: the literary tradition of the western adventure initiated by Cooper, the great popular spectacle of the Wild West Show, and the flourishing artistic tradition of representing western scenes and landscapes in painting and photography.

With the great proliferation of westerns in films and later on television, the history of the western in the twentieth century becomes very complex. Many writers, directors, performers, and technical people made important contributions to the art of the western and, in the process, created an enormous variety of westerns in many different media. In the course of this complex development, the formula was undergoing an evolution that reflected the impact not only of changing public interests and values, but of important artistic discoveries and technical innovations. Furthermore, this process of evolution was additionally complicated by the development of different types of westerns for different audiences. Popular formulas tend to generate a continuum of subformulas ranging from simple exciting stories for younger and less sophisticated audiences to more complex and "realistic" treatments for the more sophisticated adult public. Since the later nineteenth century a more or less continuing tradition of western adventure for juveniles has passed from the dime novel into movie serials, radio programs, comic books, and television series like "Hopalong Cassidy." Similarly, there has been a consistent public for the B western film and the paperback story, creations that are slightly more complex versions of the juvenile western but share its emphasis on extraordinary heroics and spectacular adventures. The evolution of the formula in these types of western is very slow and changes tend to be superficial rather than basic. A western novel written by Louis L'Amour in the 1960s is somewhat franker and more graphic in the portrayal of sex and violence, and perhaps somewhat more ambiguous about the moral qualities of its hero than one of the sagas of Max Brand from the 1920s, but the basic patterns of action and character will be similar. In these types of western, created for a special audience of western addicts, continuity is more valued than change. Just as in the case of the detective story, the true devotee prefers a new gimmick to a basic reorientation of the formula.

Yet even these more conservative types of western reflect to some extent the impact of changes that are more dramatically evident in the development of the "adult" western, where cycles of audience interest and disinterest tend to generate more fundamental changes in the formula. The process works something like this. While western devotees are likely to enjoy almost any version of the formula, the larger mass audience can make or break an expensive film production, a relatively complex novel, or a major television production. Thus while the pulp novel and the inexpensive film or television production appeal to a limited but constant audience, the big money comes from works that appeal to the general public, for these add to the basic western audience a number of other groups who are not ordinarily addicted to westerns. To attract this larger, more diverse public, western creators must not only work at a higher level of artistic effectiveness; they must manipulate the western formula so that it responds to the interests, values, and assumptions of people who are not so enamored of cowboy hats, horses, guns, and the other western paraphernalia that they will accept what seems a false or irrelevant picture of the world.

Because of this audience selectivity, the "adult" western appears to move through a cyclical process of evolution. A major new western or group of westerns attracts the attention of the large public and becomes a best-seller. Hoping to profit from the new vogue, other writers or filmmakers imitate the initial success by creating their own version of what they take to be the elements and patterns that account for its popularity. Eventually these imitations become so mechanical and uninspired that the public tires of them. At the same time public attitudes and interests change so that the current version of the formula continues to appeal only to the limited group of western devotees. From this point, profits and production will tend to fall off until a new version of the formula once again appeals to a large public and the cycle begins over again. Thus the development of the high-quality western in the twentieth century has been marked by a series of such cycles in which new "adult" westerns become temporarily appealing to the general public and then decline, only to be replaced by another version of the formula. The first such cycle followed on the success of Wister's *The Virginian* and reached a peak in the early 1920s, declining after 1925. During this period writers like Harold Bell Wright, Zane Grey, and Emerson Hough achieved a consistent best-seller status with their western novels, and their success was mirrored in the great popularity in film of W. S. Hart, Tom Mix, and of such films as *The Covered Wagon* and *The Iron Horse*. The later twenties and the thirties was a period of great flourishing for the B western and the pulp story and novel but not for the "adult" western. Few western novels reached the best-seller list and the production of high-budget western films fell off significantly. W. S. Hart retired, and John Ford, whose *Iron Horse* was one of the great successes of the twenties, did not make another western until his 1939 *Stagecoach*.

The popular success of *Stagecoach* is generally considered to be the beginning of a new cycle of "adult" western films that reached a peak in the late forties and early fifties, when films like *High Noon* and *Shane* were among the most successful and esteemed productions of 1952 and 1953. Westerns continued to be highly popular throughout the 1950s and, with the adaptation of this new "adult" version to television series like "Gunsmoke" and "Bonanza," the western probably reached a high point of appeal to the general public in the later 1950s when eight of the top ten television series were westerns. It is clear from the films of the later 1950s that the patterns of the "classic" film of the forties and early fifties were beginning to break up. Through the early 1960s the number of television westerns dropped off. Though many high-budget western films continued to be produced, few of them achieved the broad popular success of the earlier works of John Ford or of *High Noon* and *Shane*. Then, in the later 1960s, several striking new versions of the formula appeared in successful films like *Butch Cassidy and the Sundance Kid, True Grit, The Wild Bunch*, and Sergio Leone's Clint Eastwood series, and it appeared that another cycle was beginning.

To trace the evolution of the western formula in the twentieth century, and to draw some tentative hypotheses about its cultural significance, I will concentrate on these major cycles.

The two key figures of the period of great western popularity following Wister were the writer Zane Grey and the filmmaker W. S. Hart, for in these creators the dominant early twentieth-century version of the western formula came to fruition and achieved its greatest general popularity. Though many other western writers and filmmakers were important during this era, Grey and Hart produced what was unquestionably the most effective and successful work of the period 1910–25. Grey was not only the leading western writer but the single most popular author of the post-World War I era, with at least one book among the top best-sellers for almost ten years straight.[51] Hart was eventually eclipsed by other western stars, particularly Tom Mix, but during his relatively short filmmaking career he was more the exponent of the "adult" western than any other single director or star.[52] Grey and Hart never worked together, perhaps because Hart's work had begun to decline before Grey movies were being produced on a large scale (eventually over one hundred western films were based on Grey novels, several being produced in as many as four different versions over the years). Nevertheless, their works have so many points in common that it seems reasonable to view them as exponents of the same essential version of the formula. In fact, though he never appeared in a Grey film, Hart would have been the perfect embodiment of many of Grey's central figures with their mixture of maturity and innocence, of experience and purity, of shyness and latent violence. And many of Hart's stories could easily have been written by Grey, for they share the same plot patterns, the same kinds of characters and themes, the same aura of hard-bitten heroic adventure and surface concern for verisimilitude, mixed with a deep religiosity and sentimentalism.

Grey began his writing career with an attempt at historical romance in the mold of the early twentieth-century successes of Winston Churchill, but met with little public response. It was after he, like Owen Wister, took a trip to the West and began to write of western adventures in the manner of *The Virginian* that his popular success blossomed. Hart came to films through the stage, and the stamp of Wister was on him, too, since one of his most successful roles had been in a dramatic adaptation of *The Virginian*.[53] Hart certainly felt that his version of the West was more realistic than Wister's, and I suspect that Grey did, too. From today's perspective, the opposite seems to be the case. While Wister's novel remains fairly plausible, given the archetypal patterns of heroic adventure, the works of Hart and Grey seem like excessively sentimental and melodramatic treatments of Wister's formula of the drama of individual and social regeneration in the West.[54]

Grey and Hart developed the western in several new directions, but their basic indebtedness to the formulaic structure embodied in *The Virginian* is quite clear. Like Wister, Grey and Hart portray the West as a distinctive moral and symbolic landscape with strong implications of regeneration or redemption for those protagonists who can respond to its challenge by recovering basic human and American values. As in *The Virginian*, the dialectic between the cultivated but enervated East and the vigorous, vital and democratic West plays an important role in their works, commonly shaping a plot line that deals with the developing love between hero and heroine. In many instances the heroine's commitment to eastern genteel values of culture and social order provide a major obstacle to the romance, since, despite her initial attraction to the hero, she is distressed by his apparent ignorance of the finer things and his code of violent individualism. Like Wister's Molly Wood, the heroines of Grey and Hart usually come around in the end, the deep force of their love driving them back into the hero's arms when his life is threatened. There are many other important thematic and structural similarities between Wister's *Virginian* and the novels and films of Grey and Hart: all place great emphasis on the unwritten and extralegal "Code of the West" as a basic factor in the hero's identity and in the specific problems he confronts in the course of the story; all tend to build their stories around patterns of gradually increasing violence moving toward a climactic confrontation between hero and villain in what has become the classic resolution of the shootout; each in his own way develops and elaborates the same quasi-allegorical landscape of town, desert, and mountains and the same social and historical background of large cattle and sheep ranching with their attendant episodes of rustling, range wars, and wide-open towns. It is interesting to note that neither of these creators does very much with either the mining development of the West or with other types of agriculture such as wheat-raising or the family subsistence farm, probably because in the minds of both writers and their publics the uniqueness of the West and its difference from the rest of the country was most strikingly symbolized by the open-range cattle industry.

Despite their dependence on the Wister version of the western formula, Grey and Hart added important structural emphases and themes of their own. Along with other writers and filmmakers such as Harold Bell Wright, Emerson Hough, and Tom Mix, Grey and Hart were important contributors to the process by which the western formula, having passed from the adolescent fantasy of the dime novel to the more complex social and historical allegorizing of Wister, became in the first quarter of the twentieth century a popular mythology for grown-ups as well as children. Grey and Hart developed the qualities of melodramatic intensity that transformed the more sophisticated political allegory and social comedy of *The Virginian* into the incredible but immensely effective popular fantasies of *Riders of the Purple Sage* and *Hell's Hinges*. We can clearly see this process in operation in some of the new elements or emphases that Grey and Hart added to the formula, such as their treatment of the hero. Wister's Virginian, despite his skills in violence, was not a gunfighter or an outlaw. And, though he adhered to the unwritten law of the West, he was fully integrated into the community of the ranch and the town from the very beginning. As Grey and Hart developed their conception of the hero, however, he shed his close ties with society and became the more mysterious and alienated figure of the heroic gunfighter or outlaw. Grey's Lassiter, in *Riders of the Purple Sage* (1912), is probably the first widely successful version of the gunfighter in the western. Complete with fast draw, special costume, and a mysterious sinister past, Lassiter adumbrates such favorite western heroes of a later era as Shane, Destry, Doc Holliday, and Wild Bill Hickok. Hart, too, made something of a specialty of the heroic outlaw in figures like Draw Egan (*The Return of Draw Egan*) and Blaze Tracy (*Hell's Hinges*).

Unlike the Virginian, this new style western hero was typically an older man and very much a loner, at least at the beginning of his adventures. Even when he was not explicitly an outlaw, he was an outcast from society, either because of his violent past or his inability to settle down:

And he reflected that years of it had made him what he was—only a wild horse wrangler, poor and with no prospects of any profit. Long he had dreamed of a home and perhaps a family. Vain, idle dreams! The romance, the thrilling adventure, the constant change of scene and action, charac-teristic of the life of a wild-horse hunter, had called to him in his youth and fastened upon him in his manhood. What else could he do now? He had become a lone hunter, a wanderer of the wild range, and it was not likely that he could settle down to the humdrum toil of a farmer or cattleman.[55]

Yet, as is implicit in this confession, the Grey hero has a deep yearning to become part of society. This action—the domestication of the wild hero—was one essential subject of Grey and Hart's westerns. In their stories, a mature, hard-bitten hero with a violent past encounters a young woman with whom he falls in love. But there are serious obstacles to their love. As a good daughter of Wister's Molly Wood, the heroine initially rejects the hero's violence or, in some cases, finds herself committed by kinship or loyalty to the hero's enemies. There must be a climax of justifiable violence to eliminate the enemies and to overcome the heroine's scruples. In the end, hero and heroine are clearly on their way to marriage, a family, and a settled life thereafter.

The other great subject of the westerns of this period also takes off from a theme that was central to Wister. Grey and Hart were both fascinated by the idea of the West as a testing ground of character and idea. Time after time their stories represented a protagonist—usually female—whose personal qualities and attitudes, formed in the East, were challenged and tested in the western environment where situations of the most basic sort call upon the deepest resources of character and reveal what a person truly is. Grey's novels in particular are peopled with one heroine after another, who, searching for lost identity, finds regeneration and happiness in the West under the influence of its inspiring scenery, its opportunities for romance with a devastatingly glamorous and wild member of the opposite sex, and its purging, redemptive violence.[56]

Though this basic pattern is obviously reminiscent of *The Virginian*, Grey and Hart invested it with mythical and melodramatic overtones that are quite different from the political allegory and social comedy surrounding the adventures of Wister's hero. Instead of Wister's explicit treatment of political and social issues like western vigilante justice, Grey and Hart place much greater stress on sexual and religious motifs. Their leading men and women typically combine hints of dazzling erotic intensity and prowess with an actual chastity, purity, and gentility that would hardly bring blushes to the cheek of a Victorian maiden. In presenting his heroines Grey loved to dangle a seemingly corrupted and soiled dove before the reader's eyes only to assure him that the lady in question was truly virginal, sweet, and bent on monogamous domesticity. Two favorite feminine types were the eastern sophisticate whose flirtations and artificialities soon give way to deep and powerful love for the hero, and the wild heroine who appears on the scene like a sexy nature girl but soon reveals that beneath her sassy manner, her artfully torn chemise, and apparent promiscuity beats a heart as pure as the driven snow.

The same melodramatic polarities characterize the Grey-Hart hero's erotic quality. He is typically mature, experienced, and an outcast, with a past that hints not only at terrible deeds of violence but at smoldering erotic prowess. Sometimes he is suspected of perverse erotic relationships with Indian girls or Mexicans, relationships that by the racist attitudes of the period were ineffably fascinating and deeply disturbing. No decent girl could possibly be attracted to a man who ... Actually, it usually turns out that the hero's seamy past is only a myth. Though he may be a killer, his sexual life has been, despite manifold temptations, above reproach. These erotic motifs and their treatment in Grey and Hart suggest on a more sophisticated level the curious fascination with sexuality that we found so prevalent in the earlier dime novels.

In presenting the developing romantic connection between hero and heroine, Grey and Hart typically create a strong tension between symbolic sexuality and actual purity. Hero and heroine are usually brought together by emotional forces beyond their control and often against their explicit wishes. In *To the Last Man*, for example, Jean Isbel and Ellen Jorth are members of opposing families in a feud, but from their first meeting they are irresistibly drawn together. At one point in their relationship, Jean leaves a small gift for Ellen, which she is reluctant even to look at. Grey's description of her reaction to the little package is a good illustration of his technique of suggesting sexuality while maintaining chastity:

> By and by she fell asleep, only to dream that the package was a caressing hand stealing about her, feeling for hers, and holding it with soft, strong clasp. When she awoke she had the strangest sensation in her right palm. It was moist, throbbing, hot, and the feel of it on her cheek was strangely thrilling and comforting. She lay awake then. The night was dark and still. Only a low moan of wind in the pines and the faint tinkle of a sheep bell broke the serenity. She felt very small and lonely lying there in the deep forest, and, try how she would, it was impossible to think the same then as she did in the clear light of day. Resentment, pride, anger—these seemed abated now. If the events of the day had not changed her, they had at least brought up softer and kinder memories and emotions than she had known for long.[57]

For the ardent lovers of Grey and Hart, sex and religion are strangely intermixed. Sexual passion is treated as a semimystical moral and religious experience and is often associated with the redemptive and healing qualities of the simpler life and morally elevating landscape of the West. Georgianna Stockwell, the flapper heroine of *Code of the West*, at first scorns the simple, unsophisticated passion of Cal Thurman and the stringent western code of feminine behavior by which he and his family live. But she soon comes to see herself in a new perspective:

> Stranger from the East ... she had come with her painted cheeks, her lipstick, her frocks, and her bare knees, her slang and her intolerance of restraint. She saw it all now—her pitiful little vanity of person, her absorption of the modern freedom, with its feminine rant about equality with

men, her deliberate flirting habits from what she considered a pursuit of fun and mischief, her selfish and cruel desire to punish boys whose offense had been to like her.[58]

But now under the influence of her growing love for Cal Thurman, this flapper heroine becomes a new person:

Out of the pain of the succeeding days ... Georgianna underwent the developing and transforming experience of real love. It brought her deeper pangs, yet a vision of future happiness. It made her a woman. It relieved her burden. It decided the future.[59]

The same kind of total transformation takes place in the W. S. Hart character when he meets and falls in love with the heroine. Blaze Tracy, in *Hell's Hinges*, is converted from a gambling, drinking outlaw into a Bible-reading, teetotaling pillar of the church by one sweet glance from the heroine, and much the same fate befalls other Hart heroes.

This curious combination of sexuality, romance, religion, and traditional middle-class social values with the idea of the West as challenge and regeneration gave a unique flavor to the western formula in the 1910s and 1920s. The location of these values in the West is particularly striking in light of the/ fact the Grey and Hart also portray it as the land of the gun and the saloon. In *Hell's Hinges*, for example, the town is symbolically divided between the saloon and the church. Grey's novels also frequently dwell on the violence, lawlessness, and immorality that characterize the West:

He had returned to an environment where proficiency with a gun was the law. Self-preservation was the only law among those lawless men with whom misfortune had thrown him. He could not avoid them without incurring their hatred and distrust. He must mingle with them as in the past, though it seemed his whole nature had changed. And mingling with these outlaws was never free from risk. The unexpected always happened. There were always newcomers, always drunken ruffians, always some would-be killer like Cawthorne, who yearned for fame among his evil kind. There must now always be the chance of some friend or ally of Setter, who would draw on him at sight. Lastly, owing to the reputation he had attained and hated, there was always the possibility of meeting such a gunman as Mrs. Wood had spoke of—that strange product of frontier life, the victim of his own blood lust, who would want to kill him solely because of his reputation.[60]

In fact, the theme of violence in the West was much more intense in Grey and Hart than in Wister. However important violence may be to what happens in *The Virginian*, the actual quantity of mayhem is relatively small compared to the all-out range wars and violent clashes of rival groups that Grey and Hart delighted in. The image of cleansing, purging fire that Hart develops so dramatically in *Hell's Hinges* is only an extreme example of the orgies of violence in such novels as *To the Last Man*, *Riders of the Purple Sage*, and

The U. P. Trail. Of course, violence has always been a crucial element of the western formula. For Cooper, it usually resulted from the clash between Indian and white and represented the conflict between the larger forces of nature and civilization. In *The Virginian*, the hero is forced into violent acts in order to uphold the community's unwritten law and to defend his own code of honor. But Grey's heroes tend to engage in still larger orgies of violence as avengers of the innocent and destroyers of evil. Their acts of violence are carried out with a kind of transcendent religious passion that might be seen as a sort of manic blood lust were it not in such a good and holy cause. There is perhaps no better image of this special presentation of violence than the climactic scene of W. S. Hart's *Hell's Hinges* in which the religious symbolism always just beneath the surface in Grey's violent climaxes is made quite explicit as we watch Hart's avenging angel with six-guns literally purge the devil's lair by fire.

This intensification of violence is accompanied by a more mythical and symbolic treatment of the landscape in Grey and Hart. There is not, in the history of western literature, a purpler prose than that of Zane Grey. Much of his notoriously overwritten quality comes from lengthy paeans to the beauty, mystery, and moral force of the western landscape. Important as the western landscape was to Wister, his treatment of it is sober and restrained when put beside an analogous passage in Grey:

> She looked, and saw the island, and the water folding it with ripples and with smooth spaces. The sun was throwing upon the pine boughs a light of deepening red gold, and the shadow of the fishing rock lay over a little bay of quiet water and sandy shore. In this forerunning glow of the sunset, the pasture spread like emerald; for the dry touch of summer had not yet come near it. He pointed upward to the high mountains which they had approached, and showed her where the stream led into their first unfold-ings. . . . They felt each other tremble, and for a moment she stood hiding her head upon his breast. Then she looked round at the trees, and the shores, and the flowing stream, and he heard her whispering how beautiful it was.   (Wister)[61]

> He felt a sheer force, a downward drawing of an immense abyss beneath him. As he looked afar he saw a black basin of timbered country, the darkest and wildest he had ever gazed upon, a hundred miles of blue dis-tance across to an unflung mountain range, hazy purple against the sky. It seemed to be a stupendous gulf surrounded on three sides by bold, undu-lating lines of peaks and on his side by a wall so high that he felt lifted aloft on the rim of the sky. . . . For leagues and leagues a colossal red and yellow wall, a rampart, a mountain-faced cliff, seemed to zigzag westward. Grand and bold were the promontories reaching out over the void. They ran toward the westering sun. Sweeping and impressive were the long lines slanting away from them, sloping darkly spotted down to merge into the blank timber. Jean had never seen such a wild and rugged manifestation of nature's depths and upheavals.   (Grey)[62]

Hart's western landscapes are by no means visual equivalents to Grey's, which are to some extent unique. Perhaps the closest thing in film to a passage like the above is found in some of John Ford's dazzling long shots of Monument Valley. At least three of the central qualities of Grey's landscapes are found in Hart— the feeling of vastness, emptiness, and wildness. These qualities, in Wister, are distinctly subordinate to those aspects of landscape that have a human dimension and impress. To put it another way, Wister's western landscapes are often similar in character to the paintings of Remington and Russell that also focus on human activity against a spectacular background. In Grey, however, the landscape is more reminiscent of earlier painters like Albert Bierstadt or Thomas Moran in whose work the human image is swallowed up by the transcendent spectacle of mountainous vistas.

For Grey, and to a lesser extent for Hart, the western landscape becomes symbolic of the transcendent religious and moral forces of wilderness rather than, as in Wister's case, an environment for a certain kind of human culture. This vision of the landscape, combined with the image of purgative violence and the religious-erotic treatment of hero and heroine, added a new dimension to the western formula in the work of Grey, Hart, and many of their contemporaries. Culturally, the popularity of this new version of the formula suggests that the West had come to have a new meaning for many Americans. First of all, by this time the West had become more important as a moral symbol than as a social or historical reality. Of course, the American view of the West had been strongly colored by allegory from the very beginning, but with the closing of the frontier and the passage of time the distance between writers, the public, and the events of the old West increased. Many of the qualities we have discerned in the work of Grey and Hart were exemplary of that ability to color history with romance and to clothe fantasy with verisimilitude that are of the essence of the successful formulaic creator's skills.

The kind of cultural affirmations and resolutions that Grey and Hart set forth in their version of the western formula also probably played an important part both in their individual popularity and in the way in which the success of their work helped to establish the western as one of the primary twentieth-century American literary and cinematic formulas. In my view, it was their particular combination of western heroism and the wilderness, with certain traditional social patterns and values, that was the crucial element in their cultural significance. In the works of Grey and Hart, heroic deeds and character grow out of the western landscape of wild and unsettled nature and lead to fulfillment and happiness on the part of those protagonists who are strong and true enough to meet the challenge of lawless openness by purging the evil forces that also flourish in this environment. It seems important that these heroic deeds are usually individual rather than social acts that do not carry with them the broader political and social implications so important to the actions of the Virginian. In fact, the violent purgation that so often climaxes a novel by Grey or a film by Hart sometimes goes so far as to wipe out everybody but the hero and heroine. Finally, the ultimate result of this confrontation with wild nature and violent men is an affirmation of such traditional American values as monogamous love, the settled family, the basic separation of masculine and feminine roles, and the centrality of religion to life.

Thus, in a period where these traditional American values were under attack, Grey and other contemporary novelists and filmmakers transformed the western formula into a vehicle for reaffirming a traditional view of American life. Within this framework of reassertion they created stories that dealt with some of the basic conflicts in social roles and values that had begun to afflict twentieth-century Americans. Two important sources of tension were the uncertainties that had grown up around the relationship between the sexes and the meaning of nature and the natural. These tensions clearly reached a peak in the disillusion following World War I and the emergence in the 1920s of what was referred to as the "new morality" under the influence of such social and intellectual currents as Darwinian naturalism, Freudianism, feminism, and socialism. The period in which Grey and Hart reached the peak of their success and influence as popular creators was the same period in which Hemingway, Fitzgerald, T. S. Eliot, and Sinclair Lewis were major cultural spokesmen and, in this perspective, we can see some of the reasons why Grey and so many of his contemporaries turned to the fantasy of the western in order to express some of their major concerns. Like Hemingway, Grey wrote his fictions as a means of exploring and coping with the threat of a meaningless universe, but he sought to imagine an image of heroism and a vision of relation between the sexes that would bring some kind of meaning out of a world of violence and chaos. Where Hemingway confronted the tragic condition of man in a godless world, Grey, by developing his elaborate fantasy of a heroic West, passed beyond tragedy into melodrama. By absorbing many of the elements of earlier naturalistic writers like Jack London and Frank Norris— from whom he probably garnered some of the semimystical rhapsodizing about wild nature that lards his novels—and reintegrating this with a more traditional set of American values, Grey made of the West a magical enclave where the strains and uncertainties of a modern urban-industrial culture could be temporarily forgotten and where the truth of wild nature turned out to be not the meaningless Darwinian jungle but an uplifting and elevating moral force.

Along with their reassertion of the moral meaningfulness of nature, these highly popular western writers and filmmakers of the 1910s and 1920s developed the West as a place where traditional ideals of male and female roles and of moralistic romance were part of the pattern of heroic virtue. In contrast to contemporary American society where women were increasingly challenging their traditional roles, the West of Grey and Hart was, above all, a land where men were men and women were women. In novel after novel, Grey created strong, proud, and daring women and then made them realize their true role in life as the adoring lovers of still stronger, more virtuous, more heroic men:

> Those shining stars made her yield. She whispered to them that they had claimed her—the West claimed her—Stewart claimed her forever, whether he lived or died. She gave up to her love. And it was as if he was there in person, dark-faced, fire-eyed, violent in his action, crushing her to his breast in that farewell moment, kissing her with one burning kiss of passion with wild, cold, terrible lips of renunciation. "I am your wife.!" she whispered to him. In that moment, throbbing, exalted, quivering in her first sweet, tumultuous surrender to love, she would have given her all, her life, to be in his arms again, to meet his lips, to put forever out of his power any thought of wild sacrifice.[63]

In the western creations of Grey, Hart, and their contemporaries the elements of the formula are deployed to develop the image of the West as a symbolic landscape where the elevating inspiration of the vastness and openness of nature together with the challenge of violent situations and lawless men can lead to a rebirth of heroic individual morality and the development of an ideal relationship between men and women. Though the hero invariably succeeds in purging the evil and lawless forces and in establishing an ideal domestic relationship with the heroine, there seems to be an increasing sense that this happy resolution cannot be spread to society as a whole. In *The Virginian*, after his violent deeds, the hero became "an important man, with a strong grip on many various enterprises, and able to give his wife all and more than she asked or desired."[64] It is difficult to imagine a Grey or Hart hero as successful entrepreneur or to imagine the transition between the mythic landscape of their stories and the modern world, a transition of which Wister is careful to remind us. Grey's heroes and heroines existed in a timeless, suspended world where their romance and heroism could be complete and pure. As Henry Nash Smith observed of the dime novel, the cost paid for this purity was that this vision of the West could not become involved in a meaningful dialectic with the urban industrial society of modern America. Thus, in Grey's hand, and in that of the many pulp western novelists and makers of B films who followed his lead, the West became an object of escapist fantasy for adults seeking temporary release from the routine monotony and unheroic ambiguities of twentieth-century American life. There is some indication that Grey himself sensed the essential fantasy of his vision in the fact that so many of his stories eventuate in the formation of an ideal society of two people in some isolated enclave in the mountains. For me, the ultimate symbol of Grey's version of the West is the secret mountain valley into which Lassiter and Jane Withersteen flee at the end of *Riders of the Purple Sage*, sealing off forever all possibility of entrance or exit by a massive rock slide that wipes out the evil pursuers. From such a garden of Eden there can be no fall or anything else.

The Classic Western: John Ford and Others

The popularity of Grey's highly idealized and moralistic version of the western formula began to decline with the onset of the Depression. Though new Grey books were published annually until 1961, more than twenty years past his death in 1939, his amazing mass popularity of the 1920s had decidedly faded. After his record run of a decade, Grey does not appear among the top best-sellers after 1925. Similarly there is a hiatus in the western film between the silents of the 1920s—W. S. Hart, Tom Mix, and epics like *The Covered Wagon*, and *The Iron Horse*—and the new westerns of the 1940s and 1950s by directors and stars like John Ford, Howard Hawks, Anthony Mann, Fred Zinneman, William Wyler, Gary Cooper, John Wayne, Henry Fonda, and James Stewart. While there were still many westerns produced in the 1930s, they were largely for the Saturday matinee and pulp crowd. In the 1930s, westerns of this sort still strongly depended on the version of the formula articulated by Zane Grey, with the exception of a few unique writers and directors such as the novelist Ernest Haycox and the director King Vidor, who had begun to evolve a new treatment of the western formula.

This new version came to fruition at the beginning of the 1940s with John Ford's *Stagecoach* (1939), based on a story by Ernest Haycox. Its success placed a lasting mark on the western film. Still, without detracting in the least from the unique artistry of *Stagecoach*, it is worth noting that a number of contemporary westerns show some of the same transformations in the formula, among them George Marshall's *Destry Rides Again* (1939), Henry King's *Jesse James* (1940), Fritz Lang's *The Return of Frank James* (1940), and William Wyler's *The Westerner* (1940).

The differences between this new version of the western formula and the pattern found in Grey and his contemporaries becomes quite clear when we look at *Stagecoach*. As might be expected, there is considerable continuity between *Stagecoach* and the typical Zane Grey western. Like Grey, Ford emphasizes the theme of regeneration through the challenge of the wilderness, using the spectacular forms of the western landscape to give a symbolic background to the drama. Monument Valley in northern Arizona, where, beginning with *Stagecoach*, Ford shot so many of his films, is a landscape as spectacular as Grey's Tonto Basin, also in Arizona. A number of Ford's basic character types also echo Grey's—the gunfighter hero driven by an obsession to avenge a past wrong (Grey's Lassiter and Ford's Ringo Kid) and the seemingly corrupt heroine who turns out to be morally pure (Grey's Ellen Jorth and Ford's Dallas). Nevertheless, despite these indications of Grey's influence on a continuous formulaic tradition, *Stagecoach* presents a very different vision of the West from *Riders of the Purple Sage*. Compared to the highly colored ambience and melodramatic situations of Grey and his contemporaries, *Stagecoach* has restraint and subtlety that reflects a richer and more complex handling of setting, plot, character, and theme. Though Ford's landscape is certainly a symbolic one, it is not redolent of evangelical mysticism and moralistic allegory in the same way as Grey's sweeping mountains and canyons. Instead, Ford uses the landscape of Monument Valley to express subtly the ambiguous relationship of danger, the threat of death, and regeneration. Instead of filling our souls with religious awe or pure romantic passion as Grey's panoramas supposedly affect his sympathetic characters, the great isolated monoliths of Monument Valley in *Stagecoach* seem richly enigmatic. They are neither hostile nor benevolent, nor are they pretty in the sense of Grey's gorgeous, many-colored landscapes. Ford's panoramic long shots of the stagecoach threading its way among these massive rock formations suggest a sublimity and mystery beside which Grey's purple prose seems a pseudo-mystical posturing.

The same qualities of greater subtlety and richness extend to character and action. While Ford and other western directors of this period work largely with casts of stereotyped characters not unlike those in a novel by Grey or a film by W. S. Hart, these stereotypes are typically qualified and enlivened by touches of comedy and irony. In *Stagecoach* the virginally pure romantic ingenue is, in fact, a prostitute. The hero makes his *de rigueur* appearance from the middle of the wilderness, bent on revenge, but instead of being a mysterious figure in black, he is a nice young cowboy just escaped from prison and a bit shy and awkward about breaking into society on the same day, as he puts it. Larger patterns of action also have comic or ironic resonances and complexities. Like *Hell's Hinges*, much of the action of *Stagecoach* grows out of a conflict between the churchgoers and the sinners, a conflict symbolized in the town of Hell's Hinges by the church and the saloon and in *Stagecoach* by the daylight town of Tonto and the night town of Lordsburg. But where Hart melodramatizes this conflict by placing all our sympathies on the side of the church people, Ford presents the Ladies' Law and Order League as a bastion of rigid, repressive puritanism, shows Tonto's most respectable citizen as a hypocritical embezzler, and gives our fullest sympathies to a prostitute, a drunken doctor, an escaped convict, a whiskey drummer, and a dubious gambler. This unlikely group triumphs over the challenge of the enigmatic and hostile wilderness, but even regeneration has its ironic qualifications. The drunken doctor sobers up and successfully officiates at the birth of a baby in the middle of the desert, heroically faces the attacking Apaches, and, finally, helps the hero in his climactic confrontation with the villains. Yet at the end of the film it is clear that he is going to go on drinking. The hero and his prostitute-sweetheart go off together "into the sunset," though actually the departure is in the middle of the night, and they leave as fugitives to go across the border into Mexico. There is no integration into society like Hart and Grey's regenerated outlaws.

The artistic density of the westerns of the 1940s and 1950s is most strikingly evident in the work of John Ford, but a number of other directors worked very successfully with a similar version of the formula in the same period. Future generations are likely to look on this as the classic era of the western film. Several factors contributed to the special quality of major westerns during this time. First of all, for both creators and large segments of the audience, the western had become a conscious artistic genre as well as a popular story formula. In addition, there had developed a large corps of directors, writers, actors, and technicians with considerable experience in the creation of westerns. But it was, above all, what the West had come to mean to the American public and the consequent interest that the public displayed in a revitalized version of the western formula that made it possible for all this talent and creative energy to be centered around the production of western films.

The decline of the 1920s' version of the western formula into pulp novels and B western films reflected the impact of the boom and bust of the late 1920s and the depression of the 1930s.

The fate of Prohibition is somewhat analogous to that of the moralistic vision of the West. Begun as a great experiment in social morality, Prohibition became, in the booming prosperity of the later 1920s, a black comedy, no longer taken very seriously even by many of its former proponents. Like Prohibition, the westerns of Grey and Hart embodied a vision of regeneration and purgation leading to the reestablishment of the basic norms of nineteenth-century small-town society: religious piety, monogamy, feminine chastity, temperance, and the family circle. But, in an America whose moralistic assumptions had been deeply threatened by rapid urbanization, and then shattered by the chaos of Depression, the association of western heroism with this set of moral norms seemed increasingly old-fashioned and even faintly comical. One suspects that Zane Grey retained a good deal of his popularity throughout the 1930s because his gift for exciting narrative transcended to some degree his moralistic attitudes. In the case of a writer like Harold Bell Wright, or even a filmmaker like W. S. Hart, action and character were more inextricably linked with moral vision, and the decline in popularity was precipitous. Even today, while there is still a steady sale of Grey's novels, which can be fun to read in spite of their moral sentiments, the name of Harold Bell Wright has practically disappeared from the scene, and the films of W. S. Hart are largely viewed by sophisticated students of the cinema as a curious and interesting phase in the history of the film.

Another sign of this general decline of traditional moral assumptions in the late 1920s and 1930s was the rapid rise to great popularity of another film formula, the gangster melodrama. As I noted in an earlier chapter, this was the period when films like *Underworld* (1927), *Little Caesar* (1930), and *Public Enemy* (1931), with performers like Edward G. Robinson and James Cagney, eclipsed traditional western stories and heroes in mass popularity. The extent to which these films challenged traditional morality is evident from the agitation of groups like the Legion of Decency. Eventually, these groups brought enough pressure to bear on Hollywood so that some elements were censored in the new gangster films. Despite these vigorous countermeasures on the part of its moral watchdogs, the American public increasingly showed its delight in the gangster film and such related formulas as the hard-boiled detective story.

Such circumstances suggest that in the 1930s American moviegoers were deeply troubled by the gap between their inherited moral universe and their experience of social and cultural change. On the one hand, they indicated their unwillingness to give up their traditional moral values by tolerating and even supporting the moralistic censorship of self-appointed guardians of the faith, yet, on the other, they indicated their sense of the inadequacy of the traditional moral vision by turning away from novels and films that simply affirmed it in favor of works that explored its inadequacies. For the middle-class reader, Sinclair Lewis and John Steinbeck replaced Harold Bell Wright and Zane Grey on best-seller lists, while for the still broader cultural spectrum of filmgoers, Robinson and Cagney's snarling gangsters became more popular protagonists than the morally regenerate outlaws of W. S. Hart.

In the face of this change in public attitude and interest, the western either had to undergo substantial changes or to decline altogether to the level of juvenile adventure, or, possibly, faced by competition with more contemporary forms of adventure in an urban setting, to disappear altogether. Actually, the genre entered upon a new phase of creative activity that may well be its greatest period. A new vision of the meaning of the West inspired a formula more responsive to the conflicts of value and feeling that characterized the period from 1940 to 1960. Instead of simply affirming the traditional morality and dramatically resolving conflicts within it, this new image of the West encouraged a richer exploration of the tensions between old moral assumptions and new uncertainties of experience. It also expressed a sense of loss associated with the passage of a simpler and less ambiguous era while acknowledging its inevitability. Thus, in contrast to the sense of moral triumph and regeneration through violence that characterized the western of the 1910s and 1920s, the new "classic" western was typically more muted, elegaic, and even sometimes tragic in its pattern of action.

The essential feature of this new vision of the West was the notion of the "old West" as a heroic period in the past distinctly different from the rest of American society and history. The symbolic drama of the old West's passing generated new and more complex kinds of stories. To some extent, this vision of the West had always been implicit in the western. We find it in Natty Bumppo's occasional laments for the passing of the old wilderness life, or in Wister's preface to *The Virginian*, when he remarks that the cowboy "will never come again. He rides in his historic yesterday."[65] But there are two major differences between these earlier notions of the West as bygone era and the "old West" of the 1940s and 1950s. First, this earlier phase of the West was usually associated with the wilderness and the Indians. It was, in effect, a version of pastoral. The new meaning of the "old West" was, on the contrary, a vision of a particular kind of social order, a complex elaboration of the conception of a unique western society that developed in the later dime novel and in local-color writers like Bret Harte, and later, in a very different way, was conceptualized in Frederick Jackson Turner's theory of the influence of the frontier on American life. These earlier views of western society did not usually treat it as something that was irrevocably past. Even Turner was at great pains to show how the frontier had molded contemporary American society. By the 1940s, however, the "old West" was clearly seen as past, its significance lying in its discontinuity with the rest of American life. Walter Prescott Webb, a great historian of the West, eloquently expressed this view of the "old West" in his analysis of the cattle kingdom:

> The cattle kingdom was a world within itself, with a culture all its own, which, though of brief duration, was complete and self-satisfying. The cattle kingdom worked out its own means and methods of utilization; it formulated its own law, called the code of the West, and did it largely upon extra-legal grounds. The existence of the cattle kingdom for a generation is the best single bit of evidence that here in the West were the basis and promise of a new civilization unlike anything previously known to the Anglo-European-American experience. . . . Eventually it ceased to be a kingdom and became a province. The Industrial Revolution furnished the means by which the beginnings of this original and distinctive civilization have been destroyed or reduced to vestigial remains. Since the destruction of the plains Indians and the buffalo civilization, the cattle kingdom is the most logical thing that has happened in the Great Plains, where, in spite of science and invention, the spirit of the Great American Desert still is manifest.[66]

And, as Webb saw it, the central feature of the cattle kingdom was its emphasis on individual courage:

> Where population is sparse, where the supports of conventions and of laws are withdrawn and men are thrown upon their own resources, courage becomes a fundamental and essential attribute in the individual. The Western man of the old days had little choice but to be courageous. The germ of courage had to be in him; but this germ being given, the life he led developed it to a high degree.[67]

The second important difference between earlier conceptions of the "old West" and the underlying cultural myth of the classic westerns of the 1940s and 1950s was the extent to which the passing of the "old West" and the evolving pioneer society became the basic focus of western films. In *The Virginian* and in the westerns of Hart and Grey, the hero is typically integrated into the new pioneer society that is gradually evolving out of a more chaotic and lawless earlier era. The hero's culminating act of violence is a final purging of the lawless men who prevent the new society from coming into existence. It represents the culmination of the period of foundation, which seems to be the underlying mythical pattern of this version of the western formula. In the classic western, however, the story shifts from the myth of foundation to a concern with social transition—the passing from the old West into modern society. The hero becomes not so much the founder of a new order as a somewhat archaic survival, driven by motives and values that are never quite in harmony with the new social order. His climactic violence, though legitimated by its service to the community, does not integrate him into society. Instead, it separates him still further, either because a community so pacified has no need of his unique talents, or because the new society cannot aid him or do him honor. Thus, the relation of the hero to the community tends to move in a reverse direction from that of the pre-1940s western. There the hero typically made the transition from outlawry to domestication. In the classic western, the hero increasingly moves toward isolation, separation, and alienation.

This aspect of the classic western is particularly evident in a film like John Ford's *My Darling Clementine* (1946) where there is really no necessity for the hero to depart at the end. Yet Ford obviously felt that it was artistically and emotionally right for Wyatt Earp to say farewell to his new love Clementine and to leave the town he has purged of evil, dropping only a vague hint of his ultimate return. Similarly, the hero and heroine of *Stagecoach* cannot remain in the town but must take the purity of their love and their heroic courage off to some mythical ranch across the border. Again, the events of the story do not require this ending. It would certainly not have been difficult for Ford to arrange for his hero to be exonerated for killing the villains, but, again, it just seems wrong for these two representatives of the old West to stay in the orderly and pacified town, with the Indians driven back to the reservation, the unrestrained men of violence killed, and the army and the law firmly in control. In his films of the 1940s, Ford did not deal with the theme of the passing of the old West as explicitly as he did later, but part of the richness of his work comes from the way in which exciting adventure and good-humored social comedy—the dominant tones of *Stagecoach* and *My Darling Clementine*—are inextricably mixed with a subtle feeling of melancholy for a more heroic life that is passing.

Melancholy about the passing of the old West and ambiguity about the new society that has replaced it became a more explicit thematic concern in Ford westerns of the 1950s and 1960s such as *The Searchers* (1956), *The Man Who Shot Liberty Valance* (1962), and *Cheyenne Autumn* (1964). In *Liberty Valance*, for example, the old western hero, Tom Doniphon, is morally and emotionally destroyed when he purges the community of the last anarchic outlaw and enables the new-style western leader, a young lawyer from the East, to become the community's representative man. Though the result is progress and happiness, there is, nonetheless, a deep sense that something valuable has been lost. There is also an ironic twist in the fact that the young lawyer's political success is based on his false reputation as the heroic killer of the outlaw Liberty Valance, a deed actually performed by Doniphon. Thus the new society is founded on a legend of heroism, created by a man who cannot himself find what he needs in it. *Cheyenne Autumn*, based on Mari Sandoz's moving account of the attempts of a band of Cheyenne Indians to leave their arid southern reservation and return to their northern homeland, is an even more elegaic if less coherent account of the passing of the old West. With its heroic band of Indians set against the rapacity, greed, and bureaucratic inhumanity of the Indian Bureau and the government, *Cheyenne Autumn* adumbrated a new version of the formula in which the complex dramatic tensions of the classic western gave way to the quest for a new mythology in which the Indian becomes again an idealized figure. But this is one of the developments that followed after the breakdown of the classic synthesis.

The dramatic tensions created by the central theme of the passing of the old West provided the background for a particularly interesting type of hero. Unlike the natural gentleman of Owen Wister, or the romantic heroes of Zane Grey and W. S. Hart, the western hero of the classic period is largely developed through his complex and ambiguous relationship with society. Whatever romantic involvements he may have, the classic western hero's role as a man-in-the-middle between groups that represent the old and the new West is far more important than his relations with the opposite sex. Indeed, in many classic westerns there is relatively little romantic interest of the sort that was so important to Wister and Grey. Instead, the plot concerns situations in which the hero finds himself both involved with, and alienated from, society. In this type of story, the gunfighter often takes the place of the cowboy as hero, because the gunfighter's position with respect to the law is, by convention, ambiguous. According to the mythical code of the old West, the gunfighter is not a criminal, though he may have killed many men. By the standards of the new West, he is illegally taking the law into his own hands. Split between old and new concepts of law and morality, the town finds itself torn between its disapproval of what the gunfighter stands for and its need for his services. The gunfighter's own motives are also likely to be ambivalent. He may be tired of his violent way of life and hopeful of settling down to a peaceful old age, but is usually unable to do so because of his reputation and the need to prove himself anew against younger gunmen, or because of the town's inability to purge itself of evil through the regular processes of the law.

The man-in-the-middle's problem usually is that he cannot resolve his inner conflict by committing himself to one of the two courses of action or ways of life that divide him. Classic westerns often end in the hero's death or in violence, reluctantly entered upon, that does not fully resolve the conflict. Wister's Virginian chose to live out the code of the West as a matter of honor and duty, even though his sweetheart threatened to leave him. But his problem was solved when she saw him in danger and realized that her love was greater than her genteel antipathy to violence. The hero thus gained both a victory over his enemy and a respectable place in society. In contrast, the sheriff in *High Noon* is forced to fight alone by the town's failure to support him, but is left so bitter by his victory that he can only turn his back on society in disgust. In *Shane*, the hero has to take up again the role of gunfighter in order to save the farmers from being driven off their land. But once he has destroyed the old order by killing the tyrannical rancher and his hired gunfighter, he has no place in the new community and must ride into lonely exile. In a more comic vein, Howard Hawks's heroic sheriff in *Rio Bravo* destroys the tyrannical rancher and gets the girl, but the film's predominant image is that of the small heroic group isolated from the rest of society in its fortress jail.

Whether it tended toward the tragic and elegaic as in Ford, the comic as in Hawks, or the mythic as in Anthony Mann, the classic western became a vehicle for exploring such value conflicts as that between traditional ways of life and progress, individualism and organization, violence and legal process, conformity and individual freedom, and heroism and the average man. The western's traditional resolution in legitimated violence and the mythical detachment of the story from the present time implicit in the idea of the old West offered a plausible and compelling way of giving these conflicts symbolic expression. Not surprisingly, a number of westerns of the classic period such as *High Noon* and *The Ox-Bow Incident* were explicitly conceived as allegories with strong implications for the contemporary scene. Critics, also, began to interpret westerns in terms of contemporary situations and to point out analogies between the western film and such important political events of the period as the Korean conflict and McCarthy's crusade against communism. Whatever one may think about the validity of such interpretations, the tendency to make them indicates the degree to which at least some of the more sophisticated members of the public responded explicitly to the classic western's expression of American value conflicts.

The classic version of the western formula also flourished in the new medium of television as what was commonly referred to as the new "adult" western. "Bonanza" was far less pure as a western than "Gunsmoke," since its variety of central characters made it possible for the show to borrow plots from such diverse popular traditions as the detective story and the social melodrama. Still, the main line of both series was that of the classic western: the representation of a heroic figure (or in the case of "Bonanza" a group of heroes) as mediators between the aggressive individualists of the old West and the new values of the settled town.

It is certainly claiming too much to suggest that all Americans who enjoyed westerns during the classic period read the tension between American traditions of individualistic democracy and the emerging international corporate society into the conflict between the old West and the new settled society symbolized by growing towns, and orderly legal process, and the coming of the railroad and telegraph. Yet the special qualities of the classic western heroes as played by Gary Cooper, John Wayne, James Stewart, Henry Fonda, Joel McCrea, Randolph Scott, and their imitators lay in their reluctance to commit themselves to any particular social group, their ambivalence about who was right and wrong, and their strong desire to retain their own personal integrity and the purity of their individual code. As Robert Warshow so eloquently described this classic stance:

> What does the Westerner fight for? We know he is on the side of justice and order, and of course it can be said he fights for these things. But such broad aims never correspond exactly to his real motives; they only offer him his opportunity. The Westerner himself, when an explanation is asked of him (usually by a woman), is likely to say that he does what he "has to do." If justice and order did not continually demand his protection, he would be without a calling. Indeed, we come upon him often in just that situation, as the reign of law settles over the West and he is forced to see that his day is over; those are the pictures which end with his death or with his departure for some more remote frontier. What he defends, at bottom, is the purity of his own image . . . he fights not for advantage and not for the right, but to state what he is, and he must live in a world which permits that statement.[68]

The appeal of such a heroic figure is probably greatest in a time when neither tradition nor some concept of a future goal adequately defines what is virtuous for a man. In such a period, the extraordinary hero is one who, torn by the conflicting demands of different social roles and value systems, yet manages to assert his identity in action. In this respect, the classic western hero bears a strong resemblance to the hard-boiled heroes of Hemingway, Hammett, and Chandler, a heroic type who was embodied in the film performances of Humphrey Bogart at the same time that the classic western reached its peak. In fact, the classic western hero's basic pattern of initial reluctance and ambivalence finally resolved by violence was practically identical to that developed by the Bogart persona in such films as *The Big Sleep, To Have and Have Not*, and *Casablanca*. In these films, the conflict between a traditional world and a new social order is represented by urban corruption or by the coming of war. As in the western, the hero has rejected or left behind the traditional world, but he is not prepared to commit himself to the new order, for he senses that it will destroy his individual identity. In the end, he finds a mode of action, usually through violence, that reaffirms his individual code. Or, to put it in terms that were popularized by the sociologist David Riseman in the same period we are concerned with, this type of hero insists upon asserting his inner-directed self in an increasingly other-directed world.

This reflection gives us some additional insight into the way in which the meaning of the hero's violence in the classic western differs from that of the westerns of Zane Grey and W. S. Hart. In that earlier version of the western formula, the hero's violence was the means by which the evil and anarchic forces were finally purged and the hero integrated with society. But in the classic western, as in the hard-boiled detective story, the hero's violence is primarily an expression of his capacity for individual moral judgment and action, a capacity that separates him from society as much as it makes him a part of it. While in *Casablanca* Bogart's commitment to the Free French cause seems a rather romanticized expression of wartime Hollywood patriotism, the more detached and mythical setting of the classic western made the hero's violence more ambiguous and individualistic.

In general, then, the classic version of the western formula developed by projecting contemporary tensions and conflicts of values into a mythical past where they could be balanced against one another and resolved in an increasingly ambiguous moment of violent action. These conflicts were essentially expressions of the tension between those traditional values that had been so strongly affirmed in the Wister-Grey-Hart version of the western formula and the new attitudes and values of a modern urban industrial society. The basic premise of the classic western was a recognition of the inevitable passing of the old order of things, reflected in the myth of the "old West," together with an attempt to affirm that the new society would somehow be based on the older values. But, just as after World War II, Americans increasingly recognized the gap between their traditional values and goals and the new circumstances of their lives, the classic western increasingly reflected a discontinuity between the old West and the new society that had replaced it. One striking expression of this widening gap was a documentary entitled *The Real West* and narrated with great power and pathos by an aging and sick Gary Cooper. This documentary, claiming in the way of many of our best mythical treatments of the West to give us, at long last, the true story, was permeated with the sense of an exciting and heroic era, a time of great challenge and adventure, surviving only in the curious old photographs and decaying ghost towns that furnished the film's predominant visual imagery.[69] The artistic power and wide public popularity of the classic version of the western formula came from its ability to hold the vision of the old West and the emergent outlines of modern America in a dramatic tension mediated by the striking figure of the hero. But this balance could be maintained only so long as creators and audiences found satisfaction in the elegaic treatment of the old West and in the reluctant, ambiguous hero who remained torn between commitments. In the more polarized social and political atmosphere of the 1960s, the classic version of the western formula came to seem increasingly old-fashioned, and it soon became evident that the western again required some redefinition and revitalization of its formula.

The Jewish Cowboy, the Black Avenger, and the Return of the Vanishing American: Current Trends in the Formula

Since the high water mark of the late 1950s, the cultural significance of the western has perceptibly shifted. Westerns are still quite popular; at least one of the TV programs that was launched in the 1950s, "Gunsmoke," is among the longest running video series.[70] A substantial proportion of the biggest movie hits of the last few years—Leone's Clint Eastwood series, George Roy Hill's *Butch Cassidy and the Sundance Kid*, Peckinpah's *The Wild Bunch*, Hathaway's *True Grit*, and Arthur Penn's *Little Big Man*, to name a few— have been westerns. The creation of westerns continues to be a significant part of American movie production, even though it seems clear that the western no longer holds the predominant position it did twenty years ago. The number of new TV western series has slowed to a trickle. The enormous output of low-budget westerns—once a mainstay of the American film industry—has dwindled away. Directors and stars are no longer largely identified with their work in westerns as John Ford, Anthony Mann, Raoul Walsh, John Wayne, Henry Fonda, and James Stewart were in the period between 1950 and 1965. Only one major new American western director— Sam Peckinpah—has emerged since 1960. Similarly, only one new western superstar—Clint Eastwood—has come up during the same time. Even more surprising, some of the most successful westerns of the period, the group of films produced by the Italian Sergio Leone, have been international productions, largely filmed in other countries and imported into the United States in a curiously ironic cultural return.

The decline of the major Hollywood studios and the rise of independent production has inevitably affected the flow of westerns by breaking up the teams of actors, directors, cameramen, and stuntmen who used to turn out a regular quota of westerns every year. Even if we recognize the impact of changes in the film industry as an important influence on contemporary production, there are still enough differences in the form and content of current western films to suggest that the western themes and patterns of action that so deeply engaged American filmmakers and audiences for some twenty years after World War II have lost much of their interest. It seems to me that the diversity of contemporary westerns reflects a quest for new themes and meanings to revitalize the traditional western formula.

By the early 1960s the patterns of the classic western were beginning to break up. Though the classic version of the formula persisted for a somewhat longer time on television, the most creative filmmakers had already begun to depart from the traditions of the 1940s and 1950s. The swan song of the classic western was Sam Peckinpah's elegy to a disappearing heroism, *Ride the High Country* (1962). The two heroes of this film, portrayed by two aging western stars, Randolph Scott and Joel McCrea, move once more toward their redemptive gunfight, but in the end they fight not to save the decent townspeople from outlaws but as the result of an almost accidental explosion of violence. The antagonists they destroy are not evil threats to a better society, and their victory does not purge society of anything. Joel McCrea's heroic death redeems his own image of moral action; but it is also clear that, however admirable, this style of heroism is archaic—almost obsolescent— in a world where the old West is dead. Despite the traditional power of the hero's final stand, we never quite forget the film's opening images of a pathetically aged and threadbare Joel McCrea dodging cars and policemen on the streets of an already modern small city. Confusion and ambiguity in the classical formula had reached a point of such thickness by the mid-1960s that it interfered with the dramatic force of a film like Richard Wilson's *Invitation to a Gunfighter* (1964). In this story, both the hero and the social group are so mixed in their motives and so confused in their symbolic significance that it is frequently difficult to determine just what is going on.

Since the middle 1960s it has been difficult to speak of a single western formula. As Jack Nachbar puts it in an excellent essay on the recent western, the classic formula has been scattered in several different directions.[71] The only single trend that seems to mark the many different sorts of contemporary western is an emphasis on the graphic portrayal of violence, as opposed to the more bloodless and acrobatic deaths of the preceding period, together with a more explicit treatment of sex. This is hardly surprising, since it reflects a general trend in American culture and is not by any means unique to the western. This current interest on the part of filmmakers in a more intense portrayal of violence, and the audience response to that representation, may be in part a catering to jaded and corrupted taste; but, more important, I feel, this emphasis grows out of a need to arrive at some understanding of the new and terrifying mood of destructiveness and hate not only in America but in the world as a whole. With a growing sense of danger from personal and collective violence in our society, Americans have had to come to some kind of emotional terms with an unregenerate world. By looking at some of the diverse trends in the westerns of today we can define some of the new attitudes toward violence that are emerging.

One of the most widely successful new versions of the western formula was created by the Italian director Sergio Leone in a popular series of films mainly starring Clint Eastwood—*A Fistful of Dollars* (1966), *For a Few Dollars More* (1966), *The Good, the Bad, and the Ugly* (1967), *Once upon a Time in the West* (1969), and many others. The films of Leone and his imitators are full of violent action like the traditional B westerns, but in other respects they represent a major departure in theme, story, and style from the tradition. Their plots resemble Jacobean or Spanish Renaissance tragedy more than they do the traditional western, and so does their vision of a dark, corrupt, and treacherous world. Their ostensible heroes are marked not by moral purpose and righteous courage, but by superior stratagems, unscrupulousness, and skill in violence. Their style, embodied in leading actors like Clint Eastwood and Lee Van Cleef, is one of supreme detachment and coolness.

Eastwood as "the man with no name"—an anonymity that underlines his lack of human feeling and motive—performs his most violent deeds without a quiver of his characteristic cigarillo or a ripple of his serape. His role in a number of films is that of bounty hunter, a man who kills with no personal interest but the monetary reward, despicable in the moral universe of the traditional western. If the hero has any motive beyond money, it is usually to perform some terrible revenge for a long past deed, a revenge that commonly seems more like a dehumanizing obsession than a justifiable moral purpose. In many cases, the object of the hero's revenge is as interesting and sympathetic a character as he is, if not more so. In *Once upon a Time in the West*, for example, the "villain" is played by Henry Fonda, the noble hero of many classic westerns, and the "hero" by Charles Bronson, who had earlier made a specialty of villains. With such heroes, one asks, who needs villains? Yet the Leone films do arouse our interest in the hero's actions despite his morally ambiguous character by showing us a world that seems to deserve whatever violence can be wreaked upon it.

Leone's western towns are full of grotesque and ugly people in striking contrast to the decent, respectable, mildly comic townspeople of the classic western. But even more striking than the grotesque, bitterly sardonic way in which he represents his minor characters, Leone stresses their weakness and helplessness against the grasping tyrants and manic outlaws who bedevil them. These townspeople sometimes employ a vapid and impotent morality as a justification for not doing anything about the frustrated and miserable conditions of their lives, but the amoral hero has no moral pretensions—he says even less than the traditional western hero. Instead, he works smoothly and effectively against the men of power. The fact that a number of minor and relatively helpless bystanders are destroyed in the process seems more advantageous than otherwise. Because the world is violent, treacherous, and corrupt, the moral man is the one who can use violence, treachery, and corruption most effectively. The chief thing that differentiates hero from villain is the hero's coolness and lack of violent emotion; the villain is typically given to rages of greed, lust, or hatred that prevent him from effectively using the tools of power.

Public enthusiasm for the Leone films has commonly been interpreted as a simple response of salacious sadism, the cruder masses of the public taking lip-licking delight in the vivid portrayal of bloodshed and death. No doubt there are such appeals in the Leone films. Anyone who has attended one of these films in company with a large and varied audience can testify to what seems at first a shocking ghoulishness of response—applause when an innocent person is destroyed on screen, laughter at the most horrible kinds of maiming and killing. One could easily become convinced that such films are creating a bloodthirsty public who will eventually turn from fantasy to reality to satisfy their cravings. Yet few Clint Eastwood fans become mass murderers.

The orientation toward violence in the Leone films is not as simple as it seems on the surface. On closer examination, I should say that these films perhaps appeal as much to a sense of passivity as to violence. Their grotesque humor may well be more an invitation to laugh at our own sense of helplessness and victimization than an incitement to strike out against it. Their moral ambiguity, their rejection of clear distinctions between hero and villain, and their effects of grotesque horror might as well be interpreted as an attempt to transform our sense of moral paralysis and impotence in the face of worldwide violence into mockery and bitter comedy.

If this is the case, we have here one new kind of thematic portrayal of violence together with an implicit psychological strategy toward it. Violence is innate in human life, and the only defense against it is detached mockery. By avoiding emotional and moral involvement, we develop a capacity to gain pleasure from horror and outrage through identification with victimizer as well as victim. This attitude is close to the one implicit in the contemporary horror film—the current crop of Draculas, Blaculas, Frankensteins, and Wolfmen—where we are invited to identify with the monster as well as with those he victimizes, in contrast to the traditional horror story where the monster represented an outside evil that had to be purged to save the world. Like the Italian western, which it resembles in its grotesque tone and its cultivation of horrific incident, the new-style horror film has been one of the great popular successes of the last two decades.

The distinctive quality of the Leone western emerges in another way when we compare it with another type of contemporary western, a formula version that might be called the return of the rugged individual. These films, dominantly starring John Wayne, have been strongly influenced by certain aspects of the Italian western but are generally attempts to restate the traditional western themes in a slightly new fashion. Typically, this second type of contemporary western deals with an aging hero whose great days seem over but who embarks upon one more heroic quest or battle. Unlike the Italian western, this American type portrays the hero's quest as the pursuit of a clearly moral purpose. In *True Grit* the hero is a marshal who has been employed by a young lady to bring in the murderer of her father. In *Big Jake* Jake's grandson has been kidnapped by a band of outlaws and he is out to recover the child; in *Chisum* corrupt and lawless men threaten to destroy the peaceful cattle empire that John Chisum has built up through hard work and honest dealing. Similar plot devices insure that the deeds of the protagonists of *Rio Lobo* and *The Cowboys* are covered with the mantle of morality. But in many ways this air of morality seems more like a ritual than a reality, a cloak for naked aggression rather than the reluctant violence of the heroes of *My Darling Clementine, High Noon,* and *Shane.* The leading figure in these rugged individualist westerns is very different from the lyrical or stoic heroes of the forties and fifties. In fact, he resembles the official villains of the earlier westerns as much as he does the heroes. John Chisum is an overbearing cattle baron, like Stryker, the villain of *Shane*. Big Jake has the same ruthlessness and love-hate relationship with his sons as the maniacal Dock Tobin of Anthony Mann's *Man of the West*, while the Wild Bunch of Sam Peckinpah's film bears more resemblance to the vicious Clanton gang than to the gentle Wyatt Earp of *My Darling Clementine*. Yet, in these more recent films, the ruthless aggressiveness, concern with power, and penchant for violence that were seen as dangerous and even evil in the classic westerns are portrayed as positive values or moral necessities in these sagas of rugged individualism in the West. To make the contrast more precise, we might compare Howard Hawks's *Red River* (1948) and the recent *Chisum*. These two films have basic plot similarities and in both the central figure is played by John Wayne. In *Red River* Wayne's overbearing individualism, his tyrannical authority, and his ruthless appeals to violence nearly bring about the destruction of the cattle drive. It is only the rejection of violence and the concern for the welfare of others embodied in the secondary hero figure of Wayne's adopted son, played by Montgomery Clift, that finally resolves the difficulties. But in *Chisum* these very aggressive qualities make the hero successful while the more pacific and less domineering temperaments of younger men are shown to be inadequate to the overcoming of evil.

In none of these films is there much question of group regeneration associated with the hero's purging action. On the contrary, society is usually represented as weak and corrupt; its agencies—such as posses and armed forces—are given to impulsive and inefficient violence that is more likely to bring on further innocent suffering than to establish true justice. Because society is violent and corrupt, the only solution lies in the private action of a good leader who is able to overcome the outlaw's evil aggression and society's own endemic violence and corruption by superior ruthlessness and power of his own. In this emphasis on the failure of society to protect the innocent and on the need for the private leader and avenger, these new westerns clearly resemble the new gangster film and novel exemplified by *The Godfather*. I should say that the orientation toward violence and society is almost identical in these works. Because society has failed to extend its protection and order to an adequate extent, the little man is constantly threatened by violence against which he cannot protect himself. The fantasied solution is to fall back on the Godfather, or in the case of the western on the grandfather, Big Jake, and to create under his absolute authority a close-knit small group, like a family, that in return for absolute loyalty will protect its members. It is interesting that no western constructed along these lines has achieved anything like the success of *The Godfather*. Perhaps because this fantasy is so immediate a response to the tensions of modern urban life, its embodiment in a relatively contemporary urban setting, as in the gangster story, is more compelling than its displacement to a heroic past.

The westerns embodying the fantasied return of the rugged individualist bear a greater superficial resemblance to the traditional western than most other types being produced today, but I would guess the more creative potentialities for the western's future lie in a third type, which involves the attempt to create a new cultural myth of the West. In its simplest and least interesting form this new western myth is simply the old formula with an ethnic hero at the center. Thus black westerns like *The Legend of Nigger Charley*, *Buck and the Preacher*, and *Soul Soldier* are more or less traditional westerns with black heroes and plots that have some of their conflicts generated by racial tension. Because of this, the black western has heretofore been only in a minimal sense a creative transformation of the western. Like the new black police, detective, and gangster films, the black westerns are culturally important in that they represent a capturing of traditionally white legends and hero figures for black audiences. Certainly this development reflects some breakdown of traditional stereotypes. With a few notable exceptions like John Ford's unduly neglected *Sergeant Rutledge* (1960), black characters almost never appeared in earlier westerns and when they did it was in minor comic roles. A few all-black westerns were made for limited distribution, but these had no significance as far as the white public was concerned for they were never exhibited in other than totally black theaters. The new black westerns, however, import their heroes into the context of a largely white western society and are made with fair-sized budgets. Though they are particularly aimed at black urban audiences, they are seen by substantial segments of the white public as well. Doubtless it reflects some transformation of racial attitudes for audiences to accept a black man playing a formerly white heroic role and in the process saving innocent whites and avenging himself on white villains. But aside from this substitution of a black for a white hero, the new black westerns have not as yet involved any major departures from traditional western formulas. Thus it is not surprising to find critics like Clayton Riley speaking rather acerbically about them:

> The new Black movies ... have accomplished little more than a restatement of those themes the American cinema has traditionally bled dry and then discarded. Like the stepchild we get the leftover, in this case a celluloid hand-me-down. Black movies bringing color to the old movie industry Triple-S stamp: Slapstick, Sadism and Safety—from anything that might disturb the Republic's peace of mind.[72]

The black perspective may well become a source of creative transformation in the western if filmmakers begin to work the rich and fascinating vein of the actual role of black people in the history of the West. Certainly some of the black characters described by Durham and Jones in *The Negro Cowboy* could be the basis for a rich new version of the western myth. At the present time, however, the emergence of a new attitude toward the Indian in films like *A Man Called Horse*, *Soldier Blue*, and *Little Big Man* seems more important as the impetus behind a new vision of the meaning of the western experience. Since the time of James Fenimore Cooper, the serious western has often manifested a sympathetic attitude toward the Indian and has at times been openly critical of the way in which Americans have treated him. But, until recently, this sympathy has usually been focused for dramatic purposes on the tragedy of individuals. Two main story formulas would probably cover most of the serious representations of Indians in the western until the last decade or so: the elegy of the Vanishing American or the Last of the Mohicans, and the tragedy of the white man who loved an Indian maiden or vice versa. In both these stories the central point of sympathy was the plight of an individual caught in a larger clash between groups. The striking thing about the more recent Indian westerns is that they move beyond sympathy for the plight of individuals toward an attempt at a reconstruction of the Indian experience itself. Their central plot device has been the story of the white man who becomes an Indian or who, through his experiences, becomes identified with the Indian perspective in the clash between white and Indian. In effect, this amounts to an almost complete reversal of some of the symbolic meanings ascribed to major groups in the western. The pioneers become a symbol of fanaticism, avarice, and aggressive violence while the Indians represent a good group with a way of life in harmony with nature and truly fulfilling to the individual. It is through his involvement with the Indians and their way of life that the hero is regenerated. The cavalry, symbol of law and order, becomes the instrument of brutal massacre until at the end of *Little Big Man* one cheers for the Indians to destroy Custer and his men because we have seen incident after incident in which the cavalry callously and needlessly slaughters women and children.

This new Indian western is clearly a response to that complex new fascination with traditional Indian culture, particularly among the young, that Leslie Fiedler analyzes in *The Return of the Vanishing American*. In its treatment of violence as an expression of aggressive drives toward destruction in the pioneer spirit, in its negative and guilt-ridden assessment of the winning of the West, and its reversal of traditional valuations of the symbolic figures and groups of the western story this new formula has a great deal in common with another recent form that I have labeled, rather facetiously, the legend of the Jewish cowboy. The hero of this type of western is not literally Jewish, though often played by Jewish actors. Actually, I suspect that Jews are likely to be the last of the ethnic groups to insist on donning the mantle of the cowboy hero. The heroes of *Butch Cassidy and the Sundance Kid* and *McCabe and Mrs. Miller*, however, behave more like characters transported from the pages of a novel by Saul Bellow or Bernard Malamud into the legendary West than they do like the traditional western hero. They win our interest and sympathy not by courage and heroic deeds but by bemused incompetence, genial cowardice, and the ability to face the worst with buoyancy and wit. They are six-gun schlemiels and existentialists in cowboy boots. The West they inhabit is rapidly becoming the modern industrial world, and they are hopelessly out of place in the new society. Their real enemy is not the Indian or the outlaw but the corporation. They stand for a leisurely traditional way of life that is giving way to the ruthless mechanical efficiency of the corporate society. Butch Cassidy is an outlaw who is finally driven from the country by the irresistible force of organization in the form of a super-posse hired by the Union Pacific Railroad. McCabe is a small-time gambler and brothel keeper who is killed by a gang of thugs hired by a mining company that wants to take over his property. The new myth implicit in these westerns contrasts the individualistic violence of the outlaw or Indian with the brutal, streamlined force of organized society and expresses the view that the corporate violence of modern society is more dangerous and evil than the acts of individual aggression implicit in the Indian or outlaw's way of life. Thus many of the traditional meanings of the western are reversed— society cannot be purged or regenerated by heroic acts because progress means destruction of humane values. The good groups are the simpler traditional societies of outlaws and Indians, but these and the values they represent are doomed to extinction. The true hero is not the man who brings law and order but the alienated and absurd individual who cannot fit into the new society.

All three of the new western types I have discussed—the Italian western, the western Godfather, and the search for a new myth—share a disillusioned and pessimistic view of society and an obsession with the place of violence in it. As the western has always done, these new formulas project the tensions and concerns of the present into the legendary past in order to seek in the imagination some kind of resolution or acceptance of conflicts of value and feeling that cannot be solved in the present. The classic westerns of the post-World War II period seemed to reflect a balanced tension between traditional values and the sense of new social circumstances. The westerns of today, however, suggest no such balance. Instead, they seem to reflect a considerable variety of different emotional and ideological accommodations to the pessimism about society that they all share. Three major kinds of attitude seem to have emerged; first, a sense of human depravity and corruption that almost seems to take delight in the destructiveness of violence by accepting it as an inevitable expression of man's nature; second, the fantasy of a superior father-figure who can protect the innocent and wreak vengeance on the guilty, a fantasy that reflects a profound disbelief in the modern agencies of law and justice to serve their proper function. In this context, violence is the product of morally purposeful individual action in defense of the good group against the threats offered by the rest of society. Finally, the search for a new western myth expresses the view that violence has been the underlying force in the development of American society and that all modern white Americans are implicated in guilt for their aggressive destruction of other ways of life. The contemporary western reflects the conflict between these differing views of our past and present. Whether any of them will eventually serve as the basis of a new consensus about the meaning of the West only the further course of history can determine.

Nine

The Best-Selling Social Melodrama

Each preceding chapter has concentrated on a particular aspect of popular literary formulas, using various mystery and adventure formulas as instances of the problem under consideration. Here, I will attempt to apply the array of methods and analytical procedures developed in earlier chapters to a single formulaic type different from those previously studied. Since this study has not said much about the great variety of formulas that embody the archetypes of romance, alien states or beings, and melodrama, I decided to conclude by considering at least one melodramatic formula or rather set of formulas that I will designate by the term "social melodrama." I say "set of formulas" because social melodrama is not a single structural formula such as the classical detective story or the western but an evolving complex of formulas. Some elements have been relatively constant over a long period or have recurred from time to time, while others have changed considerably. In the first section, I will try to outline the common elements that define the formulaic type. Then I will discuss the distinctive aesthetic problems associated with the type. My consideration of the artistic potentials and limitations of social melodrama leads to a tentative account of the type's evolution and of its relationship to the changing imaginative needs of American culture. Finally, I will look at certain aspects of the distinctive accomplishment of a particular social melodramatist—Irving Wallace—against the background of the formulaic tradition to which most of his work belongs.

The Social Melodrama

A quick glance at any best-seller list indicates that there is no such thing as a formula for best-selling novels. Such lists range from works within the particular formulas we have already discussed such as classical detective novels by Agatha Christie to highly individual works of imaginative invention by nonformulaic writers like Saul Bellow and Thomas Pynchon. There are even novels which make use of formulaic conventions for irony and satire such as the books of Kurt Vonnegut or Thomas Berger. The diversity of best-seller lists presumably reflects the diverse interests of readers as well as differing literary types. A particular work may become popular because it is perceived by readers as a major work of literary art, because it seems to offer a particularly valuable set of insights into some problem of wide interest, because it is a particularly entertaining example of a familiar formula, or simply because the writer has a well-established reputation for satisfying one or more of these interests. Many other factors can enter into the making of best-sellers such as the effectiveness of the publisher's system of promotion and distribution and the topicality of the books in question. Because of this variety of factors, the cultural significance of many best-sellers is a matter of individual circumstances to which the method of formula analysis can make little or no contribution.

Nonetheless, within the general diversity of best-sellers there is a certain type of novel that has almost invariably been represented on best-seller lists for the last century and a half and, when effectively written and promoted, so often achieves best-seller status that it has become, in effect, a best-selling, formulaic type. I will call it the social melodrama, since it synthesizes the archetype of melodrama with a carefully and elaborately developed social setting in such a way as to combine the emotional satisfactions of melodrama with the interest inherent in a detailed, intimate, and realistic analysis of major social or historical phenomena. The structural characteristics of this formulaic type involve an interweaving of the patterns of melodrama with a particular set of current events or social institutions, the result being a complex double effect: the social setting is often treated rather critically with a good deal of anatomizing of the hidden motives, secret corruption, and human folly underlying certain events or institutions; yet the main plot works out in proper melodramatic fashion to affirm, after appropriate tribulations and sufferings, that God is in his heaven and all's right with the world. The sympathetic and the good undergo much testing and difficulty, but are ultimately saved. Evil rides high but is, in the end, overcome, at least as far as the main characters are concerned.

In describing the formula of the best-selling social melodrama, it is not possible to specify a fixed pattern of character and action as in the classical detective story, or a symbolic complex of situation and setting, as in the western. Instead of a particular formula, social melodrama is a type defined by the combination of melodramatic structure and character with something that passes for a "realistic" social or historical setting.[1] The appeal of this synthesis combines the escapist satisfactions of melodrama—in particular, its fantasy of a moral universe following conventional social values—with the pleasurable feeling that we are learning something important about reality. By way of insisting on the reality of his stories, the social melodramatist tends to take advantage of anything that can give his tale the appearance of deep social significance and truth. If the novel's setting is historical, there is usually a parade of important and well-known personalities, issues, and events. A social melodrama set at the time of the American Civil War almost invariably contains an incident or two in which the protagonist encounters Lincoln or Robert E. Lee, or at least becomes involved in one of the major battles of the time. If the setting is contemporary, the author, typically, will structure his story around an "inside" look at a major modern institution (Arthur Hailey, *Airport, Wheels*; Joseph Wambaugh, *The New Centurions*) or event (Irving Wallace, *The Prize, The Chapman Report, The Plot*). In other cases the effect of significant reality is generated by making the story a fictionalized version of the lives of some well-known group of celebrities (cf. the works of Harold Robbins or Jacqueline Susann) or of an actual place (Grace Metalious's *Peyton Place*).

The view of reality offered by the social melodramatist claims a special insight into the inner workings and motives of major institutions, personalities, and events. Typically, the melodramatist tries to make us feel that we have penetrated what shows on the surface to the inside story; he offers what appears to be the dirt beneath the rug, the secret power behind the scenes. There has been a continuing connection between the nineteenth- and twentieth-century tradition of novelistic social criticism or muckraking and the social melodrama. Indeed, a number of quite extraordinary works such as Stowe's *Uncle Tom's Cabin*, Frank Norris's *The Pit*, Lewis's *Main Street*, and Mitchell's *Gone with the Wind* lie somewhere on a continuum between the formulaic social melodrama and naturalistic novels by writers like Dreiser, Hemingway, Faulkner, and Bellow. Perhaps the deep impact such enormously popular novels have had on the American imagination is a result of their combination of fairly serious social criticism with a narrative structure that moves toward the moral fantasies of melodrama. Of course, for most social melodramatists, social criticism is generally less deep and far-reaching than in the muckraking tradition. In general, where muckraking novelists like Upton Sinclair, Theodore Dreiser, and David Graham Phillips attempted to create a systematic criticism of society that looks toward the reform of institutional abuses, social criticism in a writer like Harold Robbins tends rather to reassure the reader that little can be done to change society. The typical social melodrama reveals corrupt motives behind the scenes to assure us of the reality of the story but finally affirms the basic melodramatic principle that things are as they should be.[2]

Melodrama is, as I noted in an earlier chapter, one of the basic archetypes of moral fantasy. Its central organizing principle is the clear establishment of poetic justice in the form of a happy or morally satisfying ending. The essential shape of melodrama is the presentation of the trials and tribulations that the good are subjected to by the wicked together with the final triumph of the good and the punishment of the wicked.[3] Melodrama moves from a sense of injustice and disorder to an affirmation of a benevolent moral order in the universe. It is a highly popular form because it affirms some conventional moral or philosophical principle as the inherent basis of cosmic order by illustrating this principle at work in the lives of good and wicked characters.[4] Because of its dedication to the moral ending, melodrama bears a certain resemblance to comedy, except that, as Northrop Frye remarks, it is comedy without humor and therefore its poetic justice tends to lack the sense of human limitation enforced by laughter and foolery.

There is a special point of cultural interest about the social melodrama. Time and again, books and authors of this type have achieved an extraordinary popularity within their own era, only to lapse into almost total obscurity in succeeding generations, a pattern that is by no means equally characteristic of many of the other major formulas. Readers of detective stories frequently rediscover the delights of such major earlier authors as Conan Doyle, R. Austin Freeman, G. K. Chesterton, or Dorothy Sayers. Owen Wister's *The Virginian* is still read by devotees of the western. John Buchan's early spy stories have just recently come back into print. Even nineteenth-century dime novel westerns have their contemporary devotees. But who outside of dedicated literary scholars reads today the enormously successful nineteenth-century social melodramas of Mrs. E. D. E. N. Southworth or Susan Warner? To take a more recent example, where are the fans of Harold Bell Wright, best-selling American writer of the first two decades of the twentieth century, or of Winston Churchill, number one seller at the turn of the century. Zane Grey is a very interesting case in point here. From 1915 until 1924 Grey had at least one book among the ten top best-sellers every year except 1916. He is still read today, but by a rather limited public, for his books are only irregularly available in inexpensive paperback editions. In Grey's case I would hazard the speculation that while the western-adventure characteristics of his works remain fresh and vivid, the gamy flavor of melodrama that is so strong in his novels seems irretrievably dated to most readers. I suspect we will find the same thing to be true of such best-selling social melodramatists of the present time as Harold Robbins, Irving Wallace, and Jacqueline Susann once a similar period of time has passed by. Thus, the social melodrama seems to be the most time-bound of all the major formulas. I suspect this is because this formulaic type depends to such a great extent on the outlook and values of a particular era.

The Aesthetic of Social Melodrama

Perhaps the most important artistic skill of the successful social melodramatist is implied in such phrases as "He certainly knows how to tell a good story" or "He knows how to hold the reader's interest" or "I just couldn't put the book down." Such reader appreciation is evidently a response to the author's mastery of melodramatic character and incidents. Because the overall shape of melodrama tends to be complicated and diffuse, there is a special premium on the writer's ability to make individual episodes engrossing. Unfortunately, it is easier to note that there is such a skill than to differentiate it with any precision from the basic skills of character and incident creation that any narrative writer must possess. It is traditionally said of melodramatic incident that it calls on us to overreact—to feel happiness, sorrow, fear, or anger to a greater degree than the actual situation would seem to merit. Of course, this is for the most part not a clear description of melodramatic style but a criticism of its artistic disproportion. It is true, I think, that melodrama does require immediate and extreme reactions as well as the capacity to shift very rapidly from one extreme of feeling to another. This is not only a function of melodrama's commitment to entertainment and escape but an aspect of its basic structure. The greater gloom and uncertainty the melodramatist can plunge us into, before revealing the basic morality and order of the world, the more fully he can achieve the basic effect of melodrama. In practice, this leads to a great dependence on accident or coincidence as a melodramatic plot device. To make the swing from failure to triumph through a series of coincidental events requires a great skill in the rapid establishment and shifting of emotional responses. Thus effective melodramatic incident tends to stress single and direct emotions rather than complex explorations of motive and significance.

Since effective melodrama must arouse direct and immediate emotion in its audience, the skillful melodramatist develops an arsenal of techniques of simplification and intensification. The sort of simplification most appropriate to melodrama is that which centers our attention on moments of crisis, because it is such episodes that can most powerfully excite our emotions. The successful melodramatist has the ability to invent a great variety of plausible crises and to move us hurriedly but persuasively from one to the other. The most obvious kind of crisis is that which involves a matter of life and death, so it is not surprising to find a plethora of deaths or threats of death in the social melodrama. But death is not the only moment in life that can be treated in crisis terms; love, success, various forms of moral temptations, moments in which friends become enemies or enemies friends, moments of deep commitment or alienation, marriage or divorce, and those crucial times in life that seem to determine one's fate once and for all. But where most "serious" novels contain only a few such moments, the melodrama contains almost nothing else. Henry James may write an entire novel (*The Ambassadors*) to make us understand, in part, why a certain middle-aged American has a rather complex reaction to Europe, but his near contemporary E. P. Roe treats us to a whole succession of loves and deaths amid the burning of the city of Chicago. Even that most gothic and violent of modern novelists, William Faulkner, constructs entire novels around one or two climactic moments of decision, while contemporary melodramatists like Harold Robbins or Irving Wallace move us quickly from one critical moment to another.

Along with the principle of episodic simplicity in which each chapter confronts us with some terrible problem for the cast of characters, the successful melodramatist depends on various techniques of intensification to maintain our excited interest. One of the most important of such methods is the melodramatic use of spectacle. The good social melodramatist makes us feel that his story is involved with large events of social or historical importance that usually eventuate in some massive public spectacle or event. Our excitement about large events intensifies our feeling about the significance of individual episodes and the way in which they critically affect the fate of characters. Usually there are one or more major public spectacles—a trial, a revolution, a terrible murder, or a war—at the heart of most social melodramas.

The importance of spectacle is certainly not unique to social melodrama, since many major novels such as Tolstoy's *War and Peace*, Stendhal's *Charterhouse of Parma*, or Hemingway's *A Farewell to Arms* set the stories of their individual characters in the context of large and violent public events. But if we compare *War and Peace* with a major social melodrama involving war such as Margaret Mitchell's *Gone with the Wind*, we can see that in the melodrama historical events become a means by which morally appropriate fates are portioned out and thus both affirm the significance of individual events and the ultimate morality of the universe. In *Gone with the Wind*, the Civil War and its aftermath create the circumstances that judge and punish Scarlett for her selfish vanity and overweening egotism, while at the same time they challenge her to move in the direction of a new strength and vitality. In *War and Peace*, however, the relation between public events and private morality is a more complex dialectic. Even though Pierre Bezukhov does find a kind of salvation, it is not by taking a role in the public spectacle but by turning his back on it. The war remains an enigmatic and amoral circumstance in relation to the individual lives of the characters, despite all of Tolstoy's ruminations on historical forces. The principle of public spectacle as a moral background for individual drama is even more apparent in such works as Irving Wallace's *The Plot* or *The Seven Minutes* where a major public event functions to regenerate and bring about a higher state of happiness for the sympathetic protagonists who have been in deep moral confusion. In social melodramas the public spectacle intensifies our pleasure in the discovery of a conventional moral order in the midst of apparent chaos, while in the "serious" novel public events tend to make us increasingly aware of the limitations and complexity of reality.

As models of melodramatic incident one thinks immediately of the great set pieces from *Uncle Tom's Cabin*: Eliza's flight across the ice, the death and transfiguration of Little Eva, the martyrdom of Uncle Tom. The power of these scenes—at least for nineteenth- and early twentieth-century audiences—derived in large part from the unqualified and uncomplicated feelings they aroused. Each character is in his way a pure victim and helpless before his fate; yet each symbolizes some human quality or action for which we can feel an undivided admiration or sympathy—a mother's love, the innocent sweetness of a young child, the Christian selflessness of a noble martyr. The great gap between the characters' merits or deserts and the terrible situations in which they find themselves makes these scenes intensely powerful insofar as one can accept Mrs. Stowe's moral universe. Contemporary melodramatists assume a different moral universe and another set of fundamental concerns, but the principle of melodramatic incident is similar: intense sympathy must be aroused by placing admirable (or hateful) characters in situations where they are threatened with the wrong fate. Then, the emotion must be released either by removing the threat of an inappropriate fate, or by explaining or justifying this fate from some higher perspective. In the case of *Uncle Tom's Cabin*, we literally see Little Eva transported to heaven and are assured of a similar salvation for Uncle Tom.

Two major artistic problems arise from the nature of melodramatic incident and character: the considerable diffuseness of the structure because of the concentration on striking individual incidents, and the difficulties created by melodrama's inherently moralistic nature. The problem of structural diffusion is obvious enough in the case of the simplest and most straightforward sort of melodrama of suspense. It is further complicated by the addition of the masses of information and analysis that generally characterize the social melodrama. The writer must find an overarching structure sufficiently commodious to accommodate a vast variety of exciting incidents and a plethora of characters as well as a detailed discussion of the workings of major social institutions. To do this while still maintaining an ongoing excitement and suspense is no simple task of construction. Various solutions to this problem have been tried with more or less effectiveness. There is the structure of different groups of characters whose lives intersect at crucial moments in their history. Dickens was particularly good at developing such structures in, for example, *Bleak House* and *Nicholas Nickleby*. This is also the basic method of organization favored by Harold Robbins in most of his novels. Another common structural gambit is to center the multiple subplots around some particular social institution, thus holding our interest by the way in which the various characters and their stories develop around a behind-the-scenes view of the operations of a great hotel or a major automobile company or the United States Senate. A closely related method is to organize the incidents around some major public event in which the diverse characters are caught up—for example, the awarding of the Nobel Prize, an important trial, or a large international conference. Irving Wallace is particularly good at creating this kind of structure, as we shall see in a later section of this chapter. Still other writers have used the archetype of mystery to order their diverse characters and incidents, though this stratagem tends to shift attention from the complex social analysis of the social melodrama toward the structures of sensation or gothic melodramas, as in the novels of Wilkie Collins. But whatever the principle of structure, it must be one that can bring about the miraculous coincidences and striking reversals that are the essence of melodrama. Consequently, while exciting on first reading, social melodramas do not usually profit much from rereading because there is no further depth or richness of perception about the characters and their actions to be gained from a better grasp of the overall organization.

Another structural difficulty is nicely stated by T. S. Eliot in his essay on Collins and Dickens:

There is another characteristic of certain tales of Collins which may be said to belong to melodrama, or to the melodramatic part of drama. It consists in delaying, longer than one would conceive it possible to delay, a conclusion which is inevitable and wholly foreseen. A story like *The New Magdalen* is, from a certain moment merely a study in stage suspense; the *denoument* is postponed, again and again, by every possible ingenuity; the situations are in the most effective sense theatrical, without being in the profounder sense dramatic. They are seldom, as in *The Woman in White*, situations of conflict between chessmen which merely occupy hostile positions on the board.[5]

This problem derives from the moralistic predictability of melodrama. The good must triumph, the wicked must fail, and it is one of the prime satisfactions of melodrama that we know this from the beginning. Yet to achieve any kind of suspense or excitement the melodramatist must at least temporarily entertain the possibility that the good may fail. To balance inherent moralistic predictability against the possiblity of dramatic conflict is one of the most difficult juggling acts that must be performed by the effective melodramatist. The success of his performance will depend on his ability to dramatize the moral order in a sufficiently complex fashion that its operation allows for the trials and tribulations of the characters without basically threatening the reader's sense of a benevolent principle in action. To do this, the melodramatist must have a deep and complex insight into the moral vision of his contemporaries.

Thus a complex moralism is the crux of successful melodrama, constituting both the basis of its great popularity and the reason why so few melodramas continue to move audiences after a certain period of time has gone by. Melodrama must affirm a commonly accepted moral universe in order to give its audiences the pleasure of seeing the sympathetic and virtuous rewarded and the hateful and dastardly punished. The closer its system of rewards and punishments and its conceptions of the moral order are to the accepted ideas of its audience, the more plausible and satisfying the story will be. This is not simply a matter of manipulating puppets stereotyped as good and evil, though it may seem that way to later generations. An effective melodramatist is able to deal not only with the obvious conventional stereotypes of good and evil but with the conflicts between values and the ambiguity of latent motives and overt principles that characterize a particular period. Thus social melodrama is concerned not only with the affirmation of traditional conceptions of morality but with integrating and harmonizing what might be called the conventional wisdom with new currents of value and attitude. This gives the social melodrama a unique artistic importance for the period of its creation. But it also means that social melodrama tends to be the most perishable of popular story formulas. An analysis of the evolution of social melodrama will reveal the way in which its moralistic formula has undergone a continual process of redefinition in the last century and a half.[6]

The Evolution of Social Melodrama

If he did not invent it, Charles Dickens developed the formula for social melodrama into one of the most successful fictional genres of the nineteenth and twentieth centuries. Dickens showed conclusively that a writer could represent society in a fairly complex and critical way yet still achieve tremendous popular success if he synthesized social criticism with the archetype of melodrama and thereby gave readers the pleasure of seeing the follies of men and institutions combined with the satisfaction of witnessing the triumph of virtue and the punishment of vice.

The melodramatic conventions on which Dickens drew were the product of earlier developments in both fiction and the theater. In the last decade of the eighteenth century, a new kind of melodrama had become increasingly popular with the growing public for books and theater. The central figure in this formulaic pattern was usually a virtuous young lady of some lower or ambiguous status—village maiden, orphan, daughter of parents in reduced circumstances—who was pursued by a male character of higher status and dubious intentions, a figure of aristocratic, erotic, financial, and social power; in other words, some form of the stereotypical squire with curling mustaches. The sorely beset heroine commonly loved a more worthy and innocent young man, who was himself enmeshed in status difficulties, often because his true parentage was concealed for one reason or another. This primary triangle was the essence of melodrama and was capable of two major permutations, corresponding loosely to comic and tragic modes of action. In the first case, the heroine resisted the entreaties and threats of the villain and was ultimately united in marriage with the noble young man. In Richardson's seminal *Pamela*, the villain and the good hero were combined as phases of a single character, but in most instances hero and villain exemplified moral principles in a more stereotypical fashion. In the tragic melodrama, the heroine succumbed to the villain's plots. "When this happened," as David Grimsted puts it,

> repentance, madness, and death were all that awaited her, except in a few instances where after long suffering she was allowed a modicum of happiness. Such unhappy fate was inevitable even if the heroine had been "unfortunate, rather than guilty"—if she had been raped or deceived by a "false marriage." These were favorite plot devices because the woman's total purity of intent made her fall more pathetic, but no less inevitable.[7]

This dramatic and narrative formula, which set a supreme symbol of virtue (the beleaguered village maiden) against a potent embodiment of evil (the wicked squire), and then arranged in a particularly suspenseful and exciting manner for the success of virtue and the punishment of evil, was a highly effective version of the archetype of melodrama. But in tracing the evolution of social melodrama we must also look at the particular social and cultural themes involved. Melodrama, as we have seen, is particularly dependent on a sense of what is a proper, acceptable, and plausible means for insuring the triumph of virtue in spite of the terrible strength of vice. This sense of the proper order of things justifies the coincidences and accidents of melo-dramatic action and reveals, in a striking way, the conventional moral vision that a particular culture and period wishes to see affirmed by the striking reversals of fortune that characterize the structure of melodrama.

In the melodramas of the early nineteenth century, the principle of proper order reflected an intertwining of religious and social values. The single most important outcome of any melodrama was the marriage of the virtuous heroine to the right man—or, in the tragic version of melodrama, the degradation and death of the fallen heroine. In general, the right man was somewhat above the virtuous heroine in social status, though at the beginning of the story he may have been poor or a lost heir. When a relationship developed between a poor young man and a woman above him in status, something unfortunate usually came of it, unless by the operation of melodramatic coincidence the noble hero turned out to be the rightful heir to a still larger fortune. If a wealthy girl became involved with a hero beneath her station she often exemplified one of the favorite secondary characters of the early nineteenth-century melodramatic formula, the "other woman," who was normally more like the villain than the heroine. In fact, the "other woman," wealthy, decadent, and lustful, increasingly took on the role of villain, as later melodramatists cast about for ways to give new vitality to what were, by midcentury, somewhat tired conventions.

These stereotypes of character and action indicate the degree to which social dominance, the ideas of middle-class domesticity, the dream of romantic love, and the drive for social mobility were unified in the popular moral vision of early nineteenth-century England and America. After being threatened with a fate worse than death by an upper-class villain, the virtuous heroine settled into happy domesticity with a solidly respectable young man with whom she also, coincidently, was in love, thus neatly affirming in one stroke the nineteenth-century middle-class values of love, domesticity, social respectability, masculine dominance, and feminine purity. In the later nineteenth century, this ideal union became increasingly pre-carious and melodrama began to change in relation to new cultural tensions.

The other basic principle of the melodramatic vision in this period was the primacy of religion. Religion was, in effect, the cement tying together the other social and moral ideas. The heroine's faith in God not only helps her to endure the trials and tribulations she is subjected to by the villain, but it also leads her to make the proper romantic choice of the good hero who can share her profound faith. Moreover, the hero and heroine's Christian dedication sanctifies their union and insures that it will be a truly proper and respectable one. Above all, it is the sense of divine providence operating in the world that insures that virtue and vice will achieve their appropriate rewards. In Mrs. Southworth's *The Curse of Clifton*, Archer Clifton is deceived by the wicked "other woman" into thinking that his wife has married him for his money. Driven by suspicion, he subjects his loving and virtuous helpmeet to two years of brutal indifference. His suspicions are finally cleared up through (a) an especially selfless and heroic act on the heroine's part, (b) through Clifton's chance encounter with an even wealthier gentleman she had earlier rejected, and (c) through a deathbed confession by the villainess. Somewhat embarrassed by his lack of trust, as well he might be, Archer Clifton laments to his wife,

> "And, oh, Catherine, to think that all this trouble I have suffered, and have inflicted upon you, should have been so unnecessary."

But she, knowing better, and deeper in her faith, replies

> "Oh, no! it was *not* unnecessary. God suffered it to be, and it was well— *very* well! All things work together for good, to them that love the Lord! And every pang that has ploughed our hearts in the past, will make them fruitful of good in the future. One fruit is, that the suffering of the last two years has drawn our hearts together as nothing else could have done."[8]

Thus, the murky melodramatic triangle of virtuous heroine, noble hero, and dastardly villain was a drama of providence in which suffering and doubt challenge the heroine's religious faith, but insure that, if she remains chaste and true and submits herself to God's will, not only will she become a respectable wife and the center of a happy domestic circle but this social and romantic achievement will be sanctified and blessed by the hand of God. Thus the melodramatic formula of this period dramatized the congruence between the social ideals of domesticity, romantic love, and respectable mobility and the religious faith in the divine governance of the world. In these stories, melodramatic coincidence and apparent chance take on a special emotional and moral force because they are understood to be results of God's operative providence. When rightly understood, they show us that every worldly event is controlled by His benevolent interest and power. Henry Nash Smith is right in calling this a "cosmic success story."[9]

Beyond the basic formula of virtuous hero and heroine entangled in the toils of an aristocratic villain and saved by a providential series of revelations or happenstances, the melodrama was fleshed out by a variety of minor figures:

> The gallery of rogues was increased by such stock characters as the designing governess, preferably French; the hardhearted landlady, the cruel stepmother, the inhuman creditor, the flinty jailor, the vile procuress, and the mercenary wet nurse. Upon the side of the angels were to be found, with wearisome monotony, the noble soldier dispensing good cheer out of a meager pension, with a gesture or two borrowed from Uncle Toby; and

the generous sailor endowed with some of the more genial characteristics of Smollett's seamen. The [melodramatist's] contention that sympathy is the mainspring of human nature was exemplified in numerous instances of the good apprentice, the philanthropic merchant, the chivalrous rustic, the noble savage, the highborn benefacturess, and the long-suffering wife.[10]

Grimsted points out that the serious melodramatic triangle was often paralleled by a low comedy situation and characters whose attitudes and actions burlesqued and even sometimes cast an ironic light on the turbulent posturings of the major characters, as if, to achieve its highest effectiveness, melodramatic moralism had to be served up with a dash of comic realism. Indeed, the ideal vision of melodrama with its fundamental principle of a supremely just universe often seems a little too much for its audience to accept without some sense of basic evil or comic ridicule lurking in the wings.

Thus, from the very beginning of the nineteenth century, melodrama tended to add at least a dash of spice to its portrayal of virtue triumphant and evil defeated.[11] More sophisticated audiences were probably more responsive to the kind of story that could balance some of the satisfactions of melodrama against the claims of their sense of reality. The village virgin, her noble young swain, and the mustachioed villain may have been satisfying enough for the simpler audiences of the popular theater, but for melodrama to reach out to the more educated public as well it had to find ways of setting its stories of virtue versus vice in a context of more plausibly complex representations of the world. The result was the emergence, first in Dickens[12] and then in an almost unbroken tradition of best-sellers since his time, of what I have called social melodrama, with its basic structure of a melodramatic inner plot embodied in a more or less complex and critical treatment of society.

Perhaps because of the way in which it depends on a complex balancing of quite disparate perceptions of the world, social melodrama shades over on one side into the nonmelodramatic novel as when, in some of the novels of Dickens and almost all of Dostoevsky, strongly melodramatic elements are overpowered by a nonmelodramatic social vision. On the other side, social melodrama is closely related to other melodramatic formulas of similar character: the historical, the gothic, the religious, or the sensation melodramas. These other modes of melodramatic expression share with social melodrama the structure of a melodramatic action embedded in a more complex imaginative vision, but the nature and source of that vision reflect a religious or historical rather than a primarily social concern. Thus a truly adequate treatment of the evolution of melodrama in the nineteenth and twentieth centuries is a task of great complexity. Here I can only make a few observations about major changes in the complex of moral attitudes underlying the development of social melodrama by analyzing some exemplary works.

The basic combination of social criticism and melodramatic plot that

Dickens so brilliantly articulated was embodied in hundreds of novels and plays in mid-nineteenth-century England and America. None was more powerful and striking than Harriet Beecher Stowe's *Uncle Tom's Cabin*, which in both printed and theatrical form was the greatest nineteenth-century best-seller.

The extraordinary impact of *Uncle Tom's Cabin*—perhaps the only book other than the Bible that has been held responsible for a major war—was a testimony to Mrs. Stowe's ability to express her sense of deeply felt social wrongs in terms of the melodramatic conventions her readers were predisposed to respond to. Most important, she extended those melodramatic conventions to cover black characters as well as white and thereby accomplished one of the first major acts of racial integration on the imaginative level. Just as Dickens forced his audience to a new awareness of the urban poor by cutting through the class separation between high and low character stereotypes that had been the rule in early melodrama, Mrs. Stowe took the even more daring imaginative step of treating black characters as high melodramatic heroes and heroines. Her carefully documented account of the system of slavery and its outrages against human decency and the Christian faith was given added force by her insistence on presenting black characters as serious melodramatic protagonists. Her characterization of Eliza drew upon two of the strongest melodramatic traditions, the virtuous heroine persecuted by the brutal seducer and the suffering mother. George Harris was the noble upwardly mobile hero suddenly confronted with a dastardly plot against the woman he loved and prevented by his situation from going to her aid until it was almost too late. Uncle Tom himself embodied the convention of the benevolent father and moral spokesman who suffered and died as a martyr to the cause of Christian faith and feminine purity. Mrs. Stowe's white characters also grew out of melodramatic stereotypes: the dastardly, lascivious, mustache-twirling villain, Simon Legree; the pure and innocent young girl; the peevish spinster.

The action, too, was of the essence of melodrama. Specific scenes like Eliza's flight across the frozen river, the death of Little Eva, the sudden attack on Augustine St. Clare and the ultimate confrontation of Uncle Tom and Simon Legree possessed those qualities of suspenseful excitement, seemingly miraculous coincidence, and intensity of emotion that are essential to melodramatic incident. The overall action of *Uncle Tom's Cabin* was constructed of two large movements: the daring flight, pursuit, and eventual escape of George and Eliza Harris to the North, and the bondage, suffering, and martyrdom of Uncle Tom as he moved deeper and deeper into the hell of the slavery system of the plantation South. The happy outcome of the trials of George and Eliza obviously demonstrated the operation of providence. Not only did they escape from bondage, but they kept encountering kindly and decent people who, as agents of a higher plan, helped them on their way to freedom. The martyrdom of Uncle Tom was a less obvious but deeper portrayal of the divine governance of the world, for, in his hopeless suffering, Tom's Christian resignation to the will of God insured that he would meet his terrible fate with dignity, faith, and a growing certainty of his eternal salvation. Tom's victory was substantiated by the narrator's frequent and explicit comments on the subject, and by the two major incidents that marked important stages in the process of Tom's martyrdom: the death of Little Eva and the degeneration and damnation of Simon Legree. The manner of Little Eva's demise perfectly exemplified the striking change of tears resolved in ultimate joy that was the essence of nineteenth-century melo-drama. Eva's translation to heaven—an episode that later generations with different moral and religious attitudes would see as the quintessence of archaic melodramatic absurdity—was a scene that deeply moved nineteenth-century readers and theatrical audiences who were evidently supersensitive to the combination of childhood innocence and purity with suffering, death, and the certainty of heaven. But it also played a vital symbolic role in Tom's story, assuring us that whatever his temporal suffering might be, he was certain to join his beloved little mistress in eternal bliss. Legree's progressive deterioration was lovingly detailed by Mrs. Stowe. After Tom's death, Legree sees a diabolical figure of death beckoning to him, a vision that we are certainly intended to take as the sign of God's justice striking down the guilty.

Mrs. Stowe's work was unique in its power and impact because she integrated her attack on the social evil of slavery with the prevailing melodramatic vision of the world. Yet *Uncle Tom's Cabin* was typical of mid-nineteenth-century social melodrama in its emphasis on divine provi-dence as the agency of a benevolent moral order that rewards the good and punishes the wicked, bringing about the melodramatic triumph. The mid-nineteenth-century vision of a Christian, providential world implied several other themes. It meant that feminine purity and the ideal of motherhood were dominant symbols of virtue, the chief objects of the noble hero's protection and the villain's attack. Closely associated with the ideal of purity was the value of Christian resignation and submission to God's will. Heroine and hero both had to learn faith in God's operative providence in order to be assured of a happy resolution to their problems. The central role of the villain as seducer also grew out of this complex of values. The ideal moral order that God's providence ultimately established for the virtuous and denied to the wicked was a happy synthesis of traditional Protestant religious ideals and the middle-class social values of domesticity and respectability. The proper fate for the melodramatic hero or heroine was to learn Christian resignation by preserving moral purity in the face of great trials and temptations, with the assurance that this would lead to a happy and respectable marriage as a temporal prelude to eternal salvation in the afterlife.[13]

This divinely appointed moral order had many worldly enemies. Their attempts to draw the hero and heroine from the proper path constituted the major source of suspenseful excitement and virtuous suffering. Moreover, in social melodrama, the plots of the aristocratic rake were often supplemented or even replaced by the pressure of bad social institutions. Mrs. Stowe's analysis of the way in which the social system of slavery had corrupted government, the church, and the family was comparable to Dickens's attack on the Court of Chancery, the system of debtor's prison, the social treatment of the poor, and other institutions. These heavy indictments were echoed more thinly in Mrs. Southworth's attacks on aristocratic social prejudice and Susan Warner's pale criticisms of the worldliness and materialism of city society. It was also an important article of melodramatic faith that people were generally good when their hearts were simple and open to God's word and to love for their neighbor. Invariably the suffering, melodramatic protagonist found assistance and support among children, rural people, and the lowly, those yet uncorrupted by the artifices of society. Yet, at the same time, the successful hero or heroine was hardly fated to remain in lowly obscurity. On the contrary, having faced the dangers of social worldliness and corruption with moral purity and Christian resignation, the melo-dramatic protagonist typically achieved a marriage that placed him or her firmly within the genteel and respectable classes. Or, if the heroine ultimately succumbed to her trials, the result was a lingering death, usually among lowly, simple people who offered a final protection. If, like Uncle Tom, the tragic melodramatic protagonist had learned to accept martyrdom, the reader was usually assured in some fashion that the protagonist's death was only the prelude to a more glorious resurrection.

Culturally, the social melodrama of the mid-nineteenth century can best be interpreted as an attempt to reconcile the increasing conflict between traditional Christian views of the world and the secular values of a rapidly changing society. The formula that dominated the period's social melodrama resolved the tension between religion and the values of mobility and success by making its virtuous protagonists examples of both and by asserting a fundamental unity between the operation of God's providence and the creation of happy, prosperous, and respectable middle-class families. By the end of the nineteenth century, however, this equation of traditional religious attitudes and middle-class social values was no longer viable in the social melodrama. In the number one best-seller of 1913, Winston Churchill's *The Inside of the Cup*, the story begins with an apparent affirmation of the social and moral vision that we have just described, but the ironic tone of the narrative indicates that the traditional melodramatic version of the moral order has broken down:

> [Our story begins in] a city overtaken, in recent years, by the plague which has swept our country from the Atlantic to the Pacific—prosperity. Before its advent the [respectable families] lived leisurely lives in a sleepy quarter of shade trees and spacious yards and muddy macadam streets, now passed away forever. Existence was decorous, marriage an irrevocable

step, wives were wives, and the Authorized Version of the Bible was true from cover to cover. So Dr. Gilman preached and so they believed.[14]

In this novel, the profession of religious piety represents a residue of stultifying orthodoxy and large-scale social hypocrisy. There is a deadening separation between religion and society: "[On Sundays] the city suddenly became full of churches, as though they had magically been let down from Heaven during Saturday night. They must have been there on weekdays, but few persons even thought of them."[15]

Increasing ambivalence about divine providence as the cornerstone of society was accompanied by doubts about the two other value complexes that were basic to the earlier melodramatic vision: the purity and domestic submissiveness of women and the ideal of the respectable, middle-class family. If feminine purity, piety, and submissiveness were no longer felt to be so important as to evoke the hand of God in their defense; if the direct operation of God's providence in worldly affairs was no longer felt as an imaginative reality; if the attainment of Christian resignation in a life of domestic piety and respectability was no longer conceived to be the highest ideal; then it was not possible for melodramatists to continue writing stories in which virtuous maidens were pursued by lascivious and aristocratic rakes, saved at the last minute by providential interventions, and happily married to a lost heir of the respectable gentry. Nor could they depend on stories in which Christian innocents accepted martyrdom in the assurance of eternal happiness in a palpable heaven.

The increasing pressure on the traditional vision was reflected in two significant late-nineteenth-century developments in the formulas of social melodrama. One consisted of attempts to revitalize the traditions by expressing them in more modern terms. An example is what James Hart calls the "Gates Ajar" school in which writers tried to integrate the traditional view of divine providence and the conception of heaven and hell with contemporary social values. Even more striking was a transformation of the virtuous Christian heroine by writers like Augusta Jane Evans, whose *Beulah* (1859) and *St. Elmo* (1867) were runaway best-sellers in the 1860s and early 1870s. In these stories, the heroine retained her Christian purity and faith, but, in contrast to the early nineteenth-century image of a meek and submissive female, became a veritable tigress in the defense of her religion against aggressive and agnostic men.[16] The typical plot pattern of Miss Evans' novels restructured the traditional melodramatic triangle by setting a virtuous and dominant heroine against an aristocratic but weak male, who, converted to Christian faith by the heroine's indomitable force of will, was miraculously transformed into a noble but submissive hero. St. Elmo, for example, began as a sort of Byronic decadent, but under the avalanche of heroine Edna Earl's purity and faith was eventually converted into a pious minister and devoted husband. E. P. Roe, a best-seller in the 1870s and one of the last major social melodramatists in the earlier tradition, updated his works by giving a greater topicality to his treatment of the contemporary social scene and by inverting the traditional moral roles of men and women. In his popular *Barriers Burned Away* (1872) the heroine, initially a high-living wealthy young lady, was eventually converted to virtue and purity by her love for the noble young hero. This happy event was brought about by the great conflagration of the Chicago fire.

A second major development was the emergence of new forms of melodramatic action, and of new ways of treating society. Most important, social change and upheaval became a primary background for melodramatic action. The earlier melodrama, however much it may have advocated some kind of social reform such as the abolition of slavery in *Uncle Tom's Cabin*, tended to portray society within the story as static. Individuals rose and fell, but society went on in much the same way. This is true of the earlier novels of Dickens as it is of mid-nineteenth-century American social melo-dramas like those of Mrs. Southworth. For Dickens, a growing sense of social upheaval meant that his later novels would become less melodramatic, and increasingly dominated by a dark sense of social chaos. Later melodramatists concerned with social change developed stories in which the protagonist was morally regenerated by a new and better understanding of what was happening to society. By the end of the ninteenth century, this had become one of the standard patterns of social melodrama. The protagonist, faced with a rapidly changing society, finds his traditional religious and moral orthodoxy inadequate and finally wins through to a better relationship to the world around him. Late nineteenth- and early twentieth-century social melodramas are full of ministers who are converted from a narrow ortho-doxy to a new and more humane social gospel, of capitalists who recognize the narrow materialism of their goals and discover a new fullness of spirit in service to mankind, of tired and jaded aristocrats who sense the emptiness and futility of their lives and go west to become part of a new life.

The best-selling social melodramatists of the early twentieth century— writers like Harold Bell Wright and Winston Churchill—evolved a new melodramatic synthesis to deal with tensions between the traditional Chris-tian moral universe and the new sense of social change. Their works are a mélange of the leading social and philosophical currents of the time— Spencerian Social Darwinism, the social gospel, political reformism and progressivism, the institutional church, the new sociology of environmen-talism, even, in some writers, the intellectual and philosophical racism of the period—all stated in such a way that they can be ultimately harmonized with a more socially oriented Christianity. For these writers the traditional orthodoxies of Christian thought had to be revitalized to correspond with new realities, but they see no fundamental conflict between a religious view of the world and the new social currents. Indeed, their stories show that a regenerated religious perspective can bring about a meaningful understanding of social change. Thus Harold Bell Wright wrote in his enormously popular *Shepherd of the Hills* (1907) about a minister who had lost touch with his faith in the increasing swirl of materialism and change that characterized his fashionable urban world. His quest for regeneration takes him to the primitive Ozarks, where he learns to reaffirm his faith in a newly virile and passionate manner, freed from the sterile orthodoxies of the past. Winston Churchill's *The Inside of the Cup* (1913) told the same basic story, except that his ambivalent minister found a vital social gospel among the urban poor who lived on the margins of his upper-class parish. With his newfound strength, Churchill's John Hodder is able to confront his wealthy congregation with their selfishness and materialism while winning the love of the rebellious daughter of the city's wealthiest capitalist. In the social melodramas of the early twentieth century, the traditional plot of the embattled virgin and the lascivious seducer was typically replaced by the story of the young man or woman who recognizes the failure of success and seeks a higher ideal than material wealth and power. The aristocratic seducer was transformed into the figure of the selfish capitalist or the corrupt political boss who seeks to persuade the protagonist to give up the quest for a more humane religion and a higher concept of service to suffering mankind. The extent to which the novels of Wright and Churchill remained within the orbit of melodrama is evident by comparison with such contemporaries as Stephen Crane, Frank Norris, and Theodore Dreiser, in whose works there is no possible resolution between the traditions of Christianity and the new naturalistic determinism. Even William Dean Howells, close as he sometimes comes to social melodrama in his attempts to balance an increasingly critical view of contemporary society with a due representation of "the smiling aspects of life," cannot quite bring himself to the melodramatic reaffirmation of a benevolent moral order. For example, his novel *The Minister's Charge* (1887) deals like Wright's *Shepherd of the Hills* and Churchill's *The Inside of the Cup* with a minister's attempt to revitalize his faith by a concern for human suffering in the midst of social change, but ends up in a much more ambiguous sense of genteel futility. One might also compare Howells's *A Hazard of New Fortunes* (1890) with Wright's *Winning of Barbara Worth* (1911) as stories about the failure of capitalistic selfishness. Where Howells's Dryfoos comes to recognize an irreconcilable conflict between the power of wealth and his human needs, Wright's Jefferson Worth establishes a higher harmony between the service of God and Mammon in the gospel of the social ministry of capital.

Just as the melodramatists of the early twentieth century found ways of dramatizing the harmony between social change and Christian tradition in a vision of Christian progressivism, they also worked out new patterns for resolving the tensions created by changing conceptions of the feminine character and of relations between the sexes. In place of the traditional melodramatic incarnation of feminine purity and submissiveness, the social melodramatists of the later nineteenth century gradually evolved a morally sympathetic portrait of the new woman. While the divorcée, the promiscuous, and the prostitute remained beyond the pale and were still usually allocated an unfortunate fate, they were often treated with considerable sympathy and understanding and sometimes were even allowed to take a role as secondary heroine until their tragic fate caught up with them. The official heroine, though still usually characterized by sexual purity, gradually lost much of her submissiveness and was even granted a certain degree of wildness. One of the most popular heroines of the early twentieth century, Wright's Barbara Worth, was a vigorous horsewoman and the companion of rugged cowboys and railroad workers. Much of the drama of her romance with the upper-class eastern engineer Willard Holmes derived from the conflict between his love for her and his feeling that she was not quite respectable enough to bring home to his snobbish family, a conflict that was easily overcome when he recognized her true purity and moral worth as well as her vigor and courage. Winston Churchill went even further in the treatment of independent and self-reliant heroines. Some of his leading women were in their early thirties and had already achieved a degree of professional accomplishment before they met and fell in love with their future husbands.

Despite the greater vigor and force of the new melodramatic heroine and an increasing physicality and sensuality in her makeup, the social melodramatists of the early twentieth century strove mightily to balance these new feminine qualities with a residue of the purity and gentility so important to the traditional feminine ideal. In *Shepherd of the Hills*, Wright drew a much-loved portrait of Sammy Lane, the wild mountain girl, who, underneath her primitive and passionate exterior, has a deep desire to be a cultivated Christian lady. Before her marriage she achieves this goal under the Shepherd's tutelage. Even the free and easy Barbara Worth has a fundamental substructure of instinctive feminine modesty. Her first meeting with the man she will eventually marry goes like this:

> It was no flimsy, two-fingered ceremony, but a whole-hearted, whole-handed grip that made the man's blood move more quickly. Unconsciously, as he felt the warm strength in the touch of the girl's hand, he leaned towards her with quick eagerness. And Barbara, who was looking straight into his face with the open frankness of one man to another, started and drew back a little, turning her head aside.[17]

Zane Grey, who would carry the early twentieth-century tradition of social melodrama forward into the twenties and thirties, elaborated still further on this combination of wildness and femininity in his heroines. For example, in his *Code of the West* (1934) the heroine is a flapper from the East who is visiting her married sister in the Tonto Basin in Arizona. Her high jinks and flirtations nearly lead to tragedy until she falls deeply in love with a young westerner and changes her attitudes toward life. Yet her original wildness is only sublimated into a new and more proper form, for in the novel's climactic scene this regenerated flapper faces down the villain and so shames him that he is forced to leave the territory. In general, the melodramatic heroine of the early twentieth century was clearly evolving in the direction of what would become a favorite feminine stereotype in the novels and films of the thirties and forties: what has been labeled the "good-bad girl," a heroine who appears at the beginning of the story to be wild and even immoral but who is eventually revealed to be a truly chaste and loving woman.

In addition to its emphasis on social change, a new heroine, and the regeneration of traditional values, the early twentieth-century social melodrama explored a variety of new subjects, the most important of which were various forms of sensational crime and scandals, particularly among the upper classes, as well as the material that had been made available through the evolution of the western formula. Wister, Emerson Hough, and Zane Grey made a great success out of the western formula in the early twentieth century by giving it some important elements of social melodrama such as the multiple plot, the complex analysis of society, and an elaborate treatment of the romance between hero and heroine, qualities that were not an indispensable part of the western formula but, in this period, helped writers like Wright and Grey to achieve best-seller status. The melodramatic vision of the early twentieth century with its concern for the regeneration of traditions in the midst of a changing conception of society and sexuality was made to order for the western setting. Here it seemed appropriate that the heroine should be a more vigorous and openly aggressive type than the traditional heroine. Similarly, the portrayal of a jaded, overly genteel easterner revitalized into true manliness (or womanliness) by an encounter with the simpler and more "natural" society of the West was one effective way of dramatizing the theme of regeneration.

To sum up, the prevailing formula of social melodrama in the late nineteenth and early twentieth centuries was based on the representation of social and moral regeneration. Whether fairly conservative and orthodox in inclination like Harold Bell Wright or liberal like Winston Churchill, the social melodramatists portrayed a society that had moved from the proper course and needed to rediscover what was most important about life. In this society religion had become a sterile orthodoxy. The leading citizens had lost their humanity in the pursuit of wealth and power. Yet, underneath it all, there was an evolutionary force working to bring about a truer spirituality and a more direct and loving relationship between people. Those who discovered and aligned themselves with this deeper force were sure to become spiritually regenerated and find happiness. As a dramatization of cultural ideologies, this formula can be interpreted as a way of resolving the conflict between social and religious traditions and the new intellectual and social currents of the later nineteenth century. The social melodramas of Wright, Churchill, and many of their contemporaries were expressions in fictional form of some of the same impulses behind the more popular forms of the social gospel and the moralistic aspects of Progressive reformism. Indeed, the same emphasis on the rediscovery and revitalization of Christian ideals that we find in the social melodramas of this period is also central in the enormously popular religious best-seller of 1897, Charles Sheldon's *In His Steps*, which told the story of a group of people who sought to transcend the sterility and hypocrisy of the traditional Christian orthodoxies by applying basic Christian principles to modern social life. This was essentially the moral vision of the leading social melodramatists of the early nineteenth century: the affirmation of a new and vital social Christianity based on the spirit of love and service rather than on submission to God's will. The new vision also attempted to resolve increasing anxieties and ambiguities about the moral nature and proper social role of women by creating an active and even aggressive heroine who discovered her rightful place in a passionate and deep attachment to a morally revitalized and loving man.

To discuss the complex developments of social melodrama in the twentieth century even in the most general terms is beyond my present intention. Instead, to complete this tentative analysis of the changing formulas of social melodrama, I will consider the social melodramas of a group of writers who have dominated the best-seller lists since the mid-1960s: Irving Wallace, Harold Robbins, Arthur Hailey, and Jacqueline Susann. These writers are clearly in the tradition of social melodrama, since they typically combine a detailed and often critical analysis of contemporary society with a melodramatic plot full of surprise and suspense that brings a group of characters through a series of trials and tribulations to their appropriate rewards. Indeed, the continuity between these writers and such earlier social melodramatists as Winston Churchill and even Charles Dickens goes beyond the general synthesis of social realism and melodramatic action to specific types of melodramatic plot. Jacqueline Susann's most recent novel *Once Is Not Enough* (1973) is a classic tragic melodrama in modern dress where a heroine is "seduced" (i.e., unable to make a proper sexual adjustment because of a perverse love for her father) and goes to a lingering degradation and death, a mid-twentieth-century Charlotte Temple or Clarissa Harlowe. Irving Wallace specializes in the regeneration plot in which a hero is revitalized by new moral discoveries. Harold Robbins tends to write stories of the failure of success. His central characters pursue the phantoms of wealth and power only to discover that true fulfillment can only come through love, loyalty, and compassion. Arthur Hailey usually combines a number of these basic melodramatic plots in multiple subplots growing out of the various characters involved in the institutions his novels center upon: a hotel, an airport, a large automobile corporation.

Despite these formulaic continuities, the social melodrama of the 1960s depends upon a very different conception of the moral universe than its early twentieth-century predecessors. First of all, the religious concerns so prominent in earlier periods are almost totally absent from the contemporary best-selling blockbuster. Neither the traditional vision of God's providence nor the early twentiety-century's sense of harmony between the evolution of society and the manifestation of God's will is embodied in the current formulas. God seems to have been largely banished from the world of Robbins, Wallace, and their colleagues. This does not mean that these writers have no conception of a moral order. Melodrama would be impossible without some vision of poetic justice shaping the development of the story. But for the contemporary melodramatist, the assumption that faith in God is the ultimate test of virtue and the means by which worldly problems can be resolved is no longer tenable. Indeed, the central problem that these writers dramatize over and over again is whether modern secular man is doomed to a life without transcendent meaning or whether there is something on the human level that can offer the same sense of ultimate significance as the conception of God's providence gave to earlier generations. One of the most interesting recent social melodramas, Irving Wallace's *The Word* (1972), offered a fairly complex exploration of the meaning of religion in the modern world by confronting a representative group of modern men and women with a new gospel supposedly written by a brother of Christ. Some choose only to exploit the new gospel as a highly profitable publishing enterprise, but many people's lives are transformed by the way in which the new gospel seemingly substantiates both the historicity and the divinity of Christ. The protagonist encounters inconsistencies and anachronisms that lead him to a bitter old man who claims to have forged the document for revenge upon the church. Mysteriously, the old man dies in an accident—possibly murdered by the publishing syndicate to protect their profits—before he can give the protagonist definitive proofs of the forgery. The protagonist, a successful but frustrated public relations man who has been commissioned to direct the publicity for the new gospel, must finally decide whether to seek the truth about the forgery or to accept the fact that belief in the new gospel—even if false—has benefited many people. That he chooses in the end to commit himself to the hard road of truth is both a sign of his personal regeneration and of the ultimate inadequacy of unquestioning religious faith as a basic principle of moral order.

The Word has an unusual philosophical depth and articulateness as well as a compelling melodramatic plot. It may be Wallace's best work to the present time and the outstanding example of contemporary social melodrama. The novel illustrates the quest for order that dominates the contemporary formula: a search for transcendent significance in a secular, naturalistic age when religious faith has lost its power to inspire a basic belief in the benevolence of the world order and has come to seem only a complex psychological phenomenon. In order to fulfill the archetype of melodrama with its basic affirmation of moral significance and order in the universe, the contemporary social melodramatist has had to turn to other sources of transcendence. The most important area he looks to is that of human relations and sexuality.

It has been often observed of the writings of Wallace, Robbins, Susann, et al., that they exemplify a contemporary obsession with sexuality, and this is true. Sexual relationships of all sorts constitute the primary narrative interest in their works to the degree that one is partly constrained to agree with the critics who see such novels as *The Love Machine* (1969), *The Carpetbaggers* (1961), and *The Seven Minutes* (1969) as elaborate exercises in soft-core pornography.[18] Certainly, there is a connection between the emphasis on sexuality in these contemporary social melodramas and the flourishing in the sixties and seventies of many different kinds of pornography. Yet there is a great difference between a straight work of pornography with its primary purpose of sexual excitement and the novels of Wallace, Susann, Robbins, and Hailey where sexuality is part of a larger moral context. The contemporary social melodramatists seek to integrate new ideas of sexual liberation with traditional conceptions of romantic love and monogamy. The ideal of a full and satisfying sexuality based on a deep and lasting romantic relationship is one moral cornerstone of the new melodramatic vision. Those characters who seek and achieve this kind of experience are contemporary analogues of the pure young women and virtuous heroes who found happiness in Christian piety and faith. But those who exploit sexuality as a means to power, who deny sexual fulfillment to others, or who fail to understand the necessary relationship between sex and love are doomed to failure as contemporary incarnations of the impure heroine who yields to seductive temptation, or as melodramatic villains. In this moral universe, purity may be a form of repression, but promiscuity is still the primrose path to unhappiness. The truly virtuous are those who, like the heroine of *The Seven Minutes*, realize that happiness lies in a synthesis of full sexuality and deep love. Those who fail to find the fullness of human love and sexuality either because they are repressed or because they seek for false goals like fame, wealth, and power are on their way to "The Valley of the Dolls."

The union of romantic love and sexuality is one source of transcendent moral order in the contemporary social melodrama. The other is a concept of true success and integrity set against the evils of the unrestrained pursuit of wealth and power in the glamorous and exciting world of modern business, advertising, and the media. The novels of Wallace, Robbins, Hailey, and Susann teem with men and women who have achieved a brilliant success in glamorous careers but have not found that their accomplishment is either morally satisfying or responsive to their real human needs. Robin Stone, the hero of Susann's *The Love Machine*, rises to the top of the television industry and has innumerable casual affairs, but he does not find happiness until he gives up his position of power to become a writer and accepts his need for a woman who truly loves him. Essentially the same thing is true of the heroes of Robbins's *The Carpetbaggers* and *The Adventurers*. The lawyer protagonist of Wallace's *The Seven Minutes* is tempted by the offer of a lucrative corporate legal post and the empty and repressive sexual beauty of the tycoon's daughter, but his courageous defense of a controversial erotic novel makes him realize that he is on the path to degradation:

For Barrett [the novel] had exposed to him the ugly truth that in [the tycoon's daughter] he had sought not love but success, and the uglier truth that his goals in life were empty and that by achieving them he would find nothing that could sustain a lifetime of remaining years.[19]

True success, as opposed to the pursuit of wealth and power for their own sake, is marked by personal integrity, satisfying human relationships, and the opportunity to be of service to others. It also usually involves a fulfilling romantic sexual relationship with a loving partner. In the world of the contemporary social melodrama, those who come to realize the meaning of true success and seek it wholeheartedly usually become regenerated and their lives take on a new significance and meaning. The central antagonist, contemporary analogue to the traditional melodramatic villain, is usually not a person but the soulless modern corporation that seduces the protagonist with false ambitions and then turns him into an ulcer-ridden manipulator without the capacity for human feeling, until he has the good fortune to realize the error of his ways and turn toward a true ideal of success. No doubt the public for the contemporary melodrama takes some pleasure in vicarious participation in the protagonist's wheeling and dealing, but it has the additional satisfaction of discovering that only by a return to the basic human values of romantic love and true success that are available to everyone can the protagonist finally gain happiness.

In many ways this contemporary parable of regeneration is similar to the quest for a new sense of morality in the early twentieth-century social melodramas of Harold Bell Wright and Winston Churchill without the latter's attempt to integrate the new ideals with a revitalized sense of religious meaning. But from another point of view the novels of Robbins, Wallace, and Susann might be seen as melodramatic transformations of the naturalistic muckraking novel, as attempts to domesticate or conventionalize the naturalistic view of social, economic, and sexual determinism by leaving out its pessimistic vision and its tendency toward a radical critique of the inequities and contradictions of "the system." In general, the contemporary social melodrama arrives at its vision of a meaningful moral order by resolving the conflict between secular naturalism and the traditional faith in transcendent verities by dramatizing the process through which protagonists arrive at regeneration and happiness by discovering ultimate significance in a totally fulfilling love and a true ideal of success, both of which are viewed as possible despite the disorder, unhappiness, and corruption of modern American society. Because writers like Wallace, Robbins, Susann, and Hailey can provide this assurance and reaffirm this ultimate sense of moral order and significance in the context of what appears to be a realistic portrayal of society with all its injustices and frustrations, its glittering temptations and overwhelming constellations of wealth, power, and corruption, they have been able to hold the high but probably ephemeral place on the best-seller lists that effective social melodramatists have been able to command since the beginning of the nineteenth century.

Looking back over the evolution of the best-selling social melodrama, it appears that the type gradually shifts its formulas as each generation seeks its own means of resolving the tension between changing perceptions of the social scene and the moral ideals that define what is right and significant in life. Thus, in the mid-nineteenth century the formula of social melodrama dramatized the operation of God's providence as the primary means through which the virtuous found happiness and the evil were punished. By the beginning of the twentieth century, a new formula of social melodrama had developed emphasizing the protagonist's discovery of a revitalized Christianity that could encompass the drastic social changes threatening the religious and moral tradition. Finally, in the mid-twentieth century, the prevailing formula of social melodrama has turned away from religion to seek for other means of affirming transcendent moral truths in a secular, naturalistic world.

Despite these considerable changes in the formulas of social melodrama, there are certain basic continuities of theme and structure such as the emphasis on romantic love as an ultimate value, the defense of monogamous, family-oriented relationships between men and women, and the attempt to define true and false conceptions of success and status. These themes, which seem to prevail through the whole period of the nineteenth and twentieth century, suggest, I think, that social melodrama is primarily a genre of the well-established middle class for whom these particular values are of most importance. If this speculation is correct, then the essential social-psychological dynamic of social melodrama is one of continually integrating new social circumstances and ideas to the developing middle-class sense of social value. Perhaps, then, the social melodrama has been one of the means by which the American and English middle classes have so successfully adjusted themselves to the drastic social and cultural changes of the last century and a half. If so, it will be interesting to see how the formulas of social melodrama evolve to confront the enormous changes that will face our society in the future.

Irving Wallace

Irving Wallace has often expressed resentment at being called a formula writer who writes best-sellers according to some guaranteed recipe. In fact, he has recently published a book about his writing of *The Prize* in part to show how nonformulaic the process of creation was in this case. If we were not prepared to believe his own assertions, this book, *The Writing of One Novel* (1968), certainly shows that Wallace writes about things that concern him deeply, grow out of his own experience, and reflect the most energetic and careful research. Indeed, Wallace describes several instances where, in his handling of both particular episodes and the book's overall plot, he struggled to transcend conventionally melodramatic situations that, however successful in moving the emotions of the public, would have compromised, in his opinion, the seriousness and coherence of the story he wished to tell. In general, I see no reason to doubt Wallace's assertion that he is not a hack commercial writer for whom popularity and success are the only criteria: I accept his insistence that he does not consciously follow a formula, and that he writes as well as he can about things that are deeply important to him.

Nevertheless, it is not surprising that many critics consider him a formulaic writer, not only because of his great popular success, but because of the characteristics of his novels. Most of his highly successful works, such as *The Chapman Report*, *The Prize*, *The Seven Minutes*, *The Man*, and *The Word*, have a similarity of pattern far greater than a comparable series of novels by those writers who are commonly treated by intellectuals and academic critics as major authors, for instance, the writers discussed by Tony Tanner in his survey of contemporary American literature, *City of Words*, a book in which, rightly or wrongly, the name of Irving Wallace is not mentioned.

This pattern can be defined as follows. As a consequence of some major public event (e.g., the awarding of the Nobel Prize, a summit conference, a major trial, the publication of a new gospel) an oddly assorted group of people are brought together and faced with circumstances that bring about important crises of decision and action in their personal lives as well as in relation to the public event that is the occasion for the story. The cast of characters usually includes a protagonist whose life has been characterized by initial success followed by an increasing sense of failure and frustration. This protagonist undergoes a major regeneration as a consequence of the actions and decisions he takes in the course of the novel and this regeneration is usually accompanied by a new and better sort of success. Generally, the protagonist has experienced an unsuccessful marriage or series of affairs and has come to think himself incapable of the responsibilities and involvements of a serious love relationship. Part of his regeneration comes from the gradual development of such a relationship in the course of the story. The redemptive power of true love often works both ways, for the heroine has frequently developed some barrier to full sexuality that the hero, stirred to new life by the excitement of the action, must help her to overcome. A number of minor characters are brought into contact with the protagonist and the heroine, and they too usually find a solution to their problems, though generally a less satisfactory and fulfilling one than the protagonist.

Beneath the surface of the public event there generally lurks some kind of plot that generates a sequence of mysterious puzzles for the protagonist and his new associates to investigate and often poses serious physical danger to the protagonist. His facing of this threat is a climactic moment in his renewed commitment to life. The plot also necessitates the presence of one or more villain figures, usually characterized as ruthless men whose ambition for power and domination over others has warped their feeling for individual human beings and undermined their basic integrity. Two favorite villain figures are the great tycoon and the ambitious politician, characters whose total commitment to wealth and power contrasts with the protagonist's ultimate realization of the importance of human relations. Nevertheless, it is usually the protagonist's successful exposure or destruction of the plot that saves the world from the threat of war or tyranny.

This pattern makes possible the happy interplay of two dominant strands of reader interest, the same that have always constituted the fabric of social melodrama. First, Wallace gives us all kinds of fascinating inside information about the workings of major social institutions. He is a fanatically careful and energetic researcher and generally manages to bring together with great accuracy and liveliness a background mosaic that resembles in many ways the pattern of information that characterizes the newspaper: current news, background analyses, celebrity biography, travel tips, inside dope columns, and advice on manners and morals. In support of this interest, many of his fictional characters, like those of Hailey, Robbins, and Susann, suggestively echo the lives and characters of well-known celebrities.

The second major source of interest derives from the structure of the story itself. Because of the large number and variety of characters and the melodramatic nature of the episodes, Wallace's novels offer basic narrative interests that run the gamut of reader satisfactions. For those who enjoy adventure, there are moments of danger, which the protagonist and his friends heroically face and overcome; for mystery fans, there is the satisfaction of a hidden plot that is gradually uncovered in the course of the action; for aficionados of romance, there is the story of deepening love between the protagonist and the heroine. Finally, these different narrative segments are pulled together with a mass of background information into a unified and relatively coherent whole by the overarching pattern of poetic justice: a proper and satisfying distribution of fates. The protagonist is regenerated and restored to life, discovering at last the meaning he has been searching for. The other persons who come together in the course of the story gain their appropriate rewards and punishments. The bad secret is brought to light. The other sympathetic characters arrive at meaningful, if more limited, solutions to their problems. A potentially dangerous international crisis is averted, a socially beneficial project is accomplished, and certain conventional faiths or pieties are affirmed. The pattern of interrelated actions reveals a meaningful moral order, thus fulfilling the archetype of melodrama.

Thus Irving Wallace is a best-selling author because he has been able to develop an effective fictional pattern that reformulates a traditional popular literary genre—that of social melodrama—in a way that is responsive to central themes of concern for the contemporary public. To say that Wallace is a formulaic writer in this sense is not to say that he is a commercial hack, or that he lacks sincerity or originality, or that his work lacks artistic value. Every writer depends on conventions to some extent, and the writer who becomes especially popular in his own time is more than likely to have a greater relationship to generally accepted attitudes and conventions than most.

One of the most important traditional functions of the poet was to express the general sense of what is right, to be spokesman for the common wisdom about life. The twentieth-century separation between elite and popular culture tends to divide those serious writers who seek a unique excellence from those artists of the marketplace who necessarily depend to a large extent on the formulaic and the conventional. The modernist movement in all the arts has placed such emphasis on the uniqueness of anything worthy of being called serious art that few of our greatest writers are widely read or understood by the great mass of their countrymen, let alone conceived of as important spokesmen for their values. As Northrop Frye puts it,

> ... in the twentieth century an important and significant writer may be reactionary or superstitious: the one thing apparently that he cannot be is a spokesman of ordinary social values. The popular poems of our day are usually poems of explicit statement, continuing the sententious tradition; but such poems seem as a rule to be out of touch with the real poetic idioms of their times.[20]

Of course, we easily overstate the extent to which the greatest writers have ever been spokesmen for their own times. The traditional proposition that the greatest artists are ultimately known by transcending their times surely carries a large measure of truth and should make us pause before we analyze the current situation of the serious artist as a sad decline from some golden age when the great writer was the legislator for all mankind. Nevertheless, to effectively and imaginatively speak the common wisdom of one's times, while perhaps not the artist's highest obligation, is an important cultural function. In our day, it has become, in particular, the province of the popular comedian and the social melodramatist. Some understanding of the common sense of what is right is an integral aspect of the melodramatist's art, for he cannot achieve the archetypal pattern of melodrama without constructing a story in which his characters' fates bear out his audience's sense of a rightly ordered universe. Our judgment of the artistic merits of a melodramatist is bound up with our feeling about the extent to which his vision of the moral order of the world bears out the best potentials of the conventional moral wisdom of his time. Good melodrama is, as we have seen, an ephemeral art because the common moral sense of a particular culture at a particular time is not universal and tends to change with each generation. Yet there are writers and individual works that deserve to survive and sometimes do, because later generations find that however much they may be limited by the moral vision and artistic conventions of an earlier period, they seem to reflect the common wisdom in a particularly rich manner. Today we cherish *Moby-Dick* and *The Scarlet Letter* as works whose artistry and moral vision transcend their period and speak directly to us. But we also read *Uncle Tom's Cabin*, in spite of its melodramatic excesses and religious machinery, because it shows us some of the real depths and strengths as well as the limitations of mid-nineteenth-century American beliefs and attitudes.

In considering the art of Irving Wallace, therefore, we must analyze how his melodramatic structures reflect the common sentiments of our time and decide whether he uses these sentiments to manipulate our feelings or to speak imaginatively to his audience in an attempt to enrich its understanding of the implications of our conventional wisdom.

The treatment of sex in the contemporary social melodrama reflects one basic current conflict in attitudes. The traditional view of sex can still be summed up in the proposition that sex without love is ultimately perverse and unsatisfactory and that marriage is the final goal of love. According to the conventional wisdom, sexual relationships that are not based on love with the implication of monogamy cannot lead to happiness. And yet, this traditional moralistic vision coexists with a new sexual ideology which holds that sexual satisfaction is an end in itself. While this view is held more intensely by the younger generation, it has become very influential among the middle-aged as well. In fact, the extent to which sexual liberation has become an article of faith for the younger generation must be at least in part a reflection of implicit, if not explicit, parental acceptance. While few people probably manage to combine monogamy with complete sexual satisfaction, it is one of the functions of the common wisdom to reconcile the irrecon-cilable. Therefore, we find in the contemporary blockbuster a strong tendency to generate situations in which the conflicting claims of full sexual satisfaction and monogamous relationships are finally resolved. One of the favorite gambits is to show us a character who explores without real satisfaction a wide variety of sexual experiences and discovers that he can find true happiness only in a sexually satisfying monogamous relationship. Or we see characters helped by love to overcome the sexual hang-ups that have prevented them from finding complete satisfaction in life.

The blockbuster generally comes to some sort of affirmation of this moral synthesis of sexuality, love, and monogamy, but our judgment of the artistic level of the work must depend on the quality of the process of exploration: how fully does the writer examine the problem of contemporary sexuality and how meaningful is the way in which he relates it to the common wisdom? Does his story invite us to take a more humane and compassionate view of the world within the limits of the common wisdom, or does he use our existing attitudes and confusion solely for the purpose of excitement and suspense without seriously questioning current sexual ideologies? These are, I think, the appropriate questions to ask about this aspect of the artistry of contemporary social melodrama.

From *The Chapman Report* to *The Fan Club*, sexuality has been a fundamental narrative concern for Irving Wallace. Unlike such fellow blockbusters as Harold Robbins, Jacqueline Susann, and Arthur Hailey,

Wallace's representation of the sexual mores of contemporary American culture has deepened and become more complex. *The Chapman Report* was, in many ways, cast in the mold of *Peyton Place* or *Valley of the Dolls*, in that it exploited our fascination with the hidden sexual secrets beneath the facade of respectability and success. The tantalizing cover squib on the paperback edition nicely sums up this aspect of the book:"... as the very proper ladies of Briarwood [sic] revealed the most intimate details of their marital secrets to the eminent Dr. Chapman and his distinguished staff of researchers they found themselves face to face with long-hidden emotions and thwarted desires...." The story itself develops the usual blockbuster propositions that everybody has a sexual hang-up and that the more successful, glamorous, and promiscuous a character is, the deeper his sexual frustration. The degree to which characters deviate from the norm of monogamy becomes something of an index of their unhappiness. Insofar as characters fail to achieve a fulfilling monogamous relationship they cannot become happy. But a good monagamous relationship also demands sexual satisfaction. The sympathetic protagonists Paul Radford and Kathleen Ballard not only discover this, but they experience it:

> Suddenly the remote identity was gone and she wished only to be blended into the oneness of him. That instant, fused by passion, she let go of something held so many years—let go her separateness—and joined him without reservation. Crying out, she gave herself totally, gasping words she had never spoken aloud.... The past had dissolved, and there was left the present she could trust, and so she abandoned herself fully to carnal love ... thank God, Paul forever, forever.[21]

Significantly, our last sight of Kathleen shows her happily ensconced in "her best maternity dress."[22]

This is, of course, the essence of melodrama, both in the intensity of its language and in its happy and total resolution for the sympathetic protagonists. Like other blockbusters such as Susann and Robbins, Wallace parades before our fascinated gaze a skillful selection of sexual excesses and perversities in such a way that the reader can enjoy a voyeuristic and vicarious indulgence in promiscuous or polymorphous sex, while being assured those who indulge in such practices are in actuality unhappy and unfulfilled. Our curiosity about sexual variation and the possiblity of greater indulgence is satisfied and the conventional equation of sex, love, and monogamy is ultimately affirmed by the development of the story. Thereby the blockbusters achieve two primary melodramatic satisfactions: we have the vicarious pleasure of playing at deviant behavior without having to give up or revise our existing moral universe—the principle of having your cake and eating it too; and we have the final satisfaction of seeing the complex ambiguities of the world gradually work out so that the characters' fates substantiate a conventional moral vision.

Most contemporary social melodramatists tend, I think, to cultivate these satisfactions as ends in themselves without seriously exploring the conflicts of value that underlie the conventional wisdom. Thus in a typical Robbins novel like *The Betsy*, the central character boffs his way from boudoir to boudoir only to be converted at the end to love and monogamy. Indeed, this particular book is strikingly casual in the way the hero and heroine are finally converted to appropriately romantic erotic behavior, for the heroine is introduced to us at the beginning of the novel as a nymphomaniacal racing freak who is obsessed with having intercourse to the sound of recorded racing cars. At the end of the novel, she is suddenly converted to romantic monogamy, so that she can turn off her hi-fi set and settle down. This curious version of the girl next door is pure Robbins; he presents it as event with no suggestion that there is anything odd about this pattern of development. I should imagine that in twenty years this sudden conversion to monogamous domesticity will seem as hilariously improbable as the sudden religious illuminations that commonly transformed characters in nineteenth-century melodramas.

For Wallace, however, the melodramatic affirmation of the conventional wisdom about sex is more than an end in itself. It is, instead, a framework for a serious and complex exploration of contemporary sexual values and mores. In *The Chapman Report*, for example, the story line gives full opportunity for the tantalizing representation of the sexual peculiarities of the middle-class ladies of The Briars. But it also enables Wallace to give a detailed exposition of contemporary knowledge about sexual behavior in a fictional context where the implications of the conflict between actual behavior and traditional moral attitudes can be dramatized. Though Paul Radford and Kathleen Ballard are the human center of the story, the conflict between Dr. Chapman, who represents the new attitude of scientific objectivity toward sexuality, and Dr. Jonas, who is the spokesman for the common wisdom, gives Wallace a means of dramatizing the contemporary tension between behavioristic and moralistic visions of sexuality.

The final resolution of *The Chapman Report* may seem, in contemporary terms, something of a cop-out, since Dr. Chapman's scientific zeal turns out to have a touch of melodramatic villainy about it, making Dr. Jonas's moral victory in gaining the hero's allegiance a little too easy. Nevertheless, *The Chapman Report* remains a highly effective modern "morality play," as Wallace calls it, about the struggle of modern Americans to accept a new awareness of the actuality of their sexual behavior without destroying the traditional moral patterns of their culture.

In several novels since *The Chapman Report*, Wallace has considerably expanded the range and complexity of his treatment of the contemporary conflict between traditional sexual morals, the new ideology of sexual liberation, and the actuality of sexual behavior and fantasy. In *The Seven Minutes*, for example, Wallace uses the occasion of an obscenity trial and the various intrigues that swirl around it as a means of representing the many ways in which people can exploit sexual fantasies and fears to fulfill their various ambitions. Luther Yerkes, the business tycoon, wishes to expand his political and economic power by propelling a local district attorney into national prominence, and he lights on the obscenity issue as a means of making his candidate well known. The district attorney, though sincerely and morally concerned about the spread of pornography, accepts the tycoon's support and increasingly finds himself willing to use any stratagem to win his case. The very author of the book under attack has hidden his identity for years in order to pursue a career in politics. The wealthy, beautiful fiancée of the young defense lawyer uses her sexuality not as an expression of love but as a means to power. The central characters involved in the obscenity trial are each confronted in a different way with a choice between confirming the truth about their own sexuality or continuing to affirm the accepted myths and fantasies that prevent them from having fulfilling sexual and romantic relationships. Even the young man who is the prosecution's chief witness against the book prefers being accused of rape and murder to admitting the truth that he is sexually impotent and therefore could not possibly have raped anyone. The predicament of the various individual characters exemplifies the problem that Wallace's imaginary erotic masterpiece poses for the culture as a whole: to what extent can men accept the full truth about their sexuality without destroying the moral order of their lives?

Wallace's ultimate answer to this dilemma is, as in the case of *The Chapman Report*, melodramatic. Mike Barrett, the young lawyer who becomes the attorney for the defense, is confronted with a choice of two women, Faye Osborn, his beautiful, wealthy fiancée, and Maggie Stewart. Despite her beauty, Faye is unable to fulfill herself sexually because the drive for power has largely negated her capacity for love:

> She had emerged from the fornication as untouched and unsullied as if she had been a spectator at a sex circus, the bystander, the observer, someone superior to the ridiculous, helpless, uncontrolled, panting male member who required indulgence in this function. As ever she had survived the filth and the beast to retain on her the tiara of civilized decency and ladyship.[23]

Needless to say, Faye reads *The Seven Minutes* and is shocked and disgusted by its eroticism. Maggie Stewart, however, is deeply moved and tells Mike Barrett:

> "I sometimes think maybe I could be like that. I mean, that I have it all locked inside me, and I could find myself opening up and giving someone, the right partner, all of me, everything of me, and, in turn, being able to accept and embrace the love given to me. I hope one day I can have my own seven minutes."[24]

There is little doubt which of these ladies is fated to end up with the protagonist, so that, when, at the end, hero and heroine overcome the circumstances that have separated them and fall into each other's arms, the essential harmony between sex, love, and marriage is dramatically affirmed.

On the way to this happy conclusion, *The Seven Minutes* anatomizes and criticizes a variety of social and individual hypocrisies and mythologies based on traditionally repressive attitudes toward sexuality. The novel's climax occurs when the distinguished Senator Brainbridge confesses dramatically in the courtroom that he is the real author of the erotic story being tried for obscenity, and that his novel was based on a youthful experience of pure sexual fulfillment with a young woman he was never able to marry because of his social ambitions and obligations. Through such dramatic instances, as well as in his treatment of the hypocritical power-seeking that underlies the prosecution of this erotic novel in the first place, Wallace explores conflicts and ambiguities in our culture's sexual attitudes that make the melodramatic resolution of the story more an ideal ending for a morality play than a common and readily attainable possibility of our experience.

Wallace's most recent novel, *The Fan Club* (1974), carries this exploration of the role of sexuality in contemporary society a step further, becoming almost an inverted melodrama. *The Fan Club* is a nightmarish morality play about sexual fantasy and its relationship to contemporary life. Like most of Wallace's novels, it narrates the adventures of a group of representative individuals brought together by some major public event, in this case the abduction and rape of a major Hollywood sex symbol, loosely based on Marilyn Monroe. Unlike Wallace's earlier novels where the protagonist group is sympathetic and undergoes a process of regeneration in the course of the action, most of the central characters of *The Fan Club* are destroyed when they attempt to turn their fantasies into reality. Despite its lurid and sensational aspects—a necessary condition of successful melodrama—the story is an effective framework within which Wallace can present an anatomy of contemporary sexual fantasies. The Fan Club itself consists of three typical American males—a mechanic who is sadistically bitter at his low status and uses his desperate assertion of masculinity as a compensation; an insurance salesman whose placid suburban existence has been haunted by a sense of increasing decline since the time when he was a college football star; and an older accountant who long ago gave up his chance at a legal career to support his wife and has always regretted his lost opportunities. Each of these men has in his own way translated his resentment and frustration at life into sexual fantasies that have come to focus on the movies and, in particular, the international sex symbol, Sharon Fields. Each man believes at the outset of the story that a sexual encounter with Sharon Fields could heal his pain and somehow make his life worth living. These men are galvanized into action when they accidentally meet a fourth character, Adam Malone, an unsuccessful writer and maniacal fan of Sharon Fields. Malone persuades the others that they can actually live out their fantasies. Together they plan and successfully carry out the abduction of the star.

But as the men begin to live out their pornographic fantasies by raping Sharon Fields, they only find themselves increasingly frustrated and anxious. Even after Sharon realizes that to save her life she must herself act out the female role in each man's private sexual dream, the Fan Club's happiness is short-lived. With the exception of Adam Malone, the poet and dreamer, the men gradually turn from fantasies of sex with Sharon Fields to visions of what they can do with the large sum of ransom money they decide to demand. This money now becomes the center of their intention, even though, at the beginning of their plot it was agreed that they would never seek a ransom. Wallace points out through the shifting motivations of the Fan Club the way in which contemporary sexual fantasies are not simply a desire for physical satisfaction or love but an expression of a need for power, for domination, even for destruction.[25] The Fan Club becomes an allegorical exploration of what Wallace evidently sees as a serious human problem in contemporary mass culture. Since the average man's life in modern America provides few enduring satisfactions, he turns, in compensation, to the exciting objects for sexual fantasy offered him by the mass media. But his imagined sexual possession of the object is not only a fantasy, but irrelevant to his real need for a sense of meaning and power in relation to his own life. These fantasies may be relatively harmless, but they always pose the danger that an increase in the level of frustration and humiliation will drive the average man to try to live out his fantasies. When this happens, violence and destruction are inevitable, for the attempt to embody these mass sexual fantasies in reality exposes the terrible gap between the dream and the actual world and releases an irrational anguish that inevitably leads to violence.

One measure of the seriousness and relative complexity of The Fan Club is the degree to which it resembles the apocalyptic vision of Nathanael West's The Day of the Locust, which is an even more nightmarish account of ordinary people driven through their fantasies about the stars into a frenzy of destructiveness. This comparison also brings out in another way the importance of Wallace's role as a spokesman for the common wisdom. West's vision is dark and unredeemed. The catastrophe of The Day of the Locust is total; it overwhelms the common wisdom by representing a society that has truly fallen into chaos. Let alone the ultimate security of melodrama, West does not even offer us the harsher consolation of tragedy, since there is little that is lost. Wallace, on the other hand, takes us to the brink of disaster, but then pulls us back. Reading The Fan Club is a far more ambiguous, unpleasant, and challenging experience than was the case with any of his earlier novels. Just one of the skillful ways in which Wallace tries to make us confront our own sexual fantasies is his use of the conventional structures of pornographic writing in a highly ironic fashion. A standard episode in many pornographic books details the rape of an unwilling woman who after her initial reluctance becomes not only a willing partner but an ecstatic sex machine. Wallace places this particular fantasy in the mind of the most brutal and unsympathetic member of the Fan Club and then dramatizes its inhumanity through his narrative of this character's disgusting rape of Sharon Fields. Even when Sharon tries to act out the pornographic role of sex slave, whatever titillation the reader may derive from the episode is largely deflated by an awareness that this is a desperate woman acting a part in fear of her life. Yet in the end the framework of melodrama is restored.

In the last part of the book, the Fan Club overreaches itself by demanding ransom money. This sets into operation a chain of circumstances through which the members of the Fan Club mete out morally appropriate punishments to each other, leaving their intended victim, the character who has increasingly won our moral sympathies, triumphant. Sharon Fields's survival is finally presented to us as the act of a "tough, surviving bitch" who nevertheless hides Adam Malone's involvement in her abduction from the police and enables him to escape after the other three members of the Fan Club have been destroyed. This is particularly curious in light of the fact that the whole plot was Adam's idea in the first place. Sharon's action is appropriate, however, and shows us that she is a worthy heroine in spite of her somewhat nasty past, because she senses something missing in her life and therefore has been authentically touched by Adam's lunatic and dangerous adoration. Sharon, herself, has had her moment of truth, her realization of the degree to which she has used her sexuality as a weapon for success and has therefore never been able to know a truly loving relationship. Sharon's release of Adam tells us that her harrowing experience has not destroyed her, but has perhaps opened up new human possibilities to her. Thus, good has come out of evil in the appropriate melodramatic manner, and this good involves an affirmation of the common wisdom of sex, love, and marriage.

The final scene of *The Fan Club* is considerably more ambiguous than the typical conclusion of Wallace's earlier novels. Adam Malone, founder of the Fan Club, returns to his room and his world of make-believe, "grateful to leave behind the painful, sick and violent world of reality and return once more to the euphoric and peaceful world of make-believe, where anything you want to happen happens, no more, no less, in that best of all possible worlds."[26] Yet Adam has barely settled back into this world before he begins to turn his attention to another sex symbol and to become excited over the possibility of beginning another Fan Club. This scene suggests that Wallace has become increasingly conscious of the problematic nature of the conventional wisdom about sexuality. In his earlier books, the major protagonists are shown in the process of overcoming their sexual hang-ups and fantasies and achieving fulfillment in an enduring love relationship. In *The Fan Club*, this ideal is affirmed as a principle of the world order, but no character is shown accomplishing it in reality. Our last glimpse of the novel's central protagonist leaves us with a sense of man's overpowering need for sexual fantasy. In effect, the melodramatic transformation has taken place, but remains incomplete and ambiguous.

Thus, in his latest work, Wallace seems to be using the structures and devices of melodrama at least in part to explore the limits of the genre. It will be most interesting to see whether he will continue along this line of development and, if so, whether he will be able to take his enormous reading public with him. In any case, this tendency in his work is, I think, another sign of the seriousness and complexity with which Wallace fills his role as spokesman for the common wisdom and explorer of the limits of formulaic moral fantasy.

Conclusion

I have attempted, in the preceding chapters, to sketch out how the concept of formula analysis can be used in gaining artistic, cultural, and historical insights into a wide range of popular creations. The method is, I believe, transferable to many different areas. One major limitation of this study is that in order to make possible a certain complexity and depth of discussion I have felt constrained to limit my analyses to a very few popular formulas— the classical detective story, the hard-boiled detective story, two different kinds of gangster saga, the western, and the best-selling social melodrama. Because of this limitation, I have not really attempted any sustained analysis of, for example, the various kinds of situation comedies that have formed such an important part of the offerings of film and television, the various kinds of romance ranging from gothic through true confessions to juvenile, the formulas dealing with sports and war, the ever popular soap operas, the related professional dramas with their doctors, lawyers, and teachers, the formulaic aspects of that large and complex area of literature that goes under the label of science-fiction and fantasy, or the superheroic adventure epics that still supply much of the matter for comic books, to say nothing of many other story formulas of contemporary popular culture. If our earlier speculations on this subject are correct, the archetypal patterns embodied in popular formulas are few, but the way in which these patterns are expressed in different cultural materials leads to a great diversity of particular formulas.

It is my hope that the method of analysis tentatively developed in this study will prove useful for further investigations in at least three different directions. First, others interested in the field of popular culture may be able to use some of the techniques suggested here to examine a much wider range of contemporary popular story formulas than I have been able to deal with. Second, it should be illuminating to extend the analysis of formulas backward in time in order to trace the evolution of individual formulas, as I have done with the western, as well as the rise and decline of different formulas in various periods and cultural epochs. The formulaic approach should also make possible some interesting comparisons between the popular stories of literate societies and the folktales of traditional oral cultures, for there are many points of similarity between the techniques of formula analysis and the methods of structural analysis developed by anthropologists and folklorists. Before the kind of formulaic analysis suggested here can be synthesized with the methods of contemporary structuralism in the tradition of Lévi-Strauss and the semiologists, a number of important theoretical comparisons need to be made. Personally, I am not yet sure whether the concept of formula I have suggested is basically congruent with the structuralist approach, or whether the differences between them are so fundamental as to preclude a possible synthesis. For the time being, this is a matter readers will have to determine for themselves.

Finally, though I have applied the concept of formula and its methods of analysis exclusively to the examination of fictional structures that can be seen as stories, a third possible development of the approach would be an exploration of its usefulness in the analysis of popular constructions that do not take the form of stories. I presume there are also formulas, analogous to those discussed in this study, that have developed in music and the visual arts and are important in the evolution of the popular arts in these areas. In addition, I suspect that there are also formulas in the nonfictional literary forms of popular culture such as news, documentaries, and popular history and philosphy. In the case of news, for example, there may well be certain basic patterns that have always been present in the news media of the last three hundred years, while at the same time these underlying archetypes have been clothed in a wide variety of specific cultural materials and concerns. If we could develop a clearer idea of the evolution of the formulas for news used by different epochs and societies we would probably have a better idea of how various historical publics have understood and perceived their worlds. It would also be fascinating to be able to compare the formulas of popular fiction with the formulas of news in a more systematic fashion in order to test the speculative analogies that are often drawn between historical events and the formulas of popular fiction as, for example, between the American approach to the Vietnam war and the mythos of the western.

Such remarks may suggest that I view the concept of formula as a universal tool for unlocking the secrets of culture. I trust that any reader who gains this impression will take it with a large dose of skepticism. There are many aspects of popular culture that cannot be effectively dealt with in this way. One is the problem of medium. Whether or not one accepts the full panoply of McLuhanism, it seems clear that there are significant differences between such media as the printed book, the film, and television, and that these differences are artistic—in the sense that each medium has its own range of creative potentialities; psychological—in that media have different ranges of conceptual and perceptual implications; and social—in that media are elements in complex cultural networks that interact with both artistic and psychological dimensions. The western story *Shane* is not exactly the same in a novel as it is in a movie; there are even significant differences between the movie version of *Shane* as seen in a theater and on the television screen in one's home. The method of formula analysis has little to offer in the investigation of this kind of difference, because it must inevitably focus on that which is common to creations in these different media, the basic story patterns. The reader may have noticed that in discussing, say, detective stories or gangster sagas I made little attempt to distinguish between novels, films, or television programs. Of course, it is possible to apply the method of formula analysis to a particular medium and to seek to distinguish the formulas characteristic of that medium, as Horace Newcomb has done in his recent book on television. But this approach cannot isolate the unique characteristics of a medium unless it can be demonstrated that other media employ distinctively different formulaic patterns. To the extent that one can discover different formulas in different media, or different ways of handling the same formulas, the method may turn out to have some use in the study of media impact and cultural functions, but this remains to be seen.

Personally, I think that the most disappointing aspect of the present study is my inability to convincingly substantiate many of the speculations I have offered concerning the cultural significance of the different formulas I have discussed. In particular, there is a lack of solid data about audiences for the various formulas. To make a convincing case that our formulations of attitudes and concerns derived from the analysis of story structures are indeed characteristic of the people who enjoy these stories, we will need to have a good deal more information about who the users of different formulas are. It is my hope that the classification of formulas and the development of possible interpretations on the basis of structural analyses will provide researchers with a more sophisticated set of ideas and questions for the investigation of audiences and their attitudes. Once we have arrived at a tentative definition of the major formulas used by a culture, we can determine which subgroups of that culture constitute the primary audiences for those formulas. Our interpretive hypotheses can then be investigated both by direct questioning of the audiences and by examining their social and psychological characteristics. In this way the story formulas preferred by different groups can be compared and related to differential group characteristics. Through such inquiries, which combine the structural analysis of formulaic works with careful investigation of the conscious attitudes and social characteristics of the audiences for different formulas, we should be able to arrive at a better understanding of the cultural function of story formulas as well as new insights into differing patterns of attitude and feeling within the culture under investigation. Formula study, then, has the potential of providing a framework for cooperative inquiries by humanists and social scientists, with the different disciplines all using their own methods to develop analytical data necessary to the inquiry. In effect, the humanists can provide structural definitions and interpretations that can in turn be treated by sociologists to establish audience classifications; in turn, empirical studies should lead to a refining and a redefinition of the different formulas until the structural definitions and interpretations are substantiated by empirical research. Through this process of inquiry I believe we will eventually arrive at a much fuller understanding of the complex relation between a culture's story formulas and other aspects of individual and social behavior.

As it stands, my study seems to me more solidly grounded with respect to the aesthetic analysis of popular formula literature. At the outset my chief concern was to discover a way in which we could make persuasive cultural interpretations of those popular story formulas that seem so fundamental a part of our contemporary culture. It turned out that I could only begin to formulate a line of inquiry that, with the cooperation of empirical researchers and historians, might eventually lead to a better understanding of the cultural significance of popular formulas. But as I proceeded in this effort certain artistic implications arising from the consideration of formulaic story structures came up that gave me a new perspective on a number of interpretive and evaluative questions. When I began my study of popular genres, I assumed that popular literature was simply an inferior form of high art; that is, I viewed it as art for lowbrows or middlebrows, or as Abraham Kaplan puts it, as an immature form of art. As my thinking on this subject has developed, I have come increasingly to feel that it is important to stress that there are different kinds of artistry rather than a single standard in terms of which all fictional creations should be judged. Our age places a particularly high value on innovation and originality, to the extent that we tend to judge our most strikingly inventive writers and artists as the most significant creators of the age. But an examination of formulaic art also suggests that there is an artistry based on convention and standardization whose significance is not simply a reflection of the inferior training and lower imaginative capacity of a mass audience. Each conventional formula has a wide range of artistic potential, and it has come to seem mistaken to automatically relegate a work to an inferior artistic status on the ground that it is a detective story or a western. It seems not unlikely to me that future generations may well view certain writers of detective stories—my own predictions would be Dashiell Hammett, Ross Macdonald, Georges Simenon, and possibly Raymond Chandler—as among the major artists of our age, yet each of these writers chose to work within the narrow limits and conventional structures of the detective story formula. To effectively interpret and evaluate their work requires a clear conception of the set of conventions they chose to observe, for it is from the interplay between the detective formula and their own personal concerns that their artistry arises.

A second, more problematic, dimension of artistry arises when we consider the phenomenon of the work that achieves extraordinary popularity at the time of its creation, yet turns out to be largely ignored by later generations. The usual way of viewing such works is to conclude that they failed to meet the basic artistic test of universality. Their initial popularity is a kind of aesthetic mistake on the part of the audience that is deceived by topicality or by appeals to temporary and fleeting states of mind or mood. While one can hardly argue with the proposition that a work which does not last does not possess lasting artistic qualities, we may be closing ourselves off from an important aspect of human creation by refusing to recognize that just as there is an artistry of universality, there may also be an artistry of the moment, and that the difference between the two may be more complex than a matter of superior opposed to inferior art. It may be that, when he most powerfully embodies the thoughts and feelings unique to a particular period, the artist is, at the same time, creating something that, by virtue of its special relation to its own times, cannot attain more than an ephemeral place in the history of culture. The ability to express the spirit of the moment may not be as important an artistic characteristic as the appeal to universal human concerns in a lasting way; nonetheless, I have come to believe in the course of my explorations that this is a distinctive kind of artistry worth studying in its own right.

Finally, a third kind of popular artistry has come to seem of considerable significance to me, though perhaps I have not done it as much justice in this study as the art of the formula and of the time-bound best-seller. The sort of thing I have in mind is the work, which by most aesthetic standards is largely lacking in merit and yet clearly has a very deep and profound impact, beyond its own time. Here I am thinking of a creation like "The Lone Ranger" or Spillane's *I, the Jury*, works that would appear on the surface to be crude, simple-minded, even reprehensible, in their presentation of a vision of life, as well as lacking in the most basic unity of plot and character or eloquence of style. Yet such works do establish themselves so completely that almost everyone in the culture has some knowledge of them and what they stand for. They represent the kind of artistry that can take a popular story formula and present it in such a way that it becomes an expression of a basic pattern of meaning in the consciousness of many members of the audience. This is the kind of creativity through which a formula not only becomes an expression of cultural mythology, but becomes itself a cultural myth. This process of interplay between formulas as expressions of myths and in some instances themselves becoming myths has been explored in connection with myths of the American West by Richard Slotkin in *Regeneration through Violence*, but it is a process that needs to be studied in other areas of mythology. In addition, we need to characterize more fully the sort of creative artistry involved in those formulaic works that become basic expressions of a cultural meaning.

The shortcomings of the present study thus suggest a variety of further cultural and aesthetic inquiries that can build on the concept of formulaic analysis and bring our knowledge about this complex phenomenon to a higher level. While it is in some ways frustrating for a scholar to realize that he has been far from able to give a final and definitive treatment to his subject, it is also perhaps reassuring for him to recognize that his subject is significant and complex enough to resist the limited learning and competence of a single individual.

Notes

Chapter One

1. Robert Warshow, *The Immediate Experience* (Garden City, N.Y.: Doubleday Anchor Books, 1964), p. 85.

2. For a survey of recent experiments on the effects of pornography see *The Report of the Commission on Obscenity and Pornography* (New York: Bantam Books, 1970). For discussion of the effects of violence see Otto N. Larsen, ed., *Violence and the Mass Media* (New York: Harper and Row, 1968), and David M. Rein, "The Impact of Television Violence," *Journal of Popular Culture* 7, no. 4 (Spring 1974): 934–45. A detailed critique of the cathartic theory of represented violence based on experimental evidence can be found in Leonard Berkowitz, *Aggression: A Social Psychological Analysis* (New York: McGraw-Hill, 1962).

3. Harry Berger, Jr., "Naïve Consciousness and Culture Change: An Essay in Historical Structuralism," *Bulletin of the Midwest Modern Language Association*, 6, no. 1 (Spring 1973): 35.

4. Jean Piaget as quoted in Eric Larrabee and Rolf Meyersohn, eds., *Mass Leisure* (Glencoe, Ill.: Free Press, 1958), p. 71.

5. The Kinsey report and other surveys of sexual behavior suggest that the average middle-class couple have sexual intercourse around twice a week with a duration of less than ten minutes—weekly total: twenty minutes. Surveys of television usage indicate that the average family uses television for about six hours a day. Let us say that at a minimum this means an hour and a half for each person—weekly total: ten and a half hours.

6. Bruce Kuklick, "Myth and Symbol in American Studies," *American Quarterly*, 24, no. 4 (October 1972): 438.

7. Ibid., p. 440.

8. Umberto Eco, ed., *The Bond Affair* (London: Macdonald, 1966), pp. 59–60.

9. Raymond Durgnat, "Spies and Ideologies," *Cinema*, March 1969, p. 8.

Chapter Two

1. Throughout this chapter, I depended heavily on Northrop Frye's

treatment of archetypal forms in *Anatomy of Criticism* (Princeton: Princeton University Press, 1957). I have no doubt that most, if not all, of the categories I suggest could be subsumed under Frye's complex catalog of archetypes. I find that Frye's system, while no doubt superior as an anatomy of the whole of literature, does not systematize as clearly the relations between various types of formulas or lay as much stress on the distinction between mimetic literature and moral fantasy as I feel is necessary for the study of formula stories.

2. Cf. Elder Olson, *The Theory of Comedy* (Bloomington: Indiana University Press, 1968).

3. *True Confessions*, June 1973, p. 58.

4. M. H. Abrams, *A Glossary of Literary Terms* (New York: Holt, Rinehart and Winston, 1971), p. 91.

Chapter Three

1. A few samples of the growing literature that parallels or imitates *The Godfather*: Leslie Waller, *The Family* (New York: New American Library, 1969); Peter McCurtin, *Mafioso* (New York: Belmont/Tower, 1972); Ralph Salerno and John S. Tompkins, *The Crime Confederation* (New York: Popular Library, 1969); Goland Ziran, *The Don* (New York: Pyramid Books, 1972); Nick Quarry, *The Don Is Dead* (New York: Fawcett, 1972); Peter Rabe, *War of the Dons* (New York: Fawcett, 1972); Charles Durbin, *The Patriot* (New York: Coward McCann, 1971); Ovid Demaris, *The Overlord* (New York: New American Library, 1972).

2. A history of crime in literature would be tantamount to a history of literature, and thus there is no single work covering this immense area. The most extensive survey of pre-twentieth-century crime literature is Frank Chandler, *The Literature of Roguery* 2 vols. (Boston: Houghton Mifflin, 1907). For the immense bibliography of detective and crime stories in the nineteenth and twentieth centuries see Jacques Barzun and Wendell Hertig Taylor, *A Catalogue of Crime* (New York: Harper and Row, 1971), and Ordean Hagen, *Who Done It?* (New York: R. R. Bowker, 1969), both of which contain secondary as well as primary bibliographies. For the gangster film I have particularly depended on Stuart Kaminsky, " 'Little Caesar' and its role in the Gangster Film Genre," *Journal of Popular Film*, 1, no. 3 (Summer 1972): 209–27, and on conversations with Professor Kaminsky. I am grateful to him for sharing his immense knowledge of this type of film. Also I have extensively used John Baxter, *The Gangster Film* (New York: A. S. Barnes, 1970), and Colin McArthur, *Underworld U.S.A.* (New York: Viking, 1972).

3. Richard Altick, *Victorian Studies in Scarlet* (New York: W. W. Norton, 1970), is particularly illuminating on the nineteenth-century English public's attitude toward crime.

4. Thomas de Quincey, "Murder Considered as One of the Fine Arts," *Writings*, 23 vols. (Boston: Ticknor and Fields, 1853), 3: 20.

5. Ibid., p. 21.

6. Ibid., pp. 23–24.

7. Eric J. Hobsbawn, *Bandits* (New York: Delacorte Press, 1969).

8. Quoted in Chandler, *The Literature of Roguery*, 2: 359–60.

9. Leon Radzinowicz, *Ideology and Crime* (New York: Columbia University Press, 1966), p. 60.

10. Examples of the Capone legend in the making can be found in the newspaper and magazine articles collected by Albert Halper in *The Chicago Crime Book* (New York: Pyramid Books, 1969). The standard biographies of Capone also reflect and treat the legend; see F. D. Pasley, *Al Capone: The Biography of a Self-Made Man* (London: Faber and Faber, 1966), and John Kobler, *Capone* (New York: G. P. Putnam's Sons, 1971). The best scholarly study of Chicago crime during the Capone era is still John Landesco's report for the Illinois Crime Survey of 1929, reprinted as *Organized Crime in Chicago* (Chicago: University of Chicago Press, 1968).

11. Norval Morris and Gordon Hawkins, *The Honest Politician's Guide to Crime Control* (Chicago: University of Chicago Press, 1969), p. 203.

12. Ed Reid, *Mafia* (New York: New American Library, 1964), p. 41.

13. Demaris, *The Overlord*, p. 281.

14. Mario Puzo, *The Godfather* (New York: Fawcett, 1970), p. 146. See also Johnny Fontane's statement, "I knew you wouldn't do it without orders from the Don. But you can't get sore at him. It's like getting sore at God." (pp. 169–70).

15. Don Pendleton, *The Executioner: Chicago Wipe-Out* (New York: Pinnacle Books, 1971), p. 17.

16. Ibid., p. 187.

17. Ibid., p. 16.

18. John D. MacDonald, *Nightmare in Pink* (Greenwich, Conn.: Fawcett, 1964), p. 21.

19. Puzo, *The Godfather*, pp. 366–67.

Chapter Four

1. One can find occasional exceptions to this as to almost any generalization one can make about a formula. Several of Dorothy Sayers's Lord Peter Wimsey novels involve the detective in matters that concern friends, family, and even, in *Strong Poison*, *Gaudy Night*, and *Busman's Honeymoon*, the woman he loves. Yet the threat is perhaps more apparent than real. It always turns out that the person Lord Peter is concerned with is not guilty, in contrast to the hard-boiled story where the contrary is so often the case: see the comparison of *Strong Poison* and *The Maltese Falcon*. In the former, Lord Peter proves Harriet Vane's innocence while in the latter it is Brigid O'Shaugnessy's guilt that Sam Spade uncovers.

2. William Aydelotte, "The Detective Story as a Historical Source," in Irving and Harriet Deer, eds., *The Popular Arts* (New York: Scribner's, 1967), p. 135.

3. Edgar Allen Poe, *Works*, ed. E. C. Stedman and G. E. Woodberry, 10 vols. (New York: Charles Scribner's Sons, 1914), 3: 203.

4. There is a brilliant discussion of the significance of various kinds of evidence in the classical detective story in a recent paper by Martin Roth, "The Detective, the Clue, and the Corpse in Freud and Einstein," presented at the 1973 meeting of the Midwest Modern Language Association.

5. Poe, 3: 91–92.

6. A. Conan Doyle, *The Complete Sherlock Holmes* (Garden City, N.Y.: Doubleday, 1930), p. 739.

7. Frye, *Anatomy of Criticism*, p. 46.

8. Richard Wilbur, "The Poe Mystery Case," *New York Review*, 13 July 1967, pp. 16, 25–28.

9. Poe, 3: 72.

10. Poe, 3: 72–73.

11. Poe, 3: 74.

12. This analogy was noted at least as early as 1913 by Theodor Reik. Cf. Roth, p. 1. Also Elliot Gilbert, "The Detective as Metaphor in the Nineteenth Century," in Francis M. Nevins, Jr., ed., *The Mystery Writer's Art* (Bowling Green, Ohio: Bowling Green University Popular Press, 1970), p. 290.

13. Dorothy L. Sayers, "Introduction" to *The Omnibus of Crime*, reprinted in Howard Haycraft, ed., *The Art of the Mystery Story* (New York: Grosset and Dunlap, 1946), p. 72. "These mysteries made only to be solved, these horrors which he knows to be mere figments of the creative brain, comfort him by subtly persuading that life is a mystery which death will solve, and whose horrors will pass away as a tale that is told."

14. Cf. Howard Haycraft, *Murder for Pleasure* (New York: Appleton-Century, 1941).

15. Edward Davidson, *Poe: A Critical Study* (Cambridge, Mass.: Harvard University Press, 1957), p. 221.

16. This analysis is especially indebted to the concepts of social character propounded in David Riesman, *The Lonely Crowd* (Garden City, N.Y.: Doubleday Anchor Books, 1955).

Chapter Five

1. Good examples of this emphasis can be found in S. S. Van Dine's "Twenty Rules for Writing Detective Stories," Father Knox's "A Detective Story Decalogue" and "The Detection Club Oath," all reprinted in Haycraft, ed., *The Art of the Mystery Story*, pp. 189–99. This is also the primary interest and principle of evaluation followed by Barzun and Taylor in their *Catalogue of Crime*, which is quite rigorous in its adherence to the ideology of ratiocination.

2. Raymond Chandler, "The Simple Art of Murder," quoted in Haycraft, p. 225. Cf. Captain Hastings's comment in one of Agatha Christie's stories: "I admit that a second murder in a book often cheers things up. If the murder happens in the first chapter and you have to follow up everybody's alibi until the last page but one—well, it does get a bit tedious." *The A.B.C. Murders* (New York: Pocket Books, 1941), p. 11.

3. George Grella, "Murder and Manners: The Formal Detective Novel," *Novel* 4 (1970): 33–34.

4. Agatha Christie, *An Overdose of Death* (New York: Dell Publishing Co., 1967), pp. 140–41.

5. Ibid., p. 16.

6. Quoted in Haycraft, p. 72.

7. Dorothy Sayers, *The Nine Tailors* (New York: Harcourt, Brace and World, 1962), p. 68.

8. Ibid., p. 310.

9. Cf. Jacques Barzun's highly critical comments on Simenon's detection in *The Catalogue of Crime*, p. 14. Alme E. Murch makes a similar judgment in *The Development of the Detective Novel* (New York: Greenwood Press, 1968), p. 227.

10. Georges Simenon, *Maigret and the Reluctant Witnesses* (New York: Modern Literary Editions Publishing Co., 1959), p. 21.

11. Ross Macdonald, "The Writer as Detective Hero," in Nevins, ed., *The Mystery Writer's Art*, p. 304. I am indebted to Johnine Hazard for calling this fascinating essay to my attention. Her dissertation on Ross Macdonald deals at length with its relationship to Macdonald's own work.

12. There are a number of historical detective stories written by twentieth-century writers—the tales of Judge Dee by Robert van Gulik, those about Dr. Sam Johnson by Lillian de la Torre, and the historical mysteries of John Dickson Carr. These, however, are clearly detective stories in costume.

13. My friend Harold Boris has very powerfully urged this view upon me in conversations and letters. Cf. also Geraldine Pederson-Krag, "Detective Stories and the Primal Scene," *Psychoanalytic Quarterly* 18 (1949): 207–14, and Martin Grotjahn, "Sex and the Mystery Story," *Human Sexuality* 6, no. 3 (March 1972): 126–37.

14. Cf. several of the stories collected under the title *Knight's Gambit* (New York: Random House, 1949).

15. J. I. M. Stewart, "Introduction" to *The Moonstone* (Baltimore: Penguin Books, 1966), p. 7. Stewart is "Michael Innes," a brilliant detective story writer in his own right, one of whose stories, *Lament for a Maker*, employs a narrative procedure similar to *The Moonstone*.

16. This view of the imminent decline of the classical detective story is common to most recent historians and critics of the genre. Cf. Julian Symons, *Mortal Consequences* (New York: Harper and Row, 1972), Boileau-Narcejac, *Le Roman policier* (Paris: Petite Bibliothèque Payot, 1964), and Ross Macdonald, "The Writer as Detective Hero."

17. Michael Holquist, "Whodunit and Other Questions: Metaphysical Detective Stories in Post-War Fiction," *New Literary History* 3 (1971–72): 135. For another view of the relation between detective stories and "postmodern" fiction see William V. Spanos, "The Detective and the Boundary: Some Notes on the Postmodern Literary Imagination," *Boundary 2*, 1, no. 1 (Fall 1972): 147–68.

18. Ibid., pp. 148–49.

19. Ibid., p. 155.

Chapter Six

1. T. O. Mabbott, ed., *The Selected Poetry and Prose of Edgar Allan Poe* (New York: Modern Library, 1951), p. 166.

2. A. Conan Doyle, *The Complete Sherlock Holmes*, p. 740.

3. G. K. Chesterton, "A Defense of Detective Stories," from *The Defendant* (London, 1901), quoted in Haycraft, ed., *The Art of the Mystery Story*, p. 4.

4. Raymond Chandler, *Farewell, My Lovely* (New York: Pocket Books, 1943; orig. pub. 1940), pp. 112–13.

5. Ed McBain, *Fuzz* (New York: Signet Books, 1969; orig. pub. 1968), p. 107.

6. Mickey Spillane, *I, the Jury* (New York: Signet Books, 1968; orig. pub. 1948), p. 7.

7. Raymond Chandler, *The Long Goodbye* (New York: Pocket Books, 1955; orig. pub. 1953), p. 277.

8. Ibid., p. 146.

9. Chandler, *Farewell, My Lovely*, p. 2.

10. Raymond Chandler, *The Big Sleep* (New York: Pocket Books, 1958; orig. pub. 1939), p. 5.

11. Chandler, *The Long Goodbye*, pp. 218–19.

12. Richard S. Prather, *The Kubla Khan Caper* (New York: Pocket Books, 1967; orig. pub. 1966), p. 151.

13. Ross Macdonald, *The Doomsters* (New York: Bantam Books, 1972), p. 29.

14. Dashiell Hammett, *The Maltese Falcon and The Thin Man* (New York: Vintage Books, 1964; orig. pub. 1929), p. 3.

15. Prather, *The Kubla Khan Caper*, p. 2.

16. Ross Macdonald, *Harper* (New York: Pocket Books, 1966; orig. pub. as *The Moving Target*, 1949), p. 87.

17. Chandler, *The Long Goodbye*, pp. 309–10.

18. Mickey Spillane, *One Lonely Night* (New York: Signet Books, 1962; orig. pub. 1951), p. 25.

19. David Madden, ed., *Tough Guy Writers of the Thirties* (Carbondale and Edwardsville: Southern Illinois University Press, 1968), p. 231.

20. Raymond Chandler, "The Simple Art of Murder," quoted in Haycraft, ed., *The Art of the Mystery Story*, p. 237.

21. In his excellent essay on the hard-boiled genre, "Murder and the Mean Streets," *Contempora* 1 (March 1970): 11–12, George Grella discusses the relation between the hard-boiled story and medieval romance with several well-chosen examples.

22. From a letter by Raymond Chandler quoted in Richard Schickel, "Raymond Chandler, Private Eye," *Commentary*, February 1963, p. 159.

23. Mickey Spillane, *I, the Jury*, p. 16.

24. Ross Macdonald, *Find a Victim* (New York: Bantam Books, 1962; orig. pub. 1954), p. 105.

25. Raymond Chandler, *Farewell, My Lovely*, p. 11.

26. Brett Halliday, *So Lush, So Deadly* (New York: Dell Publishing Co., 1968), p. 59.

27. Mickey Spillane, *The Body Lovers* (New York: Signet Books, 1967), p. 46.

28. Raymond Chandler, "The Simple Art of Murder," in Haycraft, p. 236.

29. Mickey Spillane, *The Body Lovers*, p. 12.

30. Richard Prather, *The Kubla Khan Caper*, pp. 9–10.

31. Riesman, *The Lonely Crowd*, p. 37.

32. Ibid., pp. 37–38.

Chapter Seven

1. Chandler, "The Simple Art of Murder," in Haycraft, ed., *The Art of the Mystery Story*, p. 234.

2. Ibid., p. 229.

3. Lionel Trilling, "Reality in America," in *The Liberal Imagination* (Garden City, N.Y.: Doubleday Anchor Books, 1953).

4. Quoted in Haycraft, p. 417.

5. Dashiell Hammett, *The Maltese Falcon* (New York: Perma Books, 1957), p. 173.

6. Dashiell Hammett, *The Dain Curse* (New York: Perma Books, 1961), p. 3.

7. Ibid., p. 72.

8. Haycraft, pp. 417, 418, 419, 422.

9. Hammett, *The Maltese Falcon*, p. 51.

10. Hammett, *The Big Knockover* (New York: Random House, 1966), pp. 28–29.

11. Hammett, *Red Harvest* (New York: Perma Books, 1956), pp. 6–7.

12. *Red Harvest*, p. 70.

13. Ibid., p. 96.

14. Ibid., p. 127.

15. Ibid., p. 130.

16. Ibid., p. 135.
17. Ibid., pp. 136–37.
18. Ibid., p. 179.
19. Ibid., p. 178.
20. Ibid., p. 179.
21. Hammett, *The Dain Curse*, p. 86.
22. Raymond Chandler, *The Big Sleep*, pp. 203–4.
23. *The Dain Curse*, p. 87.
24. Chandler, *Farewell, My Lovely*, p. 135.
25. Ibid., p. 1.
26. *The Big Sleep*, p. 20.
27. Chandler, *Playback* (New York: Pocket Books, 1960), p. 6.
28. *Farewell, My Lovely*, p. 170.
29. Ibid., p. 190.
30. Ibid., p. 22.
31. Chandler, "The Simple Art of Murder" in Haycraft, p. 237.
32. Dorothy Gardiner and Kathrine Sorley Walker, eds., *Raymond Chandler Speaking* (London: Hamish Hamilton, 1962), pp. 248–49.
33. *Raymond Chandler Speaking*, p. 69.
34. *Farewell, My Lovely*, p. 3.
35. Ibid., p. 222.
36. Ibid., p. 216.
37. Ibid., p. 1.
38. Ibid., p. 226.
39. Ibid., p. 25.
40. Ibid., p. 230.
41. Ibid.
42. Ibid.
43. Ibid., p. 105.
44. Mickey Spillane, *I, the Jury* (New York: Signet, 1948), pp. 47–48.
45. *Red Harvest*, p. 41.
46. Ibid., p. 69.
47. *The Big Sleep*, p. 187.
48. Mickey Spillane, *The Big Kill* (New York: Signet, n.d.), p. 41.
49. Mickey Spillane, *One Lonely Night* (New York: Signet, 1951), p. 165.
50. *The Big Kill*, p. 150.
51. Ibid., p. 175.
52. *I, the Jury*, p. 174.
53. Erwin Panofsky, "Style and Medium in the Moving Pictures," in Daniel Talbot, ed., *Film: An Anthology* (Berkeley: University of California Press, 1966), pp. 17–18.
54. *One Lonely Night*, p. 9.

Chapter Eight

1. Various aspects of the West in literature and film have been extensively treated in a variety of secondary sources. For useful bibliographies see Richard W. Etulain, *Western American Literature: A Bibliography of Interpretive Books and Articles* (Vermillion, S.D.: University of South Dakota, 1972) and John G. Cawelti, *The Six-Gun Mystique* (Bowling Green, Ohio: Bowling Green Popular Press, 1970). A recent publication has dealt extensively with some of the mythical patterns that antedate the nineteenth- and twentieth-century western: Richard Slotkin, *Regeneration through Violence* (Middletown, Conn.: Wesleyan University Press, 1973). The most important studies of themes and patterns that have played a major role in the evolution of the western formula are: Henry Nash Smith, *Virgin Land* (Cambridge, Mass.: Harvard University Press, 1950); Edwin Fussell, *Frontier: American Literature and the American West* (Princeton, N.J.: Princeton University Press, 1965); James K. Folsom, *The American Western Novel* (New Haven, Conn.: College and University Press, 1966); *Le Western: source, thèmes, mythologies, auteurs, acteurs, filmographies* (Paris: Union Generale d'Editions, 1966); George Fenin and William Everson, *The Western: From Silents to Cinerama* (New York: Bonanza Books, 1962); Jim Kitses, *Horizons West: Studies in Authorship in the Western Film* (Bloomington: Indiana University Press, 1970); and Kent L. Steckmesser, *The Western Hero in History and Legend* (Norman: University of Oklahoma Press, 1965).

2. James Fenimore Cooper, *The American Democrat* (New York: Vintage Books, 1956), p. 89.

3. Marvin Meyers, *The Jacksonian Persuasion* (New York: Vintage Books, 1960), p. 67.

4. Cooper, *The American Democrat*, p. 95.

5. James Fenimore Cooper, *The Pioneers* (New York: G. P. Putnam's Sons, 1896), pp. 1–2.

6. James Fenimore Cooper, *The Last of the Mohicans* (New York: G. P. Putnam's Sons, 1896), p. 49.

7. *The Pioneers*, p. 472.

8. Ibid., p. 472.

9. Ibid., pp. 9–10.

10. James Fenimore Cooper, *The Prairie* (New York: G. P. Putnam's Sons, 1896), p. 8.

11. James Fenimore Cooper, *The Deerslayer* (Boston: Dana Estes and Co., 1909), p. 7.

12. *The Prairie*, p. 435.

13. *The Deerslayer*, p. 8.

14. Ibid., p. 129.

15. Ibid., pp. 133–34.

16. Ibid., p. 135.

17. Ibid., pp. 293–94.

18. Ibid., pp. 417–18.

19. D. H. Lawrence, *Studies in Classic American Literature* (New York: Doubleday Anchor Books, 1951), p. 72.

20. David Noble, *The Eternal Adam and the New World Garden* (New York: George Brazilier, 1968), p. 181.

21. This is the judgment so persuasively argued by Smith in *Virgin Land.*

22. Robert Montgomery Bird, *Nick of the Woods* (New York: Vanguard Press, 1928), p. 9.

23. Philip Durham, ed., *Seth Jones and Deadwood Dick on Deck* (New York: Odyssey Press, 1966), p. 4.

24. Ibid., p. 53.

25. Henry Nash Smith, *Virgin Land* (New York: Vintage Books, n.d.), p. 102.

26. Durham, p. 158.

27. Ibid., p. 181.

28. Ibid., p. 114.

29. Ibid., p. 107.

30. For a most interesting discussion of film adaptations of *The Virginian* see Joseph F. Trimmer, "The Virginian: Novel and Films," a paper delivered at the 1972 meeting of the Popular Culture Association.

31. Edward G. White, *The Eastern Establishment and the Western Experience* (New Haven, Conn.: Yale University Press, 1968).

32. Mark Twain, *Roughing It* (New York: New American Library, 1962), p. 331.

33. Ibid., p. 248.

34. Ibid., p. 34.

35. Ibid., p. 83.

36. Owen Wister, *The Virginian*, ed. Philip Durham (Boston, Mass: Houghton Mifflin, 1968), p. 10.

37. Ibid., p. 13.

38. Ibid., p. 14.

39. Ibid., p. 26.

40. Ibid., p. 265.

41. Ibid., p. 275.

42. Ibid., p. 288.

43. Ibid., pp. 291–92.

44. Ibid., p. 303.

45. Quoted in Owen Wister, *The Virginian* (New York: Pocket Books, 1956), p. vii.

46. George R. Taylor, ed., *The Turner Thesis* (Boston: D. C. Heath, 1956), p. 28.

47. Wister, *The Virginian*, p. 93.

48. *The Turner Thesis*, p. 32.

49. Wister, *The Virginian*, p. 304.

50. Ibid., p. 4.

51. Despite Grey's cultural importance, he has not received very much serious scholarly attention. The two books on him deal mainly with his life: Jean Karr, *Zane Grey, Man of the West* (New York: Greenburg, 1949), and Frank Gruber, *Zane Grey* (New York: World, 1970). An intensive study of Grey's work and its cultural significance is greatly needed. Hart's contribution to the western film is admiringly treated in Fenin and Eversen, *The Western* and in William S. Hart's charming autobiography, *My Life East and West* (New York: Benjamin Blom, 1968; a reprint of the 1929 publication).

52. Gruber has the most complete Grey bibliography and filmography.

53. Hart later claimed in his autobiography (p. 175) that no cowboy would have acted as the Virginian did in the crucial lynching scene in Wister's novel, but he is on pretty shaky grounds when he suggests that his own version of the hero is substantially more realistic.

54. Readers of Everson's excellent discussion of Hart's films may wonder why I am characterizing him as a fantasy-maker when Everson emphasizes Hart's realism. This is primarily a visual realism in Hart's films. His western towns are ramshackle and dusty, and he makes little attempt to glamorize his characters through costume, lighting, or camera work. But this is simply surface verisimilitude, of which Grey, for all his purple prose, has a good deal. Grey is often as dusty as Hart in his characterization of the hard, exhausting physicality of western life. But despite this surface verisimilitude, which has become a convention in the modern western, the characters and actions that Grey and Hart deal with are similarly melodramatic and mythical.

55. Zane Grey, *Wild Horse Mesa* (New York: Harper and Brothers, 1928), pp. 12–13.

56. Kenneth W. Scott, "*The Heritage of the Desert*: Zane Grey Discovers the West," *Markham Review* 2, no. 2 (February 1970): 10–13, does a good job in defining Grey's treatment of this theme.

57. Zane Grey, *To the Last Man* (New York: Harper and Brothers, 1922), pp. 86–87.

58. Zane Grey, *Code of the West* (New York: Pocket Books, 1963; orig. pub. by Harper in 1934), p. 219.

59. Ibid., p. 221.

60. Zane Grey, *Nevada* (New York: Bantam Books, 1946; orig. pub. by Harper in 1928), p. 9.

61. Wister, *The Virginian*, p. 295.

62. Grey, *To the Last Man*, p. 19.

63. Zane Grey, *The Light of Western Stars* (New York: Pocket Books, 1962; orig. pub. by Harper in 1913), p. 213.

64. Wister, *The Virginian*, p. 304.

65. Ibid., p. 3.

66. Walter Prescott Webb, *The Great Plains* (Boston: Ginn, 1931), p. 206.

67. Ibid., p. 245.

68. Warshow, *The Immediate Experience*, pp.93–94.

69. It is interesting to note that a somewhat similar film produced by the Canadian Film Board, "City of Gold," interprets the western experience in almost opposite terms, stressing its continuity with the present and asserting that the real essence of pioneer life was not heroic individualism but the discovery of community.

70. In 1973, NBC canceled "Bonanza" after fourteen seasons.

71. Jack Nachbar, "Riding Shotgun: The Scattered Formula in Contemporary Western Movies," a paper presented at the 1972 convention of the Popular Culture Association and reprinted in Nachbar, ed., *Focus on the Western* (Englewood Cliffs, N.J.: Prentice-Hall, 1974).

72. *New York Times*, 13 August 1972, D9.

Chapter Nine

1. Melodrama is a rather amorphous formulaic type, and what I have defined as social melodrama shades over into a variety of other melodramatic types that only a dedicated Polonius would insist on differentiating with absolute precision. Nonetheless, there are significant differences in emphasis in the different melodramatic types we encounter in the course of this chapter. For example, the social melodrama is generally given a contemporaneous setting and differs thereby from the historical melodrama, which will sacrifice a contemporaneous sense of verisimilitude in order to cultivate a romantic image of the past. There are also historical melodramas that reject romance and seek a contemporary sense of verisimilitude; a good example is *Gone with the Wind.* Similarly with the tradition of Gothic or sensation melodrama where the admixture of horror and the spice of sado-masochism is more important that "realism."

Many sensation melodramas come close to the social melodrama in their concern with detailed analysis of society, e.g., the works of Wilkie Collins. Also there is the domestic melodrama, which revolves around the problems of a family circle, with or without a complex look at social institutions. In this chapter I have tried to confine myself largely to the discussion of works that are unmistakably examples of the formulaic type of social melodrama, but there are times, particularly in the discussion of the evolution of social melodrama, when the continual interplay between social melodrama and such other formulaic types as the historical, the gothic, or the domestic melodramas cannot be avoided. I do not think this invalidates the distinction of social melodrama as a type, but it certainly cannot be defined as a formula with the same degree of differentiation as the detective story, the spy story, the romance, or the western.

2. For a more detailed comparison of the social melodrama and the

twentieth-century tradition of naturalistic muckraking see my essay "Block-busters and Muckraking: Some Reflections on Muckraking in the Contemporary Best-Seller," in John M. Harrison and Harry H. Stein, eds., *Muckraking: Past, Present and Future* (University Park: Pennsylvania State University Press, 1973), pp. 84–99

3. Tragic melodrama is a puzzling category, since it would almost seem a contradiction in terms. If we are correct that the central function of melodrama is to assure us of the benevolent moral order of the world, one would think that a tragic ending (i.e., the death or failure of the protagonist) would not be satisfying to those with a taste for melodrama. And yet there are many tragic (or at least sad) melodramas where the protagonist is not victorious. In such cases, it seems clear that the protagonist has committed some fundamental offense against the moral order. This may leave him or her still sympathetic—i.e., not a villain—and yet quite deserving of the punishment he receives. The melodrama of the "tragic" gangster is a good case in point. We may sympathize with the gangster's aggressions yet still find it right and satisfying that he be punished. There is a different artistic economy here than in tragedy. The tragic hero does not offend against morality or decency; he fights against the gods, or against the nature of things. Thus his struggle has a moral ambiguity that is not true of melodrama, where what is right and what is wrong are usually perfectly clear. Providence, but not fate, rules melodrama, providence being force that is responsive to human rights and wrongs. Another point worth noting about tragic melodrama is that many works of this type tend to shade over into the archetype of romance where another set of considerations is operative. It is often most appropriate for a romance to end with the demise of one of the lovers if, in this fashion, the power and significance of the love can be demonstrated. Again there is a useful comparison with romantic tragedy in which passion tends to be destructive. In archetypal romance, the death of one of the lovers only confirms the immortal power of love.

4. See the brilliant analytic description of nineteenth-century melodrama as the story of "cosmic success" in Henry Nash Smith, "The Scribbling Women and the Cosmic Success Story," *Critical Inquiry*, 1, no. 1 (September 1974): 47–70.

5. T. S. Eliot, *Selected Essays: 1917–1932* (New York: Harcourt, Brace, 1932), p. 380.

6. I have depended a great deal on other scholars for the nineteenth-century portion of this account of the evolution of melodrama. In particular, I have profited from Herbert R. Brown, *The Sentimental Novel in America, 1769–1860* (Durham, N.C.: Duke University Press, 1940); David Grimsted, *Melodrama Unveiled: American Theater and Culture, 1800–1850* (Chicago: University of Chicago Press, 1968); Michael Booth, *English Melodrama* (London: H. Jenkins, 1965); Frank Rahill, *The World of Melodrama* (University Park: Pennsylvania State University Press, 1967); Helen Papashvily, *All*

the *Happy Endings* (New York: Harper, 1956); Russel B. Nye, *The Unembar-rassed Muse* (New York: Dial Press, 1970); James D. Hart, *The Popular Book* (Berkeley: University of California Press, 1961); and William Veeder, *Henry James: The Lessons of the Master—Popular Fiction and Personal Expression in the Nineteenth Century* (Chicago: University of Chicago Press, 1975). I have also found two recent dissertations of enormous help in this discussion: Kay Mussell, "The World of Modern Gothic Fiction: American Women and Their Social Myths," Ph.D. dissertation, University of Iowa, 1973, and Randolph Ivy, "The Victorian Sensation Novel: A Study in Formula Fiction," Ph.D dissertation, University of Chicago, 1974. Twentieth-century social melodrama has not been as carefully studied, in part because it has not been identified as in the tradition of nineteenth-century melodrama. Both Charles Walcutt and Warren Titus treat Winston Churchill in their interesting monographs as a failed social realist rather than as the effective but ephemeral social melodramatist which I think he was. See Walcutt, *The Romantic Compromise in the Novels of Winston Churchill* (Ann Arbor, Mich.: University of Michigan Press, 1951) and Titus, *Winston Churchill* (New York: Twayne Publishers, 1963). Wright and Grey have only recently begun to receive a certain amount of scholarly attention, while contemporary melodramatists like Robbins, Hailey, Susann, and Wallace are too recent and too popular to have occupied the attention of critics other than reviewers and enormous numbers of readers. One major exception to this generalization is the very interesting recent book on Wallace by John Leverance (Bowling Green, Ohio: Bowling Green Popular Press, 1974), though this is more biographical than critical. Wallace's own *The Writing of One Novel* (New York: Pocket Books, 1971) is also very interesting for the insight it sheds on a social melodramatist's attitude toward his art.

7. Grimsted, p. 176.

8. Mrs. E. D. E. N. Southworth, *The Curse of Clifton* (New York: AMS Press, 1970), p. 465. This novel was first published in 1852.

9. Smith, p. 51.

10. Brown, pp. 170–71.

11. This may be a major reason for the perennial popularity of the Clarissa Harlowe–Charlotte Temple type of tragic melodrama, which extends down to such present-day best-sellers as Susann's *Once Is Not Enough*, a modern version of this formula. The tragic melodrama plot type allows a sympathetic and spicy portrayal of sin without disrupting the vision of the moral order, since the sin is lovingly and sado-masochistically punished at great length.

12. There seems no need for me to comment on Dickens as the founding father of social melodrama, since his works are so well known and have been subjected to such a variety of critical analysis. Of course, in saying that Dickens was the first great master of social melodrama I am not saying that he did not also transcend the formula in many if not all of his works. To understand Dickens as social melodramatist is particularly useful in grasping

the force for his contemporary readers of certain aspects of his work that twentieth-century taste tends to find dated or cloying. For instance, it is noteworthy that nineteenth-century readers were, on the whole, most enthusiastic about the earlier novels where melodramatic elements and resolutions play a much more dominant part, while more recent readers tend to approve more highly of later works like *Hard Times* and *Our Mutual Friend* where an increasingly bleak and critical view of society overpowers the melodramatic vision. *Bleak House* is perhaps a turning point in this development. In one sense we might say that melodrama and social criticism are perfectly balanced in that novel and that the two are encapsulated in the double narrative structure (i.e., the portions told by the anonymous narrator and the narrative of Esther Summerson). But the fact that the two visions are thus almost detached from each other in this structure indicates perhaps the extent to which Dickens is having more and more difficulty in holding them together in his work. Dickens himself was apparently aware of the degree to which his darker and more critical vision of society and his declining ability to qualify this with an effective sense of the benevolent order of melodrama was beginning to alienate his audience. That he turned at the last to experiment with the new structures of the sensation melodrama in the unfinished *Edwin Drood* suggests his search for a new principle of melo-drama that might be more in harmony with his bleaker view of society. See the brilliantly suggestive treatment of this issue in Randolph Ivy, "The Victorian Sensation Novel: A Study in Formula Fiction."

13. Smith comments insightfully on the prevalence of this theme, pp. 53–66.

14. Winston Churchill, *The Inside of the Cup* (New York: Macmillan, 1913), p. 1.

15. Ibid., p. 2.

16. Dee Garrison, in a forthcoming article that I had the good fortune to see in manuscript, "Immoral Fiction in the Gilded Age Library," presents a detailed analysis of the emergence of the aggressive female and her defeat of the formerly dominant male in the melodramatic novels of the later nineteenth century. Helen Papashvily suggests that women enjoyed such stories because they were essentially fantasies of feminine heroism and even conquest within the still respectable framework of domesticity.

17. Harold Bell Wright, *The Winning of Barbara Worth* (Chicago: Book Supply Co., 1911), p. 243.

18. See the discussion of Harold Robbins as soft-core pornographer in Peter Michelsen, *The Aesthetics of Pornography* (New York: Herder and Herder, 1971), chap. 2.

19. Irving Wallace, *The Seven Minutes* (New York: Simon and Schuster, 1969), pp. 244–45.

20. Northrop Frye, *The Critical Path* (Bloomington: Indiana University Press, 1971), p. 81.

21. Wallace, *The Chapman Report* (New York: Signet Books, n.d.; orig. pub. 1960), pp. 380–81.

22. Ibid., p. 382.

23. Wallace, *The Seven Minutes*, p. 232.

24. Ibid., p. 309.

25. See the provocative discussion of the psychological basis of pornography in Morse Peckham, *Art and Pornography* (New York: Basic Books, 1969).

26. Wallace, *The Fan Club* (New York: Simon and Schuster, 1974), p. 510.

Bibliographical Notes

Popular Formulaic Literature—
Theory and History
(chaps. 1–2)

My own interest in the analysis of popular formulas was initially stimulated by the combined influence of five very different but equally provocative analyses of American popular culture: Henry Nash Smith's *Virgin Land* (Cambridge, Mass.: Harvard University Press, 1950); Reuel Denney's *The Astonished Muse* (Chicago: University of Chicago Press, 1957); Peter Homans's article, "Puritanism Revisited: An Analysis of the Contemporary Screen-Image Western," *Studies in Public Communication*, no. 3 (Summer 1961), pp. 73–84; a number of the essays in the Bernard Rosenberg–David M. White anthology *Mass Culture* (Glencoe, Ill.: Free Press, 1957) and Marshall McLuhan's *The Mechanical Bride* (New York: Vanguard Press, 1951).

The analytical method developed in this book is a synthesis of three major critical traditions: the analysis of genres, patterns of conventions, and archetypes that began with Aristotle's *Poetics*; the study of myths and symbols that began in late-eighteenth- and early-nineteenth-century studies of comparative folklore and national cultures and has been elaborated in twentieth-century anthropology; and the tradition of practical manuals for writers of popular fiction that have helped me to define some of the major patterns characteristic of popular formulas.

Northrop Frye's *Anatomy of Criticism* (Princeton, N.J.: Princeton University Press, 1957), a major synthesis of generic and mythic criticism, has been the most fundamental work for me, but I have also depended heavily on insights gained from the essays in R. S. Crane, ed., *Critics and Criticism* (Chicago: University of Chicago Press, 1952); Elder Olson, *Tragedy and the Theory of Drama* (Detroit: Wayne State University Press, 1961) and *The Theory of Comedy* (Bloomington: Indiana University Press, 1968); Sheldon Sacks, *Fiction and the Shape of Belief* (Berkeley: University of California Press, 1967); and Wayne C. Booth, *The Rhetoric of Fiction* (Chicago: University of Chicago Press, 1961). E. H. Gombrich, *Art and Illusion* (Princeton, N.J.: Princeton University Press, 1961), discusses the problem of genre and convention in the visual arts.

The concept of myth is developed effectively in Frye and Smith. There is also a very good discussion of the concept in Richard Slotkin, *Regeneration through Violence* (Middletown, Conn.: Wesleyan University Press, 1973) chap. 1. Some applications of the concepts of myth and symbol to the study of American culture in the tradition of *Virgin Land* are R. W. B. Lewis, *The American Adam* (Chicago: University of Chicago Press, 1965); Ernest Tuveson, *The Redeemer Nation* (Chicago: University of Chicago Press, 1968); Leslie Fiedler, *Love and Death in the American Novel* (New York: Stein and Day, 1968); Edwin Fussell, *Frontier: American Literature and the American West* (Princeton, N.J.: Princeton University Press, 1968); John Ward, *Andrew Jackson: Symbol for an Age* (New York: Oxford University Press, 1955); John Cawelti, *Apostles of the Self-Made Man* (Chicago: University of Chicago Press, 1965); Irvin Wyllie, *The Self-Made Man in America* (New Brunswick, N. J.: Rutgers University Press, 1954); Leo Marx, *The Machine in the Garden* (New York: Oxford University Press, 1964); and Nicholas Cords and Patrick Gerster, eds., *Myth and the American Experience* (New York: Glencoe Press, 1972).

Broader studies of myth that I have found helpful include Mircea Eliade, *Myth and Reality* (New York: Harper and Row, 1963); Joseph Campbell, *The Hero with a Thousand Faces* (New York: World, Meridian Books, 1949); Carl Jung, *Flying Saucers* (New York: New American Library, 1969); Lord Raglan, *The Hero* (New York: Oxford University Press, 1937); Otto Rank, *The Myth of the Birth of the Hero* (New York: Vintage Books, 1964); Claude Lévi-Strauss, *The Savage Mind* (Chicago: University of Chicago Press, 1966) and *Structural Anthropology* (New York: Basic Books, 1963); Roland Barthes, *Mythologies* (Paris: Editions du Seuil, 1957). Some basic problems in the cultural interpretation of myths and symbols have been raised by Bruce Kuklick in "Myth and Symbol in American Studies," *American Quarterly*, 24, no. 4 (October 1972): 435–50.

Another way of looking at basic story patterns is through the eye of the professional writer. I have found a number of writing manuals very helpful in defining popular genres and formulas: Patricia Highsmith, *Plotting and Writing Suspense Fiction* (Boston: The Writer, 1966); Charles Simmons, *Plots That Sell to Top-Pay Magazines* (New York: Wilfred Funk, 1952); William Foster-Harris, *The Basic Formulas of Fiction* (Norman: University of Oklahoma Press, 1944); William Dorsey Kennedy, *The Free-Lance Writer's Handbook* (Cambridge, Mass.: Thomas Fleet Co., 1926); and Basil Hogarth, *Writing Thrillers for Profit: A Practical Guide* (London: A. and C. Black, 1936).

One basic problem that confronts any student of popular genres is the complex question of the relationship between the popular arts and the fine arts, between popular culture and high culture. Is there a distinctive aesthetics of popular culture, or are the popular arts simply degraded or naive forms of the fine arts? This issue has been discussed throughout the history of western civilization. One of its first and most brilliant formulations is in Plato's distinction between art and rhetoric in the *Gorgias*. In the nineteenth century Matthew Arnold gave an important new twist to the discussion in his *Culture and Anarchy* by suggesting that there might be as many limitations to upper-class elite culture as to the culture of the masses, a notion that was domesticated to America in Van Wyck Brooks's critique of the division of American culture into highbrows and lowbrows in *America's Coming-of-Age*. The nineteenth-century background of the high culture–popular culture issue has been most interestingly examined in the studies of Raymond Williams, *Culture and Society: 1780-1950* (New York: Columbia University Press, 1958) and *The Long Revolution* (London: Chatto and Windus, 1960). The tradition of mass culture criticism, brilliantly articulated in the writings of Ortega y Gasset and developed in more recent works like Bernard Bell, *Crowd Culture* (New York: Harper, 1952), and Deric Regin, *Culture and the Crowd* (Philadelphia: Chilton Book Co., 1968), has also been an important influence on discussions of popular culture. A number of useful anthologies include important essays on various sides of this debate: Rosenberg and White, *Mass Culture*, and *Mass Culture Revisited* (New York: Van Nostrand Reinhold, 1971); Alan Casty, *Mass Media and Mass Man* (New York: Holt, Rinehart and Winston, 1968); Norman Jacobs, *Culture for the Millions?* (Boston: Beacon Press, 1961). Barry Ulanov attempted an analysis of contemporary American culture along the lines of the high culture–popular culture polarity in *The Two Worlds of American Art: The Private and the Popular* (New York: Macmillan, 1965). See also Dwight Macdonald, *Against the American Grain: Essays on the Effects of Mass Culture* (New York: Vintage Books, 1965), and Warren French, "'An Odorous Tangle of Blossoming Vines': Popcult Confronts the Cultists," *Indiana Social Studies Quarterly* 26, no. 3 (Winter 1973–74): 14–20.

A number of critics have made important contributions to our understanding of different aspects of popular culture. Perhaps the most famous are T. S. Eliot, who wrote superb essays on Marie Lloyd and the English music hall tradition and on Wilkie Collins and melodrama, and Edmund Wilson, who wrote some delightful essays on American vaudeville and burlesque in the 1920s and a vigorous attack on detective fiction in his notorious "Who Cares Who Killed Roger Ackroyd." The most important American critical books on popular culture are Gilbert Seldes, *The Seven Lively Arts* (New York: Harper and Brothers, 1924), the first significant book-length analysis of the popular arts, and Robert Warshow, *The Immediate Experience* (Garden City, N.Y.: Anchor Books, 1964), which contains the most insightful appreciative discussions of popular genres like the western and the gangster film. Seldes has written a number of important books about popular culture since 1924, including *The Great Audience* (New York: Viking, 1950) and *The Public Arts* (New York: Simon and Schuster, 1956). Other useful critical analyses of the popular arts include: Arthur Berger, *L'il Abner: A Study in American Satire*

(New York: Twayne, 1970); Irving and Harriet Deer, eds., *The Popular Arts* (New York: Charles Scribner's Sons, 1967) and *Languages of the Mass Media* (Boston: D. C. Heath, 1965); Jonathan Eisen, ed., *The Age of Rock* (New York: Vintage Books, 1969); Ray Browne and Marshall Fishwick, *Icons of Popular Culture* (Bowling Green, Ohio: Bowling Green University Popular Press, 1970); William M. Hammel, ed., *The Popular Arts in America* (New York: Harcourt, Brace, Jovanovich, 1972); Susan Sontag, *Against Interpretation* (New York: Farrar, Strauss and Giroux, 1966); David Manning White, ed., *Pop Culture in America* (Chicago: Quadrangle Books, 1970); Edward M. White, ed., *The Pop Culture Tradition* (New York: W. W. Norton, 1972); and Tom Wolfe, *Kandy-Kolored Tangerine-Flake Streamline Baby* (New York: Farrar, Strauss and Giroux, 1965) and *The Pump-House Gang* (New York: Farrar, Strauss and Giroux, 1968).

The British have also developed a significant tradition of popular culture criticism springing from the work of George Orwell, *Shooting an Elephant and Other Essays* (New York: Harcourt, Brace, 1950), and Dr. and Mrs. F. R. Leavis—F. R. Leavis and Denys Thompson, *Culture and Environment* (London: Chatto and Windus, 1932); Q. D. Leavis, *Fiction and the Reading Public* (London: Chatto and Windus, 1932)—and Richard Hoggart, *The Uses of Literacy* (Fairlawn, N.J.: Essential Books, 1957). Other significant British popular culture criticism can be found in Stuart Hall and Paddy Whannel, *The Popular Arts* (New York: Pantheon Books, 1965); Denys Thompson, *Discrimination and Popular Culture* (Harmondsworth: Penguin Books, 1964), and Nicholas Tucker, *Understanding the Mass Media* (Cambridge: Cambridge University Press, 1966).

Other approaches to the analysis and interpretation of popular culture are developed in the works of Marshall McLuhan, particularly in *Understanding Media* (New York: McGraw-Hill, 1964); Alan Gowans, *The Unchanging Arts* (Philadelphia: J. B. Lippincott, 1971); John Kouwenhoven, *Made in America* (Garden City, N.Y.: Doubleday, 1948); Russell Lynes, *The Tastemakers* (New York: Harper, 1954), and the many writings of Ray Browne. Richard M. Dorson, *American Folklore* (Chicago: University of Chicago Press, 1959), and *Folklore and Folklife: An Introduction* (Chicago: University of Chicago Press, 1972) indicate the many ways in which the study of folk culture and popular culture overlap.

The standard historical study of the popular arts in America is Russel B. Nye, *The Unembarrassed Muse* (New York: Dial Press, 1970), which also contains an excellent annotated bibliography. Other historical studies that I have found particularly valuable are: Richard Altick, *The English Common Reader* (Chicago: University of Chicago Press, 1957); Erik Barnouw, *A History of American Broadcasting*, 3 vols (New York: Oxford University Press, 1966–70); Carl Bode, *The Anatomy of American Popular Culture, 1840–1861* (Berkeley: University of California Press, 1960); Norman Cantor and Michael Wertham, eds., *The History of Popular Culture* (New York: Macmillan, 1968); David Grimsted, *Melodrama Unveiled: American Theater and Culture, 1800-1850* (Chicago: University of Chicago Press, 1968); Alan Gowans, *Images of American Living* (Philadelphia: J. B. Lippincott, 1964); James D. Hart, *The Popular Book: A History of America's Literary Taste* (Berkeley: University of California Press, 1950); Louis James, *Fiction for the Working Man, 1830-50* (New York: Oxford University Press, 1963); Arthur Knight, *The Liveliest Art* (New York: New American Library, 1959); Gerald Mast, *A Short History of the Movies* (New York: Pegasus, 1971); Frank Luther Mott, *Golden Multitudes* (New York: Macmillan, 1947); R. K. Webb, *The British Working Class Reader, 1790-1848* (London: Allen and Unwin, 1955); J. M. S. Tomkins, *The Popular Novel in England, 1770-1800* (London: Methuen, 1932); Raymond Williams, *The Long Revolution* (London: Chatto and Windus, 1960); and Louis B. Wright, *Middle-Class Culture in Elizabethan England* (Chapel Hill: University of North Carolina Press, 1935).

The social-psychological interpretation of popular culture has been approached from many different points of view and disciplinary perspectives. One great work of cultural speculation is indispensable, Johann Huizinga's *Homo Ludens: A Study of the Play Elements in Culture* (London: Routledge and Kegan Paul, 1949). Freud's ideas about wish-fulfillment and the manifestation of unconscious impulses and basic psychological tensions in story and dream symbolism have been the most influential psychological ideas applied to the analysis of popular story patterns. Freud himself was most interested in various aspects of popular culture and in *Wit and Its Relation to the Unconscious* and in various essays like those on "Family Romances" and "The Uncanny" offered insightful analyses of certain popular story formulas. Many attempts have been made to develop a systematic method of literary analysis based on Freud. Two useful works are Norman Holland, *The Dynamics of Literary Response* (New York: Oxford University Press, 1968), and Simon Lesser, *Fiction and the Unconscious* (Boston: Beacon Press, 1957). Alan C. Purves and Richard Beach, *Literature and the Reader* (National Council of Teachers of English, 1972), is a handy survey and bibliography of psychological research on literary response, both Freudian and non-Freudian. None of these works is specifically concerned with popular culture. Martin Grotjahn, *Beyond Laughter* (New York: McGraw-Hill, 1957), and Nathan Leites and Martha Wolfenstein, *Movies: A Psychological Study* (Glencoe, Ill.: Free Press, 1950), focus on the psychology of popular forms. Harold Mendelsohn, *Mass Entertainment* (New Haven, Conn.: College and University Press, 1966), attempts to combine sociological and psychological perspectives on popular culture. Eric Klinger, *Structure and Functions of Fantasy* (New York: Wiley-Interscience, 1971), surveys psychological research into dreams and daydreams that may have important relations to popular story formulas.

Some idea of the variety of social analyses of popular culture can be gained from Ian Jarvie's *Movies and Society* (New York: Basic Books, 1970), which contains one of the best annotated bibliographies in the field. Another exceptionally useful work is the Eric Larrabee–Rolf Meyersohn anthology,

Mass Leisure (Glencoe, Ill.: Free Press, 1958), which also contains a major bibliography of studies in leisure, which is supplemented by Meyersohn, "The Sociology of Leisure in the United States: Introduction and Bibliography, 1945–65," *Journal of Leisure Research*, 1, no. 1 (Winter 1969): 53–68. Other important social analyses of aspects of popular culture are Leo Lowenthal, *Literature, Popular Culture and Society* (Englewood Cliffs, N.J.: Prentice-Hall, 1961); Leo C. Rosten, *Hollywood: The Movie Colony and the Movie Makers* (New York: Harcourt, Brace, 1941); Hortense Powdermaker, *Hollywood: The Dream Factory* (Boston: Little, Brown, 1950); Sebastian de Grazia, *Of Time, Work, and Leisure* (New York: The Twentieth Century Fund, 1962); Ernest K. Bramsted, *Aristocracy and the Middle-Classes in Germany: Social Types in German Literature, 1830–1900* (Chicago: University of Chicago Press, 1964); Albert McLean, *American Vaudeville as Ritual* (Lexington: University of Kentucky Press, 1965); Alvin Toffler, *The Culture Consumers* (New York: Macmillan, 1964); Leo Gurko, *Heroes, Highbrows and the Popular Mind* (Indianapolis: Bobbs-Merrill, 1953); and Dixon Wecter, *The Hero in America* (New York: Charles Scribner's Sons, 1941).

The area of mass communications—theory, history, and empirical research—is of particular importance to the study of popular formulas. Alfred G. Smith, ed., *Communication and Culture* (New York: Holt, Rinehart and Winston, 1966), gives some idea of the range of communications studies, while Melvin DeFleur, *Theories of Mass Communication* (New York: David McKay, 1966), explores differing conceptions of the mass communication process. Walter Lippmann, *Public Opinion* (New York: Free Press, 1965), though originally published in 1922, remains a classic in this area, particularly for its discussion of stereotyping. Other useful works are: Joseph T. Klapper, *The Effects of Mass Communication* (New York: Free Press, 1960); Wilbur Schramm, ed., *The Process and Effects of Mass Communication* (Urbana: University of Illinois Press, 1961); Theodore Peterson, Jay Jensen, and William Rivers, eds., *The Mass Media and Modern Society* (New York: Holt, Rinehart and Winston, 1965); Lewis Anthony Dexter and David Manning White, eds., *People, Society, and Mass Communications* (New York: Free Press of Glencoe, 1964); Frank E. X. Dance, ed., *Human Communication Theory* (New York: Holt, Rinehart and Winston, 1967); Edwin P. Bettinghaus, *Persuasive Communication* (New York: Holt, Rinehart and Winston, 1973); Francis and Ludmilla Voelker, eds. *Mass Media: Forces in Our Society* (New York: Harcourt, Brace, Jovanovich, 1972); Raymond Williams, *Britain in the Sixties: Communications* (Harmondsworth: Penguin Books, 1962); and Gary A. Steiner, *The People Look at Television* (New York: Alfred A. Knopf, 1963).

The Popular Literature of Crime
(chaps. 3–7)

Two major bibliographies are indispensable in this area: Jacques Barzun and Wendell Hertig Taylor, *A Catalogue of Crime* (New York: Harper and Row, 1971), and Ordean A. Hagen, *Who Done It?* (New York: R. R. Bowker, 1969). Barzun-Taylor is more reliable and has the further advantage of elaborate annotations, which are always interesting if occasionally open to argument. Hagen has a larger list and some useful supplementary features such as a list of detective films. Both include substantial secondary bibliographies as well.

The history of crime fiction has only recently begun to flourish on a large scale, but there are certain pioneer works in the field that still provide important materials. Frank Chandler, *The Literature of Roguery*, 2 vols. (Boston: Houghton Mifflin, 1907), was a momumental study that extended beyond the crime story into such areas as the picaresque novel but that still provides the broadest history of crime literature. In the more limited area of the detective story proper, Howard Haycraft was the pioneer historian with his *Murder for Pleasure* (New York: Appleton-Century, 1941). Since Haycraft there has been some excellent work, the most recent being Julian Symons, *Mortal Consequences* (New York: Harper and Row, 1972), and Colin Watson, *Snobbery with Violence* (London: Eyre and Spottiswoode, 1971). Other important works are A. E. Murch, *The Developement of the Detective Novel* (New York: Greenwood Press, 1968), which is especially good on nineteenth-century origins; Dorothy L. Sayers, *The Omnibus of Crime* (New York: Payson and Clarke, 1929), which has a historical introduction; Boileau-Narcejac, *Le Roman policier* (Paris: Payot, 1964); and Sutherland Scott, *Blood in Their Ink: The March of the Modern Mystery Novel* (London: S. Paul, 1953). See also Tage La Cour and Harald Mogensen, *The Murder Book: An Illustrated History of the Detective Story* (London: George Allen and Unwin, 1971). Continual additions to the history of the literature of crime appear in the pages of the journal *The Armchair Detective*.

Other genres of crime literature have not received as much attention as the detective novel. There have been a number of useful studies of the gothic novel such as Edith Birkhead, *The Tale of Terror* (New York: Russell and Russell, 1961), as well as some work on the "Newgate" and "Sensation" novels, which are essentially genres of melodrama in which some of the central incidents involve crime: see Randolph Ivy, "The Victorian Sensation Novel: A Study in Formula Fiction," Ph.D. dissertation, University of Chicago, 1974. Several books have been done on the gangster film, though none is truly substantial: see John Baxter, *The Gangster Film* (New York: A. S. Barnes, 1970), and Colin

McArthur, *Underworld U. S. A.* (New York: Viking, 1972). No attempt has been made to write the history of modern criminal literature except insofar as it appears tangentially in the histories of detective fiction mentioned above.

Criticism of the mystery and crime story has emerged from many different perspectives—practitioners of the art, scholars, psychologists, philosophers, and cultural historians. Two excellent anthologies represent the range of this criticism: Howard Haycraft, ed., *The Art of the Mystery Story* (New York: Simon and Schuster, 1946), and Francis M. Nevins, Jr., ed., *The Mystery Writer's Art* (Bowling Green, Ohio: Bowling Green University Popular Press, 1970). Beyond the essays in these volumes, the following are particularly recommended: W. H. Auden, "The Guilty Vicarage" in *The Dyer's Hand* (New York: Random House, 1962); Ralph Harper, *The World of the Thriller* (Cleveland: Press of Case Western Reserve University, 1969); George Grella, "Murder and Manners: The Formal Detective Novel," *Novel* 4 (Fall 1970): 30–48; W. V. Spanos, "The Detective and the Boundary: Some Notes on the Postmodern Literary Imagination," *Boundary 2*, vol. 1, no. 1 (Fall 1972): 147–68; Martin Roth, "The Detective, The Clue, and the Corpse in Freud and Einstein," unpublished paper presented at the 1973 meeting of the Midwest Modern Language Association; Michael Holquist, "Whodunit and Other Questions: Metaphysical Detective Stories in Post-War Fiction" *New Literary History* 3 (1971–72): 135–56; Geoffrey Hartman, "The Mystery of Mysteries," *New York Review of Books*, 18 May 1972, pp. 31–34; Geraldine Pederson-Krag, "Detective Stories and the Primal Scene," *Psychoanalytic Quarterly* 18 (1949): 207–14; Martin Grotjahn, "Sex and the Mystery Story," *Human Sexuality 6*, no. 3 (March 1972): pp. 126–37; Jacques Barzun, *The Delights of Detection* (New York: Criterion Books, 1961); Mystery Writers of America, *The Mystery Writers' Handbook: A Handbook on the Writing of Detective, Suspense, Mystery and Crime Stories*, ed. Herbert Brean (New York: Harper, 1956); Marie Rodell, *Mystery Fiction: Theory and Technique*, rev. ed. (New York: Hermitage House, 1952); and Edmund Wilson, "Mr. Holmes, They Were the Footprints of a Gigantic Hound!" *New Yorker* 21 (17 February 1945): 73–78.

A number of substantial studies of individual mystery writers have appeared. The literature on Poe and Conan Doyle is, of course, vast. Barzun-Taylor has a good bibliography of Sherlockiana. Other studies of this type are: G. C. Ramsey, *Agatha Christie: Mistress of Mystery* (New York: Dodd, Mead, 1967); Norman Donaldson, *In Search of Dr. Thorndyke* (Bowling Green, Ohio: Bowling Green University Popular Press, 1971); Philip Durham, *Down These Mean Streets a Man Must Go* (Chapel Hill: University of North Carolina Press, 1966); William F. Nolan, *Dashiell Hammett: A Casebook* (Santa Barbara, Calif.: McNally and Loftin, 1969); and Francis M. Nevins, Jr., *Royal Bloodline: Ellery Queen, Author and Detective* (Bowling Green, Ohio: Bowling Green University Popular Press, 1974).

In my attempts to understand the closely related formulas of the hard-boiled detective story and the gangster saga, I have found the following works particularly useful: Stuart Kaminsky, "'Little Caesar' and Its Role in the Gangster Film Genre," *Journal of Popular Film* 1, no. 3 (Summer 1972): 209–27, and his book *Don Siegel* (New York: Curtis Books, 1974), covering one of the important Hollywood directors to work in these genres; the several excellent essays in David Madden, ed., *Tough-Guy Writers of the Thirties* (Carbondale: Southern Illinois University Press, 1968); Andrew Bergman, *We're in the Money* (New York: New York University Press, 1971); Arthur Sacks, "An Analysis of Gangster Movies of the Early Thirties," *The Velvet Light Trap*, no. 1 (June 1971); Lawrence Alloway, *Violent America: The Movies, 1946–1964* (New York: Museum of Modern Art, 1971); Barbara Deming, *Running Away from Myself* (New York: Grossman, 1969); George Grella, "Murder and the Mean Streets: The Hard-boiled Detective Novel," *Contempora* 1 (March 1970): 6–15; Anthony Monahan, "The Uppity Private Eye as Movie Hero," *Midwest Magazine*, 4 June 1972, pp. 11–15; Walter Blair, "Dashiell Hammett: Themes and Techniques," *Essays in American Literature in Honor of Jay B. Hubbell* (Chapel Hill, N.C.: Duke University Press, 1967); John Paterson, "A Cosmic View of the Private Eye," *Saturday Review of Literature* 36 (22 August 1953): 7–8; Ron Goulart, ed., *The Hardboiled Dicks* (Los Angeles: Sherbourne Press, 1965); the essays on Mickey Spillane by Charles J. Rolo and Christopher La Farge in the Rosenberg-White *Mass Culture*, cited earlier; and the critical biographies of Chandler and Hammett by Philip Durham and William Nolan, mentioned above. See also the essays in my collection *Focus on Bonnie and Clyde* (Englewood Cliffs, N.J.: Prentice-Hall, 1973), and my essay "Myths of Violence in American Popular Culture," *Critical Inquiry* 1, no. 3 (March 1975): 521–41. I am also grateful for the insights into the hard-boiled detective story given to me by Johnnine Hazard, whose Ph.D. dissertation on Ross Macdonald was recently completed (University of Chicago, 1974), and by Virginia Wexman who is currently writing a Ph.D. dissertation on the hard-boiled detective film.

The literature about actual crimes and the history and theory of criminal justice offers manifold insights into the role of crime as a theme of popular literature and film. Barzun-Taylor contains an extensive annotated bibliography of true crime materials. Richard Altick, *Victorian Studies in Scarlet* (New York: W. W. Norton, 1970), is a historical study of the public fascination with crime in nineteenth-century England that is particularly illuminating. For the background of the American gangster saga the following studies of the Capone era in Chicago are particularly helpful: Albert Halper, ed., *The Chicago Crime Book* (New York: Pyramid Books, 1969); F. D. Pasley, *Al Capone: The Biography of a Self-Made Man* (London: Faber and Faber, 1966); John Kobler, *Capone* (New York: G. P. Putnam's Sons, 1971); and John Landesco, *Organized Crime in Chicago* (Chicago: University of Chicago Press, 1968). John Toland, *The Dillinger Days* (New York:

Random House, 1963), offers a broader view of American gangs in the 1930s, source of most of the literary and cinematic portrayals of the gangster.

I have found these works in the area of criminal justice and criminology eminently readable and suggestive: Norval Morris and Gordon Hawkins, *The Honest Politician's Guide to Crime Control* (Chicago: University of Chicago Press, 1969); Leon Radzinowicz, *Ideology and Crime* (New York: Columbia University Press, 1966); Don C. Gibbons, *Society, Crime and Criminal Careers* (Englewood Cliffs, N.J.: Prentice-Hall, 1968); Richard Quinney, *The Social Reality of Crime* (Boston: Little, Brown, 1970); and Edwin H. Sutherland, *On Analyzing Crime* (Chicago: University of Chicago Press, 1973).

The Evolution of the Western
   (chap. 8)

Three works contain major bibliographies on the western and its historical and cultural background: John G. Cawelti, *The Six-Gun Mystique* (Bowling Green, Ohio: Bowling Green University Popular Press, 1971); Richard W. Etulain, *Western American Literature: A Bibliography of Interpretive Books and Articles* (Vermillion, S.D.: University of South Dakota Press, 1972); and Jack Nachbar, ed., *Focus on the Western* (Englewood Cliffs, N. J.: Prentice-Hall, 1974). These works list virtually all material of consequence to the present time.

The most significant critical and historical writings on the western and the myth of the West are: Henry Nash Smith, *Virgin Land* (Cambridge, Mass.: Harvard University Press, 1960); Edwin Fussell, *Frontier: American Literature and the American West* (Princeton, N.J.: Princeton University Press, 1965); James K. Folsom, *The American Western Novel* (New Haven, Conn.: College and University Press, 1966); George Fenin and William K. Everson, *The Western: From Silents to Cinerama* (New York: Bonanza Books, 1962); Richard Slotkin, *Regeneration through Violence* (Middletown, Conn.: Wesleyan University Press, 1973); Jim Kitses, *Horizons West: Studies in Authorship in the Western Film* (Bloomington: Indiana University Press, 1970); Philip French, *Westerns* (Bloomington: Indiana University Press, 1973); André Bazin, "The Western, or the American Film par excellence," and "The Evolution of the Western" in *What is Cinema*, 4 vols., 2, tr. Hugh Grey (Berkeley: University of California Press, 1971); Robert Warshow, "The Westerner" in *The Immediate Experience* (Garden City, N.Y.: Anchor Books, 1964); Peter Homans, "Puritanism Revisited: An Analysis of the Contemporary Screen Image Western," *Studies in Public Communication*, no. 3 (Summer 1961): 73–84; Leslier Fiedler, *The Return of the Vanishing American* (New York: Stein and Day, 1968); John Williams, "The 'Western': Definition of the Myth," *Nation* 193 (18 November 1961): 401–6; Edward G. White, *The Eastern Establishment and the Western Experience* (New Haven, Conn.: Yale University Press, 1968); Roderick Nash, *Wilderness and the*

American Mind (New Haven, Conn.: Yale University Press, 1967); Roy Harvey Pearce, *The Savages of America: A Study of the Indian and the Idea of Civilization* (Baltimore: Johns Hopkins University Press, 1953); Ralph and Natasha Friar, *The Only Good Indian . . . The Hollywood Gospel* (New York: Drama Book Specialists, 1972); Kent L. Steckmesser, *The Western Hero in History and Legend* (Norman: University of Oklahoma Press, 1965); Joseph G. Rosa, *The Gunfighter: Man or Myth* (Norman: University of Oklahoma Press, 1969); Robert E. Lee, *From West to East: Studies in the Literature of the American West* (Urbana: University of Illinois Press, 1966); and Ray A. Billington, *America's Frontier Heritage* (New York: Holt, Rinehart and Winston, 1966).

The Best-selling Melodrama (chap. 9)

The indispensable work listing best-sellers of all sorts with sales statistics is Alice Payne Hackett, *Seventy Years of Best Sellers* (New York: R. R. Bowker, 1967). This book also contains a useful bibliography of books and articles about best-sellers, the most important of which are probably Frank Luther Mott, *Golden Multitudes* (New York: R. R. Bowker, 1947), and James D. Hart, *The Popular Book* (New York: Oxford University Press, 1950). Literary history is usually written from the point of view of lasting achievements—as it should be—but some literary historians have given us important insight into popular literary tastes, in particular those books that have focused on the literary and cultural history of particular decades or periods such as Grant Knight, *The Critical Period in American Literature* (Chapel Hill: University of North Carolina Press, 1951) and *The Strenuous Age in American Literature* (Chapel Hill: University of North Carolina Press, 1954); Carl Bode, *The Anatomy of American Popular Culture, 1840–1861* (Berkeley: University of California Press, 1959); and earlier studies by scholars like Fred Lewis Pattee and E. Douglas Branch. Russel B. Nye, *The Unembarrassed Muse*, has an excellent brief survey of the history of best-selling fiction and a selective bibliography.

For a list of works on melodrama see the notes to chap. 9.

Index

Alger, Horatio, 213, 224
Alice's Adventures in Wonderland, 38
Altman, Robert, *The Long Goodbye,* 140
Aristotle, *Poetics,* 7
Arthur, T. S., *Ten Nights in a Bar Room,* 189
Aydelotte, William, "The Detective Story as a Historical Source," 81

"Barnaby Jones" (TV series), 21
Barzun, Jacques, *The Catalogue of Crime,* 107
Bell, Daniel, 59
Bellow, Saul, 258, 260, 262
Berger, Harry, 16
Berger, Thomas, 260; *Little Big Man,* 13
Bierce, Ambrose, 164
Bierstadt, Albert, 230, 239
Big Jake (film), 255
The Big Sleep (film), 250
Bird, Robert Montgomery, *Nick of the Woods,* 209–10
Black Mask Magazine, 139, 163
Bogart, Humphrey, 250
"Bonanza" (TV series), 232, 249
Boone, Daniel, 197
Boorman, John, *Point Blank* (film), 69
Borges, Jorge, 133, 136–37; *Death and the Compass,* 133
Brennan, Walter, 219
Bronson, Charles, 254
Brown, Carter, 21, 139
Buchan, John, 31, 32, 93, 140, 263
Buck and the Preacher (film), 257
Burnett, W. R., *Little Caesar,* 59
Butch Cassidy and the Sundance Kid (film), 232, 252, 258

Cagney, James, 75, 244

"Cannon" (TV series), 21
Capone, Al, 59, 60, 61
Carr, John Dickson, 126, 136, 140; *The Arabian Nights Mystery,* 84, 141
Casablanca (film), 250–51
Cassil, R. Verlin, 150
Cawelti, John G., *The Six-Gun Mystique,* 194
Chandler, Raymond, 21, 108, 150, 151, 156, 166, 168, 174–82, 185, 250, 299; *The Big Sleep,* 139, 144, 147, 148, 174, 186; *Farewell, My Lovely,* 139, 141–42, 144, 153, 175–82, 183, 184, 185; *Lady in the Lake,* 153; *The Long Goodbye,* 143–44, 145; *Playback,* 175; *Raymond Chandler Speaking,* 177; "The Simple Art of Murder," 151, 155, 163, 176
Chesterton, G. K., "A Defense of Detective Stories," 140–41
Chisum (film), 255–56
Christie, Agatha, 106, 110, 129–33, 135–37, 139, 140, 148, 260; *Death on the Nile,* 118; *The Mysterious Affair at Styles,* 118; *The Murder of Roger Ackroyd,* 118, 133; *An Overdose of Death,* 112–17; *Third Girl,* 112–13, 116–19
Churchill, Winston (American writer), 233, 263, 276, 277, 278, 279, 280; *The Inside of the Cup,* 274–75, 277
Clark, Arthur, 49
Clift, Montgomery, 256
Collins, Wilkie, 266–67; *The Moonstone,* 84, 110, 134–35, 141, 148
Conan Doyle, Sir Arthur, 8, 70, 84, 99, 106, 109, 140, 229; Sherlock Holmes, 51, 58, 59; Sherlock Holmes stories, 19, 80, 82, 87, 91–95, 97; *The Hound of the Baskervilles,* 110; *The Sign of*

Four, 109, 141; *A Study in Scarlet*,
    109; *The Valley of Fear*, 109
Condon, Richard, *Mile High*, 64
Conrad, Joseph, 173
Cooper, Gary, 10, 242, 250, 251
Cooper, James Fenimore, 213–15, 216,
    221, 224, 257; *The American
    Democrat*, 195; *The Deerslayer*, 192,
    202–8; *The Last of the Mohicans*, 198,
    200–201; The Leatherstocking series,
    34, 194–209, 219; *Notions of the
    Americans*, 196; *The Oak Openings*,
    224–25; *The Pathfinder*, 203; *The
    Pioneers*, 192, 196–200, 206–7; *The
    Prairie*, 199–200, 201–2
The Covered Wagon (film), 232
The Cowboys (film), 255
Crane, Stephen, 151, 173, 216, 277
Creasey, John, 9, 127
Crime films with black heroes (*Shaft,
    Shaft's Big Score, Trouble Man,
    Super-fly*), 70
Crime in literature: the moralistic
    image, 54–55; the aesthetic image,
    55–56; the romantic image, 56–57;
    the scientific image, 57–58; the
    organizational image, 62–65
Criminals as romantic figures (Billy the
    Kid, Jesse James, John Dillinger,
    Bonnie and Clyde, Pretty Boy Floyd),
    57
Croft, Freeman Wills, 127
Cross, Amanda, 136
Cultural functions of literature: impact
    theories, 22–24; deterministic
    theories, 24–26; symbolic theories,
    26–35
Custer, George A., 219, 258

Daley, Richard J. (Mayor of Chicago),
    66
Dali, Salvador, 166
Davidson, Edward, *Poe: A Critical
    Study*, 100
Demaris, Ovid, *The Overlord*, 63
de Quincey, Thomas, *Murder
    Considered as One of the Fine Arts*,
    55–56, 60
Destry Rides Again (film), 11
Devine, Andy, 219
Dickens, Charles, 53, 189, 266, 268,
    271, 272, 274, 280; *Bleak House*, 136;
    Mystery of Edwin Drood, 135;

Oliver Twist, 58
Dickinson, Peter, 136
Dostoevsky, Fyodor, 53, 271; *The
    Brothers Karamazov*, 124; *Crime and
    Punishment*, 18, 124, 132–33, 134,
    136
Dreiser, Theodore, 151, 164, 262, 277
Durgnat, Raymond, 32
Durham, Philip, *The Negro Cowboy*,
    257

Earp, Wyatt, 12, 219
Eastwood, Clint, 253–54
Eliot, T. S., 240, 267; "Waste Land," 154
Ellis, Edward S., *Seth Jones*, 210–11, 214
Esquire Magazine, 154
Evans, Augusta Jane, 275

Fantasy, moral and physical, 38–39
Faulkner, William, 194, 262, 264;
    Intruder in the Dust, 134; *The Sound
    and the Fury*, 18, 89
Faust, Frederick ("Max Brand"), 9, 231;
    Hired Guns, 165
Fiedler, Leslie, *The Return of the
    Vanishing American*, 258
Fielding, Henry, *Jonathan Wild*, 54
Fisher, Vardis, 219
Fitzgerald, F. Scott, 165, 240; *The Great
    Gatsby*, 61, 180–81
Fleming, Ian, 93; James Bond series, 31,
    32, 39, 40, 51, 67
Fonda, Henry, 12, 242, 250, 254
Ford, John, 239, 242, 247–48; *Cheyenne
    Autumn*, 247–48; compared to
    Wister, Grey, and Hart, 248; *The Iron
    Horse*, 232; *The Man Who Shot
    Liberty Valance*, 247; *My Darling
    Clementine*, 12, 247, 255–56; *The
    Searchers*, 247; *Sergeant Rutledge*,
    257; *Stagecoach*, 232, 242, 247; *Three
    Godfathers*, 218
Formula literature: and audience
    research, 298–99; and best-sellers,
    260–61; and cultural functions, 35–36;
    and cultural selection, 20–22; and
    escapism, 13–16; and games, 19–20;
    and ideologies, 31–33; and mimetic
    literature, 13–14, 38–39; and other
    popular arts, 297; as performance, 10;
    and play, 19–20; and problem of
    media, 297–98; and standardization,
    8–10; and stereotypes, 11–12; and

uniqueness, 12–13
Fowles, John, *The French Lieutenant's Woman*, 42
Freeling, Nicholas, 131, 136
Freeman, R. Austin, 126, 136
The French Connection (film), 51, 75
Freud, Dr. Sigmund, 94–96, 103–4
Frye, Northrop, 142, 263, 287; *Anatomy of Criticism*, 90

Gangster films, 60; (Josef von Sternberg), *Underworld*, 60; (Mervyn Le Roy), *Little Caesar*, 62, 77; (William Wellman), *Public Enemy*, 62; (Howard Hawks), *Scarface*, 62, 77
Gardner, Earl Stanley: Perry Mason stories, 139; District Attorney stories, 139; Donald Lam–Bertha Cool series, 139
Gilbert and Sullivan, *Pirates of Penzance*, 57
Godwin, William, *Caleb Williams*, 102
Grella, George, "Murder and Manners: The Formal Detective Novel," 108
Grey, Zane, 218, 231, 232–41, 244, 245, 263; *Code of the West*, 236–37, 278–79; *Riders of the Purple Sage*, 234, 237, 240; *Stagecoach*, 242–43; *To The Last Man*, 236, 237; *The U. P. Trail*, 238
Griffith, D. W., *The Musketeers of Pig Alley* (film), 52
Grimsted, David, 268, 271
"Gunsmoke" (TV series), 232, 249
Guthrie, A. B., Jr. 219

Hailey, Arthur, 262, 280
Halliday, Brett, 21, 139, 183; *So Lush, So Deadly*, 154
Haggard, H. Rider, 40
Hammett, Dashiell, 12, 21, 73, 139, 143, 150, 162–76, 185, 250, 299; *The Big Knockover*, 168, *The Dain Curse*, 147, 162, 166, 174, 175, 178; *The Glass Key*, 162; *The Maltese Falcon*, 139, 146, 147,149, 162, 163, 165–67, 173, 183; "Memoirs of a Private Detective," 164, 166; *Red Harvest*, 162, 165, 168–73, 185; *The Thin Man*, 139, 163, 165
Hard-boiled detective TV series ("Peter Gunn," "77 Sunset Strip," "Call

Surfside 666," "Cannon," "Barnaby Jones"), 139
Hardy, Thomas, *The Return of the Native*, 121
Hart, James, 275
Hart, W. S., 232–41, 244; *Hell's Hinges*, 234, 237, 238, compared to *Stagecoach*, 243; *The Return of Draw Egan*, 234
Harte, Bret, 216, 218–19, 246; "The Luck of Roaring Camp," 218
Hawks, Howard, 21, 242; *Red River*, 256; *Rio Bravo*, 249
Hawthorne, Nathaniel, 194, 209; *The Scarlet Letter*, 104
Haycox, Ernest, 242
Haycraft, Howard, *Murder for Pleasure*, 98
Hecht, Ben, *Underworld* (film), 59
Hellinger, Mark, 73
Hemingway, Ernest, 73, 151, 161, 166, 173, 194, 240, 250, 262, 265; *A Farewell to Arms*, 265; *The Killers*, 73
Heroes, 39–40
Hickock, James B. ("Wild Bill"), 219
High Noon (film), 232, 249, 255
Hitchcock, Alfred, 17; *Frenzy*, 17–18; *Psycho*, 48
Hobsbawn, Eric J., 57
Holquist, Michael, 136
Homer, 5, 52
Hoover, J. Edgar, 62
"Hopalong Cassidy" (TV series), 230
Hope, Bob, *The Ghost Breakers*, 48
Horror, 47–49
Hough, Emerson, 231, 234, 279; *The Covered Wagon*, 193
Howells, William Dean, 277
Huston, John, 21; *Asphalt Jungle*, 75, 76

Identification, 18–19
Innes, Michael, 140; *Appleby's End*, 97; *Lament for a Maker*, 84, 92

James, G. P. R., *The Brigand*, 57
James, Henry, 102, 264; *The Turn of the Screw*, 48
Jones, Everett, *The Negro Cowboy*, 257
Joyce, James, 136; *Ulysses*, 18, 89

Kaplan, Abraham, 299
King, Henry, *The Gunfighter*, 195; *Jesse James*, 242

Kubrick, Stanley, *The Killing*, 76
Kuklick, Bruce, 27–30, 33
Kurosawa, Akira, *Yojimbo*, 172

L'Amour, Louis, 231
Lang, Fritz, *The Return of Frank James*, 242
Lathen, Emma, 125, 132, 136
Lawrence, D. H., 207
The Legend of Nigger Charley (film), 257
Legion of Decency, 244
Leone, Sergio, 232, 253–55; *A Fistful of Dollars*, 253; *For a Few Dollars More*, 253; *The Good, the Bad, and the Ugly* 253; *Once Upon a Time in the West*, 253–54
Levin, Ira, *Rosemary's Baby*, 156
Levi-Strauss, Claude, and structuralism, 296–97
Lewis, C. S., 49
Lewis, M. G., 97, 100; *The Monk*, 53, 102
Lewis, Sinclair, 240, 245, 262
Little Big Man (film), 252, 257–58
Little Caesar (film), 44, 244
London, Jack, 240
"Lone Ranger," 38, 68, 300

McBain, Ed, 136; *Fuzz*, 142; 87th Precinct stories, 127
McCabe and Mrs. Miller (film), 258–59
McClelland, David, *The Achieving Society*, 24
McCrea, Joel, 12, 250, 252–53
Macdonald, John D., 75; Travis McGee stories, 70, 72–73
Macdonald, Ross (Kenneth Millar), 118, 136, 139, 156, 299; *The Doomsters*, 145; *Find a Victim*, 152, 153; *Harper* (*The Moving Target*), 149; "The Writer as Detective Hero," 131
MacLean, Alistair, 40
McLuhan, Marshall, and problem of media, 297–98
Mafia, 62, 63, 67
Malamud, Bernard, 258
A Man Called Horse (film), 257
Manfred, Frederick, 219
Mann, Anthony, 242, 249; *Man of the West*, 256
Mann, Thomas, 136

"Mannix" (TV series), 21
Marsh, Ngaio, 136
Marshall, George, *Destry Rides Again*, 242
Marvin, Lee (*Point Blank* [film], *Prime Cut* [film]), 73
Marx, Karl, 96
Melville, Herman, 194, 209
Metalious, Grace, *Peyton Place*, 44, 189
Meyer, Nicholas, *The Seven-Percent Solution*, 95
"Mission: Impossible" (TV series), 75
Mitchell, Margaret, 262; *Gone with the Wind*, 19, 47, 265
Mix, Tom, 232, 234
Monroe, Marilyn, 292
Moran, Thomas, 239
Morris, Norval, and Hawkins, Gordon, *The Honest Politician's Guide to Crime Control*, 63

Nabokov, Vladimir, 136, 137
Nachbar, Jack, 253
Newcomb, Horace, 298
Newgate Calendar, 53, 54
Noble, David W., 207–8
Norris, Frank, 240, 262, 277

O'Hara, John, 162
Olson, Elder, 12, 39
Oppenheim, E. Phillips, 31, 140
Our Man Flint (film), 32
The Ox-Bow Incident (film), 249

Panofsky, Erwin, "Style and Medium in the Moving Pictures," 188
Parrington, Vernon, 164
Peckinpah, Sam, 12, 252; *Ride the High Country*, 252–53
Pendleton, Don, *The Executioner*, 70–72, 75–78
Phillips, David Graham, 262
Piaget, Jean, 20
Plato, *The Republic*, 22
Playboy Magazine, 154
Poe, Edgar Allan, 8, 80–88, 90–97, 99–102, 104, 106, 109, 134; "The Fall of the House of Usher," 48, 99–102, 104; "The Gold-Bug," 165; "The Murders in the Rue Morgue," 80–82, 85–88, 92–93, 96–97, 100, 132, 140; "The Purloined Letter," 80–82, 85–88, 91–92, 95–96, 101, 111

Polanski, Roman, 21; *Chinatown*, 140; *The Fearless Vampire Killers*, 49
Pornography, 14–15; and Wallace, Susann, Robbins; and Hailey, 282
Porter, Edwin S., *The Great Train Robbery*, 230
Prather, Richard S., 139, 183; *The Kubla Khan Caper*, 145, 149
Protocols of the Elders of Zion, 63
Public Enemy (film), 244
Puzo, Mario, *The Godfather*, 21, 51–53, 57, 61, 62, 64–69, 74, 76, 78–79, 256
Pynchon, Thomas, 260

Queen, Ellery, 126

Radcliffe, Anne, 97, 100; *Mysteries of Udolpho*, 53, 164
Radzinowicz, Leon, 59
"Ratiocinative" classical detective story writers (John Dickson Carr, Agatha Christie, Michael Innes, Ngaio Marsh, Dorothy Sayers, Josephine Tey), 80
The Real West (TV documentary), 251
Remington, Frederick, 216, 230, 239
Richardson, Samuel, *Pamela*, 268
Riesman, David, 250, *The Lonely Crowd*, 158–59
Riley, Clayton, 257
Rio Lobo (film), 255
Robbe-Grillet, Alain, 133, 136–37; *The Erasers*, 133
Robbins, Harold, 262, 264, 280; *The Adventurers*, 44; *The Betsy*, 290; *The Carpetbaggers*, 47
"Robin Hood," 56, 57, 70
Robinson, Edward G., 244
Roe, E. P., 264; *Barriers, Burned Away*, 276
Rohmer, Saxe, *Fu Manchu*, 31, 93, 141
Roosevelt, Theodore, 216, 226, 228
Royko, Mike, *Boss*, 66–67
Russell, Charles M., 230, 239

"Sapper," 31
Sayers, Dorothy, 106, 110, 119, 126, 129–30, 135–36, 140, 164; *Five Red Herrings*, 120; *The Nine Tailors*, 97, 120–25; *Omnibus of Crime*, 123; *Strong Poison*, 148
Schickel, Richard, 177
Scott, Randolph, 12, 250, 252–53

Scott, Sir Walter, 151
Segal, Erich, *Love Story*, 42
Shakespeare, William, 54; *Hamlet*, 10, 25, 54; *Macbeth*, 53; *Romeo and Juliet*, 42
Shane (film), 11, 232, 249, 255–56; effect of different media, 297, 298
Sheldon, Charles, *In His Steps*, 280
Shelley, Mary, *Frankenstein*, 49, 102
Siegel, Don, *Invasion of the Body Snatchers*, 49; *The Killers*, 73
The Silencers (film), 32
Simenon, Georges, 9, 110, 126–31, 134, 136–37, 299; *Maigret and the Reluctant Witnesses*, 128–30
Sinclair, Upton, 262
Siodmak, Robert, 73
Slotkin, Richard, *Regeneration through Violence*, 300
Smight, Jack, *Harper*, 140
Smith, Henry Nash, 197, 208, 211, 241, 270; *Virgin Land*, 195
Soldier Blue (film), 257
Sophocles, *Oedipus the King*, 26, 42, 133–34
Soul Soldier (film), 257
Southworth, Mrs. E. D. E. N., 263, 274; *The Curse of Clifton*, 270; *Ishmael*, 47
Spillane, Mickey, 13, 19, 21, 67, 139, 140, 150, 151, 170, 183–91, 300; *The Big Kill*, 186–87, 188; *The Body Lovers*, 146, 150, 154, 155; *The Erector Set*, 68; *I, The Jury*, 143, 147–48, 152, 159, 184, 187–88; *One Lonely Night*, 150, 186–87, 188, 190
"Stark, Richard" (Donald E. Westlake), "Parker" novels, 68, 73, 75
Steffens, Lincoln, 154; *The Shame of Our Cities*, 61, 155
Steinbeck, John, 162, 245; *Of Mice and Men*, 180
Stendhal, 53; *The Charterhouse of Parma*, 265
Stevenson, Robert Louis, 40; *The New Arabian Nights*, 141; *Treasure Island*, 165
Stewart, James, 250
Stoker, Bram, *Dracula*, 44, 47, 49, 102
Stowe, Harriet Beecher, *Uncle Tom's Cabin*, 46, 189, 262, 265–66, 272–74
Susann, Jacqueline, 47; *The Love Machine*, 282; *Once Is Not Enough*, 280

Suspense, 17–18
Symons, Julian, 75, 131, 136

Tanner, Tony, 285
Tey, Josephine, 136
Thoreau, Henry D., 194
Thorp, Roderick, *The Detective*, 127
To Have and Have Not (film), 250
Tolstoy, Leo, *War and Peace*, 265
Trilling, Lionel, "Reality in America,"
    164
True Grit (film), 232, 252
Turner, Frederick Jackson, 226–28, 246
Twain, Mark, 194; *Roughing It*, 216–18

Underworld (film), 244
Upfield, Arthur W., *Death of a Lake*,
    126

The Valachi Papers (film), 51
Van Cleef, Lee, 253
Veblen, Thorstein, 60
Vidor, King, 242
Violence in literature, 15
Vonnegut, Kurt, 260

Wallace, Irving, 47, 262, 264, 265, 266,
    280, 284, 295; *The Chapman Report*,
    289–90; *The Fan Club*, 292–95; *The
    Seven Minutes*, 282–83, 290–92; *The
    Word*, 281; *The Writing of One
    Novel*, 284–85
Waller, Leslie, *The Family*, 66
Walsh, Raoul, *White Heat*, 75
Wambaugh, Joseph, 262; *The New
    Centurions*, 127

Warner, Susan, 263
Warshow, Robert, 9–10, 12, 13, 59, 250
Watson, Colin, 136
Wayne, John, 242, 250, 255–56
Webb, Walter Prescott, 246
West, Nathanael, *The Day of the
    Locust*, 293
Westlake, Donald ("Richard Stark"),
    136
Wheeler, Edward L., *Deadwood Dick
    on Deck*, 211–15
White, G. Edward, *The Eastern
    Establishment and the Western
    Experience*, 216
Wilbur, Richard, 86; "The Poe Mystery
    Case," 92
The Wild Bunch (film), 232, 252
Wild West Show, 219, 230
Wilson, Edmund, 162
Wilson, Richard, *Invitation to a
    Gunfighter*, 253
Wister, Owen, *Lin Mclean*, 218; *The
    Virginian*, 11, 19, 195, 215–30, 231,
    241, 245, 279; compared to Hart and
    Grey, 233–35
Wolfert, Ira, *Tucker's People*, 66
Woolf, Virginia, 136
Wright, Harold Bell, 226, 231, 234, 245,
    263, 276, 280; *The Shepherd of the
    Hills*, 277–78; *The Winning of
    Barbara Worth*, 277–78
Wyler, William, *The Westerner*, 242

Yates, Dornford, 31, 140

Zinneman, Fred, 242
Zola, Emile, 58

John G. Cawelti is professor of English and humanities at the University of Chicago. He is author of *Apostles of the Self-Made Man* (University of Chicago Press), *The Six-Gun Mystique, Focus on Bonnie and Clyde, Why Pop?* and editor, with Alexander Kern and Marvin Meyers, of *Sources of the American Republic.*

Library of Congress Cataloging in Publication Data

Cawelti, John G
    Adventure, mystery, and romance.

    Includes bibliographical references and index.
    1. Fiction—Technique.   2. Fiction—History and criticism. I. Title.
PN3355.C36   808.3   75-5077
ISBN 0-226-09866-4